*PALGRAVE GREAT **DEBATES IN LAW***

PALGRAVE GREAT **DEBATES** *IN LAW*

Series editor
Jonathan Herring
Professor of Law
University of Oxford

Company Law
Lorraine Talbot

Contract Law
Jonathan Morgan

Criminal Law
Jonathan Herring

Employment Law
Simon Honeyball

Equity and Trusts
Alastair Hudson

Family Law
Jonathan Herring, Rebecca Probert & Stephen Gilmore

Jurisprudence
Nicholas J McBride & Sandy Steel

Medical Law and Ethics
Imogen Goold & Jonathan Herring

Property Law
David Cowan, Lorna Fox O'Mahony & Neil Cobb

If you would like to comment on this book, or on any other law text
published by Palgrave, please write to lawfeedback@palgrave.com.

PALGRAVE GREAT **DEBATES IN LAW**

GREAT DEBATES IN
JURISPRUDENCE

NICHOLAS J McBRIDE
Fellow and Director of Studies in Law
Pembroke College, Cambridge

SANDY STEEL
Fellow and Tutor in Law
Wadham College, Oxford

First published 2014 by PALGRAVE

Palgrave in the UK is an imprint of Macmillan Publishers Limited,
registered in England, company number 785998, of 4 Crinan Street,
London N1 9XW.

Palgrave Macmillan in the US is a division of St Martin's Press LLC,
175 Fifth Avenue, New York, NY 10010.

Palgrave is a global imprint of the above companies and is represented
throughout the world.

Palgrave® and Macmillan® are registered trademarks in the United States,
the United Kingdom, Europe and other countries.

ISBN: 978–1–137–32753–6 paperback

This book is printed on paper suitable for recycling and made from fully
managed and sustained forest sources. Logging, pulping and manufacturing
processes are expected to conform to the environmental regulations of the
country of origin.

A catalogue record for this book is available from the British Library.

Typeset by Cambrian Typesetters, Camberley, Surrey

Printed and bound in Great Britain by
The Lavenham Press Ltd, Suffolk

MIX
Paper from
responsible sources
FSC® C010693

For Isabel
A.N.O.

and Laura

CONTENTS

Handwritten annotations:
24
Sanctions
Claim to tell us morally what to do — read & noted / coercion
30
Moral point in 8 precepts 16
Will a wicked ruler follow them? — Read & noted / Sat. / Roh
32
Are unjust laws laws?
18
just laws of just state
unjust laws of just state 18 — Sat. / Read & noted
just & laws of wicked state
34
22
Is there a reason for the state to enforce morality? 226
Is there it wrong in principle for the state to enforce morality? — Read & noted
Is it a bad idea for the state to enforce morality?

ACKNOWLEDGMENTS

We are grateful to everyone at Palgrave for their help with the production of this book, in particular Rob Gibson, Nicola Cattini, and our copy editor, David Stott. The intellectual debts that we have incurred in preparing these chapters are obvious, in particular to H.L.A. Hart, the master from whom everything else came.

Nick McBride writes: Much of the preliminary work, preparing to write my chapters in this book, was done in Hong Kong, while lecturing out there for the University of Hong Kong (HKU). I am grateful to the members of the Law Faculty at HKU for all their support, in particular, Lusina Ho and Po Jen Yap. The actual work of writing the chapters in this book was done at a very difficult time when I was trying to combine working on the book with fulfilling my teaching responsibilities at Pembroke College, Cambridge, while helping to look after my mother, Barbara McBride, who was diagnosed with Creutzfeldt-Jakob Disease in May 2013. It simply would not have been possible to finish this book without the support of a huge number of people in the last few months, in particular: my brothers Ben and Damian, Frances Kentish, Becky Coombs, Sally Clowes, Pat Aske, Trevor Allan, John Bell, Mark Wormald, Shamima Dawood, Paul Davies, Jason Varuhas, and Sandy. They all helped lighten the load under which I was operating, in one way or another. But it was my wonderful father, and my best friend, Isabel Haskey, and her two amazingly blessed children, Ines and Luca, who gave me the energy to bear that load: I would be bereft without their love and example. In conclusion, I would like to pay special tribute to my mother, who may not live to see this book in print, but is assured of a place among the saints for her unstinting faith, hope, and love under the most difficult of circumstances. A son could not hope for a more wonderful example of how to live from his mother.

Sandy Steel writes: I would like to thank the School of Law at King's College London, where my chapters were written, and my former colleagues there. It's been a great privilege to work in such a jurisprudentially rich environment with those who have made it so: Irit Samet, Ori Herstein, Christoph Kletzer, Tim Macklem, and Lorenzo Zucca. I owe huge thanks to Nick – for his incredible efforts in the circumstances to ensure that the book was completed and for his friendship and intellectual inspiration. I am also grateful for early instruction in jurisprudential mysteries from Nigel Simmonds and David Ibbetson. A very special thank you is due to Laura, and my mum, and gran for all their love and support. Finally, thanks to our cat, Rawls, for many fruitful conversations.

INTRODUCTION

No area of legal inquiry is better suited to being dealt with in the *Great Debates* series than Jurisprudence, as so many of the major developments in jurispruden-tial thought seem to have come out of a series of great debates – between legal posi-tivists and natural lawyers over the nature of law; between Hart and Austin, and then Hart and Raz, over the nature of legal duties; between Hart and Radbruch, and then Hart and Dworkin, and then between the hard positivists and soft positivists, over how we identify what the law of a particular legal system says; between Hart and Fuller, and then Kramer and Simmonds, over whether there is such a thing as an 'inner morality of law'; between Hart and Dworkin over how judges decide hard cases; between Finnis and Raz, and then Wellman and Simmons, over whether there is a moral obligation to obey the law; between cognitivists and non-cogni-tivists about the nature of moral claims, and between consequentialists and non-consequentialists about the foundations of such claims; between Rawls and his critics over what justice requires in a democratic society; and between certain liber-als and their critics as to whether it is legitimate for the state to get into the busi-ness of enforcing morality. Our aim in this book has been to set out these debates as clearly as possible and to help the reader reach some intelligent conclusions as to which side, if any, has the better side in these debates.

This book is not meant to serve as a substitute for reading any of the great jurisprudential texts on which we have drawn in putting this book together. Rather, we hope that reading this book will help the reader understand those texts more quickly and more deeply than would otherwise be the case. In a recent review of A.W.B. Simpson's *Reflections on 'The Concept of Law'*,[1] Leslie Green remarks that

> 'before the 1960s, jurisprudence in English law schools was a realm of the amateur; people felt free to contribute to it without special training. Reflection on law in general (or on justice, or on responsibility, or on legal personality) was the kind of thing anyone might take up now and then, in their spare time, when taking a break from doctrinal work. Hart helped change that ... He wrote a book that, for all its flaws, showed that one could still write fresh works of legal philosophy, works that not only commented on Aristotle or Aquinas or Austin but also joined them in argu-ment. However, to do that one needed some philosophical tools and some skill at deploying them. That upped the barriers to entry. When jurisprudents started talk-

---

[1] Simpson, *Reflections on 'The Concept of Law'* (Oxford University Press, 2011).

ing about necessities versus contingencies, cognitivism versus non-cognitivism, sets versus systems etc., eavesdropping became less enjoyable. To actually get in on the conversation required investment.'[2]

There is no doubt that the barriers to students learning enough about jurisprudence to give them a fighting chance of making a meaningful contribution to the future development of the subject are getting ever higher, as the existing community of jurisprudents produce an ever increasing quantity of books and articles that have to be assimilated. We hope that this book will help to lower these barriers to entry somewhat, by providing students with an accessible guide to where we are at the moment in terms of the debates on which the study of jurisprudence is currently centred.

Students who are interested in exploring web-based materials on jurisprudence and associated subjects should go to the 'Jurisprudence' section of www.mcbrides-guides.com.

[2] Green, 'Jurisprudence for foxes' (2012) 3 *Transnational Legal Theory* 150.

ABBREVIATIONS

CL   H.L.A. Hart, *The Concept of Law* (Oxford University Press) (1st edn, 1961; 2nd edn with Postscript, 1994; 3rd edn with Postscript, and Introduction by Leslie Green, 2012) (all page references are to the 2nd or 3rd edn)

LE   R.M. Dworkin, *Law's Empire* (Harvard University Press, 1986)

NLNR J.M. Finnis, *Natural Law and Natural Rights* (Oxford University Press) (1st edn, 1980; 2nd edn with Postscript, 2011)

1

THE NATURE OF LAW

Debate 1

What kind of thing is law?

As Leslie Green has observed, prominent theorists of the nature of law, for all their divergences of view, agree that law is an instrument that can be used to achieve goals.[1] A major divide between these theorists lies, however, in whether they claim that an understanding of law's nature resides principally in understanding *the way in which* this instrument operates or whether the key to understanding law's nature resides principally in grasping *the specific goal* which the instrument can be used to pursue.

An analogy illustrates the contrast.[2] We understand what a Swiss army knife is less by reference to the specific purposes to which it can be put (these are many and various) and more by reference to the fact that it has many capabilities bundled together in one implement. By contrast, we understand what a saw is primarily by reference to its specific function: sawing.

So we can classify theories of law by reference to whether they consider law to be principally a *modal kind* – the sort of thing which is characterised by its *mode* of achieving various goals;[3] or whether they consider law to be a *functional kind* – the sort of thing which is characterised by the *specific* function or functions it pursues.[4]

MODAL KIND THEORIES OF LAW

The most influential theory of law's nature in the last 60 years has been that developed by H.L.A. Hart in *The Concept of Law*. In Hart's view, the only function which

---

[1] Green, 'Law as a means' in Cane (ed.), *The Hart-Fuller Debate in the Twenty-First Century* (Hart Publishing, 2010), 171–73.

[2] Ibid, 184. Aquinas was the first to compare law to a 'saw': *Summa Theologica* I-II, q.95, a.3.

[3] The terminology of 'modal kinds' is borrowed from Green, 'The concept of law revisited' (1996) 94 *Michigan Law Review* 1687, 1711. It is also used by Gardner, 'Law in general' in his *Law as a Leap of Faith* (Oxford University Press, 2012), 293.

[4] The idea of a 'functional kind' is discussed in Moore, 'Law as a functional kind' in George (ed.), *Natural Law Theory* (Oxford University Press, 1992).

law necessarily possesses is the very general one of guiding and criticising conduct.[5] This function does not distinguish law from other things like etiquette or religion. In Hart's view law is distinctive primarily in virtue of the *ways* in which it serves as a guide to conduct. The central ideas of Hart's theory describe the special way in which law guides conduct:

(1) Law guides conduct as a *system of rules* – rules which require people to do or not to do certain things (primary rules) and rules about how rules of the system come into existence, how they can be changed, and who can adjudicate upon them (secondary rules).
(2) A rule belongs to the system, and hence is a legal rule, if and only if it is recognised as a rule of the system by a master rule – *the rule of recognition.*
(3) This rule of recognition exists because of the *practice of officials* who accept the rule.

Law and games: comparisons

We can usefully introduce these ideas by an analogy to the rules of games.[6] Consider the rules of professional football. In England, the Football Association (FA) determines what these rules are. The FA recognises that the 'FIFA Laws of the Game' govern professional football matches in England. The 'FIFA Laws of the Game' include rules such as: (a) Outfield players must not handle the ball during the course of play; and (b) The referee has the power to determine whether the rules of the game have been infringed by players. Now, this set-up is in some important ways like law, on Hart's account.

(1) Games – professional football included – are constituted by rules; there are no games without rules. So, too, according to Hart, law.
(2) The rules of professional football are of different kinds. Rule (a) requires the participants in the game to refrain from certain actions. In Hart's terms, this is a primary rule of obligation – a rule which requires human beings to do or refrain from doing certain actions.[7] Contrastingly, Rule (b) does not itself require the referee to do anything – rather, it confers a power on the referee to determine whether the rules have been infringed. In Hart's terms, this is a secondary rule: a rule about the primary rules.[8] So the game of professional football, then, contains primary and secondary rules, just like law.
(3) If we consider the question – *what makes a rule a rule of English professional football?* – we can see another connection with Hart's theory. The answer to the

---

[5] CL, 249 (see list of abbreviations, p. xiii).
[6] Cf. Hart, 'Definition and theory in jurisprudence' in his *Essays in Jurisprudence and Philosophy* (Oxford University Press, 1983), 26–27: 'The economist or the scientist often uses a simple model with which to understand the complex; and this can be done for the law. So in what follows I shall use as a simple analogy the rules of a game which at many vital points have the same puzzling logical structure as rules of law.'
[7] CL, 81.
[8] CL, 94.

question is probably that a rule is one of English professional football if it is recognised by the FA as being such a rule.[9] It might be the case that football officials in England (referees and, generally, members of the FA) accept a rule that recognises 'what the FA declares as rules of English football' as the rules of English football. In Hart's view, what determines whether a rule is a rule *of law* is similarly a rule that recognises certain rules as belonging to a system of rules – the rule of recognition. Hart gives as an example of such a rule: 'what the Queen in Parliament enacts is law'. That what the law is ultimately depends upon facts about what the members of a group of officials have accepted in their practices is the core of what makes Hart a *legal positivist*.

(4) The rules recognised by the FA could be good or bad rules. Some people might think that if the FA introduced a rule that allowed goals scored in the last 10 minutes of a football match to count as two goals that this would be undesirable. Nonetheless, such a rule would become part of the rules of English football by virtue of having being recognised as such by the FA. Similarly, Hart thought that the content of the law could be good or bad – morally praiseworthy or morally heinous. Everything depends upon what rule of recognition the officials of the system accept – if they accept the rule that 'what Parliament enacts is law', then there is no logical guarantee that the content of the law will meet any moral standard.

(5) The attitudes that the players of certain games must have to the rules of the game in order to count as playing the game at all bear some important similarities to the attitudes that Hart claimed some people must have in relation to legal rules in order for law to exist. Consider the rule in chess that the bishop must be moved diagonally. A person is not playing the game of chess if they do not accept that they ought to move the bishop diagonally. In Hart's view, the officials (principally, judges) of a legal system must similarly regard the rule of recognition as a binding rule – they must think that they *ought* to follow the rule.

Hart thought that officials had to adopt this attitude to the rule of recognition in order for there truly to be a *rule* of recognition rather than a mere *habit* of recognition.[10] People may have a habit of going to the cinema on a Tuesday but, according to Hart, there is only a *rule* amongst people of going to the cinema on a Tuesday if they think that they *ought* to go to the cinema on a Tuesday. Why was Hart insistent that law requires the existence of a *rule* of recognition rather than a mere *habit*? The main reason is that a mere habit amongst officials of recognising that 'whatever Parliament enacts is law' would not explain the sense in which Parliament has *legal authority* to make law; it would not capture the sense that the officials *ought* to recognise whatever Parliament enacts as law.

---

[9] See also Green, 'The morality in law' in D'Almeida et al. (eds), *Reading HLA Hart's The Concept of Law* (Hart Publishing, 2013), at 180, comparing law to the rules of cricket, where being part of the publication, 'The Laws of Cricket', partly determines whether a rule is one of cricket.
[10] CL, 55–57.

(6) The rules of a game use normative language. For example, they tell people what they 'ought' to do – in chess, the bishop *ought* to be moved diagonally. Furthermore, the 'ought' here does not seem to be the same as the 'ought' in 'You ought not to torture children for fun'. It is not a *moral* ought. Similarly, Hart insists that legal obligation is not the same as moral obligation.[11] From the fact that one is legally obligated to do something, it does not ipso facto follow that one has a moral obligation to do it.

Law and games: contrasts

We've identified six similarities between Hart's theory of law and certain games. It is also useful in further clarifying Hart's account if we consider the limits of the analogy with games.

(1) It is a *contingent* feature of games that there is a set of officials, whilst this is, according to Hart, a *necessary* feature of law. The game of hide-and-seek goes on perfectly well without there being hide-and-seek officials.[12]
(2) It is a *contingent* feature of games that there is a rule of recognition practised by players of the game (or, should they exist, officials) identifying which rules belong to the game, whilst this is a *necessary* feature of law, according to Hart.[13] Again, there is no need to think of the participants of the game of hide-and-seek as accepting a rule of recognition determining which rules belong to the game.
(3) The rules of a game have a narrow scope of application – they govern the game-related activities. The rules of cricket govern the game of cricket only. By its nature, law, as Hart accepts, governs many activities by way of rules.

Summary

In summary, we can see that, for Hart, the key to understanding law's nature is to understand its *modes* of operation: that law governs by different kinds of rule; that those rules form a system by virtue of a master rule – the rule of recognition; that the rule of recognition exists by virtue of the practice of officials in the system; that the law imposes obligations which are genuinely obligations of a kind, but which are not moral obligations; that its rules govern all sorts of human activities.

FUNCTIONAL KIND THEORIES OF LAW (1): FULLER, SIMMONDS AND FINNIS

Lon Fuller: law is like a saw

Just as it might be said we do not understand what a saw is except by reference to its purpose, so Lon Fuller claimed in his book, *The Morality of Law*, that law's *purpose* was central to understanding its nature.[14] As Green puts it, for Fuller, law is 'an institution on a mission'.[15]

---

[11] CL, 203.
[12] Though there is a national hide-and-seek association of America: www.playhideandseek.org.
[13] CL, 116–17.
[14] CL, 145.
[15] Green, 'Law as a means' (above, n. 1), 173.

What mission? The purpose of law is 'to subject human conduct to the governance of rules'.[16] Fuller's main argument for this was that the criteria by which, in his view, we determine whether law exists are only intelligible if one presupposes that law has, by its nature, the purpose of subjecting conduct to the governance of rules. These criteria he calls the 'desiderata' or 'principles' of legality. The eight desiderata are that there must be:[17] (1) rules (2) which are published, (3) prospective (not retrospective), and (4) with which it is possible to comply; they should also be (5) intelligible, (6) non-contradictory, and (7) reasonably stable across time; in addition, (8) officials must act in accordance with the published rules.

If there is too much of a departure from these criteria, then it cannot be said that a legal system is in existence. We simply wouldn't say that there is law if, for example, there were no rules, or if the rules were entirely secret.

If this is right, Fuller says we have to ask: 'to what end is law being so defined that it cannot "exist" without some minimum respect for the principles of legality?'[18] And to that question, his answer was that law's end – law's purpose – is the governance of human conduct by rules. Only by postulating that this is law's purpose do we make sense of our settled understanding that law only exists where there are rules which are sufficiently clear, prospective, non-contradictory, and so on.

Why was Fuller so 'in love with the notion of purpose'?[19] There are at least two reasons. First, Fuller was long convinced that a central task of jurisprudence is to understand *why* law is important – *why* law is needed in human societies at all. His first book – *The Law in Quest of Itself*[20] – repeatedly criticises contemporary jurisprudence for its failure to address the 'purposive sense of why a lawgiver is needed at all'.[21] Secondly, as we explain in a later chapter, Fuller thought of law's purpose – governance by rules – as an intrinsically moral one.[22] So, for him, once we realise law's purpose, we realise that law is in pursuit of a moral aim. That would be an important property of law, if true.

Fuller's functional theory of law has been built on by two recent legal theorists: Nigel Simmonds and John Finnis.

Nigel Simmonds: law is like a triangle

If you quickly sketch a triangle, it will be an imperfect one. A triangle printed in a mathematical textbook will be a better triangle, though probably still imperfect. Both will not exactly conform to the mathematical definition of a triangle. Nonetheless your triangle and the one in the textbook *are* triangles. They are

---

[16] Fuller, *The Morality of Law*, rev'd edn (Yale University Press, 1969), 106.

[17] Ibid, ch. 2.

[18] Ibid, 198.

[19] A remark made by H.L.A. Hart in his review of *The Morality of Law*: (1968) 78 *Harvard Law Review* 1281, 1296.

[20] Fuller, *The Law in Quest of Itself* (Foundation Press, 1940).

[21] See Rundle, *Forms Liberate* (Hart Publishing, 2012), 28.

[22] See ch. 4, below.

triangles by virtue of their approximation to the mathematical definition of a triangle. And one is *more* of a triangle by more closely approximating the mathematical definition.

Compare the concept of a 'bachelor'. A bachelor is an unmarried man. A man is either a bachelor or he is not. It is not a question of degree or approximation to a definition of bachelorhood which determines whether some particular person is a bachelor or not.

Nigel Simmonds offers a theory of law's nature, in his book *Law as a Moral Idea*, which says that law is more like 'triangle' than 'bachelor'. Simmonds describes concepts like *triangle* as 'archetypal' concepts.[23] Something counts as an instance of an archetypical concept in virtue of its approximation to an abstract definition – and this will be a matter of degree. By contrast, he designates concepts like *bachelor* as 'class concepts'.[24] Something counts as an instance of a class concept only if it meets certain criteria and, upon meeting those criteria, its being an instance of the concept is not a matter of degree.

In Simmonds' view, whether something counts as an instance of *law* depends upon the extent to which it conforms to Fuller's eight desiderata, and the more that it does, the more that it counts as an instance of law – the more *law-like* it is. Law's archetype, then, involves conformity to Fuller's desiderata.[25] However, conformity to Fuller's desiderata is only a first layer in an understanding of law's archetype for Simmonds. Upon further reflection, the archetype reveals itself to have a deeper layer. His further claim is that law's archetype also reflects *a moral aspiration*. Although law is like a triangle, it differs, according to Simmonds, in so far as law's archetype is a *moral aspiration*.[26]

What, then, is this moral aspiration? It is that compliance with Fuller's desiderata is intelligible as realising an ideal of liberty.[27] Complying with the desiderata (to sufficient extent that the resulting rules would be counted as 'law' by virtue of sufficient proximity to the Fullerian archetype) confers a distinctive kind of liberty on persons subject to the law.[28] This is because a system of rules announced prospectively, with which it is possible to comply, will always grant subjects some options as to how to comply with the rules (for example, the law might require a person to drive on the left hand side of the road, but leave open all sorts of things the person can do whilst driving (like whether the person wears a hat or not whilst driving)). Furthermore, these options will enjoy some protection against interference by other subjects, says Simmonds, if the system is concerned (as all legal systems, to some extent, are) with ensuring the effectiveness of the rules of the

---

[23] Simmonds, *Law as a Moral Idea* (Oxford University Press, 2007) (henceforth, *Law as a Moral Idea*), 52–54.
[24] Ibid.
[25] *Law as a Moral Idea*, 65–66. See also Simmonds, 'The nature of law: three problems with one solution' (2011) 12 *German Law Journal* 601, 615–16.
[26] *Law as a Moral Idea*, 54, distinguishing aspirational and non-aspirational archetypes.
[27] See, further, ch. 4, below.
[28] *Law as a Moral Idea*, 101–10.

system.[29] In short, we can make sense of law's archetype if we come to see it as geared towards serving liberty.

Why should we think of law as an *archetypal* concept rather than a *class* concept in the first place? Simmonds' basic argument is that the archetypal nature of law is reflected in our ordinary discourse about law. On the one hand, we think of law as a 'mundane' instrument, capable of serving good and bad purposes equally; on the other hand, we think of law as embodying a moral ideal. This is so in three ways:

(1) *The rule of law.* Simmonds writes: 'Governance by law is regarded as being in itself a virtue of a just political community.'[30] We tend to think of the *rule of law* as an ideal or aspiration. For Simmonds, there is an intimate connection between 'law' and the 'rule of law'. The 'rule of law' is just the situation where law rules.[31] So, if it's right to think that law and the 'rule of law' are deeply connected, and the rule of law is an aspiration, then there is a deep connection between law and an ideal or aspiration.[32]

(2) *Law is invoked as a justification for sanctions.* Judges offer the fact that a person has breached a rule of law as a justification for sanctioning that person. The fact that the person has breached a rule of *law* (rather than some other rule) is thought to be crucial to justifying the outcome that the person should be sanctioned. Simmonds says that this ordinary understanding we have of the way law is invoked by judges to justify sanctions cannot be understood *simply* by reference to Hart's idea of a master rule of recognition, which could be followed by officials for any reasons whatever.[33] It would not be intelligible, Simmonds claims, for a judge to offer, as a justification for a sanction, the fact that a person has breached a rule, which is identified by a rule (the rule of recognition), which the judge follows purely for, say, selfish or malicious reasons. Rather, the practice of invoking the *law* as a justification for a sanction only makes sense if the status of a rule as one of law is thought by the person invoking it to have some moral significance. So, implicit in our ordinary understanding of law, according to Simmonds, is the idea that law has some special moral quality that could justify imposing sanctions on a citizen. This points towards an aspirational understanding of law as embodying a moral ideal.

(3) *Doctrinal argument.* The aspirational aspect to our ordinary understanding of law is also revealed, Simmonds claims, when we consider doctrinal argument about the law in particular cases. Textbook writers often offer, as claims about what the law is, propositions that have never been authoritatively determined

---

[29] Ibid, 104.
[30] Ibid, 37.
[31] Ibid, 46–47.
[32] Ibid, 46–52.
[33] Ibid, 130–36.

by courts. For Simmonds, these kinds of claim can be understood as attempts to move our understanding of particular rules or doctrines of law towards the archetype of law.[34]

John Finnis: law is like a house

John Finnis has written that it is a 'philosophical mistake', in developing a theory of law's nature, to think that '... you can answer the question[:] What is it? [b]efore you tackle the question[:] Why choose to have it, create it, maintain it, and comply with it?'[35] We'll explore his reasons for this view in the next debate. The point for now is that, for Finnis, law's *purpose* is central to understanding law's nature. For Finnis, Fuller's understanding of law as simply existing to guide people's behaviour is too thin. The purpose of having law is not *just* to guide people's behaviour, but to guide people's behaviour in order to enable people to participate in the sort of states and activities that it is good for human beings to participate in: life, knowledge, play, marriage, friendship, aesthetic experience, spirituality, and practical reasonableness.

For Finnis, then – though this is not a comparison he has himself made – law is like a house. To define a house in functional terms as simply existing to provide its occupants with a roof over their head would be to offer an account of the nature of the house that is just as thin and as impoverished as Fuller's account of the purpose of law. Rather, a house, properly understood and properly constructed, exists to provide its occupants with a place to participate in virtually all of the goods that Finnis identifies law as existing to enable people to enjoy. And for Finnis, law is like a house in another sense – and this is a comparison he has made in the past. There are thousands of different ways of designing a house in order to enable the occupants of the house to enjoy the kinds of goods that the occupants of a properly designed house will enjoy. So if a house is to function in the way a house is supposed to, it needs an architect: someone who will *decide how* the house will be designed. In the same way, there are thousands of different combinations of laws that would work equally well to enable the members of a particular community to enjoy the goods that law exists to enable them to enjoy. So if a legal system is to operate in the way it is supposed to do, someone or some body or some combination of bodies needs to *determine* what combination of laws will be given effect to by that legal system.

We will discuss Finnis's theory of law in much greater detail in a later chapter.[36] For now, we will turn to consider another functional theory of law that sees the function of law as lying not so much in its directive quality, but in its justificatory quality.

---

[34] Ibid, 167.
[35] Finnis, 'Law and what I should truly decide' (2003) 48 *American Journal of Jurisprudence* 107, 129.
[36] See ch. 5, below.

FUNCTIONAL KIND THEORIES OF LAW (2): DWORKIN

Ronald Dworkin's theory of law's nature can be summarised in four propositions:

(a) Law is an interpretive concept.
(b) The function of law is to insist that force be used only to the extent that it is justified by past political decisions about when collective force is justified.
(c) The law in a system consists of the best moral justification of the past political decisions of that system.
(d) Law is a branch of morality.

To understand (a)–(c), it will be helpful to consider an analogy drawn between law and the social practice of *courtesy*, an analogy which Dworkin himself deploys in Chapter 2 of *Law's Empire*.[37] We'll consider (d), which is developed in Dworkin's more recent book, *Justice for Hedgehogs*,[38] later.

Dworkin introduces his theory of law by developing a story about the practice of courtesy in an imaginary community. The story has two important stages:

Stage one. At this stage, the community follows a set of rules, which they call rules of 'courtesy', in certain social interactions. They say things like: 'Courtesy requires that peasants take off their hats to nobility.'[39] The practice of courtesy, during this time, goes largely unquestioned and unchanged by the members of the community. It has the character of taboo: the community thinks that the rules of courtesy just ought to be followed, full stop.

Stage two. At a later stage, there develops in the community what Dworkin calls an 'interpretive attitude' towards the rules of courtesy. This attitude has two distinct components: (1) it involves an assumption that the practice of courtesy has some *point or value or purpose*, which can be stated independently of simply describing the rules of courtesy themselves; (2) it involves a further assumption that what courtesy requires in a particular situation is not wholly determined by what people have thought courtesy requires in the past – rather, the requirements of courtesy are sensitive to its *point, value or purpose*.

To understand what (2) means, think again of the rules of football. We might think that the game of football has some value, or set of values at the heart of it (sometimes people might talk of 'the spirit of the game'), and we might appeal to that value in arguing about whether the rules of football *ought to be changed*. But in arguing about what the rules of football *are right now*, we would not appeal to the value or purpose of the game: the rules are determined by whatever the FA says they are. If, however, we adopt the second aspect of the interpretive attitude, we think that *what the rules of a practice currently are* (not what they *ought* to be) is directly determined by *the point, value or purpose* of the practice (and not just by

---

[37] LE, 46–49.
[38] Dworkin, *Justice for Hedgehogs* (Harvard University Press, 2011). We discuss the arguments in this book below, at pp. 18–20, 23–24.
[39] LE, 47.

what anyone actually says the practice requires). So even if a number of the members of the community think that courtesy requires one to say 'Hello' to one's neighbour in the morning, this is not conclusive of what courtesy *actually* requires. Rather, what courtesy actually requires depends upon the conclusion of an argument about what the value of courtesy is and what that value requires in the circumstances.

If the practice described by some concept – like the concept of courtesy – is one to which participants have taken up the interpretive attitude (that is, they assume (1) and (2)), then that concept is an *interpretive concept*, in Dworkin's terminology.

It is a crucial feature of an interpretive concept, according to Dworkin, that if one makes a claim about what the practice to which that concept refers requires, one necessarily takes a stand on the value of the practice. So if I claim that courtesy requires that men rise when women enter the room, I am implicitly taking a view on what the value of courtesy is. This follows simply from the fact that the community has taken up the interpretive attitude to courtesy. If the interpretive attitude is taken up in relation to some practice like courtesy, it is accepted that what that practice requires is sensitive to the *value* or *purpose* of that practice. So when I say that the practice requires *x*, I am always going to be taking a position on the value of the practice. For example, if I say that courtesy requires you not to try to start a conversation with me about my private life when we are in a public place, I might implicitly be assuming that courtesy serves the value of fostering privacy. According to Dworkin, if someone were to ask you to say what courtesy requires in a particular situation without taking a stand on the *value* of courtesy, you would be like 'a man at the North Pole who is told to go any way but south'.[40]

Dworkin claims, then, that *law*, like courtesy in his imaginary community, is an interpretive concept. Consequently, whenever we seek to determine what the law on a particular question is, we are always going to be making a claim about what the point, purpose, or value of law is. What, then, does Dworkin contend the *point* of law to be? He writes that:

> 'the most abstract and fundamental point of legal practice is to guide and constrain the power of government in the following way. Law insists that force not be used or withheld, no matter how useful that would be to ends in view, no matter how beneficial or noble these ends, except as licensed or required by individual rights and responsibilities flowing from past political decisions about when collective force is justified.'[41]

From this abstract starting point, which he claims to be 'uncontroversial',[42] Dworkin goes on to offer an account of a fundamental part of this starting point: namely, the way in which individual legal rights and responsibilities *flow from* past political decisions. In his words, he goes on to offer an account of the *grounds* of

[40] LE, 69.
[41] LE, 93.
[42] LE, 94.

law.[43] The grounds of law are what make it the case that a certain proposition is a proposition of law.[44] For example, someone might claim that one ground of law is 'what Parliament enacts'.

So what is Dworkin's theory of what it is that makes something a proposition of law – what is his account of the *grounds* of law? It needs to be remembered what kind of question this is for Dworkin. Because law is an *interpretive concept*, answering the question involves offering an *interpretation* of legal practice – principally, the practice of recognising the enactments of legislatures as law and the practice of following previous court decisions.[45]

This interpretive exercise involves a working-through of the interpretive attitude in relation to those practices. Dworkin provides an account of how an interpreter should proceed in this task. The account involves three stages of interpretation.[46] The first 'pre-interpretive' stage involves the identification of the 'rules and standards taken to provide the tentative content of the practice'. In the second stage, the interpreter settles upon a justification of the 'main elements' of the practice identified at the pre-interpretive stage. In the final, 'post-interpretive' stage, the interpreter comes to a better sense of what the practice really requires, in light of justification he or she has identified as being the point of the practice. Dworkin calls the entirety of this process *constructive interpretation*.

To illustrate, consider again the example of courtesy. At the pre-interpretive stage, we might find in our imaginary community that there are many rules identified as rules of courtesy which are concerned with showing due respect for the aristocracy. At the second stage, we might come to think that the best justification for this practice lies in a respect for noble people in general. Although this justification might not fit with all aspects of the practice – perhaps there is also a rule which requires one to doff one's cap to women, regardless of their nobility – it provides a justification of most aspects of the practice and is superior to alternative justifications. It is superior, let us suppose, both in the extent to which the justification *fits* with the rules of courtesy (it explains why we have the rules we do) and in the extent to which it is a *morally good* justification (other justifications, say, claim there is value in servility). At the post-interpretive stage, we might find that the justification of the practice requires us not only to show due respect for the aristocracy, but also to show respect – hitherto unrecognised by the practice – for heroic acts of bravery.

Applying this strategy of constructive interpretation to legal practice, Dworkin arrives at a theory of law which he calls 'law as integrity'. According to *law as integrity*, the law of a community consists in the most morally coherent justification of the community's legal practice. Notice that this isn't merely to re-state the claim that law is an interpretive concept and that therefore, in order to understand

---

43 LE, 4–5.
44 LE, 5.
45 LE, 99.
46 LE, 65–68.

what it requires, one needs to determine what the best justification of legal practice is. Rather, Dworkin arrives at law as integrity by arguing that, on the best interpretation of legal practice, the point of legal practice is itself to come up with the best justification of a community's legal practice. This is why he says that law as integrity is 'relentlessly interpretive' and why 'it is both the product of and the inspiration for comprehensive interpretation of legal practice'.[47] Unlike other theories of law (which equally must be arrived at by offering interpretations, since law is an interpretive concept), law as integrity is not *merely* an interpretation of legal practice, but also claims that legal practice *is itself fundamentally interpretive*. Law as integrity itself requires judges themselves to engage in a process of constructive interpretation of the community's legal practices.

IN PLACE OF A CONCLUSION

It would be premature to reach any conclusions at this stage as to which theory of law's nature is superior to the others: there would be little point in the rest of this book if we could. However, we can make some preliminary observations about the contrasts between Hart's modal way of thinking about law, and the two principal functional theories of law advanced by Fuller and Dworkin, respectively.

Hart v Fuller

On the face of it, there is a clear disagreement between Hart's modal theory, which claims that law is primarily distinguished by its *mode* of performing the various functions to which it is put, and functional theories like Fuller's, which claim that law must be understood by reference to a distinctive *function*.

Yet, on closer inspection, this disagreement between Hart and Fuller is thin. Hart accepts that law necessarily, by its nature, has the function of guiding and criticising conduct and that it does so by the *modality* of primary and secondary rules. Fuller accepts that law necessarily, by its nature, has the *function* of subjecting conduct to the governance of rules. The difference here is simply that, for Hart, guiding is the function, and rules are the modality, whilst for Fuller, *guiding by rules* is the composite function. This is a terminological difference about what goes to 'function' and what goes to 'mode'.

Hart and Fuller do disagree in two respects, however. First, even if both accept that guiding conduct by rules is central to law's nature, Hart thinks that this feature only goes part of the way to distinguishing law from other kinds of thing. Quite apart from the existence of *rules*, Hart would importantly add: (1) the rules of any legal system gain their status as law by virtue of the actions (whether deliberate or not) of officials of the system; (2) in any legal system, the practice of officials gives rise to a rule of recognition which determines which rules are rules of law. By contrast, these ideas seem to play little role in Fuller's theory, though they are logically consistent with it. Secondly, they disagree about the moral value of

---

[47] LE, 226.

one of law's *modal* features. They disagree about the moral value of Fuller's eight desiderata. We discuss this disagreement in much more detail in a later chapter.[48]

Hart v Dworkin

The extent to which Hart and Dworkin truly disagree, as opposed to simply being engaged in different enterprises – one (Hart's) concerned with *describing* the concept of law and one (Dworkin's) concerned with *normatively justifying* law – is a notoriously tricky issue.[49] However, there seem to be three ways in which they do genuinely disagree:

(1) Hart does not share Dworkin's supposedly 'uncontroversial' starting point that law's function is to justify coercion. Of course, Hart accepts that law is often invoked as the reason for state coercion. However, Hart denies that the existence of sanctions for the breach of legal obligations is a conceptually necessary condition for the existence of law.[50] This is a topic that we discuss in much more detail in Chapter 2.

(2) Dworkin denies Hart's claim that what the law is necessarily depends upon criteria identified by the rule of recognition. There are disagreements – 'theoretical disagreements' – about what the law is in certain cases which, Dworkin claims, cannot be modeled as disputes about whether the criteria under the rule of recognition have been satisfied. We discuss and reject this argument in Chapter 3.

(3) In Dworkin's view, it is *necessarily* the case that whether a proposition is a proposition of law depends, even if wholly implicitly, upon the conclusion of a *moral* argument, whereas Hart thinks that this is a *contingent* matter, dependent upon the criteria contained in the rule of recognition. Dworkin's position follows from his insistence that law is an interpretive concept. If law is an interpretive concept, then what it requires depends upon coming up with the best justification for its main features.

Dworkin seems to have two main arguments for the claim that law is an interpretive concept. The first argument is simply that this is the only explanation of the phenomenon of theoretical disagreement. To the extent that this argument fails – as we later suggest it does – this undermines Dworkin's position on this third disagreement.

Dworkin's second argument seems to rest upon a general thesis that the only way to interpret social practices is to engage in the process of constructive interpretation.[51] This thesis is quite distinct from the claim about theoretical disagreement. It is possible to reject Hart's position on the rule of recognition for reasons

---

[48] See ch. 4, below.
[49] See Shapiro, 'The Hart-Dworkin debate: a guide for the perplexed' in Ripstein (ed.), *Ronald Dworkin* (Cambridge University Press, 2007).
[50] CL, 219–20.
[51] See LE, 64–65.

relating to the phenomenon of theoretical disagreement, without buying into Dworkin's claim about interpretation. One might simply think that Hart provided a poor description of the nature of law. The converse is also true. One might think that there is no such thing as theoretical disagreement, and yet think that the interpretation of social practices always involves the three-stage inquiry that Dworkin describes. Ultimately, this second argument is an independent thesis about jurisprudential methodology. We discuss and reject this thesis, in the next debate.

Debate 2

Can there be purely descriptive theories of law's nature?

Hart insisted that his account of law in *The Concept of Law* was '*descriptive* in that it is morally neutral and has no justificatory aims'.[52] However, the possibility of remaining aloof from *evaluative* questions in developing a theory of law's nature has been challenged. We discuss two primary challenges here: that made by John Finnis in Chapter 1 of *Natural Law and Natural Rights*, and that made by Ronald Dworkin in *Law's Empire* and later writings. Before we address the criticisms made of purely descriptive legal theory, it is necessary first to set out in more detail Hart's own conception of descriptive theory.

HART: DESCRIPTIVE LEGAL THEORY AS CONCEPTUAL ANALYSIS

In the preface to *The Concept of Law*, H.L.A. Hart wrote that his book could be considered as both 'an essay in analytical jurisprudence' and 'an essay in descriptive sociology'.[53] By the former, he seemed to mean that the book could be understood as an exercise in analysing the meaning of and interrelationships between the concepts (like obligation, rule, validity) which are essential to the concept of law, and which, combined in certain way, differentiate law from other phenomena. Thus he writes:

> 'My aim in this book has been to further the understanding of law, coercion, and morality as different but related social phenomena.... The lawyer will regard the book as an essay in analytical jurisprudence, for it is concerned with the clarification of the general framework of legal thought ... [A]t many points, I have raised questions which may well be said to be about the meanings of words. Thus I have considered: how "being obliged" differs from "having an obligation"; how the statement that a rule is a valid rule of law differs from a prediction of the behaviour of officials ...'[54]

---

[52] CL, Postscript, 240 (emphasis in original).
[53] CL, vi–vii.
[54] CL, vi.

After giving this flavour of what is meant by 'analytical jurisprudence', Hart *then* says that the book could *also* be regarded as an essay in descriptive sociology. The reason he gives is that:

> 'the suggestion that inquiries into the meanings of words merely throw light on words is false. Many important distinctions, which are not immediately obvious, between types of social situation or relationships may best be brought to light by an examination of the standard uses of the relevant expressions. In this field of study it is particularly true that we may use, as Professor J.L. Austin said, "a sharpened awareness of words to sharpen our perception of the phenomena".'[55]

The reason the book is *also* an exercise in descriptive sociology, then, is not because it adopts some *additional* method – above and beyond the analysis of concepts – but because the analysis of concepts itself gives us access to the nature of the thing to which those concepts refer.

The reason this can be described as *sociological* is – as John Gardner plausibly maintains – because sociology has itself been concerned with *conceptual, classificatory* questions and not the purely empirical questions of clipboard-carrying field work. As Gardner writes:

> 'Are their [sociologists'] questions only the empirical ones that arise in applying classifications provided by others, perhaps philosophers? It is hard to see how this could be so. It would expel from the sociological canon the most celebrated work of such major figures of the discipline as Durkheim, Tönnies, Weber, and Mauss, archclassifiers all four.'[56]

It follows, then, that we can safely describe Hart's method as one of *conceptual analysis,* the aim of which is to describe the features in virtue of which some phenomenon should be classified as 'law'.

What does Hart understand by 'conceptual analysis'? Frequently, he writes of providing an 'elucidation' or 'clarification' of the concept of law.[57] However, as Schauer notes, Hart does not give sustained attention to the question of what it is to *analyse* a concept.[58] Nonetheless, Hart's intentions seem to be reasonably clear from various scattered remarks in *The Concept of Law*. In Chapter 1, Hart emphasises that he is not attempting to provide a set of necessary and sufficient conditions for the appropriate use of the word 'law', such that we can definitively determine whether we ought to describe a certain phenomenon as law or not.[59] Rather his aim is to identify, and explain the nature of, the features of the 'central' or 'standard' or 'paradigm' case of law.[60] This leaves open the possibility that an instance of law might lack some of the features of the paradigm or standard case,

---

[55] CL, vi.
[56] Gardner, 'Law in general' (above, n. 3), 278.
[57] See, for example, CL, 219.
[58] Schauer, 'Hart's anti-essentialism' in *Reading HLA Hart's The Concept of Law* (above, n. 9), 241–44.
[59] CL 4, 17.
[60] CL, 16–17

and yet still be classifiable as such. The conclusion to be drawn from something's lacking all of the features of the paradigm case is only that this instance is less law-like: it is a non-central case of law.

Furthermore, according to Hart, the extent to which a potential instance of law, which lacks all of the features of the paradigm case, is classifiable as law is a question of how far removed it is from the standard or paradigm case. As Endicott points out, it doesn't follow that Hart's method is not concerned with finding necessary truths about law.[61] On Hart's method, something counts as an instance of law only if it is sufficiently analogous to the paradigm case of law. Necessarily, then, something only belongs to the concept 'law' if it partakes of sufficient features of the paradigm case. This rules out – as a matter of necessary truth – many things as *not-law* (dogs, houses, rain, the Isle of Skye, John Finnis).

FINNIS'S CHALLENGE TO DESCRIPTIVE LEGAL THEORY

In Chapter 1 of *Natural Law and Natural Rights*, John Finnis argues that a descriptive theory of law cannot be developed without the theorist becoming involved in evaluation. In his words:

> 'no theorist can give a theoretical description and analysis of social facts [law being such] without also participating in the work of evaluation, of understanding what is really good for human persons, and what is really required by practical reasonableness.'[62]

It will be useful to set out the general structure of Finnis's argument first, before going on to reflect upon each stage. In essence, the argument is:

(1) Descriptive theories of law need to make judgments about what is *important* and *significant* to include within a general description of law. If they do not, they will just list a miscellaneous bunch of facts about law.

(2) The descriptive theorist must treat as important and significant the perspective of those within the law who consider the law as potentially giving them reason to take certain actions.

(3) Having identified as important the internal perspective of those within the law, one ought to accept that the 'central case' of that perspective is the one which regards the creation of law as a moral requirement. The descriptive theorist, whose primary concern is with law's central case, must consequently build up a general picture of law from the perspective of one who considers the establishment of law as morally required.

Consider (1). The basic point is quite simple. It is obvious that in constructing a theory of law's nature, some judgments need to be made as to what to include and what to leave out. For example, the average size of the judges' shoes in each system

---

[61] Endicott, 'The generality of law' in *Reading HLA Hart's The Concept of Law* (above, n. 9), 28–33.
[62] NLNR, 3.

would not merit inclusion, nor would the dimensions of court buildings. And this is true even if it turned out that the average judicial shoe size was the same in every recorded historical instance of a legal system. Consequently: 'there is no escaping the theoretical requirement that a judgment of *significance* and *importance* be made if theory is to be more than a vast rubbish heap of miscellaneous facts ...'[63]

So the issue is then: how is a theorist to go about making these judgments of significance and importance? This is stage (2). Finnis says that he or she must place significance on the perspectives of people within the social practice of law. Recall that in our description of Hart's theory above, we noted that Hart draws attention to the particular kinds of 'internal' attitude which officials must have towards the rule of recognition if law, in his view, is to exist. Hart said that the officials must *accept* the rule as binding – although their reasons for acceptance, he claimed, could vary entirely from self-interest to a sense of moral duty. At stage (2) of the argument, Finnis is simply agreeing with Hart that it is crucial for the theorist to reflect the internal point of view of participants to legal practice in constructing a general descriptive theory. Why, though, is the internal perspective so important – why was Hart right to focus on it in the first place? The reason, for Finnis, is that it is impossible to understand a practice which exists partly by virtue of the understandings of participants to the practice 'without understanding their point, objective, significance or importance *"as conceived by the people who performed them, engaged them, etc."'*.[64]

The crucial move comes at stage (3). Here Finnis argues: once the theorist has accepted the internal perspective as crucial to constructing a descriptive theory of law, the theorist is committed to taking up the internal perspective of a fully reasonable agent within the practice. So instead of describing the attitudes of the judge who follows the rule of recognition for purely self-interested reasons, or the anarchist judge who follows the rule merely to defeat the system from within, the theorist should describe law through the lens of a person within the practice who is fully reasonable. If the fully reasonable agent would consider the creation of law to be 'a moral ideal if not a compelling demand of justice', that is the perspective which should be taken up in constructing a general theory of law's nature. In determining what aspects of the law the fully reasonable person would consider to be central to law's nature, the theorist will become entangled in evaluative questions.[65]

What reasons does Finnis give for his claim that there is an inexorable path from taking into account the internal attitudes of participants in law to describing law from the perspective of a fully reasonable participant in law? There are two reasons. First, this follows from the 'central case' method.[66] The theorist should

---

[63] NLNR, 17.
[64] Finnis, 'Law and what I should truly decide' (above, n. 35), 118 (emphasis in original). See also 112: 'The primary reality of the law is rather in its claim ... on my deliberating about what to decide ... to choose and do.'
[65] NLNR, 15.
[66] NLNR, 10–11.

seek to identify the *central case* of some concept, not the borderline or watered-down version of the concept. So the theorist of tables (a strange character) does not, we might say, identify a *broken* table as the central case of a table, albeit that it is still a table in virtue of its sharing features with the central case. Finnis claims that the central case of law is morally good law. Morally good law is a more central case of law than morally wicked law. Notice that this is not simply the tautology that *good* law is *better* law – it is that that *good* law is *more* law-like, just as the unbroken table is more table-like than the broken.

The second reason seems to be that, if the theorist does not take up the evaluative stance of a fully reasonable agent within law, the resulting theory of law will be overly parochial or insufficiently *general*. Finnis begins Chapter 1 of *Natural Law and Natural Rights* by observing that jurisprudence aspires to do more than provide a 'local' lexicography of the concept of law – it aims to do more than simply to set out the rules which particular societies use or have used in deciding whether a social institution counts as law. Jurisprudence aims to provide a *general* theory of the nature of law, by reference to which particular social formations throughout different cultures can be understood as more or less central instances. Unless the theorist describes law from the perspective of a fully practical reasonable agent – which Finnis would say is a universal, objective perspective, cutting across all cultures – it is difficult to see how jurisprudence could meet its aim to be more than a local history of the use of the word 'law'. So the generality of jurisprudence's aspirations is met by the generality and universality of the perspective of the practically reasonable agent.

DWORKIN'S CHALLENGE TO DESCRIPTIVE LEGAL THEORY

Consider the following conversation:

A: Abortion is always wrong.
B: You're wrong: abortion is permissible sometimes.
C: You're both wrong – abortion is neither morally prohibited nor morally permissible – it's like washing your hair; morality has nothing to say about it.
D: This conversation is really weird: you are all assuming that there is a right answer here – morality is totally subjective and none of you can be said either to be right or wrong.

It's clear in this conversation that A, B and C are all taking a (different) moral position on abortion. On the face of it, though, D is not taking a moral position. D is just making a descriptive claim *about* morality, not a claim *within* morality – D is saying that morality, as a descriptive matter, is purely subjective.

Ronald Dworkin rejects this characterisation of what D is saying. Dworkin says that D is actually making a claim *within* morality – just like A, B and C.[67] This is

[67] Dworkin, 'Objectivity and truth: you'd better believe it' (1996) 25 *Philosophy and Public Affairs* 87, 96–97; *Justice for Hedgehogs* (above, n. 38), ch. 1.

because it follows from D's position that there are no moral prohibitions or moral permissions in relation to abortion. So if A said to D: 'Abortion is morally wrong', D would be committed to saying: 'No, it's not true that abortion is morally wrong (it's neither true nor false).' So, although D's position looks to be a purely factual and descriptive one about the nature of morality, Dworkin says that taking such a position ultimately means taking a stand on questions *within* morality. Do you want to deny that moral claims can be true or false? Then you must accept that propositions like 'Torturing babies for fun' are neither true or false and so, it follows, no one has a duty not to torture babies for fun.

Dworkin thinks that descriptive theories of law make claims about law like D makes about morality. On the face of it, these theories of law are purely descriptive, and make no moral claims, but in reality, once we see what those theories entail, they do end up making moral claims. If so, then descriptive theories are ultimately always normative, evaluative, theories.

Dworkin illustrates this argument with a hypothetical legal case which he calls *Sorenson's Case*.[68] The claimant in this case, Mrs Sorenson, suffered from rheumatoid arthritis for many years and took a drug caiied 'inventum' to relieve her suffering. During that period, inventum was manufactured by 11 different drug companies under different trade names. In fact the drug had serious undisclosed side-effects, about which the manufacturers should have known, and Mrs Sorenson suffered permanent cardiac damage from taking the drug. She sues the manufacturers and argues that, although she cannot prove which manufacturer's drug was a cause of her injury, each manufacturer should be liable in proportion to the share of the market it had during the period in which she took the drug.

Dworkin then asks: How should people decide what the law requires in *Sorenson's Case*?[69] On his theory of law – law as integrity – the judge ought to look at the past precedents and interpret them in their best light, trying to identify the most morally coherent principle which underlies those precedents, and ask whether that principle would justify recovery for Mrs Sorenson. The result of that inquiry identifies what the law is in *Sorenson's Case*. By contrast, he says, on Hart's theory of law, the judge must look only to whatever sources of law are incorporated within the rule of recognition. The rule of recognition might require the judge to look to a certain moral principle, but it might not – it all depends upon what rule the officials have followed in a certain system. So, on Hart's view, if the past precedents do not support Mrs Sorenson, and there is no principle incorporated in the rule of recognition which would allow the judges to go beyond those past precedents, then Mrs Sorenson – so far as the law is concerned – should lose. The difference between Hart's and Dworkin's view here, according to Dworkin, is that in Dworkin's view, identifying what the law says *necessarily* involves making a

---

[68] See Dworkin, 'Hart's Postscript and the character of political philosophy' (2004) 24 *Oxford Journal of Legal Studies* 1, 3–5. The case is based upon the Californian case, *Sindell v Abbott Laboratories*, 607 P 2d 924 (1980).

[69] Dworkin, 'Hart's Postscript and the character of political philosophy' (above, n. 68), 4.

moral argument, whilst for Hart, identifying what the law says may or may not – it all depends upon the content of the rule of recognition.

Now here is where Dworkin makes the analogy with Hart's supposedly descriptive theory and his characterisation of D's position in the conversation about abortion. He says: Hart's supposedly descriptive account of law's nature, in terms of a rule of recognition, is 'far from neutral between the parties in Mrs Sorenson's case'.[70] It is not neutral because it means that, unless the rule of recognition has already incorporated moral principles into the law, Mrs Sorenson must lose. And more generally:

> 'Hart's view is not neutral in the argument: it takes sides. It takes sides in fact in every difficult legal dispute, in favour of those who insist that the legal rights of the parties are to be settled entirely by consulting the traditional sources of law.'[71]

So Hart's descriptive account, Dworkin claims, has knock-on effects on how cases like Mrs Sorenson's are to be decided. The theory implicitly takes a stand on the moral issue of how such cases are to be decided. Consequently, Hart's theory is ultimately evaluative in nature. Any descriptive theory, it seems, will end up taking a stand on moral questions about how cases are to be decided.

CONCLUSIONS

Are Finnis and Dworkin successful in establishing that a purely descriptive theory of law is impossible? Let's begin with Finnis.

Finnis's arguments

Must the descriptive theorist inevitably engage in moral evaluation in order to construct a theory of law's nature? If Finnis is right, then that will be true. So is Finnis's argument sound? It seems to us that virtually everyone will accept his first premise (1) – that we have to avoid presenting a rubbish heap of miscellaneous facts in coming up with a theory of law. And it also seems hard to deny (2) – surely any account of law that misses out what the people within law think will miss something 'important and significant'. So it is stage (3) that is attackable, if any is. More precisely, it is that part of stage (3) that claims that the theorist *must* take up the viewpoint of someone who thinks that bringing law as a social order into existence is morally required. What's controversial about (3) is thus not the *central case* method itself – it's hard to deny that there are more and less central instances of a concept – but rather the *criteria by which we determine whether something counts as central or not*. Finnis thinks these criteria are moral in nature. There are at least three objections one can make to this.

---

[70] Ibid, 20.
[71] Ibid.

(1) Objection 1: Importance and significance can be determined indirectly by non-moral criteria

First, one might contend that it is possible to make judgments of importance and significance which do not involve moral evaluation of law's features. Julie Dickson develops a position of this kind.[72] Dickson rejects the distinction between 'descriptive' and 'evaluative' theories, partly for the reason that the distinction creates the impression that descriptive theories are entirely value-free. As she points out, even Hart – arch-descriptivist that he was – accepted that a theory of law's nature 'will be guided by judgements, often controversial, of what is important and will therefore reflect such meta-theoretic values and not be neutral between all values'.[73]

However, Dickson insists that not all evaluation need be *moral* evaluation. She draws a distinction between *indirectly* and *directly* evaluative theories. Finnis's theory is directly evaluative, requiring the theorist directly to make judgments as to the moral value of law. The *indirectly* evaluative theorist, however, makes judgments of importance and significance by reference to features of the law which are 'already considered important and significant about law by those living under and guiding their conduct by it'.[74] The indirectly evaluative theorist, then, makes evaluations *indirectly* in the sense that his or her primary source of what to include within a theory of law's nature are the judgments of *other people* – the judgments of importance and significance already made by those living under the law.[75] So it would be important for a theory of law's nature to explain the role of coercion because this is judged important by those living under the law.

An objection to Dickson's approach is that there will be many different perspectives upon what is central and important to law adopted by those living under it.[76] In a recent essay, she herself draws attention to the attitudes to the law of those who engaged in rioting in London in 2011, as reported by empirical studies. To these people, she says, a core characteristic of the law is its (overbroad) use of force.[77] But one wonders how the theorist is to do justice to different (potentially conflicting) perspectives of what is important and significant about the law, without having some criterion of ranking or priority. As Finnis himself says: 'any general theory of law, however merely descriptive its ambition, necessarily prefers one concept of law over countless others'.[78] Finnis at least has a clear account of how to make such a choice: the viewpoint of those who morally support law's existence is central.

---

[72] Dickson, *Evaluation and Legal Theory* (Hart Publishing, Oxford, 2001). For a short introduction to her position, see Dickson, 'Descriptive legal theory' (available on the online *IVR Encyclopaedia of Jurisprudence, Legal Theory and Philosophy of Law*).

[73] Hart, 'Comment' in R. Gavison (ed.), *Issues in Contemporary Legal Philosophy: The Influence of HLA Hart* (Oxford University Press, 1987), 39.

[74] Dickson, 'Descriptive legal theory' (above, n. 72), section 2.

[75] Dickson, *Evaluation and Legal Theory* (above, n. 72), ch. 3.

[76] For a similar objection, see Madden Dempsey, 'On Finnis' way in' (2012) 57 *Villanova Law Review* 827, 838.

[77] Dickson, 'Law and its theory: a question of priorities' in Keown and George (eds), *Reason, Morality, and Law: The Philosophy of John Finnis* (Oxford University Press, 2013), 372.

[78] Finnis, 'Law and what I truly should decide' (above, n. 35), 119.

(2) Objection 2: Law's function is less central to its nature than Finnis claims: law is more like the concept of a 'painting' than the concept of 'medicine'

In a footnote to his article, 'Law and what I truly should decide', Finnis recounts the following objection made to his methodological arguments by Joseph Raz, and a response to it:

> 'Joseph Raz asked why law should be thought to be like argument, medicine or contracts, rather than like novels or paintings, or people, that are still novels or paintings, or people, even if they are bad. One answer is that, like argument, medicines, and contracts, law has a focused and normative point to which everything else about it is properly to be regarded as subordinate. Novels and paintings, on the other hand, can have incompatible points, e.g. to entertain or arouse (like kitsch or porn) or to tell a truth with artistry.'[79]

It seems true to say that my terrible attempt to paint a portrait of van Gogh is just as much a painting as van Gogh's splendid self-portrait, but that medicine which doesn't work is no medicine at all, or only medicine in a diluted sense. To be sure, van Gogh's is a much better painting than mine. But it is not *more* painting-like in virtue of being a better painting. So, Raz's question is – Why think of law as becoming more law-like the more morally good it is (or, conversely, less law-like the more morally problematic it is)?

Finnis's response is a little obscure, but it seems to be that law's main point – to co-ordinate activity for the sake of the common good – is so central to its nature that its failure to achieve that purpose is much more determinative of whether we say that an object is law than a novel's being bad. This is because a novel's being bad might only constitute a failure to achieve *one* of its *many* possible purposes. Even if a novel failed in some of those purposes, it might still achieve others and so merit its status as a 'novel'. By contrast, since law's *central* purpose is to achieve the common good, if it fails in that central purpose, it becomes less law-like.

It seems to us that Raz's objection is ultimately misplaced, though not for the reason Finnis says. The whole point of Finnis's argument is that in constructing a *general* theory of law, which is more than just a collection of various views about the concept of law, the theorist will have to make judgments about what is practically reasonable in order to select between these competing concepts. This argument is quite distinct, and untouched, by whether law's function is central to its nature.

(3) Objection 3: The theory of law does not claim the universality which Finnis alleges

The major appeal of Finnis's argument is that it provides the theorist with a way of deciding between competing judgments of what is important and significant about law in developing a theory of law's nature. In this way, the theorist avoids the charge – so long as we assume, with Finnis, that morality is objective and universal – of producing a parochial history of the concept of law as it was understood in, say, 1950s Oxford.

---

[79] Ibid, 114, fn. 9.

Joseph Raz denies that descriptive theories of the concept of law need to be non-parochial. In Raz's view, descriptive theories of law *do* simply provide analyses of *our* concept of law.[80] Raz is not particularly clear on what he means by 'our' concept of law. He simply speaks of 'our society's' concept of law.[81] It does not follow, according to Raz, that legal theory is wholly parochial. It is general in two respects. First, he claims, 'our' concept of law has itself evolved so as to take into account our engagement with other cultures and our increased knowledge of history.[82] Secondly, we can still ask whether *other* societies or cultures have the social institutions which our concept of law picks out as central to law. So we can sensibly ask whether ancient Egyptian society had *law* in our sense.[83] The reason this is possible is that other societies can have law in our sense – that is, they can have the social institutions to which our concept of law refers – without themselves possessing our concept of law.

It is difficult to assess Raz's view without his clarifying further to whom he is referring in speaking of *our* concept of law. It seems to us that the wider the group of people to whom this refers, the more likely it is that Raz will face the problem with which Finnis's argument is intended to deal. That is – the more perspectives on what is important and significant about law that one takes into account in developing a general theory of law's nature, the more likely it is that one will be faced by multiple views as to law's nature and, in order to decide between them, moral criteria will need to be used.

Dworkin's arguments

In our view, Dworkin's argument fails for two reasons:

First, his own theory of law relies upon making purely descriptive claims about law's nature. Take the claim that law is an interpretive concept. As this idea is presented in Chapter 2 of *Law's Empire*, by reference to the imaginary community's concept of courtesy, it seems that whether a concept is an interpretive concept is a descriptive or analytical issue. Dworkin says that a concept becomes an interpretive one once the interpretive attitude sets in in relation to that concept. But surely whether the interpretive attitude exists is itself a descriptive claim. It requires no moral argument to establish that people do in fact have a certain attitude towards their practices. So Dworkin's argument is self-defeating. If Dworkin is right that descriptive legal theories are untenable, then his own theory of law is in trouble.

Secondly, the analogy Dworkin draws between the conversation about abortion and *Sorenson's Case*, and law in general, is not convincing. First, unlike (arguably) D's position in the abortion conversation, Hart's argument has no significant moral consequences. It simply does not follow on Hart's account of the concept of

---

[80] Raz, 'Can there be a theory of law?' in his *Between Authority and Interpretation* (Oxford University Press, 2009), 36.
[81] Ibid, 32.
[82] Ibid, 33.
[83] Ibid, 37.

law that people like Mrs Sorenson should lose their cases; nor are people like Mrs Sorenson systematically disadvantaged by Hart's account. That would only follow if Hart *also* claimed that, *as a moral matter* or as a *moral principle of adjudication*, judges should not develop the law in accordance with the moral principles underlying it. But Hart makes no such claim.[84] Secondly, Dworkin's argument proves way too much. In essence, Dworkin's argument is: If a descriptive account of some concept leads to some moral consequence, then that account makes a moral argument and needs to defend itself on moral grounds. But the idea that a claim which has moral consequences is itself a moral position is far too broad. The claim that water is H_2O has moral consequences (if you know that water is H_2O, you oughtn't to tell schoolchildren that it is HO), but whether it is true or not has nothing to do with morality. Dworkin would, of course, accept this – he would say that 'water' is different from 'law'. Water is a 'natural kind' concept – it has a definite, scientifically determined nature, a nature constituted wholly independently of human evaluations. Nonetheless, Dworkin's argument that law is different, so that law requires a moral argument in order to say what it is, seems to rest on the overly broad claim that defining law in one way or another has moral consequences for people. As such, it is subject to the objection that it proves too much.

Further Reading

Hart, CL, ch. I, Postscript, 239–44.

Hart, 'Definition and theory in jurisprudence' in Hart, *Essays in Jurisprudence and Philosophy* (Oxford University Press, 1983).

Dworkin, LE, chs 1–3.

Finnis, NLNR, ch. 1, Postscript 417–19, 426–36.

Finnis, 'Law and what I truly should decide' (2003) 48 *American Journal of Jurisprudence* 107.

Madden Dempsey, 'On Finnis' way in' (2012) 57 *Villanova Law Review* 827.

Green, 'Law as a means' in Cane (ed.), *The Hart-Fuller Debate in the Twenty-First Century* (Hart Publishing, 2010).

Simmonds, *Law as a Moral Idea* (Oxford University Press, 2007), chs 1–2.

Steel, 'Shapiro's planning theory of law' at <www.mcbridesguides.com/category/jurisprudence/sandy-steel/>.

---

[84] See, further, Endicott, 'Adjudication and the law' (2007) 27 *Oxford Journal of Legal Studies* 311.

2

THE NORMATIVITY OF LAW

The existence of law can give us reasons to act in particular ways. Most obviously, the fact that we are required to drive on the left in the UK gives each of us a reason to drive on the left: driving on the right becomes extremely dangerous if everyone else is driving on the left. The assurance the law gives us that it will give us a remedy if someone breaches a contract with us, can give us reasons to trust someone to perform a contract that would not be present in the absence of that assurance. The prospect that we might be held liable if someone is injured on a school trip that we are supervising may give us reason to scrap the idea of taking 30 schoolchildren camping. Some of these effects are intended; some not. This chapter is about situations where the law intends to supply us with a reason to act in a particular way by requiring us to act in that way.

For example, s. 1(1) of the Protection from Harassment Act 1997 (PHA) provides that: 'A person must not pursue a course of conduct– (a) which amounts to harassment of another, and (b) which he knows or ought to know amounts to harassment of another.' This provision obviously seeks to influence our behaviour – but how does it seek to do this? When the law tells us not to pursue a course of conduct which (as we know or ought to know) amounts to harassment of another, is it telling us 'Don't engage in conduct which (as you know or ought to know) amounts to harassment of another, or else you will be punished'? Or is it telling us 'Not engaging in conduct which (as you know or ought to know) amounts to harassment of another is the right thing to do'? Or is it saying something else entirely? The debates in this chapter are all about how the law purports to give us reasons to act (or not act) in a particular way when it tells us to act (or not act) in that way.

Debate 1

Are legal requirements simply orders backed by threats?

Until the publication of H.L.A. Hart's *The Concept of Law* in 1961, it was popular to think that provisions such as s. 1(1) of the PHA were simply saying 'Act in this way, or you will incur some kind of legal sanction'. This view was most closely associated with the English legal philosopher John Austin, and the American jurist Oliver Wendell Holmes. So Austin wrote:

'Every *law* ... is a *command* ...

A command ... is a signification of desire. But a command is distinguished from other significations of desire by this peculiarity: that the party to whom it is directed is liable to evil from the other, in case he comply not with the desire.

Being liable to evil from you if I comply not with a wish which you signify, I am *bound* or *obliged* by your command, or I lie under a *duty* to obey it. If, in spite of that evil in prospect, I comply not with the wish which you signify, I am said to disobey your command, or to violate the duty which it imposes.

Command and duty are, therefore, correlative terms ...'[1]

And Holmes took much the same view:

'If you want to know the law and nothing else, you must look at it as a bad man, who cares only for the material consequences which such knowledge enables him to predict, not as a good one, who finds his reasons for conduct, whether inside the law or outside of it, in the vaguer sanctions of conscience. ...

Take ... the notion of legal duty ... We fill the word with all the content which we draw from morals. But what does it mean to a bad man? Mainly, and in the first place, a prophecy that if he does certain things he will be subjected to disagreeable consequences by way of imprisonment or compulsory payment of money.'[2]

H.L.A. Hart rejected what he called this 'gunman' theory of law, where legal requirements such as that contained in s. 1(1) of the PHA are viewed as akin to a gunman's 'Do this, or else!'. He made a number of arguments against this view:

(1) People say that s. 1(1) of the PHA imposes an *obligation* on us not to harass other people. But no one handing over their money to a gunman would say that they had an *obligation* to hand over their money to the gunman. Instead they would say that they were *obliged* to hand over their money.[3]

(2) Moreover, when someone is punished for failing to comply with s. 1(1) of the PHA, we say that he is being punished *because* he had an obligation under s. 1(1) of the PHA not to harass other people; we don't say (as the 'gunman' theory of law would have us say) that he had an obligation under s. 1(1) of the PHA not to harass other people because he was liable to be punished if he did harass other people.[4]

(3) Furthermore, we would still say that someone had an obligation not to harass other people under s. 1(1) of the PHA even if his situation meant that it was highly unlikely that he would ever face any kind of sanction for harassing someone else[5] – for example, if he were an extremely powerful and wealthy mobster and the targets of his harassment were either too well paid or too frightened ever to make an issue of the way they were treated by him.

---

[1] Austin, *Lectures on Jurisprudence, Volume I*, 3rd edn (John Murray, 1869), 90–91.
[2] Holmes, 'The path of the law' (1896–97) 10 *Harvard Law Review* 457, 459, 461.
[3] CL, 88 (see list of abbreviations, p. xiii).
[4] CL, 84.
[5] CL, 84.

Hart argued that these differences in language show that s. 1(1) of the PHA is fundamentally different from a gunman's 'Do this, or else!'. What s. 1(1) of the PHA is doing is laying down a *rule* that establishes a standard of behaviour that we are expected to live up to. Those who are disposed (for whatever reason) to comply with this rule – in Hart's terminology, those who adopt an 'internal attitude' towards the rule – will regard themselves, once the rule is laid down, as having an obligation to comply with it, and will regard themselves as having good reason for criticising those who fail to comply with the rule and for taking steps to see that other people do comply with the rule.[6] Austin and Holmes' theory of what provisions such as s. 1(1) of the PHA are doing fails to account for the way such provisions offer themselves as a *guide to conduct*, and are accepted as such both by the courts that give effect to the law and the vast majority of the population that are subject to the law.[7] Holmes made a mistake, Hart thought, in insisting on looking at law through the eyes of a 'bad man' who was only worried about what would happen to him if he acted in this or that way: 'Why should the law not be equally if not more concerned with the "puzzled man" or "ignorant man" who is willing to do what he is required, if only he can be told what it is? Or with the "man who wishes to arrange his affairs" if only he can be told how to do it.'[8]

Under Hart's theory of law, we can say that A has a legal obligation to do *x* even if there exist no legal sanctions for failing to do *x*. All that is required for such a legal obligation to exist is that there exist some rule which is recognised as a valid rule of the relevant legal system under which people like A are required to do *x*.[9] For Hart, sanctions for failing to adhere to what he called the 'primary rules' of a legal system were required, not in order for us to be able to say that people have legal obligations under those primary rules, but as a matter of fairness, 'in order that those who would voluntarily submit to the restraints of law shall not be mere victims of malefactors, who would, in the absence of such sanctions, reap the advantages of respect for law on the part of others, without respecting it themselves.'[10]

Hart is generally seen as having convincingly won the debate with Austin and Holmes about the nature of legal obligation – we cannot say that the essence of having a legal obligation to act in a particular way is that you will face some kind of sanction under the law if you do not act in that way. But note that Hart's victory is purely negative in nature. His arguments establish that whatever s. 1(1) of the PHA might be saying, it is *not* saying that 'If you engage in conduct that (as you know or ought to know) amounts to harassment, you will be punished.' But what, then, *is* it saying? It is when we look to Hart for a *positive* account of what such provisions *are* saying that doubts creep in as to how total his victory over Austin

[6] CL, 55–56.
[7] CL, 90–91.
[8] CL, 40.
[9] CL, 216.
[10] CL, 218. See also CL, 198.

and Holmes was. For Hart never offered a convincing account of what provisions such as s. 1(1) of the PHA are *actually* saying.

Hart thought that he could account for the way in which people think of provisions such as s. 1(1) of the PHA as creating obligations through the 'internal attitude' towards rules – the idea being that someone who has a standing disposition to obey the rules of (say) the UK legal system will regard himself as having, among other things, an obligation under s. 1(1) of the PHA not to engage in conduct which (as he knows or ought to know) amounts to harassment in the sense that he will regard the existence of s. 1(1) of the PHA as giving him a conclusive reason not to engage in such conduct, regardless of whatever other reasons he might have for and against engaging in such conduct.[11] But this misses the point, which is that the rule set out in s. 1(1) of the PHA *itself* purports to make not engaging in harassing conduct obligatory and we want to know in what sense *that rule* makes not engaging in harassing conduct obligatory. Asking about people's attitudes towards the rule cannot tell us anything about what the rule is actually saying.[12]

For example, suppose that I ask my best friend's daughter, Ines, what she wants for Christmas. She replies, 'You should get me a chess set' or 'You must get me a chess set'. My standing disposition to get Ines whatever she wants for Christmas (within limits) will mean her words will produce in me a feeling of having an obligation to get her a chess set for Christmas, but that tells us nothing about what *she* meant by saying 'You *should* get me a chess set' or 'You *must* get me a chess set'. After all, I would have had exactly the same feeling of obligation even if she had simply said 'A chess set' in response to my question – using words which did not purport to impose any kind of obligation on me at all. So my attitudes towards Ines' words do not give us any insight into what the words she used actually mean.

When we look to Hart's writings for some account of what a provision like s. 1(1) of the PHA is actually saying, he tells us in *The Concept of Law* that

> 'Rules are conceived and spoken of as imposing obligations when the general demand for conformity is insistent and the social pressure brought to bear upon those who deviate or threaten to deviate is great.'[13]

and

> 'To say that at a given time there is a rule requiring judges to accept as law Acts of Parliament ... entails, first, that there is general compliance with this requirement ...; secondly, that when or if [deviation from or repudiation of this requirement]

---

[11] See Hart, *Essays on Bentham* (Oxford University Press, 1982), 253–55 for the clearest statement to this effect.

[12] See Endicott, 'The subsidiarity of law and the obligation to obey' (2005) 50 *American Journal of Jurisprudence* 233, at 235: 'the existence of an attitude to an obligation does not explain the nature of the obligation ...' Also Endicott, 'Law and language' in Zalta (ed.), *Stanford Encyclopedia of Philosophy* (at <http://plato.stanford.edu/entries/law-language/>), §3.2: 'Hart had nothing to say about the *meaning* of normative expressions such as "ought" and "must" or "obligation" or "right" ... He only pointed out that people display an attitude when they use it.'

[13] CL, 86.

occurs it is or would be treated by a preponderant majority as a subject of serious criticism and as wrong ...'[14]

But this all goes to people's attitudes towards a rule and infractions of that rule, and tells us nothing about what the rule itself actually says.

Later on, in his *Essays on Bentham*, Hart argued that

'to say that an individual has a legal obligation to act in a certain way is to say that such action may be properly demanded or extracted from him according to the legal rules or principles regulating such demands for action'[15]

and

'where the law is clearly settled and determinate, judges, in speaking of the subject's legal duty, may mean [simply] ... to draw attention to what by way of action is 'owed' by the subject, that is, may legally be demanded or exacted from him.'[16]

However, such an analysis produces the uncomfortable conclusion that when s. 1(1) of the PHA says that (A) 'You must not pursue a course of conduct that (as you know or ought to know) amounts to harassment', it is actually saying (B) 'You may be required or compelled by the authorities to refrain from engaging in a course of conduct that (as you know or ought to know) amounts to harassment'.

The conclusion is uncomfortable for two reasons. First, (B) does not seem that different from the Austin–Holmes analysis of (A) as saying 'You will be punished if you engage in a course of conduct that (as you know or ought to know) amounts to harassment'. Secondly, (B) seems inconsistent with Hart's arguments that legal rules offer themselves as guides to conduct and are accepted as such by those who adopt an 'internal attitude' towards those rules: there seems nothing in (B) for a member of the general public (to whom s. 1(1) of the PHA seems to be addressed) to adopt an 'internal attitude' towards.

Hart's failure[17] to produce a convincing *positive* account of what a provision like s. 1(1) of the PHA is actually saying may account for why legal theorists writing after *The Concept of Law* was published still find themselves attracted by the Austin–Holmes account of what such provisions are actually saying, and are uneasy with the idea that A can be said to have a legal obligation to do *x* even if there exist no legal sanctions for failing to do *x*.

For example, Patrick Atiyah has questioned whether A can be really said to have a legal duty to fulfil his contract to buy a car from a second hand car dealer when a failure to purchase the car will result in A incurring no sanction so long as the

---

[14] CL, 146.

[15] Hart, *Essays on Bentham* (above, n. 11), 160.

[16] Ibid, 266.

[17] Self-confessed: see Lacey, *A Life of HLA Hart: The Nightmare and the Noble Dream* (Oxford University Press, 2004), 335–37.

second hand car dealer can sell the car at an equivalent price to someone else.[18] And Donal Nolan has dismissed the suggestion that the law of negligence imposes on people duties to take care not to expose others to unacceptable risks of physical harm, as A will not incur any sanction if he merely exposes someone else to an unacceptable risk of harm by, for example, careering down Piccadilly at 60 miles an hour.[19] More generally, Frederick Schauer asks whether Austin was right after all, arguing that (1) most people living under modern legal systems experience the law's demands as being orders backed by threats; and (2) the most obvious distinction between *legal* duties and other kind of duties (such as moral duties, or duties in playing a game) are that legal duties stand to be coercively enforced by the State.[20]

Whether these challenges to Hart's negative project of demolishing the Austin–Holmes view of the law's requirements can be dismissed depends on whether we can come up with a positive account of what those requirements entail that can replace the Austin–Holmes view. Fortunately, one of Hart's students, Joseph Raz, has supplied us with such an account. Discussing Raz's views will take us onto our second debate about law's normativity.

Debate 2

Does the law claim to tell us what we, morally, ought to do?

Raz argues that s. 1(1) of the PHA is telling us that we have a *moral* obligation not to engage in conduct that (as we know or ought to know) amounts to harassment of another. More generally, all our legal obligations are moral obligations which our law-makers recognise us as having. Raz makes two arguments in favour of this position that 'normative terms like "a right", "a duty", "ought" are used *in the same sense* in legal, moral and other normative statements'.[21]

(1) *The argument from language.* When you tell someone that they *ought* to do x, you are telling them that they have reason to do x.[22] If you have reason to act in a particular way, that reason must either be a *prudential* reason ('You have reason to do x because it is in your interests to do so') or a *moral* reason ('You have reason to do x irrespective of whether it is in your interests to do so').[23] Section 1(1) of the PHA is telling you that you ought not to engage in conduct that (as you know or ought to know) amounts to harassment, and therefore

---

[18] Atiyah, *Essays on Contract* (Oxford University Press, 1987), 62–63, citing *Lazenby Garages v Wright* [1976] 1 WLR 459.

[19] Nolan, 'Deconstructing the duty of care' (2013) 129 *LQR* 559, 561.

[20] Schauer, 'Was Austin right after all? On the role of sanctions in a theory of law' (2010) 23 *Ratio Juris* 1.

[21] Raz, *The Authority of Law*, 2nd edn (Oxford University Press, 2009), 158 (a statement endorsed by Raz at 159).

[22] Raz, *Practical Reason and Norms* (Princeton University Press, 1990), 29–33.

[23] Cf. Kramer, 'Requirements, reasons, and Raz' (1999) 109 *Ethics* 375, at 379: 'morality and prudence exhaust the realm of reasons.'

that you have reason not to engage in such conduct. It is unlikely that the reason that s. 1(1) of the PHA is telling you that you have not to engage in harassing conduct is a prudential reason, so it is very likely that s. 1(1) is telling you that you have a moral reason not to engage in such conduct. So the best analysis is that s. 1(1) is telling you that, morally, you ought not to engage in harassing conduct.

(2) *The argument from a claim to authority*. Law, and the institutions associated with law, claim legitimate authority over us.[24] In other words, they claim that we will do better, in terms of acting in accordance with the reasons that apply to us, if we act in accordance with the law's demands than if we simply make up our own minds as to what is the best thing to do in any given situation.[25] Insofar as those reasons are moral reasons – reasons to act in particular ways irrespective of whether acting in those ways is in our interest – the law claims legitimate *moral* authority over us. In other words, the law claims that we will do better, in terms of doing what we, morally, ought to do, if we act in accordance with the law's demands than if we make up our own minds as to what is the right thing to do in any given situation. So when the law requires us to act in a particular way, the law is simply exercising a power, to tell us what we, morally, ought to do.

It should be noted that neither of these arguments are arguments that legal obligations *are* moral obligations. Just because the law tells you that you ought to do something does not necessarily mean that you *really* ought to act in that way. And the law's claim to possess legitimate moral authority over us is not necessarily justified. So Raz, like Hart, is a *legal positivist*. He does not believe that there is anything in the nature of law that guarantees that the law's demands on us are morally justified. However, Hart was troubled by Raz's account of law's normativity. He raised a couple of objections to Raz's account that are worth considering.

Hart's *first objection* to the idea that when the law says that you should act in a particular way, the law is telling you that you should, morally, act in that way is that there seem to be many examples of cases where the law tells us to do *x* where no one would say that you have an underlying moral obligation to do *x*. And these are not cases where the law has missed its mark and failed accurately to tell us what we morally ought to do – these are cases which seem to show that the law is doing something completely different from what Raz says that it is attempting to do. Take, for example, the requirement that we should drive on the left hand side of the road. In *The Concept of Law*, Hart observed that,

'it is possible, though difficult, to imagine that men with general beliefs very different from ours, might come to attach *moral* importance to driving on the left instead of the right of the road ... Though such strange moralities are possible, it yet remains true that a morality cannot (logically) contain rules which are generally

---

[24] Raz, *The Authority of Law* (above, n. 21), 29–33; Raz, 'Authority, law, and morality' in his *Ethics in the Public Domain* (Oxford University Press, 1994).

[25] Raz, *The Morality of Freedom* (Oxford University Press, 1986), 53.

held by those who subscribe to them to be in no way preferable to alternatives and of no intrinsic importance. Law, however, though it also contains much that is of moral importance, can and does contain just such rules, and the arbitrary distinctions, formalities and highly specific detail which would be most difficult to understand as part of morality, are consequently natural and easily comprehensible features of law.'[26]

Raz would seem to have a good counter to this objection. While we might not, in the absence of the law, have a reason to drive on the *left*, we do all have a moral reason – in order to avoid accidents and traffic chaos – to drive on the *same side of the road*. And we will do far better, in terms of acting in accordance with that reason, if we act in accordance with the law's requirement 'You should drive on the left' than if we all make up our own minds as to what side of the road we will drive on.

Hart's *second objection* to Raz's account of what the law is telling us when it tells us to act in a particular way is that a judge need not take any view as to what someone's moral obligations were in a particular case in order to reach a view as to what that person's legal obligations were.[27]

For example, consider the case of *R v Evans*.[28] In that case, the defendant was convicted of the manslaughter of her sister, Carly. It was held that the defendant had a legal duty to go to her sister's assistance when Carly overdosed on heroin that the defendant had supplied her, and that Carly died because the defendant breached that duty. There seems no reason why the Court of Appeal that decided *Evans has* to be taken as claiming, when it found that the defendant had a *legal* duty to go to Carly's aid, that the defendant had a *moral* obligation to help her sister. The judges in the Court of Appeal who decided *Evans* might have thought that the defendant did nothing morally wrong in failing to go to Carly's assistance. They might have thought that Carly was entirely to blame for what happened to her and no one else had a moral obligation to help her out when she overdosed on heroin that she chose to take herself. But they could have thought all that, but still convicted the defendant on the basis that, *as a matter of law*, the defendant *did* have a duty – not a moral duty, but a legal duty – to go to Carly's assistance based on the fact that she helped to put Carly in physical danger by supplying her with heroin that she knew Carly was going to take.

More generally, the judges in the Court of Appeal who decided *Evans* might – if asked – confess that they felt themselves incompetent to pronounce on moral issues, and disclaim any intention of acting as moral authorities, determining for the rest of us how we ought, morally, to behave. But at the same time the judges in the Court of Appeal in *Evans* would probably claim to be authorities on what the *law* says we should do, and feel very confident in reaching conclusions on what the *law* required the defendant in *Evans* to do for her sister.

---

[26] CL, 229.
[27] See Hart, *Essays on Bentham* (above, n. 11), 159.
[28] [2009] 1 WLR 1999.

In response to this objection, Raz would argue that a judge cannot avoid acting as a moral authority when he or she determines what legal obligations people have. It is a necessary part of a judge's job that he or she perform (or appear to perform) this role. As Raz observes, 'the claim [to have authority] is made by legal officials wherever a legal system is in force.'[29] So in a case like *R v Evans*, in finding that the defendant in that case had a legal duty to go to her sister's aid, the Court of Appeal is *necessarily* claiming that if A supplies drugs to B and B subsequently (to A's knowledge) overdoses on those drugs, then A has a moral obligation to try to help prevent B dying from the overdose. This claim might be made insincerely – the Court of Appeal might privately believe that no one should raise a finger to stop B getting what's coming to her – but the claim is still made.[30]

The debate between Hart and Raz on these issues was cut short by Hart's death in 1992. However, seven years later, the debate was revisited by Matthew Kramer who sought to do what Hart never did – supply a positive account of what the law is saying when it tells us to act in a particular way, but which does not take the Razian turn of arguing that when the law tells us to act in a particular way it is telling us that we morally ought to act in that way.[31]

Kramer argues that the law need not be viewed as telling us what we *ought*, morally, to do when it requires us to act in a particular way. Instead, the law's requirements can be seen as a set of *imperatives* – a set of statements as to what we *must* do, issued by someone in a position of overwhelming superiority over us. (It may be interesting to note that s. 1(1) of the PHA says that a person *must* not pursue a course of conduct that he knows or ought to know amounts to harassment, not that a person *ought* not pursue such a course of conduct.) Kramer takes the view that A will enjoy the sort of overwhelming superiority over B that will allow A to issue imperatives to B if

'A has ... power to, and is prepared to, inflict undesired harm on B without present risk of equal or similarly undesirable retaliation; there is at least some range of acts which B is prepared to do, however unwillingly, in order to avoid suffering the harm which A can inflict; and A and B both know all this, or at least suppose it to be the case.'[32]

---

[29] Raz, 'The problem about the nature of law' in his *Ethics in the Public Domain* (above, n. 24), 202. See also Gardner, 'What law claims, how law claims' in his *Law as a Leap of Faith* (Oxford University Press, 2012).

[30] It might be worth a footnote to point out how unsatisfactory arguments that someone is *necessarily* saying or claiming something are: they are a way of winning an argument without making one. See, for example, the funny story told by Derek Parfit in the Preface to his *On What Matters: Volume One* (OUP, 2011) about asking a Kantian philosopher about Kant's Categorical Imperative: 'I asked a Kantian, "... if I don't give myself Kant's Imperative as a law, I am not subject to it?" "No," I was told, "you have to give yourself a law, and there's only one law." This reply was maddening, like the propaganda of the so-called "People's Democracies" of the Soviet bloc, in which voting was compulsory and there was only one candidate. And when I said, "But I haven't given myself Kant's Imperative as a law", I was told "Yes you have." This reply was even worse.' (xlii–xliii).

[31] See Kramer, 'Requirements, reasons, and Raz' (above, n. 23).

[32] Ibid, 383, quoting MacCormick, 'Legal obligation and the imperative fallacy' in Simpson (ed.), *Oxford Essays in Jurisprudence, 2nd series* (Oxford University Press, 1973), 106–7.

Recasting legal requirements as imperatives ('must' statements) rather than prescriptions ('ought' statements) allows Kramer to avoid Raz's first argument in favour of his analysis of the nature of legal obligations. But what of Raz's second argument – that law necessarily claims the moral authority to tell us what we should, morally, do and that legal obligations spring from the law's exercising that moral authority?

Kramer takes on this claim by considering whether we would ever say that a Mafia syndicate, which seeks to gain control over a particular region by laying down a set of rules for how people living in that region are to behave and seeks to enforce those rules, is operating an effective *legal* system in the region that it is seeking to control.[33] If we would, then we have to reject Raz's claim that the officials of any legal system effectively claim moral authority over the subjects of that system, as the Mafia bosses and soldiers are not claiming the authority to determine how the people in the region they seek to control ought, morally, to behave: they are merely seeking to ensure that those people do exactly what the Mafia want them to do. Kramer sees no reason why we should not characterise the set of rules laid down by the Mafia in this scenario as amounting to a legal system – so long as those rules are sufficiently general, are adhered to by the officials of the Mafia (in the sense that they will only use force against those who break the rules), and are the only rules that are effectively enforced in the region we are concerned with. The important point is that the fact that the rules make no claim to moral respectability is neither here nor there so far as the issue of whether they amount to a legal system is concerned.[34]

Kramer's views seem to provide a viable alternative to Raz's insistence that legal obligations amount to moral obligations that the legal authorities claim we have. However, they may come at a price: viewing legal obligations as imperatives issued by someone in a position of overwhelming superiority over the people to whom those imperatives are issued comes close to resurrecting the Austin–Holmes view of the nature of legal obligations. If the overwhelming superiority that A (who issues the imperatives) enjoys over B (to whom the imperatives are addressed) consists in A's being able to harm B without fear of being harmed in retaliation by B, then are we not close to saying that if the law tells us to act in a particular way, it is really telling us that if we do not act in that way we are liable to suffer some kind of harm at the hands of the proper authorities?

---

[33] Kramer, 'Requirements, reasons, and Raz' (above, n. 23), 390–95.

[34] John Finnis takes the same position, arguing that 'It seems entirely possible for a regime to proclaim: "Our law, which satisfies all the (say) Hartian criteria … imposes legal duties and confers legal rights that have nothing to do with moral rights. Our law imposes legal obligations that are not moral obligations, and has nothing to do with justice in the moral sense etc. but is instead a structure of ordered power designed to pursue our sectional purposes. We as a regime will mercilessly enforce this law." I see no compelling reason why this "would not be a legal order" (still less why it is conceptually impossible). It is simply very deviant…': Finnis, 'Reflections and responses' in Keown and George (eds), *Reason, Morality and Law* (Oxford University Press, 2013), 538. See also Finnis, 'Introduction' in Finnis, *Philosophy of Law: Collected Essays of John Finnis Volume IV* (Oxford University Press, 2011), 8, fn. 18.

Kramer denies this, arguing that his account of the nature of legal obligations remains 'as warily distant from Austin's account as did Hart himself'.[35] A key difference, for Kramer, is that under his theory, you can have a legal obligation to act in a particular way even if there exists no realistic prospect of your incurring a sanction for failing to act in that way. The crucial point is that you have a legal obligation to act in a particular way if you have been told you *must* act in that way by officials who *generally* enjoy a position of overwhelming superiority over you – there is no need that that superiority be employed in every case to threaten you with harm if you fail to act in accordance with the imperative.

Kramer's theory of legal obligation deserves greater attention than it has received so far, though the lack of attention means that it can at least claim to be unrefuted for the time being. However, it would be foolish to think – as with many of the debates addressed in this book – that we have heard the final word on this fundamental issue.

Further Reading

Hart, CL, chs II, III.1, V.1, V.2.
Raz, *The Authority of Law*, 2nd edn (Oxford University Press, 2009), chs 1 and 2.
Hart, *Essays on Bentham* (Oxford University Press, 1982), chs VI and X.
Gardner, 'What law claims, how law claims' in Gardner, *Law as a Leap of Faith* (Oxford University Press, 2012).
Kramer, *In Defense of Legal Positivism* (Oxford University Press, 1999), ch. 4.

---

[35] Kramer, 'Requirements, reasons, and Raz' (above, n. 23), 396.

3

THE RULE OF RECOGNITION

One of the greatest contributions that H.L.A. Hart's *The Concept of Law* made to the study and understanding of the nature of law was his insight that a legal system is not just made up of *primary* rules that require people to act in particular ways (such as not harassing other people). A legal system will also contain within it a number of *secondary* rules, which regulate the creation and application of the system's primary rules. Hart identified three such secondary rules:[1] (1) a *rule of recognition*, which determines when a particular rule will be a primary rule of the legal system; (2) a *rule of change*, which lays down procedures for altering the primary rules of the legal system; and (3) a *rule of adjudication*, which empowers individuals to determine authoritatively whether a primary rule has been breached. Since *The Concept of Law* was published, a number of debates have developed around Hart's suggestion that every legal system contains a rule of recognition; this chapter is devoted to those debates.

Debate 1

Does every legal system have a rule of recognition?

H.L.A. Hart would have been reluctant to accept that there could be a legal system without a rule of recognition. In *The Concept of Law*, he argued that 'the ... social situation where a secondary rule of recognition is accepted and used for the identification of primary rules of obligation ... deserves, if anything does, to be called the foundation[ ] of a legal system.'[2] However, in order to consider this issue fully, we need to consider two different kinds of society: a primitive society (which we call *Arcadia*), and a modern society (which we will call *Metropolis*).

THE POSITION IN *ARCADIA*

Hart begins his discussion of why a society might need secondary rules such as a rule of recognition by describing a 'primitive' society 'without a legislature, courts,

---

[1] See, in particular, CL, 94–97 (see list of abbreviations, p. xiii).
[2] CL, 100.

or officials of any kind'.[3] Such a society will have a number of 'primary rules of obligation' 'contain[ing] in some form restrictions on the free use of violence, theft, and deception'[4] and there will exist various unofficial social pressures on members of society to conform to these primary rules. Hart argues that such a society can only successfully exist if amounts to a 'small community closely knit by ties of kinship, common sentiment, and belief, and placed in a stable environment'.[5] As we will see, if these conditions did not obtain (as they do not in *Metropolis*), it would not be possible for *Arcadia* simply to rely on primary rules of obligation enforced through informal social pressure to hold itself together.

Arcadia lacks a rule of recognition because there exists no basic rule which we can use to tell whether or not a given rule is one of that society's primary rules of obligation. In *Arcadia*, 'we must wait and see whether a rule gets accepted as a rule or not: in a system with a basic rule of recognition we can say before a rule is actually made, that it *will* be valid *if* it conforms to the requirements of the rule of recognition.'[6] But this is not a problem. *Arcadia* does not need a rule of recognition to identify what its primary rules of obligation are as the close ties of common sentiment and belief that unite the members of *Arcadia* mean that everyone knows what those primary rules of obligation are.

Does the existence of *Arcadia* show that you can have a legal system without a rule of recognition? Hart would say 'no' on the basis that there is no legal *system* in *Arcadia*: the primary rules of obligation in *Arcadia* 'do not form a system, but a mere set'.[7] This seems a slim basis on which to deny that *Arcadia* has a legal system. A more promising argument might be that the *Arcadian* primary rules of obligation are merely enforced through informal social pressures, rather than through the sort of organised central authority that would be constituted by a set of rules of *adjudication*. Were *Arcadia* to have such a central authority in charge of enforcing the primary rules of obligation that are accepted in *Arcadia*, we might be much more inclined to say that *Arcadia* was a society governed by law, and in possession of a legal system. But even that case would probably not disprove Hart's thesis that you cannot have a legal system without a rule of recognition. As Hart observes,

> 'a system which has rules of adjudication is necessarily also committed to a rule of recognition of an elementary and imperfect sort. This is so because, if courts are empowered to make authoritative determinations of the fact that a rule has been broken, these cannot avoid being taken as authoritative determinations of what the rules are. So the rule which confers jurisdiction will also be a rule of recognition, identifying the primary rules through the judgments of the courts and these judgments will become a "source" of law.'[8]

---

[3] CL, 91.
[4] Ibid.
[5] CL, 92.
[6] CL, 235.
[7] CL, 234; also CL, 92.
[8] CL, 97.

THE POSITION IN *METROPOLIS*

Whatever might be the position in *Arcadia*, rules of recognition and the other secondary rules identified by Hart come into their own in a society like *Metropolis*.[9] In such a society, which lacks the close ties that unite the members of *Arcadia*, and which lacks the stable environment that *Arcadia* enjoys, a set of widely accepted primary rules of obligation reinforced by informal pressures to abide by those rules could not work to hold *Metropolis* together. The size of *Metropolis* and the consequent lack of common sentiment and belief among *Metropolitans* will create uncertainty about what *Metropolis*'s primary rules of obligation are (or, indeed, we might add, whether it has any). The lack of stability in *Metropolis*'s environment will create the need to be able deliberately to change *Metropolis*'s primary rules of obligation (and, indeed, we might add, the need to empower *Metropolitans* to order their own affairs through exercising various powers). And the size of *Metropolis* and the lack of any close ties of kinship between *Metropolitans* means that unofficial social pressures are likely to be singularly ineffective in inducing people to abide by *Metropolis*'s primary rules of obligation. If *Metropolis* is to survive, it needs a fully-fledged legal system – not only primary rules of obligation, but secondary rules that will clearly identify in advance what those primary rules are, provide for ways of deliberately altering those primary rules, and a set of officials charged with the task of determining when those rules have been broken and empowered to sanction those who break those rules.

It would seem then that in a modern society like *Metropolis*, there is no question of *Metropolis* having a legal system without a rule of recognition. However, Jeremy Waldron has recently questioned whether even a modern society like *Metropolis* *needs* a rule of recognition as part of its legal system.[10] He has two main arguments. First, all of the work that is done by rules of recognition in determining what the rules of a legal system are can be done by rules of change. If we know what the rules of change of a system are, all we have to do is see how those rules of change have been used to alter the law to know what the law now says. Secondly, we can get along perfectly well in making legal arguments without a rule of recognition. All we need is a rule of *sources of law* that tells us what sort of things may and may not be validly taken into account in coming to a conclusion as to what the law says on a particular issue and what principles we should be faithful to in coming to that conclusion. Such a rule would provide us with sufficient guidance as to what the law said on particular issues while leaving 'advocates and judges free to experiment with new and unusual ways of extrapolating norms from decided cases, as well as tried and true ways.'[11]

---

[9] This paragraph follows Hart's argument in CL, 92–97.

[10] Waldron, 'Who needs rules of recognition?' in Adler and Himma (eds), *The Rule of Recognition and the US Constitution* (Oxford University Press, 2009).

[11] Ibid, section VIII.

A number of objections can be made to Waldron's first argument. First, we would need a rule of recognition to determine the validity of rules that do not owe their existence to the fact that they have been introduced into a legal system through the exercise of the system's rules of change. Secondly, we would need a rule of recognition to determine what the legal position is when a rule of change has been exercised and then the exercise of that rule of change has been reversed. This would be the case, for example, if one line legislation were passed which purported simply to repeal the European Communities Act 1972, or the Human Rights Act 1998. A rule of change would tell us that after the repeal of these statutes it is *no longer* the law that ..., but it could not tell us what it is *now* the law that .... Thirdly, we may need a rule of recognition to clear up uncertainties over what the law says that may be created by uncertainties over whether a legal system's rule of change has been validly exercised.

Waldron's second argument has more merit, but one suspects that were he to set out his rule of sources of law it would end up resembling a Hartian rule of recognition. Two things indicate that this is a real possibility. First, Waldron says that in suggesting that a modern legal system does not need a rule of recognition but a rule of sources of law, he is simply following the views of Hart's greatest critic, Ronald Dworkin. However, as we will see, Dworkin's masterwork *Law's Empire* could be interpreted as arguing that Anglo-American legal systems should (and do?) adopt a particular rule of recognition (though Dworkin preferred to use the phrase 'grounds of law' rather than 'rule of recognition'). So Dworkin himself did not seem to see a significant difference between a rule of recognition and a rule of sources of law. Secondly, in the Postscript to the second edition of *The Concept of Law*, Hart significantly softened his views on what a rule of recognition does. He protested against the idea that

> 'the rule is meant to determine completely the legal result in particular cases, so that any legal issue arising in any case could simply be solved by mere appeal to the criteria or tests provided by the rule ... [T]his is a misconception: the function of the rule is to determine only the general conditions which correct legal decisions must satisfy in modern systems of law.'[12]

Given this, a Waldronian rule of sources of law could easily count as a valid rule of recognition in Hart's eyes.

Debate 2

How does the rule of recognition come into existence?

In *The Concept of Law*, H.L.A. Hart argued that the rule of recognition of a legal system exists by virtue of the fact that the officials of that system employ that rule in determining what does and does not count as a valid statement of law. 'Its

---

[12] CL, Postscript, 258.

existence is a matter of fact' and depends purely on 'a complex, but normally concordant, practice of the courts, officials and private persons in identifying the law by reference to certain criteria.'[13] So when we say that under the rule of recognition that governs UK law, 'the enactments of the Queen in Parliament are valid law', we are saying no more and no less than that legal officials – and in particular judges – generally accept that 'the enactments of the Queen in Parliament are valid law' and would regard any legal official who did not accept that 'as a subject of serious criticism and as wrong'.[14] It follows that there is no test for the validity of a rule of recognition. In Hart's famous comparison, it would make no more sense to ask whether a rule of recognition is valid than it would to ask whether the 'standard metre bar in Paris'[15] is *really* a metre long. The rule of recognition is a test for whether a given proposition is a valid rule of law; we cannot therefore ask whether that rule is valid itself. There is no rule of recognition for the rule of recognition.

Basing the existence of a rule of recognition on the practice of the officials of a legal system seems to give rise to what Scott Shapiro has termed a 'chicken and egg' problem.[16] If you can't have a rule of recognition without legal officials, where did the legal officials come from? The existence of legal officials seems to *presuppose* the existence of a system of which they are officials, and under which those officials are endowed with legal powers. Hence the chicken and egg problem. You can't have a rule of recognition without legal officials; but it would seem that you also can't have legal officials without a legal system, and for that you need a rule of recognition. So what came first – the officials or the rule of recognition? Obviously, Hart wants to say 'the officials' (otherwise he would have to abandon his claim that the existence of a rule of recognition depends on the practice of the system's officials) but that still leaves unresolved the problem of where the officials came from.

In our view, the 'chicken and egg' problem is illusory. Let's return to Hart's description of the kind of society that does *not* need a full-blown legal system – the society we have called *Arcadia*. The problem is – How does a society like *Arcadia* transition into becoming a society like *Metropolis* that has a fully developed legal system? We know from Hart's account that *Arcadia* will seek to develop something like a legal system as it becomes a more complex and populated society. But it is hardly likely that the transition to developing a fully-fledged legal system will happen overnight. It is likely that of the secondary rules identified by Hart, rules of adjudication will come first – the population of *Arcadia*, or someone to whom the population usually defers, will respond to the increasing number of infractions of its traditional primary rules of obligation by empowering a group of people ('enforcers') to investigate complaints of such infractions, and take measures

[13] CL, 110.
[14] CL, 148.
[15] CL, 109.
[16] See Shapiro, 'On Hart's way out' (1998) 4 *Legal Theory* 469; and his book *Legality* (Harvard University Press, 2010), 36–40.

against those who have infringed the rules.[17] Once you have rules of adjudication in place, the 'chicken and egg' problem disappears. Those who incur sanctions at the hands of *Arcadia*'s 'enforcers' may well complain that they had no means of knowing that they were doing anything wrong under *Arcadia*'s customary primary rules, and demand that those enforcers make it public what those customary rules are. Once those rules are published, it is a natural step for *Arcadia*'s enforcers to act on the basis that the published text of *Arcadia*'s rules provides the 'rule of recognition' for determining what *Arcadia*'s primary rules of obligation are: if a rule is in the published text, then it is part of *Arcadia*'s primary rules of obligation; if it is not, it is not. And once there is a published text of *Arcadia*'s primary rules of obligation that is accepted by *Arcadia*'s enforcers as authoritatively determining what *Arcadia*'s primary rules of obligation are, then it would again be a natural step for the 'enforcers', either at their own initiative or at the prompting of *Arcadia*'s population (or whoever the population normally defers to), to adopt procedures – or rules of change – for altering the published text from time to time. By this stage, the journey from *Arcadia* to *Metropolis* is well under way.

Debate 3

Do all the judges of a legal system agree on what its rule of recognition is?

Ronald Dworkin spent his academic life assaulting the picture of a legal system that Hart propounded in *The Concept of Law* – that of a legal system consisting in a union of primary rules and secondary rules. His attack on Hart's concept of law reached its high point with the publication in 1986 of *Law's Empire*. *Law's Empire* begins with the seemingly innocent observation that judges 'disagree about the grounds of law, about which other kinds of propositions, when true, make a particular proposition of law true'.[18] Dworkin called that kind of disagreement a '"theoretical disagreement" about the law' and said that *Law's Empire* was all 'about theoretical disagreement in law'.[19]

Why did Dworkin think that the phenomenon of 'theoretical disagreement' (if it exists) deserved such attention? The reason is that, if theoretical disagreements over the grounds of law do exist, then Hart's picture of a legal system seems to be radically inadequate. This is because 'grounds of law' is just another term for 'rule of recognition', and Hart's account of how a legal system works does not seem to allow for the possibility that the judges in a legal system might disagree over what the rule of recognition of that legal system is. If – as Hart seemed to contend – a legal system's rule of recognition owes its existence to the fact that it is generally

---

[17] To the same effect, see Waldron, 'All we like sheep' (1999) 12 *Canadian Journal of Law and Jurisprudence* 169, 173.

[18] LE, 5.

[19] LE, 11.

accepted and applied by the officials of that legal system in determining what counts as a valid proposition of law and what does not, then how could the officials of a legal system disagree over what that system's rule of recognition is? If we all accept that *x* is true, then how could we simultaneously disagree over whether *x* is true?

In order to account for the reality of 'theoretical disagreement' (if it is real), Dworkin argued that we need to adopt a radically different picture of how judges arrive at conclusions as to what the law says in a particular case. All judges employ a rule of recognition (or an understanding of what the 'grounds of law' are) in reaching such conclusions, but the rule of recognition that each judge employs will reflect, and is accountable to, the judge's vision of what law is. The judge's vision of what law is does not come out of thin air but instead reflects the position that the judge has adopted in an 'interpretive debate' over the nature of law, which takes as its starting point the idea that 'Law insists that force not be used or withheld, no matter how useful that would be to ends in view, no matter how beneficial or noble those ends, except as licensed or required by individual rights and responsibilities flowing from past political decisions about when collective force is justified.'[20] The debate over the nature of law is over what concrete understanding – or conception – of law best makes sense of this central feature of our understanding of what law is. What rule of recognition a judge adopts in determining what the law says in a concrete case will depend on what position the judge takes in that debate.

Dworkin canvasses a variety of different conceptions of law – conventionalism, pragmatism, and law as integrity – and argues that law as integrity makes best sense of the 'pre-interpretive' idea of law as justifying coercion that underlies, and allows us to engage in, debates about the nature of law.

> 'Law as integrity asks judges to assume, so far as possible, that the law [or, rather, past decisions of the courts and statutes passed by the legislature] is structured by a coherent set of principles about justice and fairness and procedural due process, and it asks them to enforce these in the fresh cases that come before them, so that each person's situation is fair and just according to the same standards.'[21]

Law as integrity, then, yields the following

> 'thesis about the grounds of law. According to law as integrity, propositions of law are true if they figure in or follow from the principles of justice, fairness and procedural due process that provide the best constructive interpretation of the community's legal practice.'[22]

This, in turn, requires judges, in determining what the law says in a particular issue, to determine first of all what 'principles of justices, fairness and procedural

---

[20] LE, 93.
[21] LE, 243.
[22] LE, 225.

process' could be said to *fit* the past decisions of the courts and statutes passed by the legislature, and then if more than one such set of principles fit those decisions and statutes, to give effect to those principles that cast those previous decisions in their *best light*.

There are a number of significant differences between Hart's picture of how a legal system operates, and the alternative vision that Dworkin offers. According to Dworkin's account:

(1) There *is* a rule of recognition for the rule of recognition: what rule of recognition a particular judge will adopt (and will think he or she ought to adopt) depends on what position he or she takes in the debate over the nature of law, and what that position implies for what the 'grounds of law' are.

(2) What rule of recognition a judge adopts is therefore a matter of personal conviction – as to what position he or she takes in the debate over the nature of law – rather than, as Hart would argue, common convention among judges generally.[23]

(3) A judge cannot determine what the law says on a particular issue without taking a position in the debate over the nature of law. In that sense then, 'Jurisprudence is the general part of adjudication, silent prologue to any decision at law.'[24] In contrast, Hart would argue that judges can perfectly well determine what the law says on a particular issue, and have done so for centuries, without having to get into jurisprudential arguments about the nature of law. As he says in the Postscript to the second edition of *The Concept of Law*: 'propositions of law are typically statements not of what "law" is but of what *the law* is, i.e. what the law of some system permits or requires or empowers people to do.' And Hart insists that 'there is no trace ... in my work' of the 'doctrine' that 'the criteria provided by a system's rule of recognition and the need for such a rule [are] derived from the meaning of the word "law".'[25]

(4) The task of determining what the law says on a particular issue is inescapably value-laden, at two levels. First, in order to determine what rule of recognition he or she will adopt, a judge has to take a stance on what conception of law best makes sense of law's claims to *justify* coercion by reference to past political decisions. This will obviously involve the judge having to take a view on moral questions about when coercion is or is not justified. Secondly, a judge who adopts law as integrity as his or her preferred conception of law (as Dworkin thinks he or she should) will, in determining what the law says on an issue where more than one interpretation of the law fits the legal materials that he or she has to work with, have to decide which interpretation casts the

---

[23] See CL, 256, arguing that the rule of recognition is a 'conventional social rule[ ]' and 'is in effect a form of judicial customary rule existing only if it is accepted and practised in the law-identifying and law-applying operations of the courts.'

[24] LE, 90.

[25] CL, 247.

law in its best light – which is, again, a moral issue. In contrast, Hart would argue that the task of determining what the law says on a particular issue (as opposed to what it *should* say on a particular issue) will only be value-laden if the rule of recognition of the legal system that we are concerned with requires the courts to take moral considerations into account in determining what the law says.

The stakes could not be higher, then, in relation to the issue of whether the judges disagree over what the rule of recognition in their system is: Hart's theory of law would seem to stand or fall over whether there is, as Dworkin contended there was, such a thing as 'theoretical disagreement'.[26] It is not surprising, then, that those who want to defend Hart's picture of a legal system have rushed to address this issue and have sought to argue that Dworkin was mistaken. When he thought that he had detected in the caselaw examples of the judges disagreeing of what the rule of recognition in their system was, Dworkin's critics argue what he had actually found was:

(1) DISAGREEMENT OVER HOW A PRIMARY RULE SHOULD BE APPLIED

One of Dworkin's stock examples of 'theoretical disagreement' in the caselaw is the decision of the US Supreme Court in *Tennessee Valley Authority v Hill*[27] (referred to by Dworkin as the 'snail darter case').[28] The snail darter is a type of perch that was discovered in 1973, and listed in 1975 as an endangered species under the Endangered Species Act (which was passed by Congress in 1973). Under the Act, government agencies were required to ensure that they did not do anything to jeopardise the continued existence of an endangered species. Unfortunately, in 1967 the Tennessee Valley Authority had started work on constructing the Tellico Dam. The location of the dam meant that when it was completed it would obstruct the snail darter's migratory path. As soon as environmental activists – who were opposed to the construction of the dam on principle – learned of the effect that the dam would have on the snail darter, they brought an action to halt the construction of the dam.

---

[26] Brian Leiter disagrees with this, arguing that even if Hart's theory of law cannot explain 'theoretical disagreement', it is hard to see why we would get rid of it given its overwhelming success in explaining most features of our legal system: see his 'Explaining theoretical disagreement' (2009) 76 *University of Chicago Law Review* 1215, 1220, 1226–28. He draws an analogy with the theory of gravity: we would not think that theory wrong just because it makes it difficult to explain why the universe is expanding. But – to draw another scientific analogy – Newton's laws of motion were hugely successful in explaining the movement of bodies in the solar system, except for the one tiny fact that Mercury was always slightly out of the position one would predict it would occupy applying Newton's laws. This fact resulted in the eventual overthrow of Newton's laws of motion in favour of Einstein's theory of relativity. Scott Shapiro's 'The Hart-Dworkin debate: a short guide for the perplexed' in Ripstein (ed.), *Ronald Dworkin* (Cambridge University Press, 2007) is more acute to recognise the importance of the phenomenon (if such it is) of 'theoretical disagreement' for the validity of Hart's concept of law.

[27] 437 US 153 (1978).

[28] LE, 20–23.

The case went to the US Supreme Court, with the Court ruling 6:3 that an injunction halting construction of the dam should be issued under the Endangered Species Act. Burger CJ held for the majority that the plain words of the Act required that the construction work stop. Powell J dissented, arguing that the words of the Act should be construed with a modicum of common sense, and as a matter of common sense it was hard to think that Congress intended that the Act should apply to projects that had already been started by the government before the Act was passed. It is hard to see how this is an example of 'theoretical disagreement'. Both Burger CJ and Powell J agreed that the Endangered Species Act was valid law. They also agreed that the US Supreme Court should give effect to the intention of Congress in applying the Act. They simply disagreed over what Congress had intended in passing the Act. It is hard to see how this very low-level disagreement could be characterised as a fundamental disagreement over what the rule of recognition in US law was.

(2) DISAGREEMENT OVER HOW THE RULE OF RECOGNITION SHOULD BE APPLIED

We might be able to make the snail darter case more dramatic – from a jurisprudential point of view – by supposing that the different constructions that Burger CJ and Powell J put on the Endangered Species Act were due to the fact that they thought that the rule of law established by the Endangered Species Act was *not* the *only* rule of law relevant to the outcome of the case. Perhaps Burger CJ thought there was a rule of law that in construing the Endangered Species Act, one should give effect to its plain words. And maybe Powell J thought that in interpreting the Act, the law told him that he should – so far as is possible – read it in a way which accorded with common sense. If this were the case, then we might be able to say that the snail darter case is an example of 'theoretical disagreement' – the different rules of law that Burger CJ and Powell J thought applied in the snail darter case may have reflected a more fundamental disagreement between them over what rule of recognition applied in US law.

There are two problems with this analysis. The first is that there is no evidence that Burger CJ and Powell J thought that there was anything more than just one rule of law applicable in the snail darter case: the rule of law laid down by the Endangered Species Act. We have to be very careful not to fall into adopting what has become known as a 'King Midas theory of law', under which everything that the courts take into account in determining the outcome of a case gets turned into law.[29] Just because Burger CJ thought that we should determine what Congress meant by passing the Endangered Species Act by looking at the plain words that Congress used does not mean that he thought there was a rule of law requiring him to do this; likewise with Powell J's more commonsensical approach.

---

[29] The phrase originates from the work of Hans Kelsen, who argued – using the Midas analogy – that everything the state touches turns into law, and that everything the law refers to turns into law.

Secondly, even if Burger CJ and Powell J thought that different legal rules for construing an Act of Congress applied in the snail darter case, that does not necessarily mean they disagreed over what the rule of recognition in US law was. They might have agreed on what the rule of recognition in US law said, but disagreed over how it applies, with the result that they ended up thinking that they were required under the law to construe the Endangered Species Act in different ways.[30] This is obviously possible. For example, suppose that the rule of recognition that judges generally accepted in their legal system happened to be the same as that supplied by 'law as integrity'. There would be obvious scope for different judges to reach different conclusions as to what counted and did not count as a rule of law under that rule of recognition.

Unless we are given some reason to believe that neither of these obstacles to seeing the snail darter case as an example of 'theoretical disagreement' apply in that case, the more natural analysis of the snail darter case is that it is not an example of 'theoretical disagreement'.

(3) DEVELOPMENT OF THE RULE OF RECOGNITION

Suppose – to consider an example first propounded by Sir Leslie Stephen – Parliament passed a statute requiring some government body to slaughter all blue-eyed babies.[31] Stephen assumed – as did A.V. Dicey, following Stephen[32] – that such a statute would count as valid law under the rule of recognition that currently obtains in UK law, under which 'the enactments of the Queen in Parliament are law'.[33] But, in fact, the practice of the UK courts does *not* allow us to say that the courts accept as a rule that *whatever* the Queen in Parliament enacts will be law. The practice of the UK courts of accepting as a rule that whatever the Queen in Parliament enacts is law has grown up around statutes that do not come anywhere close to being as outrageous as a statute requiring the slaughter of all blue-eyed babies would be.

So all the practice of the UK courts allows us to say that is that they accept as a rule that whatever the Queen in Parliament enacts is law *so long as* the Queen in Parliament continues to enact statutes that are merely guilty, at most, of the kind of low-level outrageousness that we have become used to from our governments. Were the Queen in Parliament to enact a statute requiring the slaughter of all blue-eyed babies, all bets would be off and it would be genuinely uncertain what the

---

[30] For the possibility that different judges who are committed to the same rule of recognition might disagree over how it applies, see Coleman, 'Negative and positive positivism' (1982) 11 *Journal of Legal Studies* 139, 152–54, 157. Also CL, 148–50, 258; Endicott, 'Are there any rules?' (2001) 5 *Journal of Ethics* 199.

[31] See Stephen, *Science of Ethics*, 1st edn (1882), 137.

[32] Dicey, *Introduction to the Study of the Law of the Constitution*, 1st edn (1885), ch. 1 ('The nature of Parliamentary sovereignty'), text at fn. 56.

[33] CL, 145.

courts would do.[34] Such a statute would go beyond the scope of the current rule of recognition accepted and given effect to by the courts, and the courts would have to decide what their practice *will* be in relation to that kind of statute. If the courts ruled that they would not give effect to the statute, and held firm in that refusal over a sufficient period of time, then we could say that the rule of recognition employed by the UK courts had *developed* so that we can now say that whatever the Queen in Parliament enacts will normally be law unless the statute in question does something like requiring the slaughter of all blue-eyed babies. If, on the other hand, the courts ruled that they would give effect to the statute, and they continued to accept over a sufficient period of time that they would give effect to statutes of this degree of monstrousness, then we could say that rule of recognition employed by the UK courts had *developed* so that it *is* true to say that *whatever* the Queen in Parliament enacts will be law.[35]

Now in the *first* case ('the blue-eyed baby case') where the UK Supreme Court had to decide whether the killing of a blue-eyed baby was lawful under the Slaughter of the Innocents (Blue-Eyed Babies) Act 2065, one could imagine that each of the Supreme Court Justices ('SCJs') would be genuinely uncertain as to what they should do, and a SCJ who decided to uphold the Act as valid law would certainly not regard another SCJ who decided not to uphold the Act 'as a subject of serious criticism and as wrong';[36] the same would be true *vice versa*. But one could *also* imagine that a SCJ who decided to uphold the 2065 Act as valid law would *say* in his or her judgment that 'A fundamental principle of our constitution is that Parliament is sovereign, and that whatever legislation is validly enacted by Parliament is valid law. This principle applies here to establish that the 2065 Act is valid law and should be given effect to by the courts.' And one could imagine that a SCJ who decided not to uphold the 2065 Act as valid law would *say* in his or her judgment, 'There is actually no authority that establishes that an Act as monstrous as this is valid law, for the simple reason that no Act as iniquitous as this one has ever been passed before. So there is nothing that compels us to rule that this Act is valid law, and nothing to stop us reaching the obvious conclusion that killings of blue-eyed babies are not rendered lawful by this statute.'

---

[34] Stephen argued (and Dicey agreed) that 'If a legislature decided that all blue-eyed babies should be murdered, the preservation of all blue-eyed babies would be illegal; but legislators must go mad before they could pass such a law, and subjects be idiotic before they could submit to it.' But as Trevor Allan has pointed out to one of us in private conversation, the judges are 'subjects' too – so by Stephen's own lights, we could expect the judges to refuse to give effect to the statute, thereby establishing a practice of refusing to accept, as a rule, that this kind of statute was valid law.

[35] Hart coined the memorable phrase 'all that succeeds is success' (CL, 153) to describe this process of development of the rule of recognition: 'when courts settle previously unenvisaged questions concerning the most fundamental constitutional rules, they *get* their authority to decide them accepted after the questions have arisen and the decision has been given. Here all that succeeds is success. ... a ... piece of judicial law-making concerning the very sources of law may be calmly "swallowed". Where this is so, it will often in *retrospect* be said, and may genuinely appear, that there always was an "inherent" power in the courts to do what they have done. Yet this may be a pious fiction, if the only evidence for it is the success of what has been done.'

[36] CL, 148.

As both of these judgments are couched in terms of what the law *says*, they may appear to provide us with an obvious example of 'theoretical disagreement'. However, appearances deceive. The Supreme Court Justices in the blue-eyed baby case are not disagreeing over what the rule of recognition *says* – at the moment, it does not say anything about the validity of the Slaughter of the Innocents (Blue-Eyed Babies) Act 2065 as no practice has yet developed around statutes that are as iniquitous as that one is. What they are disagreeing about is what the rule of recognition *will* say about statutes such as the 2065 Act. The fact that their judgments are phrased to give the impression of disagreement over what the rule of recognition *says* is simply a matter of judicial habit: judges are used to couching their judgments in terms of what the law says, rather than acknowledging frankly that they are striking new ground in deciding a case in the way they have.

(4) DIFFERENCES, BUT NOT DISAGREEMENTS, OVER WHAT THE RULE OF RECOGNITION SAYS

However, most cases do not explicitly give rise to issues over what the rule of recognition in a legal system is in the way that the blue-eyed baby case does. In most cases, the rule of recognition employed by the courts is, as Hart observed, 'not stated, … its existence is *shown* in the way in which particular rules are identified, either by courts or other officials or private persons or their advisers.'[37] This point has been taken up by John Gardner, who argues that the rule of recognition changes over time *accidentally*.[38]

This happens when one judge (call him *Herbert*) decides a case (call it *A v B*) on the *assumption* that the rule of recognition says *x* (when actually there is no warrant for thinking that at the time he is making his decision because there is no established practice at that time which warrants that conclusion), and then other judges follow that judge's decision, thereby making it the case that the rule of recognition *does* say *x* (because now there is an established practice that supports the idea that the judges accept *x*, as a rule). No one intended to change or develop the rule of recognition in the way it did, but it still changed or developed.

While this change or development is occurring, it would not be surprising to find a judgment in another case (call it *C v D*, and the judge deciding the case *Ronnie*) which assumes that the rule of recognition does *not* say *x*. Over time, the judgment in *C v D* will fall by the wayside and will be forgotten. But at the time they were decided, the decisions in *A v B* and *C v D* would seem to provide us with an example of 'theoretical disagreement' – *Herbert* and *Ronnie* took different views as to what the rule of recognition in their legal system said, so they disagreed about what the rule of recognition said in their legal system. But this does not follow.

While *Herbert* and *Ronnie* did take different views, they did *not* disagree. The reason *Herbert* and *Ronnie* did not disagree was that they were not *intending* to take

---

[37] CL, 101.
[38] Gardner, 'Some types of law' in *Law as a Leap of Faith* (Oxford University Press, 2012), 71–72, 73–74.

different views from each other as to what the rule of recognition is in their legal system. Had *Herbert* become aware that *Ronnie* did not share his assumption that the rule of recognition in their legal system says *x*, then *Herbert* may well have dropped that assumption, realising that there is in fact no shared practice that would warrant that assumption. And *Ronnie* might have done the same had she become aware that *Herbert* did not share her assumption that the rule of recognition in their legal system does not say *x*. So there was no disagreement – there was just, in both cases, a mistaken assumption of agreement.[39]

(5) OPPORTUNISTIC DISTORTION OF THE RULE OF RECOGNITION

Finally, we may be fooled into thinking we have stumbled across an example of 'theoretical disagreement' because a judge in a particular case is lying about what he thinks the rule of recognition in his system says. The way this works is this.

In a particular case (call it *X v Z*), *Faithful*, *Chancer* and *Clueless* are the judges. *Faithful* gives effect to the rule of recognition that is generally accepted by him and his fellow judges, and finds for *X*, the claimant. *Faithful* regrets having to find for *X*: *Z* seems like a decent person who made some foolish choices, and *X* does not really need the money that he is suing *Z* for. But the law seems clearly in *X*'s favour. *Chancer* is of exactly the same mind as *Faithful*: she wishes she could find in favour of *Z*, but she also knows that the law is clearly in favour of *X*. However, *Chancer* chooses to lie. She plays fast and loose with the existing authorities and conjures up a judgment in favour of *Z*. *Clueless* hasn't been paying attention for the entire case, and simply rules in favour of *Z* because he likes *Chancer*. So *Z* wins. In the chambers after the judgments have been handed down, *Faithful* reproves *Chancer* for departing from the established rule of recognition. *Chancer* chuckles and says, 'Yes – I'm very bad. But I just couldn't let *X* win.'

To an outsider, the decision in *X v Z* would seem to provide an example of 'theoretical disagreement'. *Faithful* and *Chancer* seem to disagree over what the rule of recognition in their legal system is. But, in fact, there is no disagreement. The two judges agree on what the rule of recognition is, and what it implies for their case, but *Faithful* chooses to follow the rule, while *Chancer* chooses not to. Instead, *Chancer* pretends to the outside world that in fact a different rule applies in the legal system in which she and *Faithful* are judges, while acknowledging in private that she can be rightfully criticised by her fellow judges for failing to adhere to the rule of recognition that is generally accepted by her and other judges.[40]

Brian Leiter brilliantly exposes another of Dworkin's stock examples of 'theoretical disagreement' as in fact based on *two* judges being disingenuous about what the law required in the case they had to decide.[41] The case is *Riggs v Palmer*.[42] Elmer

---

[39] Brian Leiter calls this the 'error theory' explanation of 'theoretical disagreement' in his 'Explaining theoretical disagreement' (above, n. 26), 1224.

[40] Brian Leiter calls this the 'disingenuity account' of 'theoretical disagreement': ibid.

[41] Leiter, 'Explaining theoretical disagreement' (above, n. 26), 1241–46.

[42] 22 NE 188, 115 NY 506 (1889).

Palmer knew that he stood to inherit a lot of money under his grandfather Francis's will. But Elmer was scared that Francis might change his will and write Elmer out of the new will. So Elmer killed Francis before Francis got the chance to make a new will. Francis's two daughters went to court, asking for an order invalidating Francis's will, on the basis that if the will was given effect to then Elmer would benefit from his crime. The problem was that the New York statute of wills did not provide that a will could be invalidated in this kind of case. No matter: the New York Court of Appeals ruled, by a majority, that it had the power to make the order. Earl J, giving the majority judgment, ruled that it was 'inconceivable' that the New York legislature could have intended Elmer to inherit in circumstances such as these when it passed the statute of wills. Gray J dissented: invalidating the will would involve going against the express words of the statute of wills, and impose an additional punishment on Elmer for what he had done.

We may doubt, as we did with the snail darter case, whether *Riggs* provides us with a genuine example of 'theoretical disagreement' as opposed to a more low-level disagreement over what the New York legislature might have intended when it passed the statute of wills. Be that as it may, even if *Riggs* can be read as presenting us with an example of 'theoretical disagreement', Brian Leiter provides us with good reason to think that both Earl J and Gray J were deliberately massaging their reading of the law in order to reach the result that they wanted to reach. In an earlier case, Earl J had argued – but this time on the losing side, in the minority – that a convict lost all his property rights: a result that would have meant there was no chance of Elmer inheriting under Francis's will. So invalidating Francis's will was a way of achieving the result that Earl J had unsuccessfully argued for in the earlier case. And Gray J was a conservative who was hostile to the courts fiddling with the rules governing the transmission of property rights. In the terms used here, *both* were *Chancers* who had made up their mind what they wanted the result of the case to be, and were willing to say anything about the law in order to reach their desired result.

CONCLUSION

Dworkin's claim that there exists 'theoretical disagreement' among judges over what the rule of recognition is in their legal system is not made out. We have judges who agree on what the rule of recognition is, but disagree on how it applies in particular cases. We have judges who disagree about what should happen in cases that go beyond the current boundaries of the currently accepted rule of recognition. We have judges who proceed on the mistaken assumption that other judges accept that the rule of recognition obtaining in their legal system says one thing rather than another. We have judges who lie about what the rule of recognition is in their legal system, or what it implies for a case at hand. But what Dworkin has not shown is that we have judges who flat out disagree with each other as to what the rule of recognition in their system is. If Hart's picture of the legal system is correct, we would not expect such flat out disagreements to exist. The fact that

Dworkin is not able to come up with convincing examples of such disagreements provides strong evidence in favour of Hart's views.

Debate **4**

Can the rule of recognition have a moral component?

Dworkin's attacks on Hart's theory of law were motivated by Dworkin's basic hostility to *legal positivism*. Dworkin thought that Hart's *The Concept of Law* was the most sophisticated and intelligent statement of what legal positivists believe, so if he was to refute legal positivism, he would have to take on Hart's theory of law. But what do legal positivists believe?

In his earliest attacks on Hart, Dworkin assumed that legal positivists (including Hart) all thought that legal rules could 'be identified and distinguished by specific criteria, by tests having to do not with their content but with their *pedigree* or the manner in which they were adopted or developed.'[43] Dworkin thought that he could refute legal positivism by pointing to the fact that in the Anglo-American legal systems, certain rules and principles were accepted by judges as being part of UK or US law not because they had gone through some deliberate process of being made part of UK or US law but because of their content – and more particularly, their ability to explain or make sense of the past decisions of the courts in the UK or the US.

So, for example, the principle that was relied on in *Riggs v Palmer* as a reason for invalidating Francis Palmer's will in favour of his murderous grandson – the principle that 'no man should profit from his wrong' – could not be said to be a legal principle of UK or US law because it has a certain pedigree. There was no initiation ceremony that made that principle part of UK or US law. Instead, that principle counts as being a legal principle of UK or US law because there are so many decided cases – most of them dealing with situations where a claimant is allowed to sue a defendant for money that the defendant has made by committing some kind of legal wrong in relation to the claimant – that can be explained as giving effect to that principle. The validity of the principle that 'no man should profit from his wrong' rests on its explanatory power, and therefore its content, rather than its source or pedigree.

Some legal positivists[44] reacted to Dworkin's early attack on legal positivism by arguing that his attack missed its mark. Legal positivists are not, they argued, committed to believing that what we can call the *pedigree thesis* is correct. The rule of recognition of a given legal system *can* make the validity of a legal rule dependent on its content rather than its pedigree. They argued that the defining feature

---

[43] Dworkin, 'The model of rules I' in his *Taking Rights Seriously* (Duckworth, 1977), 17.

[44] Soper, 'Legal theory and the obligation of a judge: the Hart/Dworkin debate' (1977) 77 *Michigan Law Review* 473; Lyons, 'Principles, positivism and legal theory' (1977) 87 *Yale Law Journal* 415; Coleman, 'Negative and positive positivism' (above, n. 30).

of legal positivism lies elsewhere – either in the belief that it is not *necessary* for the rule of recognition of a legal system to make the validity of a legal rule dependent on its content, or in the belief that the content of the rule of recognition of a legal system is a matter of social fact rather than moral argument. The sort of legal positivism that these positivists argued for became known as *soft* legal positivism or *inclusive* legal positivism.[45]

In the Postscript to the second edition of *The Concept of Law*, H.L.A. Hart 'came out' as a soft (or inclusive) legal positivist, arguing that Dworkin's criticisms of his theory of law had ignored the fact that even in the first edition of *The Concept of Law*, he had 'expressly state[d] … that in some systems of law, as in the United States, the ultimate criteria of legal validity might explicitly incorporate besides pedigree, principles of justice or substantive moral values, and these may form the content of legal constitutional restraints'[46] and that he had explicitly acknowledged 'that the rule of recognition may incorporate as criteria of legal validity conformity with moral principles or substantive values'.[47]

However, the soft (or inclusive) legal positivist idea that the rule of recognition *can* make the validity of a legal rule dependent on its conformity to certain moral principles has not won universal acceptance. It has been attacked by both Dworkin, and by legal positivists – most notably, Joseph Raz – who endorse the pedigree thesis and have as a result come to be known as *hard* or *exclusive* legal positivists. But before we join the debate over whether a rule of recognition *can* make the validity of a legal rule dependent on its moral content – as the soft (or inclusive) legal positivists argue it can – we should note two different ways in which a rule of recognition could do this.

(1) The first is to say that a rule with a particular pedigree will count as a valid legal rule *unless* it violates some moral standard. Some would say that this is the position under the US Constitution, where a legal rule contained in an Act of Congress will count as a valid legal rule unless it violates a moral standard set out in the US Constitution such as the 8th Amendment to the Constitution which forbids, among other things, the infliction of 'cruel and unusual punishments'.

(2) The second is to say that a rule will count as a valid legal rule *if* it satisfies a test that requires one to evaluate the content of the rule. An example might be the mini rule of recognition for determining whether or not one person will owe another a duty of care under the test laid out in the case of *Caparo Industries plc v Dickman*.[48] Under the *Caparo* test, a defendant will owe a claimant a duty of care if (1) it is foreseeable that the claimant would suffer some kind of harm if the defendant were careless; (2) the defendant and the claimant were in a suffi-

---

[45] The most extended treatment of this form of positivism is Waluchow, *Inclusive Legal Positivism* (Oxford University Press, 1994).

[46] CL, 247.

[47] CL, 250.

[48] [1990] 2 AC 605.

ciently proximate relationship; and (3) it would be 'fair, just and reasonable' to find that the defendant owed the claimant a duty of care.[49]

There is no good, established terminology for these two different ways in which a rule of recognition can make the content of the law dependent on morality. We will say that a legal system where the rule of recognition says that a rule with a particular pedigree will be legally valid unless it violates a moral standard is one where *law is bounded by morality*. We will say that a legal system where the rule of recognition says that a rule will be legally valid if it satisfies a test requiring one to evaluate the content of the rule is one where *law is generated by morality*.[50]

So another way of putting the question of whether the rule of recognition of a legal system *can* make the validity of a legal rule dependent on morality is to ask whether one can have a legal system where law is bounded by morality, or where law is generated by morality, or both. Soft (or inclusive) legal positivists say that you can. A number of different attacks have been made on this position.

DWORKIN'S ATTACK

Dworkin would not, of course, have denied that you can have a legal system where law is both bounded and generated by morality. As we have seen,[51] for Dworkin, the exercise of determining what the law says on a particular issue was an inescapably value-laden one, and at a number of different levels. What Dworkin denied was that a *positivist* could believe that a legal system can make the validity of a legal rule dependent on morality. Dworkin made a couple of arguments for thinking this: the argument from *uncertainty*, and the argument from *controversy*.

The argument from *uncertainty* goes as follows.[52] According to the positivists (though not Dworkin) the whole point of having a rule of recognition is to cure the uncertainty that would otherwise obtain in a place like *Metropolis* over what the primary rules of obligations in *Metropolis* are. This certainty would be lost were the rule of recognition to make the validity of a rule dependent on morality. Hart's response to this criticism was that it

'exaggerate[s] both the degree of certainty which a consistent positivist must attribute to a body of legal standards and the uncertainty which will result if the criteria of legal validity include conformity with specific moral principles or values. It is of

---

[49] Ibid, 617–18.

[50] Confusingly, Matthew Kramer reserves the term 'inclusive legal positivism' for the claim (1) that you can have a legal system where law is bounded by morality, and uses the term 'incorporationism' for the claim (2) that you can have a legal system where law is generated by morality: Kramer, 'How moral principles can enter into the law' (2000) 6 *Legal Theory* 83. There seems no reason for using the term 'inclusive' for claim (1), and doing so creates a lot of confusion as the term 'inclusive legal positivism' is used by others to describe the belief that claims (1) or (2) or both (1) and (2) are true. In the text we repeatedly use the term 'soft (or inclusive) legal positivism' to describe this belief, in order to make it clear at every turn that we are not using the phrase 'inclusive' in the restricted way that Kramer does.

[51] See above, pp. 43–44.

[52] See Dworkin, 'A reply by Ronald Dworkin' in Cohen (ed.), *Ronald Dworkin and Contemporary Jurisprudence* (Duckworth, 1984), 247–48.

course true that an important function of the rule of recognition is to promote the certainty with which the law may be ascertained. This it would fail to do if the tests which it introduced for law not only raise controversial issues in some cases but raise them in all or most cases. But the exclusion of all uncertainty at whatever costs in other values is not a goal which I have ever envisaged for the rule of recognition.'[53]

Dworkin had two versions of the argument from *controversy*. The first was to argue that if, as the positivists contend (while Dworkin does not), the rule of recognition employed by the judges in a legal system owes its existence to its shared acceptance by those judges, that shared acceptance must go all the way down, to the level of issues about how the rule of recognition applies in concrete cases.[54] But this depth of shared acceptance could not be maintained if the rule of recognition required the judges to make moral judgments in order to determine whether a particular legal rule is valid: differences in the judges' moral views would mean that they would end up disagreeing about how the rule of recognition applied in particular cases. However, as we have seen,[55] there is no reason why we cannot say that judges agree that a particular rule will be a valid rule if *x* is true, and at the same time disagree as to when *x* will be true.

The second version of Dworkin's argument from controversy was that it is a controversial issue in moral theory as to whether moral statements express beliefs about the world which can be correct or incorrect, so that when someone says 'It is wrong to torture someone' we can ask whether the belief about the world expressed in that statement is actually true or not. 'Moral cognitivists' say that moral statements *do* express beliefs about the world that can be correct or incorrect. 'Moral non-cognitivists' disagree, arguing that a statement such as 'It is wrong to torture someone' is really just a statement about the speaker, where the speaker is really saying 'I don't want you to torture other people' or 'I don't like the idea of you torturing other people' or 'I don't approve of you torturing other people'. Dworkin argued that if the rule of recognition of a legal system made the validity of a legal rule dependent on morality, then what the law said on a particular issue would depend on which of these philosophical theories about the nature of moral statements was true. For Dworkin this was not a problem: he was more than happy with the idea of judges wrestling with complex moral issues to reach conclusions about the law.[56] However, he thought that positivists would reject the possibility that the content of the law might depend on the outcome of controversies over whether cognitivism or non-cognitivism is correct.[57] In the Postscript to the

---

[53] CL, Postscript, 251.

[54] Dworkin, 'The model of rules II' in his *Taking Rights Seriously* (Duckworth, 1977); and Dworkin, 'A reply by Ronald Dworkin' (above, n. 52), 253

[55] See above, pp. 45–46.

[56] Indeed, Dworkin discusses precisely these issues in LE, 80–85. See also his *Justice for Hedgehogs* (Harvard University Press, 2011).

[57] See Dworkin, 'A reply by Ronald Dworkin' (above, n. 52), 250: 'I had thought it was part of Hart's ambition (and of the ambition of positivists generally) to make the objective standing of propositions of law independent of any controversial theory either of meta-ethics or of moral ontology.'

second edition of *The Concept of Law*, Hart accepted that this criticism did have a great deal of force as he thought that 'the question of the objective standing of moral judgments [should be] left open by legal theory.'[58] Given this, he conceded that the soft (or inclusive) positivist claim that a rule of recognition could make the validity of a law dependent on morality might need to be replaced by a claim (advanced by Raz) that a legal system could include a secondary rule requiring the judges, when developing or changing the law, to do so in accordance with various moral values or precepts.[59]

RAZ'S ATTACK

We saw in the previous chapter that Joseph Raz argues that law necessarily claims that it is a *legitimate authority*. In other words, in requiring people to act in a particular ways, law – of its nature – claims that people will do better, in terms of conforming to the reasons that apply to them, if they simply do what the law tells them to do rather than making up their own mind as to what to do. But if law is to make the claim to be a *legitimate authority*, then it must be capable of being *authoritative*. And it cannot be authoritative if the law is either bounded or generated by morality. So law's claim to be a legitimate authority makes it impossible for soft (or inclusive) legal positivism to be correct. All this needs much more explanation.

Suppose that *Guru* claims to be a legitimate moral authority. He tells anyone who will listen that 'If you just do what I tell you to do, you will do the right thing far more often than if you make up your own mind what's the right thing to do.' *Seeker* hears about *Guru*, and the claims he makes for himself, and travels many hundreds of miles to meet *Guru*. On being ushered into *Guru*'s presence, *Seeker* falls to his knees and says, 'Tell me, o wise master, how should I live?' *Guru* stays silent for a long time, thinking deeply, and eventually says, 'Do the right thing.' It would not be surprising if *Seeker* were outraged at *Guru*'s response; at the very least, he will be immensely puzzled by it. *Seeker* will rightly think, 'I have come all this way and he has told me absolutely nothing. I already know that I should do the right thing – that's why I'm here. I want to know what's the right thing to do, and he hasn't told me anything about that.'

In this story, *Guru* has not only failed to be a legitimate authority – he has failed even to be an authority. A directive can only be authoritative if it settles the issues it is supposed to settle. *Guru*'s directive 'Do the right thing' does not do anything to tell *Seeker* what exactly is the right thing to do, which is the issue he was seeking guidance from *Guru* on, and which *Guru* claimed he would supply people with when he said that if they just did what he told him to do, they would do the right thing far more often than if they made up their own mind what to do. As it is,

---

[58] CL, Postscript, 254.
[59] Ibid.

Seeker is left no choice but to continue to make up his own mind as to what is the right thing to do.[60]

Raz argues that were soft (or inclusive) legal positivism to be correct, then on the occasions where a rule of recognition in a legal system made the validity of a legal rule dependent on morality, that legal system would fail to be an authority in the way that *Guru* fails to be an authority for *Seeker*. As Raz observes, the subjects of a legal system can only regard the legal rules to which they are subject as authoritative if they can establish

> 'which rules were made or endorsed by the authorities. This can involve establishing the acts of the authority and their meaning. But it cannot consist of establishing which law the authority should have passed. Authorities ... exist precisely to avoid the need for their subjects to base their actions on their own estimation of what is best to do. That is their main rationale, and it will be defeated if to establish the content of the law they would have to deliberate the very considerations the law exists to pre-empt ... So for the law to be able to fulfil its function, and therefore to be capable of enjoying moral authority, it must be capable of being identified without reference to the moral questions which it pre-empts, i.e. the moral questions on which it is meant to adjudicate.'[61]

If the rule of recognition of a legal system makes the validity of a legal rule contingent on morality, it would seem that the subjects of that legal system can only determine what the law is requiring them to do by going behind the law and making up their own mind as to what the law *should* require them to do. But that is precisely what law exists to save people from having to do.

Raz's arguments against soft (or inclusive) legal positivism can be criticised in a number of different ways.

(1) Raz's arguments rest on the idea that law necessarily claims legitimate authority over its subjects. However, as we have seen,[62] it may be doubted whether this is true.

(2) It is not clear that the hard (or exclusive) legal positivism that Raz favours – according to which one can determine what counts as a valid rule of a legal system without engaging in moral argument – offers a more faithful account of the workings of the sort of legal systems with which we are familiar than soft (or inclusive) legal positivism does.[63] Most importantly, judges frequently

---

[60] Raz makes the same point with the example of an arbitrator, who is asked to decide what is fair in a dispute between two parties. All the parties to the dispute are told is that the arbitrator has reached his decision and he has made the right decision. See Raz, 'Authority, law and morality' in his *Ethics in the Public Domain* (Oxford University Press, 1994), 203.

[61] Raz, 'On the nature of law' in his *Between Authority and Interpretation* (Oxford University Press, 2009), 114–15.

[62] See above, p. 34.

[63] For a very balanced discussion of the issue, see Waluchow, 'Four concepts of validity: reflections on inclusive and exclusive positivism' in Himma and Adler (eds), *The Rule of Recognition and the United States Constitution* (above, n. 10).

do resort to moral considerations in determining what the law says: witness the already mentioned *Caparo* test for determining when one person owes another a duty of care.

Raz attempts to reconcile this feature of our law with his hard (or exclusive) positivism in two ways. First, he argues that the fact that the courts routinely refer to moral considerations in determining what the law says in a particular case is not enough to make such considerations part of the law, in the same way that when a UK court refers to, or even applies, some provisions of US law raising conflicts of law issues, those provisions of US law do not become part of UK law.[64] To think otherwise is to fall into the trap of adopting a King Midas theory of law, according to which anything the courts touch turns into law.[65] Secondly, Raz argues that where the courts do refer to moral considerations in determining what the law says in a particular case, that is because the law directs them to exercise their power to develop or change the law in a way that is faithful to morality.[66]

(3) Ronald Dworkin criticises Raz's hard (or exclusive) legal positivism by pointing out that if we accept Raz's arguments that law, in its nature, has to be authoritative, then it would seem to follow that if 'a nation's legislature adopts a [statute] declaring that henceforth, on pain of severe criminal punishment, subjects must never act immorally in any aspect of their lives ... it would be a conceptual mistake to describe the statute as law at all.'[67] This is because the statute does nothing to settle the issue of how the subjects of the statute should behave: it is the equivalent of our *Guru* telling *Seeker* 'Do the right thing'. But, as Dworkin observes, saying that the statute in Dworkin's example is not law at all

> 'seems too strong. The statute, after all, has normative consequences for those disposed to accept its authority. They now have an additional reason to reflect carefully on the moral quality of everything they do and to act punctiliously, not only because they are now subject to official sanction, but also because their community has declared, through its criminal law, the cardinal importance of moral diligence.'[68]

(4) Raz's objections to soft (or inclusive) legal positivism seem to work in relation to a legal system where law is *generated* by morality, but may not work where law is *bounded* by morality. A legal system that employed a mini rule of recognition

---

[64] Raz, 'Incorporation by law' in his *Between Authority and Interpretation* (above, n. 61), 193–202.

[65] See above, p. 45.

[66] Raz, 'The inner logic of the law' in his *Ethics and the Public Domain* (above, n. 60), 225–234. In his *The Authority of Law*, 2nd edn (Oxford University Press, 2009), 47, fn. 8, Raz argues that positivists who believe that 'Sometimes the identification of some laws turns on moral arguments' have to provide 'an adequate criterion for separating legal references to morality, which makes its application a case of applying pre-existing rules, from cases of judicial discretion in which the judge, by resorting to moral considerations, is changing the law. I am not aware of any serious attempt to provide such a test.'

[67] Dworkin, 'Thirty years on' (2002) 115 *Harvard Law Review* 1655, 1673.

[68] Ibid.

that said 'You are legally required to do x if you ought, morally, to do x' would be incapable of being an authority for its subjects on the issue of whether they should do x. In order to work out whether or not the law required them to do x, people would have to work out whether or not they *should* do x – but that is precisely what the law is meant to save them from doing if it is to be an authority on the issue of whether the law's subjects should do x. However, where the law is *bounded* by morality, things are more complicated.

To use an example first put forward by Jules Coleman,[69] suppose that the rule of recognition of a legal system says that rules contained in statutes passed by the legislature will be valid legal rules unless they are unfair; and the legislature passes a statute prohibiting intentional killing. The fact that the statute is liable to be struck down if it is unfair will not prevent the statute being authoritative on the issue of whether people shouldn't kill others intentionally. This is because in order to determine whether the statute is unfair, people don't have to work out for themselves whether they shouldn't kill other people intentionally. That issue is settled by the statute: the issue of whether the statute is fair is completely different.

So it seems that the fact that law in the legal system we are considering is *bounded* by morality does not necessarily stop law in that legal system being authoritative on the issue of how people should behave. However, it must also be admitted that there may be many examples of situations where a moral limit on the validity of law undermines its capacity to be authoritative. For example, suppose that an Act of Congress is passed providing that any state that employs the death penalty should use a particular method for executing prisoners who have been sentenced to death. The Act of Congress will be invalid if the prescribed method of execution amounts to a 'cruel and unusual' punishment.[70] This would seem to prevent the Act of Congress being authoritative on the issue of whether states should use the prescribed method of execution, as whether the prescribed method is 'cruel and unusual' is intimately bound up with the issue of whether it should be used.

CONCLUSION

It seems to us that the debate between legal positivists over whether the rule of recognition of a legal system *can* contain a moral component should be scored a win for the soft (or inclusive) legal positivists. They start with the advantage that given the social roots of the rule of recognition, they *must* win unless a convincing argument can be made that there is some reason why the judges of a legal system simply could not adopt a rule of recognition that made the validity of a legal rule dependent on morality. No such convincing argument can be made out.

---

[69] Coleman, 'Authority and reason' in George (ed.), *The Autonomy of Law* (Oxford University Press, 1996), 307.
[70] Eighth Amendment to the US Constitution.

The argument that comes closest is Dworkin's argument that soft (or inclusive) legal positivism would make the content of the law dependent on the outcome of another debate between moral cognitivists and moral non-cognitivists. But even that argument melts away if we assume that debate has finished with a convincing win for the cognitivists.[71]

Debate 5

Must the rule of recognition have a moral component?

We finish this chapter with a debate in which all positivists, of whatever description, are on the same side. All legal positivists would agree that there is no reason to think that the rule of recognition in a particular legal system *must always* have a moral component that would deny legal validity to rules of a certain level of iniquity. However, this position has not gone unchallenged. A number of distinguished legal philosophers have attempted to argue that the rule of recognition of *any* legal system *must* deny the status of law to rules that approach a certain extreme level of odiousness. In this section, we look at what these philosophers have had to say, and the arguments that have been made by legal positivists against their positions.

GUSTAV RADBRUCH

Gustav Radbruch was a German jurist who died in 1949. Early in his career, Radbruch was a hard (or exclusive) legal positivist who took the view that the validity of a legal rule could never turn on the content of the rule. However, the rise of the Nazis in Germany changed his mind. He thought that the widespread endorsement of legal positivism among German lawyers had made it too easy for the Nazis, once they took power in Germany in 1933, to take control of the German legal system and bend it to their terrible ends. After World War II ended, Radbruch argued that law has to be responsive to three different values: certainty, 'purposiveness', and justice.[72] The idea that a statute is a source of valid law irrespective of its content promotes certainty but does nothing to ensure that law responds to the need to be just. For that to happen, we need to adopt what has come to be known as 'Radbruch's Formula':

> 'The positive law, secured by legislation and power, takes precedence even when its content is unjust and fails to benefit the people, unless the conflict between statute and justice reaches such an intolerable degree that the statute, as "flawed law", must yield to justice.'[73]

---

[71] On which debate, see Parfit, *On What Matters: Volume Two* (Oxford University Press, 2011), and below, ch. 8.

[72] Radbruch, 'Statutory lawlessness and supra-statutory law (1946)' (2006) 26 *Oxford Journal of Legal Studies* 1 (trans. Bonnie and Stanley Paulson).

[73] Ibid, 7.

Radbruch went on to argue that while there might be cases where it would be diffi-cult to determine whether his Formula applied, there could be no doubt that it did in the case 'Where there is not even an attempt at justice, where equality, the core of justice, is deliberately betrayed in the issuance of positive law'. In such a case, Radbruch argued 'the statute is not merely "flawed law", it lacks completely the very nature of law.' Radbruch went on to conclude that 'Measured by this standard, whole portions of National Socialist law never attained the dignity of valid law.'[74]

The post-war German courts went on to apply Radbruch's Formula, or some-thing like it, in determining the criminal guilt of defendants who had executed people for violating Nazi 'law', or had exploited Nazi 'law' to inform on their enemies and have them executed, or had used force to defend themselves against being killed by officials acting under Nazi 'law'. Holding that Nazi 'law' was no law at all allowed these defendants to be tried on the basis that they had no justifica-tion for their actions, or ample justification in the case of someone who used force to defend himself from being killed by officials acting under Nazi 'law'. Lecturing at Harvard in 1957, H.L.A. Hart criticised the view that in cases like these Nazi 'law' could be set aside as no law at all as 'hysteria'.[75]

Both in that lecture and later on, in *The Concept of Law*, Hart argued that the real solution to the problem that Radbruch's Formula was meant to address – that of judges unthinkingly giving effect to iniquitous rules on the basis that they were legally binding because they complied with the laid down forms for creating law – is to help people realise that just because the law requires you to do *x*, that does *not* mean you should, morally, do *x*. So for Hart, legal positivism was not the source of the problem of German courts between 1933 and 1945 going along with *diktats* issued by Nazi officials: it was the potential solution. The real source of the problem was the identification of law with what ought to be done – a problem that could only be accentuated by Radbruch's Formula, which attempts to guarantee that what the law requires will coincide with what is to be done. A more clear-sighted view of the nature of law – such as that offered by Hart and other legal positivists – would help 'preserve the sense that the certification of something as legally valid is not conclu-sive of the question of obedience' and create some conceptual space for a judge faced with an evil law to say 'This is law but too iniquitous to obey or apply'.[76]

---

[74] Ibid.

[75] Hart, 'Positivism and the separation of law and morals' (1958) 71 *Harvard Law Review* 593, 619.

[76] CL, 210. Hart also argued in *The Concept of Law* that from an academic point of view 'nothing is to be gained in the theoretical or scientific study of law as a social phenomenon by adopting the [view that iniquitous rules cannot have the status of law]: it would lead us to exclude certain rules even though they exhibit all the other complex characteristics of law. Nothing, surely, but confusion could follow from a proposal to leave the study of such rules to another discipline, and certainly no history or other form of legal study has found it profitable to do this' (CL, 209). However, mindful of Hart's later admo-nition that 'the criteria [for legal validity] provided by a system's rule of recognition' are *not* 'derived from the meaning of the word "law"' (CL, 247) this academic argument as to the desirability of extend-ing the term 'law' to cover iniquitous rules cannot be used as an argument for saying that a rule of recognition in a particular legal system *will* allow iniquitous rules to count as valid law. And indeed, as we have seen (above, p. 52) Hart did accept the soft (or inclusive) positivist position that in a particular legal system, its rule of recognition could be such that iniquitous rules do not count as valid law.

So Hart thought that what happened to the German legal system after 1933 did not indicate that we *must* say that the rule of recognition of *any* legal system will deny that an iniquitous rule is valid. Rather it emphasised the need to remember that the rule of recognition of a legal system is simply a matter of social fact and is as a result, in John Gardner's phrase, 'normatively inert'.[77] Just because a rule counts as valid under a legal system's rule of recognition does not mean that you ought to obey it or give effect to it. However, there is a problem with Hart's position.

Suppose the judges in a particular legal system are both morally virtuous and cannot be cowed by the government into doing whatever the government wants. They also accept Hart's advice that just because a particular legal rule is valid, that does not mean they should necessarily give effect to it. So they get into the habit, when faced with an iniquitous legal rule created by the government, of saying, 'This is law, but it is too iniquitous for us to apply.' There seems to be no practical difference between their doing that, and their saying 'Under the rule of recognition that we all accept for determining what counts as valid law, an iniquitous rule will not count as valid law.' There is a verbal difference – in the legal system we are imagining the judges say 'Under the rule of recognition that we all accept, an iniquitous rule will count as valid law – but of course, even if it does, we won't give effect to it.' But in terms of what the judges *do*, there is no difference at all.

Given this, it is almost inevitable – because doing so would be simpler and more straightforward and efficient – that our virtuous judges would in time reformulate the rule of recognition that they mutually accept so that it said that 'A rule that is too iniquitous for us to apply will not count as valid law.' If this is right, then we might be able to say that the rule of recognition in a legal system where the judges are both morally virtuous and able to act independently of government pressure *will* have a moral component, under which rules that achieve a certain level of odiousness or iniquity will not count as valid legal rules. It is in legal systems where the judges are not particularly morally virtuous – but are instead happy to be timeserving hacks, or unscrupulously self-serving, or are easily cowed by the government into not doing anything to rock the boat – that it is possible that the rule of recognition in those legal systems will not have a moral component.

LON FULLER

Lon Fuller was an American jurist who served as H.L.A. Hart's principal living antagonist until the advent of Ronald Dworkin. As we saw in Chapter 1,[78] Fuller took a purposive view of the nature of law, arguing that 'law is the enterprise of subjecting human conduct to the governance of rules.'[79] That enterprise, he argued, is subject to both a 'morality of duty' and a 'morality of aspiration'.[80] The

---

[77] Gardner, 'Legal positivism: 5½ myths' (2001) 46 *American Journal of Jurisprudence* 199, 202.
[78] See above, pp. 4–5.
[79] Fuller, *The Morality of Law*, rev'd edn (Yale University Press, 1969), 106.
[80] Ibid, ch. 1.

use of the term 'morality' here is seriously confusing and prejudicial, so we will substitute for these terms 'standards of competence' and 'standards of excellence'. Standards of competence define the minimum standards that you have to live up to even to be able to claim that you are engaged in a given enterprise. Standards of excellence define what it means to do really well in engaging in a given enterprise.

So, for example, standards of competence for writing an introductory book on jurisprudence might include 'Deal with H.L.A. Hart's theory of law and how it relates to theories of law that preceded and succeeded his *The Concept of Law*'. If you don't do that, you can't really claim to have written an introductory book on jurisprudence. You may have *aimed* to write an introductory book on jurisprudence, but you have completely failed in that task. Standards of excellence for writing an introductory book on jurisprudence might include 'Explain as clearly as possible in what respects H.L.A. Hart's theory of law is superior and inferior to theories of law that preceded and succeeded his *The Concept of Law*.' If you do that, to some extent, then you can claim to have produced a good introductory book on jurisprudence. It is in the nature of standards of excellence that they are *inexhaustibly demanding*, in that even if you live up to them to some extent, it is always possible to fulfil them more completely. You can always write more clearly; you can always find more ways in which *The Concept of Law* is superior and inferior to what came before and after it.

The standards of competence and excellence for 'the enterprise of subjecting human conduct to the governance of rules' are both centred round a number of different precepts that govern the enterprise of rule-making, and were identified by Fuller in his great work *The Morality of Law*. These precepts require that the rules laid down by a law-maker be (1) general, (2) publicised, (3) prospective and not retrospective in their effect, (4) clear and understandable, (5) non-contradictory, (6) not such that they require people to do the impossible, (7) relatively stable and not changing so often as to make it impossible for someone to keep up with them, (8) adhered to by the government in that the government will only use force against someone when authorised to do so under the rules.[81] These precepts define both standards of competence and excellence for law-makers.

Fuller argued that 'a total failure' to give effect to just one of these precepts 'does not simply result in a bad system of law; it results in something that is not properly called a legal system at all.'[82] Fuller demonstrates this with his parable of a failed law-maker Rex, who fails to provide his subjects with general rules by which they can guide their lives; then fails to publicise the code of rules that he has drawn up and intends to use in determining the outcome of legal cases; then decides all cases on a retrospective basis, determining after the event what the parties in a particular case ought to have done; then attempts to govern using a code that is completely contradictory; then governs using a code that is subjected

---

[81] Ibid, 39.
[82] Ibid.

to daily amendments in order to try to keep it up to date; and then handed down a long series of decisions which bore absolutely no relation to the code by which he was purporting to follow in making those decisions.[83] As Fuller relates, Rex 'never made any' law.[84] He failed at every turn to live up to the standards of competence that governed his chosen career as a law-maker.

But even if Rex had managed to live up to each of Fuller's eight precepts to some extent, that would not have made him an excellent law-maker. Achieving excellence as a law-maker would have required Rex to move closer and closer to 'a utopia of legality in which all rules are perfectly clear, consistent with one another, known to every citizen, and never retroactive. In this utopia the rules remain constant through time, demand only what is possible, and are scrupulously observed by courts, police, and everyone else charged with their administration.'[85]

We are not concerned at the moment with the standards of excellence that Fuller claimed govern the activity of law-making. Our interest is in the idea that there exist standards of competence the failure to observe which would prevent us saying that a law-maker had created a valid legal rule. An example might be the grant of a power to a public body accompanied by an ouster clause preventing the courts from judicially reviewing the exercise of that power. It might be argued that the rule granting the power and the rule containing the ouster clause contradict each other: the power-granting rule meant to give the public body a limited power while the ouster clause makes that power unlimited. If that is the case, the law-maker cannot do what he is trying to do: either the grant of power is a nullity, or the ouster clause is. Does this mean that Fuller's precepts amount to a necessary limit on the validity of law under any rule of recognition, so that a *complete* failure to observe one of those precepts will prevent us from saying that a particular rule counts as valid law? H.L.A. Hart never tried to deny that this might be the case. However, what he did argue was that even if this were the case, this would not mean that the rule of recognition in a legal system had a *moral* component. An unjust law, Hart insisted, could perfectly well observe all of Fuller's eight precepts[86] with the result that even if Fuller's arguments were correct, there is nothing in them to indicate that a grossly unjust law could not count as valid law under the rule of recognition of a legal system.

---

[83] Fuller, *The Morality of Law* (above, n. 79), 33–38.

[84] Ibid, 41.

[85] Ibid.

[86] CL, 207 (observance of Fuller's precepts is 'unfortunately compatible with very great iniquity'); Hart, 'Review of *The Morality of Law*' (1965) 78 *Harvard Law Review* 1281, 1284 (Fuller's eight precepts 'are essentially principles of good craftsmanship ... They are independent of the law's substantive aims just as the principles of carpentry are independent of whether the carpenter is making hospital beds or torturers' racks').

ROBERT ALEXY

Robert Alexy is another German jurist, who was born just a few months after the end of World War II. Alexy has become famous in jurisprudential circles for his defence of Radbruch's Formula. His most well-known argument in favour of the Formula is what is known as the *argument from injustice*.[87] The idea underlying this argument is that the law, of its nature, claims to be just. It follows that, in some sense, a grossly unjust law is a contradiction in terms. It claims to be just, but obviously fails to live up to the claims that it makes for itself. By its own lights, it fails to be what it claims to be: by failing to be just, it fails to be law.

The argument is easily refuted, and has been by John Gardner.[88] We have no reason to think that law necessarily claims to be just. The most that thinkers like Raz and Gardner say that law claims for itself is that it is a *legitimate authority*. It claims – they say – not that every law is just, but that if we do as the law says then we will do better, over time, in terms of acting in accordance with the reasons that apply to us than we would if we made up our own minds what to do. So law admits that it *will* get things wrong from time to time: it merely claims that it will get things right more often than we could if we were left to rely on our own resources. If this is right, then the argument from injustice fails. And if this is wrong, then even then the argument from injustice fails because if it is right to reject – as thinkers like Matthew Kramer do[89] – the idea that the law claims to be a *legitimate authority*, then we could hardly accept the much stronger claim that the law claims to be *just*.

However, if thinkers like Raz and Gardner are correct that the law, of its nature, claims to be a legitimate authority then that might provide the basis for an Alexy-style argument in favour of the view that there *will* exist a necessary limit on what kind of rules can be regarded as legally valid under the rule of recognition of a legal system. The suggested limit is this: a rule that on its face cannot maintain a claim of legitimate authority could not be regarded as legally valid under the rule of recognition of any legal system.[90]   Dworkin

For example, suppose that the UK is taken over by a fascist government that acts in such a militarily provocative way that countries on the Continent make plans for the invasion of the UK and the overthrow of its fascist regime. The UK government passes legislation that provides that if London falls to enemy forces, all farms, factories, roads and bridges in the UK must be blown up, and suicide pills distributed to the entire UK population, who are required under the legislation to

---

[87] Alexy, *The Argument from Injustice: A Reply to Legal Positivism* (Oxford University Press, 2002) (trans. Bonnie and Stanley Paulson). See also Alexy, 'A defence of Radbruch's formula' in Dyzenhaus (ed.), *Recrafting the Rule of Law* (Hart Publishing, 1999).

[88] Gardner, 'How law claims, what law claims' in Klatt (ed.), *Institutionalized Reason: The Jurisprudence of Robert Alexy* (Oxford University Press, 2012).

[89] See above, p. 34.

[90] For the same point, see Dworkin, 'Thirty years on' (2002) 115 *Harvard Law Review* 1655, 1668–69.

take the pills unless their conscience dictates otherwise.[91] No one – even with a pretence of sincerity – could claim that we would do better abiding by such legislation than we could do if we made up our own minds what to do. That is not the point of the legislation: it is seeking, not to help people comply with the reasons that apply to them, but to get them to act in defiance of reason either to ensure that the victory of the UK's enemies is as bitter as possible or because the UK government thinks that if it is going down to defeat, it wants to take as many people as possible down with it, *Götterdämmerung*-style. So if law does, of its nature, claim to be a legitimate authority, then it might be argued that this kind of suicidal legislation cannot count as valid law whatever the nature of the legal system under which it was passed. (Of course, one could draw the opposite conclusion: that this kind of legislation obviously counts as valid law, and this shows that law does not, of its nature, claim to be a legitimate authority.)

CONCLUSION

While none of the theorists discussed in this section were able to make a convincing case for thinking that the rule of recognition of a legal system will necessarily include some kind of moral component, their arguments do enough to force us seriously to consider the possibility that there may exist substantive limits on what can count as valid law under the rule of recognition of any legal system. That, in turn, would indicate that there is more to the nature of law than simply a Hartian union of primary and secondary rules.[92]

Further Reading

Hart, CL, chs V.3 and VI.
Green, 'The Concept of Law Revisited' (1996) 94 *Michigan Law Review* 1687.
Raz, 'Authority, law, and morality' in *Ethics in the Public Domain* (Oxford University Press, 1994).
Gardner, 'Legal positivism: $5\frac{1}{2}$ myths' (2001) 46 *American Journal of Jurisprudence* 199.
Dworkin, *Taking Rights Seriously* (Duckworth, 1977), chs 1 and 2.
Dworkin, LE, ch. 1.
Shapiro, 'The Hart-Dworkin debate: a short guide for the perplexed' in Ripstein (ed.), *Ronald Dworkin* (Cambridge University Press, 2007).
Leiter, 'Explaining theoretical disagreement' (2009) 76 *University of Chicago Law Review* 1215.
Gardner, 'Some types of law' in *Law as a Leap of Faith* (Oxford University Press, 2012).

---

[91] This is not so different from the way the German Nazi government reacted to the prospect of impending defeat at the end of World War II.
[92] This was something that Hart himself was happy to concede: CL, 155, 213.

4

THE MORALITY OF LEGALITY

As we saw towards the end of the last chapter, Lon Fuller argued that in a legal system that is working properly, a number of different precepts – what we can call *precepts of legality* (and what other thinkers refer to when they are talking about *the rule of law*) – will be observed by the system's law-makers in laying down rules to guide the conduct of the subjects of the legal system. Those rules will be, to some degree or other: (1) general, (2) publicised, (3) prospective and not retrospective in their effect, (4) clear and understandable, (5) non-contradictory, (6) not such that they require people to do the impossible, (7) relatively stable and not changing so often as to make it impossible for someone to keep up with them, (8) adhered to by the government in that the government will only use force against someone when authorised to do so under the rules.[1]

The debates in this chapter are over whether there is any connection between morality and observance of these precepts. The debates take as their starting points two rulers, *Justin* and *Vlad*. *Justin* is always concerned to do the right thing morally, and attempts to be a morally good ruler. *Vlad* does not care at all about morality, but is simply concerned to do what is in his self-interest. If acting in his self-interest coincides with what is the right thing to do, then all well and good; but if it conflicts, *Vlad* will think nothing of doing the wrong thing. Both *Justin* and *Vlad* have chosen for the time being to govern their subjects through law, which in turn involves their observing – at least to some degree – Fuller's eight precepts.

The first debate is over whether *Justin* will see any moral value or point in following Fuller's eight precepts. If he will, then he won't just think of Fuller's precepts as wise pieces of advice designed to help him govern his subjects through law that he has strong prudential reasons for following: he will think that he is morally bound to observe those precepts.

The second debate is over whether *Vlad* will in the long term stick to his choice to govern his subjects through law and seek to adhere to Fuller's eight precepts. If he will not – if *Vlad* will, at some point, decide that he would be better off departing from Fuller's eight precepts – then that would seem to show that in the long

---

[1] Fuller, *The Morality of Law* (Yale University Press), 1st edn (1964; rev'd edn, 1969) (henceforth, Fuller, *Morality of Law*).

term Fuller's precepts will only be observed (if they were observed at all) in coun-tries governed by people like *Justin*; that is, morally good rulers.

Whether you think there is any connection between morality and the obser-vance of Fuller's eight precepts depends on what position you take in these debates. The possible positions one could take in these debates, and the conclu-sions one will consequently draw as to the connection between morality and the eight precepts, are charted in the table below:

	First Debate (Is there a moral point or value in observing Fuller's precepts?)	Second debate (Will a ruler who is indifferent to morality stick to Fuller's precepts in long term?)	Strength of connection between morality and Fuller's eight precepts
(1) *Primus*	No	Yes	None
(2) *Secundus*	No	No	None or weak
(3) *Tertius*	Yes	Yes	Weak
(4) *Quartus*	Yes	No	Strong

The debates that we are going to look at in this chapter were pursued first by Hart and Fuller,[2] and then – more recently and at much greater length – by the two Cambridge jurists, Matthew Kramer and Nigel Simmonds.[3] Jeremy Waldron has also made distinguished contributions to the discussion of these issues.[4] But before we get into seeing what all these different thinkers have had to say about the debates discussed in this chapter, it might make those debates easier to follow if we briefly sketch out the four different positions that someone might take in those debates, and what they imply. //

Someone who adopts position (1) – let's call him *Primus* – will first of all deny that there is any moral point or value in a ruler like *Justin* or *Vlad* adhering to Fuller's eight precepts. *Primus* will say that those precepts are merely ones of *efficacy*:

---

[2] Hart, 'Positivism and the separation of law and morals' (1958) 71 *Harvard Law Review* 593; Fuller, 'Positivism and fidelity to law – a reply to Professor Hart' (1958) 71 *Harvard Law Review* 630; CL (see list of abbreviations, p. xiii), ch. VIII.1, ch. IX.3; Fuller, *Morality of Law*; Hart, 'Book review of *Morality of Law*' (1964–5) 78 *Harvard Law Review* 1281; Fuller, 'A reply to critics' in *The Morality of Law*, rev'd ed (Yale University Press, 1969).

[3] See the articles cited at nn. 12, 13, 19, 21, 24, 29, 30, 41, 42, below.

[4] Waldron, 'Why law? – efficacy, freedom or fidelity?' (1994) 13 *Law and Philosophy* 259; Waldron, 'Positivism and legality – Hart's equivocal response to Fuller' (2008) 83 *New York University Law Review* 1134; Waldron, 'Hart and the principles of legality' in Kramer et al (eds), *The Legacy of HLA Hart: Legal, Political, and Moral Philosophy* (Oxford University Press, 2008); Waldron, 'The concept and the rule of law' (2008) 43 *Georgia Law Review* 1; Waldron, 'How law protects dignity' (2012) 71 *Cambridge Law Journal* 200.

if you want to govern people effectively via law, then it would be a good idea to adhere to Fuller's precepts. [But morality does not demand that *Justin* or *Vlad* govern their people through law, and therefore does not demand that they adhere to Fuller's precepts of legality.] *Primus* will go on to insist that a wicked ruler like *Vlad* will – having initially chosen to govern his people through law – stick with that choice even if doing so might cause him some short term inconvenience. The reason is that the advantage of governing his people through law – the same sort of advantages that, in the previous chapter, accounted for why a society like *Arcadia* might develop a full-blown legal system – are such that *Vlad* would be foolish to seek to govern his people in any other way, even though doing so might every so often get in the way of what *Vlad* really wants to do. *Primus* will conclude that there is no connection between morality and Fuller's precepts of legality. Morality does not demand that rulers like *Justin* or *Vlad* abide by those precepts; and we cannot even say that in the long run only benevolent rulers like *Justin* will abide by those precepts – *Vlad* will have more than enough reason to adhere to them in the long run, despite his wicked nature.

Secundus, who adopts position (2), will agree with *Primus* that there is no moral point or value in adhering to Fuller's eight precepts. However, she will be more sceptical than *Primus* as to whether *Vlad* will be able to abide by those precepts in the long term. She thinks that *Vlad* will eventually grow weary of the constraints placed on him by those precepts. In particular, the eighth precept – which prevents *Vlad* using force against a subject unless such force is authorised under the rules that *Vlad* laid down for the governance of his subjects – will prove particularly vexing and is the precept that *Vlad* is most likely to abandon, in the long term. If that is the case, then there *may* exist a *weak* connection between morality and Fuller's precepts of legality. Such a weak connection *would* exist if it were true that only a virtuous ruler such as *Justin* would abide by Fuller's precepts in the long run. However, it is not clear whether that is true.

If, as *Secundus* argues is the case, *Justin* only has prudential reasons for giving effect to Fuller's precepts of legality, then *Justin* may be just as tempted as *Vlad* to depart from those precepts when adhering to them gets in the way of what he wants to do. That virtuous rulers like *Justin* may be subject to such temptations is well illustrated by the following exchange in Act One of Robert Bolt's play *A Man For All Seasons*, where Sir Thomas More clashes with his daughters and his son-in-law William Roper, who are urging him to arrest Richard Rich, a spy sent by the King's representatives to catch More out in some indiscretion for which he can be imprisoned:

'Margaret: Father, that man's bad.
More: There is no law against that.
Roper: There is! God's law!
More: Then God can arrest him.
Roper: Sophistication upon sophistication!
More: No, sheer simplicity. The law, Roper, the law. I know what's legal not what's right. And I'll stick to what's legal.

...

Alice (exasperated, pointing after Rich): While you talk, he's gone!

More: And go he should, if he was the devil himself, until he broke the law!

Roper: So now you'd give the devil benefit of law!

More: Yes. What would you do? Cut a great road through the law to get after the devil?

Roper: I'd cut down every law in England to do that!'

So the fact that *Secundus* takes position (2) does not – yet – allow her to determine whether there is a connection between morality and legality. There will be a weak connection, in her view, if virtuous rulers like *Justin* are more likely in the long run to adhere to Fuller's precepts than wicked rulers like *Vlad*. But whether that is the case will depend on: (a) whether wicked rulers like *Vlad* are likely to be tempted to depart from Fuller's precepts more often than virtuous rulers like *Justin*;[5] and (b) whether, when such temptations arise, the prudential reasons for sticking to Fuller's precepts would weigh more heavily in *Justin*'s deliberations than they would in *Vlad*'s.[6] Until we know what the position is with (a) and (b), all we can say is that someone like *Secundus* will think that there is either no connection between morality and legality, or a weak connection.

Tertius adopts position (3). *Tertius* thinks that *Primus* and *Secundus* are wrong to think that there is no moral value or point in giving effect to Fuller's precepts of legality, but agrees with *Primus* that a wicked ruler like *Vlad* will have sufficient prudential reasons for wishing to adhere to Fuller's eight precepts, even in the long run. So, for *Tertius*, there is a strong similarity between Fuller's precepts and the requirement that a shopkeeper give his customers the right change when they buy goods from him.[7] Obviously, morality demands that a shopkeeper give his customers the right change, but even an unscrupulous shopkeeper will have very good prudential reasons for being punctilious about giving his customers the right change as he will soon go out of business if he acquires a reputation for being

---

[5] It is worth noting here (as our conclusion that positions (1) and (2) are incorrect will mean that the issue will not arise for consideration later on) that Fuller thought that wicked rulers would chafe against his precepts much more than virtuous rulers: Fuller, 'Fidelity', 636–37 (arguing that 'coherence and goodness have more affinity than coherence and evil' and that wicked rulers would find it very difficult to comply with the requirement that laws be made public as no one wants to make a public spectacle of their iniquities).

[6] In *A Man For All Seasons*, Sir Thomas More gives Roper the following prudential reason for not cutting down every law in England to get after the devil: 'And when the last law was down, and the devil turned on you – where would you hide, Roper, the laws all being flat? This country's planted thick with laws from coast to coast – man's laws, not God's – and if you cut them down – and you're just the man to do it – d'you really think you could stand upright in the winds that would blow then? Yes, I'd give the devil benefit of law, for my own safety's sake.' It is not clear whether a ruler like *Vlad* – who, let's suppose, is tempted to use extra-legal violence against an enemy – could be deterred from doing so by similar arguments: even if his departure from the demands of legality ushered in an era of anarchy, he would still fancy his chances against all-comers.

[7] This is an adjusted version of the example discussed in Kant, *Groundwork of the Metaphysics of Morals* (1785), §10, where Kant considers the motivations for a shopkeeper's adhering to the requirement that he not overcharge his customers.

dishonest. *Tertius* will think, then, that there is a *weak* connection between moral-ity and legality: morality demands that rulers adhere to Fuller's precepts; but even people who don't care about morality will be careful to adhere to those precepts so that in the end whether you adhere to the precepts or not will not be affected by how virtuous you are.

Finally, *Quartus* adopts position (4). He agrees with *Tertius* that there is a moral value or point in giving effect to Fuller's precepts of legality. *Quartus* also agrees with *Secundus* that a wicked ruler like *Vlad* can hardly be expected to adhere to those precepts in the long run. Given the fact that *Quartus* thinks that there is a moral value or point in giving effect to Fuller's eight precepts, *Quartus* is confident (in a way that *Secundus* cannot be, without further research) that a virtuous ruler like *Justin* will adhere to those precepts in the long run; or, at the very least, *Justin* is far more likely to adhere to those precepts than someone like *Vlad*, who is indifferent to the fact that he is morally required to comply with those precepts.[8] So *Quartus* will think that there is a *strong* connection between morality and legality. Not only does morality demand that rulers adhere to Fuller's eight precepts; the only kind of ruler who can be expected to adhere to those precepts in the long run is a virtuous ruler.

Now that you understand a bit more about the different positions people might take in the debates that we are going to be looking at in this chapter, and the impli-cations those positions have for what you think the connection between morality and legality is, we can plunge into the details of those debates.

Debate 1

Is there any moral value or point in following Fuller's eight precepts?

All but one of the academics that we have mentioned as contributing to the debates considered in this chapter have acknowledged – with more or less enthu-siasm (more in the case of Fuller, Simmonds and Waldron; much less in the case of Hart) – that there is some moral value or point in adhering to Fuller's precepts of legality. However, they differ slightly over what that moral value or point is. For Simmonds and (much more reluctantly) Hart, the moral value of adhering to Fuller's precepts lies in the way that adhering to those precepts guarantees to the subjects of the law a degree of *independence* that they could not enjoy under any other form of government. For Fuller and Waldron, a ruler who complies with Fuller's precepts in governing her subjects recognises them as possessing a *dignity* that she would fail to acknowledge if she attempted to govern her subjects in some other way. All this needs more explanation.

---

[8] We cannot rule out the possibility that there may exist circumstances where *Justin* will think that he is morally required to depart from Fuller's precepts. But, under the assumption that position (4) is correct, those circumstances will be few and far between, and insignificant compared with the situations where *Vlad* will be unable to resist the temptation to depart from Fuller's precepts.

SIMMONDS/HART

As Jeremy Waldron has noted, Hart was ambivalent on the issue of whether there is any moral point or value in adhering to Fuller's eight precepts.[9] In his review of Fuller's *Morality of Law*, Hart was dismissive of Fuller's claim that Fuller's precepts amounted to an 'inner morality of law'. Instead, Hart argued that they were merely principles of 'efficiency', comparable to the advice that you might give to a would-be poisoner that he should avoid using poisons that will cause the victim to vomit, or are too big to swallow.[10] However, in his writings on criminal law, Hart was much more willing to condemn on moral grounds departures from Fuller's precepts of legality, arguing that doing so would deprive us of 'the ability ... to predict and plan the future course of our lives within the coercive framework of the law'.[11]

This is a point that has been made in much more detail by Nigel Simmonds, arguing that the choice to govern one's subjects through law rather than some other means serves the distinct moral value of preserving for those subjects *independence* from the will of others.[12] Someone who lives under a system of law is left free to choose what to do within the limits imposed upon him or her under the rules of law. Those limits might place very severe limits on what he or she can do, but that is irrelevant: he or she is still left free to choose what to do within those limits and as a result enjoys a kind of freedom which, say, a slave never does. A slave is always subject to his master's will; someone who lives under the rule of law has no master. So respect for people's independence demands that governments govern through law rather than through other means. It follows that any failures to give effect to Fuller's precepts *are* a matter of moral regret – though they may be justifiable when other moral values are at stake.[13]

While, as we will see, Jeremy Waldron nowadays locates the moral value of adhering to Fuller's precepts of legality in the fact that doing so honours the dignity of the law's subjects, in an earlier essay, he pointed out how the choice to govern people through law evinced respect for people's independence as agents.[14] A government that makes that choice is effectively saying to its subjects:

> 'We respect your agency and your goals. We are asking you also to cooperate in the pursuit of a certain social goal G, and to give us your support. And we know we are

[9] Waldron, 'Positivism and legality – Hart's equivocal response to Fuller' (above, n. 4).

[10] Hart, 'Book review of *Morality of Law*' (above, n. 2), 1286.

[11] Hart, *Punishment and Responsibility: Essays in the Philosophy of Law* (Oxford University Press, 1968), 181.

[12] Simmonds, 'Straightforwardly false: the collapse of Kramer's positivism' (2004) 63 *Cambridge Law Journal* 98, 129–30; 'Law as a moral idea' (2005) 55 *University of Toronto Law Journal* 61, 87–88; 'Freedom, law and naked violence' (2009) 59 *University of Toronto Law Journal* 381, 394–95.

[13] Simmonds, 'Kramer's High Noon' (2011) 56 *American Journal of Jurisprudence* 135, 147–48.

[14] Finnis runs the two ideas – of the principles of legality honouring people's independence and their dignity – together in NLNR, at 272: 'Individuals can only be *selves* – i.e. have the "dignity" of being "responsible agents" – if they are not made to live their lives for the convenience of others but are allowed and assisted to create a subsisting identity across a "lifetime". This is the primary value of the predictability which the law seeks to establish through [its] formal features ....'

asking that of some of you who do not actually agree with G. But we give you this guarantee: the demands we make in the name of G, will never be made on the basis that your own goals do not matter. Our demands will always be made in a way that takes seriously the fact that you are an agent and that [you] have business and purposes of your own. For that reason, we will pursue G only through institutional forms that provide a predictable environment for your action. That's the deal: and that's the price we are offering for your co-operation.'[15]

FULLER/WALDRON

At one point in *The Morality of Law*, Lon Fuller argued that:

> 'To embark on the enterprise of subjecting human conduct to the governance of rules involves of necessity a commitment to the view that man is, or can become, a responsible agent, capable of understanding and following rules, and answerable for his defaults.
>
> Every departure from the principles of law's inner morality is an affront to man's dignity as a responsible agent. To judge his actions by unpublished or retrospective laws, or to order him to do an act that is impossible, is to convey to him your indifference to his powers of self-determination.'[16]

This is a point that Jeremy Waldron has made the focus of his arguments as to the moral value of adhering to Fuller's precepts of legality.[17] Governing people through law is quite different, he argues, 'from (say) herding cows with a cattle prod or directing a flock of sheep with a dog'. A government that chooses to govern its subjects through law recognises that those subjects have the 'capacities for practical understanding, for self-control, for self-monitoring and modulation of their own behaviour in relation to norms that they can grasp and understand' and pays them the tribute of expecting them to co-operate in achieving the law's goals by applying the law's norms to themselves. In this way, law 'presupposes a commitment to human dignity. Law assumes that ordinary people are capable of applying norms to their own behaviour and it uses this as a pivot of their being governed.'[18]

KRAMER'S RESPONSE

Matthew Kramer thinks that these arguments for thinking that there is some moral value or point in complying with Fuller's eight precepts do not stand up. His views focus exclusively on Simmonds' arguments, but they are capable of being adapted to Fuller and Waldron's arguments as well.

---

[15] Waldron, 'Why law? – efficacy, freedom or fidelity?' (above, n. 4), 280.

[16] Fuller, *Morality of Law*, 162.

[17] See also, to the same effect, Raz, *The Authority of Law*, 2nd edn (Oxford University Press, 2009), 221: 'observance of the rule of law [= Fuller's precepts of legality] is necessary if the law is to respect human dignity. Respecting human dignity entails treating human beings as persons capable of planning and plotting their future.'

[18] All quotes from Waldron, 'How law protects dignity' (above, n. 4), 206, 208.

One of the objections that Kramer makes to the idea that adherence to Fuller's precepts of legality ensures that people who live under the rule of law enjoy independence from the will of others is that 'the rule of law can serve to establish the institution of chattel slavery.'[19] In other words, far from guaranteeing people independence from the will of others, law can be used to take people's independence away by enslaving them. And it is questionable how far even those who are not enslaved can be said to enjoy any 'independence' from the will of others given that, at any moment, the government could use its legal powers to enslave them.[20] The same objection could be made to Fuller and Waldron's arguments that the moral value or point of adhering to Fuller's eight precepts lies in the respect for human dignity that is involved in adhering to those precepts. The institution of slavery obviously involves a serious affront to human dignity: so it is hard to see how a system of law that recognises slavery could be said to honour human dignity even if it adheres to Fuller's eight precepts.

One possible response – and one which Simmonds has made[21] – is to say that law-established slavery is a special case because someone who is made a slave effectively exists outside the law and its protections. So the existence of law-established slavery does not disprove any claims as to what those who exist under the law enjoy. Indeed, the fact that a slave – by virtue of no longer existing under the law's protections – loses his independence shows a close affiliation between existing under the rule of law and enjoying independence from the will of others. Kramer, however, objects to this move on the ground that:

> 'it does not counteract the damagingness of the fact that the rule of law can serve to establish the institution of chattel slavery. After all, the slaves remain human beings when they are excluded from the status of jural subjects. Their very exclusion from that status within a particular legal system is inimical to the notion that every such system serves the value of liberty. Simmonds cannot vindicate that mistaken notion by pointing out that the unprotected slaves are not jural subjects; the very fact that they are not jural subjects within the legal-governmental system that presides over them and defines the nature of their slavery is precisely what renders so ludicrous the idea that that system serves the value of liberty.'[22]

It looks like Kramer wins this point, but that does not mean he wins the match. It might be argued that while adherence to Fuller's precepts may not be *sufficient* to ensure that people's independence or dignity is honoured by the law, it is *necessary* in that a legal system that did not adhere to Fuller's precepts would definitely violate people's independence or dignity. The fact that adhering to Fuller's precepts is a necessary, albeit not sufficient, condition for honouring people's independence as agents or their dignity is enough to establish that there is some moral point or value in giving effect to those precepts.

---

[19] Kramer, 'Freedom and the rule of law' (2009–10) 61 *Alabama Law Review* 827, 844.
[20] Ibid, 841–44.
[21] Simmonds, *Law as a Moral Idea* (Oxford University Press, 2008), 101.
[22] Kramer, 'Freedom and rule of law' (above, n. 19), 844–45.

Kramer rejects this counter-argument because it relies on a *moral transmissibility thesis* according to which if B is good and depends for its existence on A, then A is good as well.[23] Kramer thinks that adopting the moral transmissibility thesis results in a paradox when applied to Fuller's precepts of legality because it is not only goods such as independence and dignity that depend for their existence on adherence to Fuller's precepts: there are also a large number of evils that could not exist outside a society that was governed by the rule of law.[24] This is a point that Hart was keen to emphasise – that the transition from a primitive society like *Arcadia* to a society like *Metropolis* with a full-blown legal system is not risk-free:

> 'the step from the simple form of society, where primary rules of obligation are the only means of social control, into the legal world with its centrally organised legislature, courts, officials and sanctions brings its solid gains at a certain cost. The gains are those of adaptability to change, certainty, and efficiency, and these are immense; the cost is the risk that the centrally organised power may well be used for the oppression of numbers with whose support it can dispense, in a way that the simpler regime of primary rules could not.'[25]

Hart went on to observe, pessimistically, that 'So long as human beings can gain sufficient co-operation from some to enable them to dominate others, they will use the forms of law as one of their instruments. Wicked men will enact wicked rules which others will enforce.'[26]

Kramer argues on the basis of reflections such as these that if the moral transmissibility thesis were correct, then we would have to conclude that adhering to Fuller's precepts is both good and evil – good because of all the goods (not just independence and dignity, but also a huge range of material goods)[27] that depend for their existence on adherence to those precepts, but also evil because of all the evils that could not exist except under a system where Fuller's precepts were adhered to. Given this paradox, we should drop the moral transmissibility thesis and with it arguments that there is a moral value or point in adhering to Fuller's eight precepts based on the fact that adhering to those precepts is necessary if we are to enjoy certain goods.

Kramer notes that this argument does not work if there are *no* evils that depend for their existence on a government's scrupulously adhering to Fuller's principles

---

[23] Fuller seems to rely on such a thesis when he argues that 'If respect for the principles of legality is essential to produce ... a system [for the realization of moral objectives in life], then certainly it does not seem absurd to suggest that those principles constitute a special morality of role attaching to the office of law-maker and law-administrator. In any event the responsibilities of that office deserve some more flattering comparison than that offered by the practices of [a] thoughtful and conscientious poisoner': Fuller, 'A reply to critics' (above, n. 2), 206.

[24] Kramer, 'Once more into the fray: challenges for legal positivism' (2008) *University of Toronto Law Journal* 1, 34–38.

[25] CL, 202.

[26] CL, 210.

[27] For arguments that adherence to Fuller's precepts is valuable because our prosperity depends on it, see Hayek, *Law, Legislation and Liberty* (Routledge, 1976).

of legality.[28] And, indeed, it could be argued that we need to be careful here not to mix up *law* and *legality*. Terrible evil is done when the law requires that people be locked up, or worse, because they belong to a certain race or religion. But the generality, clarity, no-contradictoriness, and so on and so on of the rules under which those people are locked up does not contribute in any way to that evil.[29] Kramer seeks to forestall this counter-argument by observing that the degree of co-ordination among government officials to perpetrate nationwide evils is crucially dependent on the rules under which they operate adhering to Fuller's precepts.[30] However, Fuller might have criticised Kramer at this point, arguing that Kramer is confusing two different forms of social ordering here: managerial direction, and law.[31] All we need, for government officials to get organised to do evil together, is that they are brought under some kind of managerial control, which will – of course – involve them accepting and following *diktats* that need to be clear, non-contradictory, stable, and capable of being followed. But we do not need law – which is primarily addressed to the governed, not the governing – for that kind of system of control to exist.

CONCLUSION

It seems to us that the majority of academics writing in this area are correct and that there is some moral value or point in observing Fuller's precepts. If the government is thinking of passing legislation that violates in a serious way one of Fuller's precepts, a prudential 'That's not a good idea – you are in danger of not achieving what you are trying to achieve' is not *all* that can be said in opposition to what the government is proposing to do. The point is most obvious in respect of retrospective legislation, which authorises the punishment of acts that were lawful at the time they were committed. As Fuller observed, such legislation could actually be very effective in achieving what the government wants to achieve in passing it.[32] What, if any, prudential considerations militate against passing retrospective legislation cannot account why even H.L.A. Hart – who was generally allergic to invocations of morality – was still willing to describe such legislation as 'odious' and the principle against retrospective legislation as 'a very precious principle of morality endorsed by most legal systems'.[33] The same point could be made about laws that contradict each other, with the result that the law's subjects are trapped into breaking the law whatever they do. As John Finnis has pointed out, a government might well have very sound prudential reasons for passing such legislation:

---

[28] Kramer, 'Once more into the fray' (above, n. 24), 35.

[29] See Simmonds, 'Freedom, law and naked violence' (2009) 59 *University of Toronto Law Journal* 381, 393–94.

[30] Kramer, 'Once more into the fray' (above, n. 24), 35–36. See also Kramer, 'On the moral status of the rule of law' (2004) 63 *Cambridge Law Journal* 65, 69 and 'For the record: a final reply to N.E. Simmonds' (2011) 56 *American Journal of Jurisprudence* 115, 125.

[31] Fuller, 'A reply to critics' (above, n. 2), 207.

[32] Ibid, 202–203 (the object of the legislation considered by Fuller – authorising the retrospective application of the death penalty for economic crimes – was to get people to stop stealing from the state).

[33] Hart, 'Positivism and the separation of law and morals' (above, n. 2), 619.

'Why should not some regime wish to use the law's norm-creating capacities to keep the population at its mercy by confronting them with contradictory legal requirements, so that the regime's judges and other officials can enforce against selected persons whichever of a pair of contradictory legal norms those officials choose: either, or both, or neither?'[34]

Objecting to such laws on the basis that 'You are in danger of not achieving what you want to achieve' is to miss, quite spectacularly, the point of such laws. The real objection to these laws is moral in nature. Passing laws in the hope or expectation that they will be broken is a kind of fraud on the subjects of the law.

Debate 2

Will a wicked ruler seek to follow Fuller's eight precepts in the long term?

Lon Fuller was sceptical as to whether a wicked ruler would follow his eight precepts in the long term: either he would eventually abandon the precepts, or the effort to abide by the precepts would in the long term moderate his wickedness.[35] However, a full exploration of the issue had to wait until Matthew Kramer and Nigel Simmonds began their extended debate over the question of what connections, if any, there were between morality and legality.

Their debate over whether a wicked ruler could be expected to follow Fuller's eight precepts of legality in the long term centred over whether such a rule could be expected to abide by Fuller's *eighth* precept, which requires that the ruler only use force against a subject if authorised to do so under the rules he has laid down for the guidance of his subjects. Simmonds argued that in the long term a wicked ruler could be expected to disregard that requirement in favour of using extra-legal force against those who get in his way. In so arguing, Simmonds hoped to establish that, in the long term, only a benevolent ruler could be expected to abide by Fuller's precepts of legality, thus strengthening the connections between morality and legality. Kramer sought to undermine those links by arguing that even a wicked ruler would have strong prudential reasons for adhering to Fuller's precepts in the long term. If this is right, there is considerable reason to think that even a wicked ruler will respect the demands of legality in the long term.

The Kramer–Simmonds debate over this issue had four basic moves before it turned into a debate over whether there was a moral value or point in following Fuller's precepts of legality. The four moves can be described as follows:

---

[34] Finnis, 'Law and what I truly should decide' (2003) 48 *American Journal of Jurisprudence* 107, 124.
[35] Fuller, 'Positivism and fidelity to law – a reply to Professor Hart' (above, n. 2), 636–37.

SIMMONDS' OPENING MOVE

Simmonds initially argued that a wicked government will inevitably end up using extra-legal force against opponents of the government who have managed to comply with all of the government's legal directives. For example, a religious fundamentalist government might want to eliminate all manifestations of atheism. It may initially try to do this through law, by compelling people to go to religious services, or daily prayers, and banning certain irreligious books. But opponents of the government may find ways of signalling their atheist beliefs through ways that the government did not, and could not, have expected – by wearing baseball caps, for example.[36] And if the government tries to pass a law against wearing baseball caps, then people will find some other way of expressing their opposition. Faced with this problem, the government will simply stop trying to stamp down on opposition through law, and will start using extra-legal violence against its opponents, thus violating Fuller's eighth precept. So only a benevolent government will, ultimately, have reason to observe all of the precepts that are summed up by the ideal of the rule of law.

KRAMER'S INITIAL DEFENCE

Kramer countered by arguing that it wasn't necessarily true that a wicked government – frustrated at its inability to stamp down on its opponents through law – would end up resorting to extra-legal violence. A wicked government may have good, prudential reasons from abstaining from using extra-legal force against its subjects, because its doing so will reduce people's incentives to obey the law. If people know that even if they obey the law, they may still end up having force used against them by government agents, they will see less reason why they should obey the law. So in order to maintain the law as an effective agent for getting people to do what the wicked government wants them to do, the wicked government may well abstain from using extra-legal violence against its subjects.[37]

SIMMONDS' RIPOSTE

Simmonds argued that Kramer's position was 'straightforwardly false'.[38] In a society where even those who obey the law might still face having force used against them by their government, your chances that force will be used against you will still be less if you obey the law than if you break the law. Let's say if you break the law, it is 90% likely that you will be subject to some sort of sanction from the government. But if you obey the law, the fact that the government is willing to use extra-legal force against its opponents means that there is a 20% chance that you will still be beaten up or imprisoned by government agents. So if you break the law,

---

[36] Simmonds, 'Straightforwardly false: the collapse of Kramer's positivism' (above, n. 12), 101.

[37] Kramer, 'On the moral status of the rule of law' (above, n. 30), 88–89.

[38] Simmonds, 'Straightforwardly false: the collapse of Kramer's positivism' (above, n. 12), 108.

your chance of being subject to some kind of government action is 92%,[39] whereas if you don't break the law your chance of being subject to some kind of government action is 20%. In this case, you still have an obvious incentive to obey the law. Even if we assume that this wicked government is *very* ready to resort to extra-legal action – say there's a 90% chance of being subjected to extra-legal force by the government even if you obey the law – that would still mean that if you obey the law, you have a 90% chance of having the government do something to you, while if you break the law, you have a 99% chance of having the government do something to you. You still have an incentive to obey the law, even in that extreme scenario. However, this extreme scenario is highly implausible as even under the most wicked government you can dramatically reduce your chances of being the subject of extra-legal action by keeping your head down, not showing any visible signs of dissent, and being careful who you are friends with.[40] So there's no reason to think that a wicked government which was thinking about using extra-legal force against its opponents would forebear for fear of sapping people's incentives to obey the law.

KRAMER'S FULL DEFENCE

Kramer responded by arguing that people will be more likely to break the law *the less they think they have to lose* by breaking the law.[41] Suppose we compare two wicked regimes. Under both regimes, if you break the law there is a 90% chance of incurring some sort of government sanction. The first regime tries to adhere quite faithfully to Fuller's eighth precept, so that if you obey the law, there is only a 2% chance you will be subjected to some kind of extra-legal violence by the government. The second regime doesn't care about Fuller's eighth precept, so that even if you obey the law, there is still a 30% chance you will be subjected to some kind of extra-legal violence by the government. Under the first regime, it's 45 times more likely that you will be subjected to some kind of government action if you break the law than if you obey it. Under the second regime, it's three times more likely that you will be subjected to some kind of government action if you break the law than if you obey it. So you have much more to lose by breaking the law under the first regime than the second regime.

Kramer conceded that it might at first sight seem irrational for someone living under the second regime to be *more* willing to break the law than someone living under the first regime. This is because whatever regime you live under, breaking the law will increase your chances of being punished. However, Kramer argued that

---

[39] We calculate this by saying that if you break the law, your chances of escaping any kind of government sanction are 10% (chance of escaping action for breaking the law) x 80% (chance of escaping an extra-legal beating or imprisonment) = 8%. So your chances of facing some kind of sanction if you break the law are 92%.

[40] Simmonds, 'Law as a moral idea' (above, n. 12), 61, 79.

[41] Kramer, 'Incentives, interests and inclinations: legal positivism defended' (2006) 51 *American Journal of Jurisprudence* 165, 167–69.

what we can call the *less to lose effect* is an observable feature of human nature, and means that people living under the second regime (which couldn't care less about Fuller's eighth precept) will be more willing to break the law than people living under the first regime (which tries, on the whole, to respect Fuller's eighth precept). Kramer gave two examples of this less to lose effect in action.

First, suppose that someone wants to buy a book and he finds the book in a bookstore; the price is £52. Now – he knows that if he walks to another bookstore at the other end of town, there is a 30% chance that he will be able to get the same book for £2. It's very likely that he will check out the other bookstore to see if it has the book at the much cheaper price. Now let's suppose that someone wants to buy a car and she finds the car she wants and it costs £15,500. She also knows that if she walks to another car dealership at the other end of town, there is a 30% chance that she will be able to buy the same car for £14,450 – that is, for £50 less. It's highly unlikely that she will walk to the other dealership to check out its cars. Now – why would the book buyer check out the other bookstore in our first scenario, but our car buyer would not check out the other dealership in the second scenario when both are presented with a 30% chance of saving £50? The answer is that, judged proportionately, the book buyer has a lot more to lose by not checking out the other bookstore than the car buyer does. If the book buyer goes to the other store there is a 30% chance that he will get the book 96% cheaper. If the car buyer goes to the other store there is a 30% chance that she will get the car 0.3% cheaper. The car buyer has much less to lose by not checking out the other dealership so she won't go there.[42]

Secondly, Kramer argued that it is a well-established fact that when the Japanese randomly killed British prisoners of war that they were holding in order to reduce the numbers of prisoners of war that they had in their camps, the Japanese found that it was then much more difficult to get the remaining prisoners of war to obey the camp rules. Before the random killings occurred, the prisoners of war had a lot to lose by disobeying the rules – they would be subjected to punishment beatings and maybe even killed on the spot. But after the random killings occurred, the prisoners of war realised that they had less to lose by disobeying the rules – they knew that even if they obeyed the rules, they might still be killed anyway. So as a result they had less of an incentive to obey the rules. This might strike us as irrational, but that is what happened – and when the Japanese realised that their random killings were making it more difficult to control the remaining prisoners of war, they stopped the random killings.[43]

CONCLUSION

So far as we can see, these were the main points of argument between Kramer and Simmonds on the subject of our second debate. Their debate turned into a debate

---

[42] Kramer, 'The big bad wolf: legal positivism and its detractors' (2004) *American Journal of Jurisprudence* 1, 9; Kramer, 'Incentives, interests and inclinations: legal positivism defended' (above, n. 41), 170–72.
[43] Ibid, 172–73.

about whether there was a moral point or value in giving effect to Fuller's precepts via an observation of Simmonds that if the less to lose effect is correct, then even a wicked government would have good, prudential reasons to provide its citizens with some degree of security against natural and economic disasters that might, because of the less to lose effect, reduce people's incentives to obey the law – but the fact that a wicked regime protected people against such disasters would not mean that there was no moral point or value in protecting people against such things. Likewise, even if a wicked regime might have good, prudential reasons for complying with Fuller's eight precepts, that does not establish that there is no moral point or value in abiding by those precepts.[44] And so debate was then joined on the issue of whether, irrespective of what a wicked regime might do in practice in terms of abiding by Fuller's precepts of legality, we could say that there was a moral point or value in adhering to those precepts.

In terms of *this* debate, Kramer's less to lose effect seems to have some validity and gives us *a* reason to think that a wicked ruler like *Vlad might* have long term prudential reasons to adhere to Fuller's precepts of legality even when doing so will frustrate his short term goals. However, we must set against this two weighty considerations. First, there is the possibility that the less to lose effect can be made to dwindle into insignificance, and incentives to obey the law maintained, under a truly wicked regime that is regularly willing to engage in extra-legal violence against its opponents. This could be done either by the penalties for breaking the law being made extremely serious so that you will still have a lot to lose by breaking the law,[45] or by it becoming clear to the general population that so long as they keep their head down and do not make a fuss then their prospects of being subjected to extra-legal violence will be low (though not zero). Secondly, there is the experience of history, which teaches us that there is no wicked regime on earth that has ever abided by all of Fuller's eight precepts. That, more than anything, should weigh in favour of a negative conclusion to the second debate.

Further Reading

Hart, CL, ch. VIII.1, ch. IX.3.

Fuller, *Morality of Law*, rev'd edn (Yale University Press, 1969), especially chs II, IV and V.

Hart, 'Book review of Morality of Law' (1964–5) 78 *Harvard Law Review* 1281.

Simmonds, 'Freedom, law and naked violence' (2009) 59 *University of Toronto Law Journal* 381.

Kramer, 'Freedom and the rule of law' (2009-10) 61 *Alabama Law Review* 827.

Kramer, 'For the record: a final reply to N.E. Simmonds' (2011) 56 *American Journal of Jurisprudence* 115.

---

[44] Simmonds, 'Law as a moral idea' (above, n. 12), 82–85; 'Evil contingencies and the rule of law' (2006) 51 *American Journal of Jurisprudence* 179, 187–88.

[45] Ibid, 186.

Simmonds, 'Kramer's High Noon' (2011) 56 *American Journal of Jurisprudence* 135.

Waldron, 'Why law? – efficacy, freedom or fidelity?' (1994) 13 *Law and Philosophy* 259.

Waldron, 'Positivism and legality – Hart's equivocal response to Fuller' (2008) 83 *New York University Law Review* 1134.

Waldron, 'How law protects dignity' (2012) 71 *Cambridge Law Journal* 200.

5

NATURAL LAW

Debate 1

What is natural law?

One of the things that is most off-putting about the label 'natural law' is that it has no natural meaning. So it is not immediately clear what is being said if we say of some thinker, *Leia*, that she is a 'natural lawyer' or that she believes in 'natural law'. As Philip Soper has observed: 'natural law refers both to a moral theory and a legal theory' where the moral theory insists 'that moral principles are objectively valid and discoverable by reason'[1] and the legal theory 'denies that a sharp separation of [law and morality] is possible'.[2] But even this is too simple. There are no less than eight different positions, the adoption of any one of which by *Leia* might lead someone to categorise her as a 'natural lawyer'. There is, first of all, the position that:

(M) There are moral facts.

This is Soper's moral theory version of natural law.[3] As for legal theories that might be categorised as 'natural law' theories, there are seven versions of those:

(L1) Law necessarily makes moral claims for itself.
(L2) Law necessarily provides us with reasons for acting.
(L3) Law necessarily performs certain moral functions.
(L4) Law necessarily aims at performing certain moral functions.
(L5) The central case of law performs certain moral functions.
(L6) We cannot determine what the law says without engaging in moral argument.
(L7) Unjust laws are not laws.

---

[1] Soper, 'Some natural confusions about natural law' (1992) 90 *Michigan Law Review* 2393, 2394.
[2] Ibid, 2395.
[3] John Finnis seems to endorse this as *the* meaning of natural law in Finnis, 'Natural law: the classical tradition' in Coleman and Shapiro (eds), *The Oxford Handbook of Jurisprudence and Philosophy of Law* (Oxford University Press, 2002), 1.

We'll now look at each of these positions in more detail.

(M) THERE ARE MORAL FACTS

Leia will believe that there are moral facts if, when she claims that 'slavery is wrong' (or, what comes to the same thing, that 'no should engage in slavery' or 'we have compelling reason not to engage in slavery'), she is stating that it is a fact that 'slavery is wrong' (or that 'no one should engage in slavery' or 'we have compelling reason not to engage in slavery'). If *Leia* does think in this kind of way, then she will reject the claims of *non-cognitivists*, who argue that when *Leia* claims that 'slavery is wrong', *all* that *Leia* is saying, at base, is that 'I don't like slavery' or 'I don't want people to be enslaved' or 'I disapprove of slavery' or 'Boo to slavery!'. There may be – non-cognitivists argue – facts on the ground that account for why *Leia* adopts this position, but the fact that 'slavery is wrong' cannot be one of them as there is no such fact. There is only – in the case of slavery – suffering and domination. Most people respond to those facts with repugnance and a desire to see less slavery and they express all that – the non-cognitivists argue – by saying 'slavery is wrong'; while a tiny minority respond to those facts with glee and a desire to see more slavery and they express all that by saying 'slavery is not wrong'. Someone who is a natural lawyer – in this first sense of the term, of believing that there are moral facts – will reject this non-cognitivist way of thinking, and any other way of thinking that denies that there are moral facts.[4] So any thinkers who reject the idea that there are no moral facts[5] can be classed as natural lawyers in this first sense, even if they know nothing about law. Of the legal theorists discussed in this book, most are or were natural lawyers in this first sense – the most notable exceptions are Ronald Dworkin[6] and Brian Leiter,[7] and possibly H.L.A. Hart.[8]

(L1) LAW NECESSARILY MAKES MORAL CLAIMS FOR ITSELF

We have already seen that Joseph Raz believes that the law necessarily makes moral claims for itself: he believes that law, to be law, must claim moral authority over its subjects. In this sense, then, Raz is a natural lawyer. Others are not natural

---

[4] In addition to non-cognitivism, there is the so-called 'error theory' (see Mackie, 'The subjectivity of values' in his *Ethics: Inventing Right and Wrong* (Penguin Books, 1977)) which allows – as non-cognitivism does not – that someone who says that 'slavery is wrong' is stating that it is a fact that slavery is wrong, but argues that they are simply wrong to say that, as there are no moral facts. In his *On What Matters, Volume Two* (Oxford University Press, 2011), at 384, Derek Parfit remarks that 'I was present when the most notorious "Boo-Hurray" Theorist, [AJ] Ayer, heard Mackie present his ... Error Theory. Ayer's first comment was: "That's what I should have said". Ayer happily gave up his Non-Cognitivism, turning instead to the view that most people misunderstand morality, since most people mistakenly believe that there are moral truths.' See, further, below, p. 151.

[5] Such as Derek Parfit: ibid, chs 27–30.

[6] See his *Justice for Hedgehogs* (Harvard University Press, 2011), which seems to take the position that there are no moral facts, just interpretations of moral concepts.

[7] See his *Naturalizing Jurisprudence* (Oxford University Press, 2007), Part III.

[8] See Hart, *Essays on Bentham* (Oxford University Press, 1982), 266–67.

lawyers in this sense: as we have also seen, Matthew Kramer and John Finnis reject the idea that law necessarily claims to have moral authority.[9] And Ronald Dworkin[10] and H.L.A. Hart[11] were sceptical as to whether law makes claims of the kind Raz argues it does.

(L2) LAW NECESSARILY PROVIDES US WITH REASONS FOR ACTING

This position is most closely associated with Lon Fuller and Ronald Dworkin. Fuller argued that 'laws, even bad laws, have a claim to our respect' and Dworkin argued that law has what he called '*force*'[12] – that 'law provides a justification *in principle* for official coercion ... [so that] in a flourishing legal system the fact of law provides a case for coercion that must stand unless some exceptional counterargument is available.'[13] As we have seen, both Hart and Raz reject the idea that law necessarily provides us with reasons for acting.[14] John Finnis's position is that law, of and in itself, only provides us with reasons for acting within a legal system that counts as a 'central case' of a legal system – that is, a legal system that is working well to help its subjects flourish as human beings. The law of a legal system that is a degraded imitation of the central case of a legal system does not, of and in itself, provide its subjects with reasons for acting – though there may exist strategic reasons, supplied by considerations external to the law, for complying with the law despite the sorry state of the legal system from which that law comes.[15]

(L3) LAW NECESSARILY PERFORMS CERTAIN MORAL FUNCTIONS

As we have just seen, Ronald Dworkin took the view that law does perform a moral function – that of justifying official coercion. In the Postscript to *The Concept of Law*, H.L.A. Hart unsurprisingly and flatly rejected this view of law:

> 'Since the occasions for legal coercion are mainly cases when the primary function of the law in guiding the conduct of its subjects has broken down, legal coercion, though of course an important matter, is a secondary function. Its justification cannot be sensibly taken to be the point or purpose of law as such.'[16]

However, in *The Concept of Law*, Hart was prepared to concede that if a legal system was to have any hope of being long-lived, it would *have* to give effect to certain rules of conduct that he styled 'the minimum content of natural law'.[17] These rules of conduct (forbidding murder, violence, providing for a system of private property,

---

[9] See above, p. 34.
[10] Dworkin, 'Thirty years on' (2002) 115 *Harvard Law Review* 1655, 1666.
[11] Hart, *Essays on Bentham* (above, n. 8), 157–59.
[12] LE, 110 (emphasis in original) (see list of abbreviations, p. xiii).
[13] Ibid (emphasis in original).
[14] See above, p. 31.
[15] NLNR, 359–61. For further discussion, see ch. 7, below.
[16] CL, Postscript, 249.
[17] CL, 193.

and for sanctions to be applied to those unwilling to abide by the legal system's requirements)[18] are all geared towards securing the survival of the subjects of the legal system. Without these rules there could be no legal system in the long run because the society governed by that legal system would turn into a 'suicide club'[19] and there would in the end be no one left for that legal system to govern. So, Hart argued, there is a 'natural necessity'[20] for law to perform certain moral functions if we are to have any law at all in the long run.

(L4) LAW NECESSARILY AIMS AT PERFORMING CERTAIN MORAL FUNCTIONS

This claim has been made by Scott Shapiro in his book *Legality*.[21] Law, he argues, aims at resolving moral problems 'that are numerous and serious, and whose solutions are complex, contentious and arbitrary' and that cannot therefore be solved through non-legal means such as 'improvisation, spontaneous ordering, private bargaining, communal consensus, or personalized hierarchies'.[22] This claim would have puzzled Hart, who thought it 'quite vain to seek any more specific purpose which law as such serves beyond providing guides to human conduct and standards of criticism of such conduct'.[23]

(L5) THE CENTRAL CASE OF LAW PERFORMS CERTAIN MORAL FUNCTIONS

This claim is most closely associated with John Finnis, who argues that the best way to understand the nature of law is not to try to come up with a definition of law that 'will extend to *all* circumstances in which, regardless of particular points of view, the word ["law"] could "correctly" be employed'[24] but to look at the *central cases* of law – ones which best exemplify why we might 'choose to have [law], create it, maintain it, and comply with it'.[25] But, of course, we would – as reasonable people – only choose to have law, create it, maintain it, and comply with it, if there is something about law that means that it is *good* to have law; in other words, if there is something about law that means that our ability to enjoy various human goods is dependent on our living under a legal system. So, for Finnis, the central case of law – the one which best exemplifies why law is something we would want to have – is the case where law performs the moral function of helping us to enjoy various human goods.[26] H.L.A. Hart rejected this view in the 'Introduction' to his collected *Essays in Jurisprudence and Philosophy*,[27] arguing that

[18] CL, 194–98.
[19] CL, 192.
[20] CL, 199.
[21] Shapiro, *Legality* (Harvard University Press, 2010).
[22] Ibid, 170.
[23] CL, Postscript, 249.
[24] NLNR, 265 (see also NLNR, 10).
[25] Finnis, 'Law and what I truly should decide' (2003) 48 *American Journal of Jurisprudence* 107, 129.
[26] NLNR, ch. 1.
[27] Hart, *Essays in Jurisprudence and Philosophy* (Oxford University Press, 1983).

'the identification of the central meaning of law with what is morally legitimate, because orientated towards the common good, seems to me in view of the hideous record of the evil use of law for oppression to be an unbalanced perspective, and as great a distortion as the opposite Marxist identification of the central case of law with the pursuit of the interests of a dominant economic class.'[28]

(L6) WE CANNOT DETERMINE WHAT THE LAW SAYS WITHOUT ENGAGING IN MORAL ARGUMENT

As we have seen in a previous chapter, this was a central claim of Ronald Dworkin's jurisprudence.[29] And Dworkin's arguments have led some legal positivists – soft (or inclusive) legal positivists – to concede that in a legal system where the rule of recognition makes the content of the law dependent on morality, then in such a system we won't be able to determine what the law says without engaging in moral argument.[30] However, hard (or exclusive) legal positivists like Joseph Raz insist that what the law *says* can *always* be determined without engaging in moral argument, though judges may be required under the rules of their legal system to take into account moral considerations in developing or changing the law.

(L7) UNJUST LAWS ARE NOT LAWS

This last claim is the one that is most associated with the 'natural law tradition' in the popular imagination (insofar as anyone has heard of 'natural law'). This is because this claim appears in the writings of classical thinkers who are regarded as the founders of the 'natural law tradition'.[31] As we have already seen,[32] more modern legal theorists like Gustav Radbruch and Robert Alexy have sought to argue that this classical natural law position is correct, at least insofar as laws that approach a certain level of gross iniquity are concerned. H.L.A. Hart was prepared to concede that unjust law might not be law – but only if the rule of recognition in a particular legal system made the validity of a law dependent on its moral content. Joseph Raz disagrees. In his view, the unjustness of a law cannot make it invalid as a law – provided it has the right pedigree then it will count as valid law. John Finnis and Ronald Dworkin have much more complex views on whether unjust laws count as being laws, which is why we have not considered them until now. Their views are considered in the second debate in this chapter.

CONCLUSION

Some of what has been said above can be summed up in the table below, where we list some major jurisprudential figures and identify in what respects they can be said to be natural lawyers:

---

[28] Ibid, 12.
[29] See above, pp. 43–44.
[30] See above, pp. 51–53.
[31] Plato, *Laws*, IV, 715b; Cicero, *On the Laws*, II.v.11; Augustine, *On The Free Choice of the Will*, I.v.11.
[32] See above, pp. 59–61, 64–65.

Legal theorist ...	... is a natural lawyer in sense ...
H.L.A. Hart	(L3)
Joseph Raz	(M), (L1)
Ronald Dworkin	(L2), (L3), (L6), (L7)?
John Finnis	(M), (L5), (a version of) (L7)
Lon Fuller	(M), (L1)?, (L2), (L3)?, (L5)?, (L6)

It might be thought that a term that is capable of meaning so many different things – with the result that it can be applied to so many different thinkers – is of severely limited usefulness, and should perhaps be dispensed with. However, it seems that there are two positions for which we still need to use the term 'natural law' as no other term is apt to describe these positions. The first is the position that 'an unjust law is not law'. The second is the position adopted by John Finnis about the nature of law. Tradition demands that we style the first position as being a 'natural law' position. The complexity and range of John Finnis's theory of law – and his position as the foremost proponent of 'natural law' in the 20th century – means we have no choice but to identify his theory of law as being a 'natural law' theory. So we can say that if *Leia* believes that an unjust law is not law, *or* if *Leia* endorses John Finnis's theory of law, then she is a 'natural lawyer'. But if *Leia* takes any other position – such as endorsing (M) or any of the legal positions set out above other than (L5) and (L7) – then there seems no point in identifying her as a 'natural lawyer'. If she endorses (M) then she is a *moral realist*. If she endorses one of the legal positions set out above other than (L5) and (L7), then she is simply someone who endorses that position – there is no need to stick a further label on her.

The next two debates in this chapter are about whether we should adopt the two positions that we have identified as worthy of the label 'natural law' – the proposition that an unjust law is not law, and John Finnis's theory of law.

Debate 2

Are unjust laws laws?

So far, we have not been given any good reason to think that an unjust rule will not count as valid law by virtue of its injustice.[33] However, a complete discussion of this issue requires us to consider the views of Ronald Dworkin and John Finnis. Only after we have taken account of their views can we be confident of reaching a fully informed conclusion on this matter.

---

[33] For discussion of Radbruch and Alexy's positions to the contrary, see above, pp. 59–61, 64–65.

RONALD DWORKIN ON UNJUST LAWS

In *Law's Empire*, Ronald Dworkin searched for a conception of law that would account for why law has *'force'* – why we 'think the law should be obeyed and enforced' unless 'strong competing considerations of justice' apply.[34] Dworkin thought that the idea of *law as integrity* best explained why law has force.

Law as integrity is based on the 'political ideal' of integrity, which requires the

> 'government [to] speak with one voice, to act in a principled and coherent manner toward all its citizens, to extend to everyone the substantive standards of justice or fairness it uses for some.'[35]

But why is it important for the government to 'speak with one voice' in determining what rights and duties we have under the law? It is important because the state cannot claim that it is treating its subjects with *equal concern and respect* if it applies one set of standards about justice (which, for Dworkin, is concerned with what 'moral and political rights' we should have)[36] and fairness (which, for Dworkin, is concerned with arriving at 'political procedures ... that distribute political power in the right way')[37] and procedural due process (which, for Dworkin, is concerned with determining what are 'the right procedures for judging whether someone has violated' the law)[38] to one group of people, and a completely different set of standards of justice and fairness and procedural due process to another group of people:

> '[the] command of integrity assumes that each person is as worthy as any other, that each must be treated with equal concern according to some coherent conception of what that means.'[39]

And why is it important for the government to treat everyone with equal concern and respect in determining what rights and duties we have under the law? The reason is that the obligations we are recognised as having under the law will have no *force* unless they count as *associative obligations* – obligations that are binding on us merely by virtue of the fact that we are members of a 'bare' community (a group of people linked by location or history or genetics) that is also a 'true' community, one which recognises the members of the community as having responsibilities to each other that: (1) are *special* to the group; (2) are *personal*, in that 'they run directly from each member to each other member'; (3) flow from 'a more general responsibility each has of *concern* for the well-being of the members of the group'; and (4) reflect an '*equal* concern for all members' of the community, an assumption that the community's 'roles and rules are equally in the interests of all, [and] that no one's life is more important than anyone else's'.[40]

---

[34] LE, 111.
[35] LE, 165.
[36] LE, 97; see also LE, 165, 404.
[37] LE, 164; see also LE, 404.
[38] LE, 165; see also LE, 404–405.
[39] LE, 213.
[40] This paragraph sums up LE, 195–201, especially 199–201. All emphases in the quotations are in the original.

So, working our way back up to law as integrity: the rights and duties we are recognised as having under the law will only have force if they are associative in nature; they will only be associative in nature if the government treats us with equal concern and respect in determining what rights and duties we have under the law; the government will only treat us with equal concern and respect if it speaks with one voice in determining what rights and duties we have under the law; and, of all the competing conceptions of law that are on offer to us, only law as integrity satisfies the requirement that the government speak with one voice in determining what rights and duties we have under the law. This is because:

> 'Law as integrity asks judges to assume, so far as possible, that the law [or, rather, past decisions of the courts and statutes passed by the legislature] is structured by a coherent set of principles about justice and fairness and procedural due process, and it asks them to enforce these in the fresh cases that come before them, so that each person's situation is fair and just according to the same standards.'[41]

Dworkin argues that implementing the idea of law as integrity will require a judge who has to decide a case – Dworkin calls his ideal judge *Hercules*, so we will do the same – to go through a three-stage process:

(1) *The pre-interpretive*[42] *stage. Hercules* starts with the materials – statutes and cases in our system – that are generally acknowledged as being sources of law in his community. These are the past political decisions out of which *Hercules* will construct his vision of what the law says.

(2) *The interpretive stage.*[43] *Hercules* then has to ask himself – What set of principles about justice and fairness and procedural due process provides the best interpretation of what has been done so far in the name of the law?

In determining what interpretation counts as 'best', he must first look at what legal principles can be said to 'fit' the materials that he is seeking to interpret. Principles that are wildly inconsistent with what those materials say – for example, principles that 'deny legislative competence or supremacy outright' or that say that 'the rich [are legally] required to share their wealth with the poor' – must be discarded. It may be that this winnowing process will leave *Hercules* with only one principle that fits the existing sources of law and is relevant to the case he has to decide. If this is so, then the case is an *easy* one: it is clear what law as integrity requires – give effect to the principle as legally binding in this case.

But it might be that the case is *hard*. In a *hard* case, there will be two or more competing principles that pass the 'rough threshold requirement' of fitting the available sources of law. In such a case, *Hercules* has to 'choose between [these]

---

[41] LE, 243.
[42] We follow Dworkin in using the word 'interpretive' rather than the more normal 'interpretative'. (Though Dworkin does use the word 'interpretative' twice at LE, 107 – it may be that he originally used 'interpretative' throughout the book and then switched to 'interpretive' as less of a mouthful.)
[43] The quotations in this section come from LE, 255–56.

eligible interpretations [of what the law says] by asking which shows the community's structure of institutions and decisions – its public standards as a whole – in a better light from the standpoint of political morality'. The principle that stands out as providing the most attractive account of the community's standards on justice, fairness, and procedural due process will, under law as integrity, determine what the law says in the case *Hercules* has to decide.

(3) *The decision stage.* Having, through this interpretive process, determined what the law says in the case at hand, *Hercules* has to decide what to do. Law, under law as integrity, has *force* – so there is a presumption that *Hercules* should decide the case in accordance with the understanding of what the law says that he has developed at the interpretive stage. But:

> 'the adjudicative principle of integrity [is not] absolutely sovereign over what judges must do at the end of the day. That principle is decisive over what a judge recognizes as law. It is sovereign, that is, over the grounds of law, because it admits no other view of what "flows from" past political decisions. But we saw ... that any theory about the grounds of law abstracts from detailed issues about the force of law. A judge who accepts integrity will think that the law it defines sets out genuine rights litigants have to a decision before him. They are entitled, in principle, to have their acts and affairs judged in accordance with the best view of what the legal standards of the community required or permitted at the time they acted, and integrity demands that these standards be seen as coherent, as the state speaking with a single voice. But though this requirement honours the political virtue of procedural due process, which would at least prima facie be violated if people were judged against standards other than the legal standards of the day, other and more powerful aspects of political morality might outweigh this requirement in particular and unusual circumstances. Perhaps the law of the United States, properly interpreted in deference to integrity, did include the Fugitive Slave Act enacted by Congress before the Civil War. If a judge's own sense of justice condemned that act as deeply immoral because it required citizens to help send escaped slaves back to their masters, he would have to consider whether he should actually enforce it on the demand of a slave owner, or whether he should lie and say that this was not the law after all, or whether he should resign. The principle of integrity in adjudication, therefore, does not necessarily have the last word about how the coercive power of the state should be used. But it does have the first word, and normally there is nothing to add to what it says.'[44]

So Dworkin admits that: (1) propositions of law that are unjust can still count as law under law as integrity; and (2) in such cases a judge will have reason to give effect to the law, though the injustice of the law might give the judge a greater reason not to give effect to the law – which reason he might act on by either lying about what the law says, or by simply resigning from the Bench.

---

[44] LE, 218–19.

At first sight, there is nothing strange about (1). (1) will occur under law as integrity where (a) the only principle relevant to the case that *Hercules* had to decide that passed the 'threshold requirement' of fit was a morally unattractive one, or (b) the legal materials that provided *Hercules* with the basis for his decision yielded two or more principles that fit those materials, but both principles were morally unattractive, with the result that when *Hercules* had to decide which principle showed his community's legal practices in a better light, *Hercules* had to choose which principle was least bad.

And yet – as Trevor Allan has pointed out[45] – there is at the same time something paradoxical about (1). Recall that for Dworkin, the rights and duties that we are recognised as having under the law can only have *force* – and therefore, for Dworkin, can only count as 'legal' – if they are *associative* in nature, and they will only be associative in nature if they flow from a general responsibility that each of us has to show *concern* for the well-being of others in our community, and if they reflect an *equal* concern for all members of the community under which no one is treated as more important than anyone else.

These conditions will *never* be fulfilled in a *wicked* legal system where the raw legal materials that a judge – we can follow Dworkin in calling him Judge *Siegfried*[46] – has to work with cannot be interpreted in any way that would allow us to claim that they demonstrate equal concern and respect for the subjects of the legal system. As Dworkin himself admitted, 'integrity makes no sense except among people who want fairness and justice as well.'[47] So if we adopt law as integrity as our preferred conception of law, then we would have to say that there is no law among a people who (or whose leaders) do not want fairness and justice.[48] *Siegfried* could go through the motions of the three-stage process set out above to determine what the 'law' in his country says, but doing so would be meaningless.[49] It only makes sense to practise law as integrity in what Jeremy Waldron has called 'the circumstances of integrity', where:

---

[45] Allan, 'Law, justice and integrity: the paradox of wicked laws' (2009) 29 *Oxford Journal of Legal Studies* 705.

[46] LE, 105–107.

[47] LE, 263.

[48] See LE, 103–104, 108, arguing that Nazi Germany might not have had law in any sense that would allow us to say that coercion under the 'legal' rules and procedures existing in Nazi Germany was justified. See also Dworkin's remarks in Cohen (ed.), *Ronald Dworkin and Contemporary Jurisprudence* (Duckworth, 1984), at 260 that we should not just assume that people in Nazi Germany had legal rights: 'this is not given; on the contrary we need a theory of legal rights in order to decide whether there were legal rights out there.' However, we could go further and say while the Nazis did not have law by our lights (assuming, for the sake of argument, that we adopt law as integrity) they did have *something* that *approximated* the force that law has for us, by virtue of the fact that past decisions by even a corrupt regime give people (very weak) rights that a case be decided in their favour if a failure to do so would disappoint their legitimate expectations, on which they have relied. In support of the claim that this was the state of things in Nazi Germany, see Dworkin, 'Reply' in Cohen (ed.), *Ronald Dworkin and Contemporary Jurisprudence* (Duckworth, 1984), at 258.

[49] A comparison could be drawn with the 'cargo cult islanders' who – having experienced numerous drops of Japanese and American equipment onto their islands during World War II – thought that they could bring back the drops of cargo after hostilities had ceased by re-enacting the various things that were done on the islands at the same time equipment was being dropped onto their islands.

'the various political decisions currently in force in a given society, coming as they do from different sources, are not guaranteed to cohere with each other. The task of integrity is to deal with what happens when principles of political fairness legitimate the making and enforcement of decisions in one and the same political system by partisans of competing views about justice.'[50]

In a society where past political decisions are dominated not by 'competing views about justice' but (say instead) a desire to get one's own way at any cost, such decisions cannot yield anything that would have any force for us here and now, no matter how many times we processed such decisions through the 'law as integrity' mixer that Dworkin has provided for us.

And even in a society that *is* animated by a desire to be just and fair, in a situation where (because either (a) or (b), above, apply) *Hercules* has ended up concluding that a morally unattractive principle is part of the law, it is hard to see how such a principle – given its unattractiveness – could be said to show equal concern and respect for the law's subjects and thus have the force of law for us. As Allan observes:

'It is true that departures from justice will often be warranted by conflicting considerations of fairness and due process, insofar as integrity permits and requires; but very grave injustice to any particular group of citizens would undermine the idea of the true community of principle. For those citizens would then be denied any *plausible* version of equal concern and respect; their associative obligations would be counterfeit ...'[51]

Dworkin seeks to show that even a morally unattractive principle might satisfy his requirements for an associative obligation to exist by discussing the example of a daughter who grows up in a culture that says that parents have the power to choose spouses for their daughters but not their sons.[52] We might, he argues, come to the view that the daughter's cultural obligation to defer to her parents when it comes to deciding who she marries *does* flow from a genuine concern for the daughter's welfare that *does* (despite appearances) treat her and her needs as just as important as everyone else's. In such a case, the daughter's obligation would be associative in nature, and should have some force for her, so that if she were to marry against her parent's wishes (for perfectly good and acceptable reasons), she 'has something to regret. She owes [her parents] at least an accounting, and perhaps an apology ...'[53] Allan is unconvinced:

'this account is surely confused ... If she owes "an accounting, and perhaps an apology", it must be because her principled stance has caused offence that she naturally regrets. She is free to marry against her father's wishes, however, only because she insists that, *properly interpreted*, her family responsibilities permit her to do so; or else

---

[50] Waldron, *Law and Disagreement* (Oxford University Press, 1999), 189.
[51] Allan, 'Law, justice and integrity: the paradox of wicked laws' (above, n. 45), 713 (emphasis in original).
[52] LE, 204–205.
[53] LE, 205.

because, if that view is quite untenable, such responsibilities are sham – imposed by an oppressive tradition that she now rejects.'[54]

In conclusion, then, *if* we accept that law – of its nature – has force for us, and *if* we accept that law as integrity provides us with the best account of why law has that force, then the idea of law as integrity provides us with sufficient resources to (1) deny that wicked societies have any law at all (as we know it), and (2) deny legal validity to a manifestly unjust principle that somehow manages to provide us with the best interpretation of our past political practices. Dworkin was prepared to concede that (1) was true,[55] but (for no good reason we can see) not (2).[56]

However, this entire argument in favour of thinking of that unjust laws are not laws falls apart if we refuse to accept (as Hart refused to accept) (L2) – the idea that law, of its nature, should be enforced and obeyed.

JOHN FINNIS ON UNJUST LAWS

John Finnis does *not* think that (1) the validity of a law within a legal system can be affected by its justice or not, unless the legal system itself provides resources for saying that it is not valid.[57] But he also repeatedly *endorses* the classical natural law position that (2) 'an unjust law is not law'.[58] How can he take both of these positions at the same time? Finnis argues that, properly understood, the classical natural law position that 'an unjust law is not law' uses the word law in two different ways. The 'law' of 'an unjust law' is a law that is recognised as being valid under the rules of a legal system and which also happens to be unjust. The 'law' of 'is not law' should be interpreted as meaning 'authoritative in the way that the central case of law is authoritative'. So the statement (2) 'an unjust law is not law', properly interpreted, simply means 'a law that is recognised as being valid under the rules of a legal system but which is unjust is not authoritative in the way that the central case of law is authoritative'. Read this way, (2) is perfectly consistent with (1) – indeed (2) presupposes that (1) is true: that a law can be valid under the rules of a legal system despite the fact that it is unjust. This is sufficient to summarise Finnis's position on the status of unjust laws, but it might give rise to some questions in the mind of the reader, to which we will now turn.

First, *is Finnis's reading of the classical natural law position that 'an unjust law is not law' plausible?* – in particular, is it plausible to think that one sentence could use the same word in two different ways? Finnis sees nothing implausible about this. One of his favourite analogies is with the statement 'an invalid argument is not an

---

[54] Allan, 'Law, justice and integrity: the paradox of wicked laws' (above, n. 45), 718.

[55] See above, n. 48.

[56] See the quotation at n. 44, above.

[57] NLNR, 355–57.

[58] NLNR, 359–61; Finnis, 'Law and what I truly should decide' (above, n. 25), 114: 'Unjust laws are not laws, though they may still count in reasonable conscientious deliberations, and certainly warrant attention and description.'

argument'.[59] The first 'argument' in this sentence means 'something with premises and a conclusion reached on the basis of those premises'. The second 'argument' in this sentence means 'something that compels one to accept a certain conclusion'. So 'an invalid argument is not an argument' means 'If a chain of reasoning from premises to conclusion is not valid (because the premises are invalid or the conclusion does not follow logically from the premises) then we are not compelled to accept that conclusion' – which makes perfect sense and is perfectly correct. The same could be said of the statements 'A quack medicine is not medicine' (which, expanded, means 'A useless remedy that is administered to a sick person will not help her get better') or 'A disloyal friend is not a friend' (which, expanded, means 'Someone who acts as if they like you but will drop you if it's in their interests to do so is not someone you can trust to support you whatever the circumstances').[60] What all these statements have in common is that they are all directed at what you should do, and are basically saying that some X that would normally give you reason to act will no longer give you a reason to act if it is deprived of some quality Y – so an X without Y is not an X.[61]

Secondly, *why would a legal system not make the validity of a rule dependent on its justice?* Finnis would respond that the 'definition, specificity, clarity, and thus predictability' that law brings 'into human interactions'[62] – and therefore its value in shaping, supporting and furthering 'patterns of co-ordination'[63] – would be impaired if the law made it too easy to question the validity of the rule on the basis that it offended this or that precept of justice. As Finnis argues:

> 'authority is useless for the common good unless the stipulations of those in authority ... are treated as exclusionary reasons, i.e. as sufficient reason for acting notwithstanding that the subject would not himself have made the same stipulation and indeed considers the actual stipulation to be in some respect(s) unreasonable ...'[64]

Thirdly, *when will a legal rule count as being unjust for the purposes of the statement 'an unjust law is not law'?* Finnis identifies four senses in which a legal rule might be unjust:[65] (1) if the rule has been promulgated, not for the purpose of furthering the interests of the law's subjects but for the ruler's own advantage, or out of malice; (2) if the rule has been promulgated by someone who was not empowered to do this; (3) if the manner and form in which the rule has been promulgated violates one of the precepts of legality identified in the previous chapter (which Finnis prefers to refer to as requirements of the 'rule of law'); (4) if the rule offends

---

[59] NLNR, Postscript, 438.

[60] See Finnis, 'Natural law theories' in Zalta (ed.), *The Stanford Encyclopedia of Philosophy* (<http://plato.stanford.edu/entries/natural-law-theories>), §4.

[61] See Finnis, 'Law and what I truly should decide' (above, n. 25), 114, fn. 9 (responding to Joseph Raz's question why law should be thought to be like arguments or medicine, 'rather than like novels or paintings, or people, that are still novels or paintings, or people, even if they are bad.')

[62] NLNR, 268.

[63] NLNR, 267.

[64] NLNR, 351–52.

[65] NLNR, 352–54.

against requirements of reasonableness in distributing goods that are initially held in common, or in determining what rights and duties we owe each other.

Fourthly, *why will an unjust rule not be authoritative in the way that the central case of law is authoritative?* For Finnis, authority is, first and foremost, a matter of fact: A has authority over a group of people if, as a matter of fact, they will, by and large, do what he tells them to do, whether or not they themselves can see that there is a good reason for doing what A is telling them to do.[66] If they *will* do what A tells them to do, they *should* do what A tells them to do *so long as* A is using the authority he has over them for their benefit. But if A starts using the authority he has over them to act for his own benefit, or starts misusing that authority in some other way, then they have no good reason for going along with what A tells them to do *just because* he has told them to do it.[67]

Fifthly, *does that mean we have no reason to obey an unjust law?* Finnis would reject this suggestion. A *public* act of disobeying an unjust law that is *likely to be seen* may well bring the law into disrepute and encourage other people not to obey the law, even when it is just and they have good reason to go along with what it says.[68] As a result, we may have reason to avoid being 'observed defying [an] unjust law',[69] at least where the legal system is basically just.

CONCLUSION

argues against Radbruch's formula

We began this debate by observing that we had not yet come across a good argument that: (A) a rule will not count as being legally invalid simply because it is unjust. We conclude that we still have not. While John Finnis accepts that 'an unjust law is not law', the interpretation that he puts on that statement means that he does not support (A), and in fact his interpretation of the statement 'an unjust law is not law' would make no sense if (A) were true. While Ronald Dworkin's theory of law as integrity does provide us with sufficient resources to endorse (A), that theory of law rests on a premise – that law necessarily has *force*, in that law justifies coercing us to obey it – that we have no reason to accept. So the classical natural law position that an 'unjust law is not law' should be rejected *if* we read that statement – contrary to the way Finnis would read it – as saying that an unjust rule cannot amount to a rule of law. Whether we should accept that 'an unjust law is not law' in the way that Finnis would have us read that statement depends on whether we have an obligation to obey *just* laws. After all, the statement 'an unjust law is not law' would become pretty meaningless if it were also the case that a just law is not morally obligatory either. We will defer consideration of this issue to a later chapter.[70]

---

[66] NLNR, 246, 233.
[67] NLNR, 359–60.
[68] NLNR, 361.
[69] NLNR, Postscript, 476.
[70] See below, ch. 7.

Debate 3

Should we accept Finnis's theory of law?

John Finnis's *Natural Law and Natural Rights* (first published in 1980) is the only book that can challenge Hart's *The Concept of Law* for the title of 'greatest work of jurisprudence published in the 20th century'. The source of that challenge lies in the comprehensiveness of Finnis's theory of law, which goes much further than Hart's theory in explaining *why* law has the features that Hart identified it as having, and in providing us with answers to questions that legal positivists generally steer clear of as none of their business; questions such as: *When* can we say that the law is just? *When* do we have an obligation to obey the law? *What* functions is law designed to perform? *How* can and how does law play a role in helping us to decide what to do?

It is little wonder that in a 2003 lecture, Finnis should have exclaimed that 'it is a mistake to talk about positivism at all' and 'there's no such thing as positivism'.[71] From the perspective of his legal theory, there is no need for anyone to identify themselves as a legal positivist.[72] His theory can account for everything the legal positivists emphasise about law, and does so much more on top of that, that to remain *simply* a legal positivist and not endorse Finnis's much larger and richer theory of law would seem as perverse as refusing to abandon Newton's account of how the universe operates in favour of Einstein's account, when Einstein's account can explain all of Newton's results and explain much that Newton's account cannot.

Given the importance of Finnis's theory of law, it is a pity that there exists no canonical statement of his theory of law. A second edition of *Natural Law and Natural Rights* was published in 2011, but – just as with the second edition of *The Concept of Law* – the text of the first edition was left untouched and a Postscript commenting on that text was simply added at the end. In the Postscript, Finnis commented that 'the book has significant weaknesses. But its main purposes and main positions remain intact.'[73] As a way of remedying the weaknesses, the

---

[71] Finnis, 'Law and what I truly should decide' (above, n. 25), 127. Finnis's earlier essay 'On the incoherence of legal positivism' (2000) 75 *Notre Dame Law Review* 1597 provides an alternative interpretation of what he is getting at here. At 1611, he says 'Positivism does no more than repeat (1) what any competent lawyer – including every legally competent adherent of natural law theory – would say are (or are not) intra-systemically valid laws, imposing "legal requirements", and (2) what any street-wise observer would warn are the likely consequences of non-compliance ... Positivism is in the last analysis redundant.'

[72] See Finnis, 'Natural law theories' (above, n. 60), §5: 'Might it not be better to say: no legal philosopher need, or should, be a legal positivist? For law's dependence on social facts is fully acknowledged, and also accounted for, in natural law theories of law' (Internet accessed December 15, 2013); and 'Law and what I truly should decide' (above, n. 25), 115: 'a complete and fully realistic theory of law can be and in all essentials has been worked out from the starting point of the one hundred per cent normative question, what should I decide to do and, equivalently, what kind of person should I resolve or allow myself to be. I can think of no interesting project of inquiry left over for a philosophical theory of law with any different starting point.'

[73] NLNR, Postscript, 425.

Postscript repeatedly refers the reader to various books[74] and articles of Finnis's that improved on, or clarified, points made in *Natural Law and Natural Rights*. So gaining a full appreciation of Finnis's legal theory requires one to have read *Natural Law and Natural Rights*, the Postscript to the second edition of *Natural Law and Natural Rights*, and the various books and articles written by Finnis between 1980 and 2011 that modify or expand on the positions adopted by Finnis in *Natural Law and Natural Rights*.

So Finnis has not made it easy for his readers to understand his theory of law, or for us to present *our* readers with a summary of that theory of law. But if we are going to decide whether or not we should adopt his theory of law, we have to try.

FINNIS'S THEORY OF LAW: AN OVERVIEW

It seems to us that Finnis's theory of law can be summed up by reference to the following seven key ideas:

(1) *The basic goods.* Finnis's theory of law begins with the statement that 'There are human goods that can be secured only through the institutions of human law ...'.[75] So if we are to understand what is (or can be) good about law, then we first have to understand what is good for human beings. Understanding what is good for human beings requires not that we reflect on our desires – because our desires may be unreasonable[76] – or that we understand human nature – because we only come to understand our nature by coming to understand what is good for us[77] – but that we think intelligently about *why* we make the choices that we do.[78]

Doing so allows us to see that there exist a range of *basic goods*, which give us reasons for choosing and acting that require no further support or justification.[79]

The 1980 first edition of *Natural Law and Natural Rights* set out a comprehensive list of what these basic goods are: (i) life (defined as 'every aspect of the vitality ... which puts a human being in good shape for self-determination');[80] (ii) knowledge; (iii) play; (iv) aesthetic experience; (v) sociability (friendship); (vi) practical reasonableness (defined as 'the basic good of being able to bring one's own intelligence to bear effectively ... on the problem of choosing one's actions and lifestyle and shaping one's character');[81] (vii) 'religion' (defined as thinking 'reasonably and

---

[74] Finnis, *Fundamentals of Ethics* (Oxford University Press, 1983); Finnis, Boyle and Grisez, *Nuclear Deterrence, Morality and Realism* (Oxford University Press, 1987); Finnis, *Moral Absolutes: Tradition, Revision and Truth* (Catholic University of America Press, 1991); Finnis, *Aquinas* (Oxford University Press, 1998).

[75] NLNR, 1.

[76] NLNR, Postscript, 449.

[77] NLNR, Postscript, 416; Finnis, 'Foundations of practical reason revisited' (2005) 50 *American Journal of Jurisprudence* 109, 117; Finnis, *Aquinas* (above, n. 74), 29.

[78] Ibid, 31–34.

[79] Finnis, Boyle and Grisez, *Nuclear Deterrence, Morality and Realism* (above, n. 74), 278.

[80] NLNR, 86.

[81] NLNR, 88.

(where possible) correctly' about the issue of whether there 'is a transcendent origin of the universal order-of-things and of human freedom and reason').[82]

Over time, this list evolved. The 2011 second edition of *Natural Law and Natural Rights* endorsed as 'best'[83] the following list of basic goods from an article published in 1997:

> '(1) *knowledge* (including aesthetic appreciation) of reality; (2) *skilful performance*, in work and play for its own sake; (3) *bodily life* and the components of its fullness, viz. health, vigour and safety; (4) *friendship* or harmony and association between persons in its various forms and strengths; (5) the sexual association of a man and a woman which ... should be acknowledged to be a distinct basic good, call it *marriage*; (6) the good of harmony between one's feelings and one's judgments (inner integrity), and between one's judgments and one's behaviour (authenticity), which we can call *practical reasonableness*; (7) *harmony with* the widest reaches and most *ultimate source* of all reality, including meaning and value.'[84]

(2) *Incommensurability*. The reasons for choosing and acting that the basic goods give us 'lay down for us the outlines of everything one could reasonably want to do, to have and to be'.[85] They therefore define for us what it is to flourish as a human being. Someone whose life participates in these goods, insofar as they are available to him, is doing better, is in better shape, than someone whose life does not. A crucial point is that all of the basic goods are *equally* basic in the sense that 'each can reasonably be focused upon, and each, when focused upon, claims a priority of value. Hence there is no objective priority of value amongst them.'[86] As such the basic goods are *incommensurable*. So, for example, we have no reason to think that enjoying a certain amount of play is *better* than enjoying a certain amount of knowledge.

Given this, Finnis argues, there is no *one right way* of flourishing as a human being. We cannot say a flourishing life *will* involve *x* amount of play, *y* amount of study, and *z* amount of friendship. A flourishing life will simply participate in those goods – or, at least, be open to the possibility of participating in those goods – in proportions and intensities to be determined by the individual leading that life. And because each of the basic goods 'can be participated in, and promoted, in an inexhaustible variety of ways and with an inexhaustible variety of combinations of emphasis, concentration and specialization',[87] there are an inexhaustible variety of ways in which someone can lead a life that can truly be said to be flourishing.

---

[82] NLNR, 89–90.
[83] NLNR, Postscript, 448.
[84] Finnis, 'Commensuration and public reason' in Chang (ed.), *Incommensurability, Comparability and Practical Reasoning* (Harvard University Press, 1997), 244, fn. 25 (emphasis in original).
[85] NLNR, 97.
[86] NLNR, 93.
[87] NLNR, 100.

(3) *Practical reasonableness.* The good of practical reasonableness allows a person to knit together all the other basic goods – insofar as participation in those goods is open to her – into her life.[88] As such, the 'good of practical reasonableness rules over the [other goods] – not because it is more valuable than them, but because such rule is what it is about ...'.[89] The master principle that underlies practical reasonableness is: 'all one's choices and other kinds of willing should be *open to integral human fulfilment*'[90] both in oneself and other people. The concrete requirements of practical reasonableness – 'have a coherent plan of life',[91] 'don't rule out participating in a particular basic good',[92] 'don't arbitrarily prefer your own fulfilment over other people's',[93] 'don't put all your eggs in one basket, so that if one project does not come off you feel like your life is over',[94] 'don't be apathetic about your commitments or your life',[95] 'make the most of your time and resources',[96] 'don't intentionally damage any basic good',[97] 'do what you are required to do to foster the conditions required for everyone, including you, to participate in the basic human goods',[98] and 'don't act contrary to what your conscience tells you should not be done'[99] – all identify ways in which someone can fail to be open to integral human fulfilment in their choices and tell people not to fail in those ways.

(4) *The common good.* If people are going to flourish as human beings by participating in all of the basic human goods that are available to them, they need to live in

> 'a "complete community", an all-round association in which would be co-ordinated the initiatives and activities of individuals, of families, and of the vast network of intermediate associations. The point of this all-round association would be to secure the whole ensemble of material and other conditions, including forms of collaboration, that tend to favour, facilitate, and foster the realization by each individual of his or her personal development. (Remember: this personal development includes, as an integral element and not merely as a means or pre-condition, both individual self-direction and community with others in family, friendship, work, and play.)'[100]

The securing of this 'ensemble of material and other conditions' is referred to by John Finnis as 'the common good'[101] because securing this ensemble is good for

---

[88] NLNR, 100-103.
[89] Finnis, 'Response' (2012) 57 *Villanova Law Review* 925, 929, n 3.
[90] NLNR, Postscript, 420.
[91] NLNR, 103-105.
[92] NLNR, 105-106.
[93] NLNR, 106-109.
[94] NLNR, 110.
[95] Ibid.
[96] NLNR, 111.
[97] NLNR, 118–25; Finnis, *Moral Absolutes: Tradtion, Revision and Truth* (above, n. 74), 54–55.
[98] NLNR, 125.
[99] NLNR, 125–26.
[100] NLNR, 147–48.
[101] NLNR, 155.

every individual, in that it favours 'the realization, by each individual in the community, of his or her personal development'.[102] While Finnis used to categorise 'the common good' as 'instrumental',[103] in the Postscript to the second edition of *Natural Law and Natural Rights* he points out that living in a 'complete community' and contributing to its existence is itself a feature of human flourishing.[104]

(5) *The need for authority.* But this common good can be secured in thousands, if not millions, of different ways, each of which involve a slightly different – but equally acceptable – way of co-ordinating the activities of people in the complete community so as to favour, facilitate and foster their mutual flourishing. In order to determine in *what* way the common good is to be realised, decisions have to be made:

> 'Somebody … must decide how children are to be educated; … there must be deci-sions about the management and use of public resources, about the use of force, about permitted forms or content of communication, and about the many other problems of reconciling aspects of justice with each other … and of reconciling human rights with each other and with other 'conflicting' exercises of the same right and with public health, public order, and the like.'[105]

And, in the end, there are only two ways of making these decisions: 'There must be either unanimity, or authority. There are no other possibilities.'[106] Where unanimity is impossible, authority is vital and whoever happens (for whatever reason) to have authority in a community – in the sense that the members of that community (for whatever reason) will do what that person or institution tells them to do regardless of their own views as to the wisdom of doing what they have been told to do – comes under an obligation to exercise that authority for the sake of securing the common good.[107]

Finnis follows Aquinas in calling the process of deciding how the common good is to be secured – out of the thousands, or millions, of different ways of doing that – *determinatio*:

> '*Determinatio* is best clarified by Aquinas' own analogy with architecture. The general idea or form of a dwelling-house (or a hospital), and the general ideas of a door and a doorknob (or a labour ward), must be made determinate as this particu-lar design and house (or hospital), door, doorknob, etc.; otherwise nothing will be built. The specifications which the architect or designer decides upon are certainly derived from and shaped by the primary general idea, e.g. the commission to design

---

[102] NLNR, 154.

[103] Finnis, 'Is natural law theory compatible with limited government?' in George (ed.), *Natural Law, Liberalism and Morality* (Oxford University Press, 1996), 5–6.

[104] NLNR, Postscript, 459, referring the reader to Finnis, *Aquinas* (above, n. 74), 235.

[105] NLNR, 232. For a concrete example of a co-ordination problem that can be 'solved' a variety of ways, see Finnis, 'The authority of law in the predicament of contemporary social theory' (1984–85) 1 *Notre Dame Journal of Law, Ethics and Public Policy* 115, 133–35 (how to deal with the pollution of a river).

[106] Ibid.

[107] NLNR, 246.

a dwelling-house (or maternity hospital). But the specifications decided upon could reasonably have been rather different in many (even in every) dimension and aspect, and require of the designer a multitude of decisions which could reasonably have been more or less different.'[108]

(6) *The importance of law.* There are a variety of ways in which the authority to make decisions could be exercised: by example, or exhortations, or directives. But a number of features of law make it especially well suited to being *the* way through which decisions as to how the common good is to be secured are made.

First, law's *positivity* – the fact that 'The identification of the existence and content of law does not require resort to any moral argument'[109] – allows determinations made through law to be clearly identified and acted on,[110] thus bringing 'definition, specificity, clarity, and thus predictability into human interactions ...'.[111]

Second, law's *integrity* – understood in a much weaker sense than Dworkin's to refer to the fact that law attributes 'authoritativeness to past acts' – 'provides a stable point of reference unaffected by present and shifting interests and disputes' and 'the present will soon be the past; so [law] gives people a way of now determining the framework of their future.'[112]

Third, law's *coerciveness* – the fact that people can be forced to comply with the law's requirements – does not just enhance the authoritativeness of law among those who might otherwise be disposed to decide for themselves what to do; it also enhances the authoritativeness of law among those who are pre-disposed to be law-abiding but are afraid that they will be suckers for obeying the law while 'the lawless are ... left to the peaceful enjoyment of ill-gotten gains.'[113]

Fourth, law's *seamlessness* – the fact that people are not allowed to pick and choose which laws they are going to obey – further enhances the authoritativeness of the law, as someone who is disadvantaged by a particular legal provision can reconcile himself with complying with that provision by reflecting that he has benefited from other provisions elsewhere in the law.[114]

Fifth, law's *gaplessness* – 'the working postulate ... that every present practical question or co-ordination problem has, in every respect, been ... "provided for" by some ... past juridical act or acts'[115] – means the law is always on hand to answer any such question or problem.[116]

---

[108] Finnis, *Aquinas* (above, n. 74), 267; also NLNR, 284.

[109] Raz, *The Morality of Freedom* (Oxford University Press, 1986), 81–82.

[110] Cf. Waldron, 'Normative (or ethical) positivism' in Coleman (ed.), *Hart's Postscript* (Oxford University Press, 2001).

[111] NLNR, 268.

[112] NLNR, 269.

[113] NLNR, 262. The same point is made in CL, 198: '"Sanctions" are therefore required not as the normal motive for obedience, but as a *guarantee* that those who would voluntarily obey shall not be sacrificed to those who would not. To obey, without this, would be to risk going to the wall.'

[114] Finnis, 'Law as coordination' (1989) 2 *Ratio Juris* 97, 137.

[115] NLNR, 269.

[116] NLNR, 148.

Sixth, law's *supremacy* – the fact that law claims to be the ultimate determinant of how its subject are to behave, even above morality – makes it a reliable source of solutions to co-ordination problems: people will know what the law says goes, irrespective of what other considerations apply to those subject to the law; and also means there are no limits on what co-ordination problems might be solved through law.[117]

Seventh, law's *openness* – the fact that the law can give legal force to 'rules and normative arrangements (e.g. contracts) from other associations within and without the complete community'[118] – means that law can provide authoritative support to solutions to co-ordination problems that members of the community have come up with themselves.

Eighth, law's *flexibility* – established through its Hartian rules of change – means that it can generate 'relatively prompt but also relatively clear and subtle solutions to coordination problems as they emerge and change'.[119]

(7) *The two types of law.* In employing the authority of law to secure the common good, two types of law emerge.[120]

The first type might be styled as *deductive*. This type of law gives concrete effect to some of the abstract principles of practical reasonableness that we are all subject to. So the requirement of practical reasonableness (based on the requirement 'don't intentionally damage any basic good') that 'one is not to deliberately kill the innocent'[121] gets turned into a set of legal provisions making it an offence to murder someone and defining murder as causing another's death with the relevant *mens rea*. The point of these deductive rules is not to coerce those who are subject to them into acting reasonably, but rather to make sure that people's unreasonable actions do not impede others' abilities to flourish as human beings.[122] So the 'coercive jurisdiction of the state's government and law … is limited to interpersonal relations and external acts which impact directly or indirectly on others.'[123]

The second type of law is made up of what we might call *determinations* – provisions designed to settle an issue that could have been settled in two, or three, or a thousand, or a million different equally reasonable ways, but which needs to be settled if the common good is to be secured.[124] Of course, in settling those issues, there are quite a few ways of settling them in an *unreasonable* way. So in order to

---

[117] Ibid.

[118] Ibid.

[119] Finnis, 'Law as coordination' (above, n. 114), 137.

[120] NLNR, 289.

[121] NLNR, 281.

[122] Finnis, 'Law, morality and "sexual orientation"' (1995) 9 *Notre Dame Journal of Law, Ethics and Public Policy* 11, 37_39.

[123] NLNR, Postscript, 459. In 'Kant v Neo-Kantians' (1987) 87 *Columbia Law Review* 433, Finnis says (at 447) that 'the harm principle … [is not] entitled to a place in a sound political philosophy'; but it is hard to see what basis there is for Finnis's stated limit on the coercive powers of the state other than something like the harm principle.

[124] For examples, see NLNR, 284–86.

ensure that they do not stray from the path of determining which of the reasonable ways of settling an issue will be adopted, law-makers are required to comply with a number of different maxims – requirements of practical reasonableness for law-makers, if you will. These maxims 'express the desirability of stability and predictability' and require law-makers to attend to the need to preserve these values, so far as they can, in arriving at their *determinations*. The maxims require:

'(i) compulsory acquisition of property rights to be compensated ...; (ii) no liability for unintentional injury, without fault; (iii) no criminal liability without *mens rea*; (iv) estoppel ...; (v) no judicial aid to one who pleads his own wrong ...; (vi) no aid to abuse of rights; (vii) fraud unravels everything; (viii) profits received without justification and at the expense of another must be restored; (ix) *pacta sunt servanda* (contracts are to be performed); (x) relative freedom to change existing patterns of legal relationships by agreement; (xi) in assessments of the legal effects of purported acts-in-the-law, the weak to be protected against their weaknesses; (xii) disputes not to be resolved without giving both sides an opportunity to be heard; (xiii) no one to be allowed to judge his own cause.'[125]

Finnis's theory of law is a magnificent achievement – but should we adopt it? Two lines of attack can be, and have been, made on his theory.

FINNIS'S ACCOUNT OF HUMAN FLOURISHING

In discussing 'What makes someone's life go best', Derek Parfit distinguishes between

'three kinds of theory. On *Hedonistic Theories*, what would be best for someone is what would make his life happiest. On *Desire-Fulfilment Theories*, what would be best for someone is what, throughout his life, would best fulfil his desires. On *Objective List Theories*, certain things are good or bad for us, whether or not we want to have the good things, or to avoid the bad things.'[126]

Finnis's account of what human flourishing entails looks like an *Objective List Theory*: the basic goods are objectively good, and your life goes better the more you have them in your life (insofar as they are available to you). As such, Finnis's account of human flourishing can be criticised from two angles. The first criticism – the *external* criticism – argues that an *Objective List Theory* of human flourishing is simply wrong: some other theory should be adopted instead. The second criticism – the *internal* criticism – argues that an *Objective List Theory* of human flourishing is correct but Finnis's list of objective goods is incorrect: some other list works better to explain what human flourishing entails. Let's look at each type of criticism in turn.

---

[125] NLNR, 288.
[126] Parfit, *Reasons and Persons* (Oxford University Press, 1984), 493 (emphasis in original).

(1) *External criticisms*. Finnis might have thought – and certainly assumes in his writing – that his account of human flourishing is immune from external criticism. The reason is that of the three theories of what makes someone's life go best identified by Parfit, *Hedonistic Theories* and *Desire-Fulfilment Theories* seem inherently implausible. So far as *Desire-Fulfilment Theories* are concerned, the mere fact that all my desires are being fulfilled would not seem to tell us anything about whether things are going well for me or not. If my desire is to eat coal all day[127] and I am rich enough to purchase all the coal I need to fulfil that desire, no reasonable person would think that I am doing well by gnawing on coal all day.

Hedonistic Theories are more attractive (especially to students) but are generally thought – and certainly thought by Finnis[128] – to have been refuted through Robert Nozick's 'experience machine' thought experiment:

> 'Superduper neuropsychologists could stimulate your brain so that you would think and feel you were writing a great novel, or making a friend, or reading an interesting book. All the time you would be floating in a tank, with electrodes attached to your brain. Should you plug into this machine for life, preprogramming your life's experiences? If you are worried about missing out on desirable experiences, we can suppose that business enterprises have researched thoroughly the lives of many others. You can pick and choose from their large library or smorgasbord of such experiences, selecting your life's experiences for, say, the next two years. After two years have passed, you will have ten minutes or ten hours out of the tank, to select the experiences of your next two years. Of course, while in the tank you won't know that you're there; you'll think it's all actually happening. ... Would you plug in?'[129]

If *Hedonistic Theories* are correct then you should plug in – you will certainly be far happier inside the experience machine than outside. But most people would think that you should not plug in. Inside the experience machine, you could not be said to be 'doing well' as a person. In fact, it is hard to see how you would count as being a person at all – you would just be a piece of meat that was being subjected to electrical stimuli. As Nozick observes, 'Plugging into the machine is a kind of suicide.'[130]

This leaves *Objective List Theories* as the only acceptable theories of human flourishing, and that would seem to leave external critics of Finnis's account of human flourishing with nowhere to go. However, *Objective List Theories* are vulnerable to *Mixed Theories* of what makes someone's life go best. A *Mixed Theory* proposes that human flourishing consists in a *mixture* of happiness, desire fulfilment, and participation in things that are objectively good. Parfit attempted to put forward a *Mixed Theory* of human flourishing when he argued in his essay on 'What makes someone's life go best' that:

[127] Aristotle, *Nicomachean Ethics*, 1148–27; NLNR, Postscript, 449.
[128] NLNR, 95–97; Finnis, *Fundamentals of Ethics* (above, n. 74), 37–42; NLNR, Postscript, 450.
[129] Nozick, *Anarchy, State and Utopia* (Basic Books, 1974), 42–43.
[130] Ibid, 43.

'What is good for someone is neither just what Hedonists claim, nor just what is claimed by Objective List Theorists. We might believe that if we had *either* of these, *without the other*, what we had would have little or no value. We might claim, for example, that what is good or bad for someone is to have knowledge, to be engaged in rational activity, to experience mutual love, and to be aware of beauty, while strongly wanting just these things. On this view, each side in this disagreement saw only half of the truth. Each put forward as sufficient something that was only necessary. Pleasure with many other kinds of object has no value. And, if they are entirely devoid of pleasure, there is no value in knowledge, rational activity, love, or the awareness of beauty. What is of value, or is good for someone, is to have both; to be engaged in these activities, and to be strongly wanting to be so engaged.'[131]

However, this *Mixed Theory* is insufficiently distinct from Finnis's account to count as a genuine challenger to that account. Finnis could easily claim that someone who is flourishing by his standards will be engaged in the activities Parfit identifies as objectively valuable *and* (because he participates in the good of practical reasonableness) will strongly want to be so engaged. The *Mixed Theory* put forward by Thomas Scanlon poses a more severe challenge to Finnis:

'any plausible theory of well-being would have to recognize at least the following fixed points. First, certain experiential states (such as various forms of satisfaction and enjoyment) contribute to well-being, but well-being is not determined solely by the quality of the experience. Second, well-being depends to a large extent on a person's degree of success in achieving his or her main ends in life, provided that these are worth pursuing. This component of well-being reflects the fact that the life of a rational creature is something that is to be *lived* in an active sense – that is to say, shaped by his or her choices and reactions – and that well-being is therefore in large part a matter of how well this is done – of how well the ends are selected and how successfully they are pursued. Third, many goods that contribute to a person's well-being depend on the person's aims but go beyond the good of success in achieving those aims. These include such things as friendship, other valuable personal relations, and the achievement of various forms of excellence, such as in art of science.'[132]

Finnis's account of what it means for someone's life to go well does not accommodate the first two 'fixed points'. In particular, in (rightly) dismissing the possibility that having pleasurable experiences or avoiding painful experiences is *all there is* to human flourishing, Finnis overlooks the possibility that having pleasurable experiences and avoiding painful experiences may be *part* of what it is to do well as a human being.[133]

---

[131] Parfit, *Reasons and Persons* (above, n. 126), 502.

[132] Scanlon, *What We Owe To Each Other* (Harvard University Press, 1998), 124–25.

[133] See Crisp, 'Finnis on well-being' in Keown and George (eds), *Reason, Morality and Law: The Philosophy of John Finnis* (Oxford University Press, 2013) (arguing that participation in the basic goods will not be of much value unless that participation is *enjoyed*) and McBride, 'Tort law and human flourishing' in Pitel, Neyers and Chamberlain (eds), *Tort Law: Challenging Orthodoxy* (Hart Publishing, 2013) (pointing out various negative mental states – misery, anxiety, hatred, boredom – that are incompatible with human flourishing).

Finnis could try to accommodate this point by arguing: (1) that he does not at all deny that pleasure and pain are relevant to human flourishing, and (2) that his theory actually explains what is good and bad about pleasure and pain – pleasure is good insofar as it is a necessary component of the enjoyment of some of his basic goods, and pain is bad insofar as it disrupts someone's ability to enjoy the basic goods.[134] However, this would imply that a pleasure which is not bound up with the enjoyment of a basic good (for example, the pleasure involved in just sitting in a chair and watching a funny film) is valueless. It would also imply that a pain that is sudden, severe, but very temporary with no effects beyond the period during which the pain is experienced is not a bad thing. Most people would find it very hard to accept either of these claims.

If this response of Finnis's does not work, then it would seem that Finnis's theory of human flourishing needs to be adjusted to take account of the point that a lack of pleasure or presence of pain can make a person's life go less well *whether or not* that person is otherwise participating in the basic goods identified by Finnis in a practically reasonable way. One way to do this would be to retain Finnis's *Objective List Theory* and simply tack on 'pleasure' and the 'avoidance of pain' to Finnis's list of basic goods. However, this would not work. The *unfocussed* nature of pleasure and pain mean that if we were to start regarding 'pleasure' and the 'avoidance of pain' as basic goods, scope for pervasive conflicts between the basic goods would be introduced and it might become impossible for a person to adhere to the requirement of practical reasonableness that he should not intentionally damage a basic good.

So it seems we have no choice but to adopt a *Mixed Theory*. Under such a theory, to assess someone's flourishing we have to look at them in more than one dimension – we not only have to ask how far they are participating in the basic goods (insofar as they are available to them) but also how far their lives are enjoyable or painful; and other dimensions (such as – How successful are they in achieving their goals?) may be relevant as well.

(2) *Internal criticisms.* Let's go back. Even if we abandon an *Objective List Theory* of human flourishing like Finnis's in favour of a *Mixed Theory*, internal criticisms of Finnis's *Objective List Theory* will still be of interest to us as they will help us to decide how someone's flourishing should be assessed along what we might call the 'objective' dimension for assessing how well they are doing. Internal criticisms of Finnis's *Objective List Theory* can be divided into two – *weak* criticisms, and *strong* criticisms.

Weak criticisms suggest that Finnis's list of basic goods just needs tweaking a bit to be made perfect. We just need to add good X or subtract good Y from Finnis's list, or slightly alter the definition of good Z in Finnis's list, and all will be well. *Weak* criticisms have tended (1) to question whether Finnis is right to include marriage in his list of basic goods; and (2) to question whether knowledge is a basic

---

[134] This is the line Finnis takes in NLNR, Postscript, 450.

good given that there are some forms of knowledge that are valueless – for example, knowing how many cats there were born on 20 November 720 AD.[135] It seems to us (and Finnis!)[136] that Finnis's list of basic goods stands up pretty well to these weak criticisms. The amount of time people spend searching for 'the one' that they can spend the rest of their lives with can only be made intelligible if we suppose that marriage is a basic human good. That some forms of knowledge may be useless or harmful does not bring into question knowledge's status as a basic good. A practically reasonable person will acknowledge that it is better *not* to be in a state of 'ignorance and muddle ... error, misinformation, and delusion'[137] than it is to be in such a state. But at the same time he will disdain the pursuit of useless or harmful knowledge as practically unreasonable – either because it is a waste of time, or because it will damage his or someone else's participation in the basic goods.

Strong criticisms argue that Finnis's list of basic goods is basically wrong. Such criticisms get their force from the suggestion that reflecting on why we choose to do the things that we do will *not* help us to understand what is good for us because we are *continually* operating in a state of 'ignorance and muddle ... error, misinformation, and delusion' that means the choices we make bear *no relation* to what is actually good for us. That we live in such a state of delusion has been suggested, in their *very* different ways, by Jesus Christ, the Buddha, and Friedrich Nietzsche. It is because of the mismatch between their understanding of what is good for us and our – they claim – delusions about what is good for us that their recommendations as to how we should live seem very strange to us, and hard to accept:

'Then Jesus told his disciples: "If anyone would come after me, let him deny himself and take up his cross and follow me. For whoever would save his life will lose it, but whoever loses his life for my sake will find it. For what will it profit a man if he gains the whole world and forfeits his soul?"'[138]

'Who so delights in corporeality, or feeling, or perception, or mental formations, or consciousness, he delights in suffering; and whoso delights in suffering, will not be freed from suffering. Thus I say.'[139]

'You higher men, overcome the small virtues, the small prudences, the grain-of-sand consideration, the ants' riff-raff, the wretched contentment, the "happiness of the greatest number"! And rather despair than surrender. And verily, I love you for not knowing how to live today, you higher men! For thus *you* live best.'[140]

---

[135] Raz's example: Raz, 'Value: a menu of questions' in Keown and George (eds), *Reason, Morality and Law: The Philosophy of John Finnis* (above, n. 133), 23.

[136] See his 'Introduction' to *Reason in Action: Volume I of the Collected Essays of John Finnis* (Oxford University Press, 2011).

[137] Finnis, 'Reflections and responses' in Keown and George (eds), *Reason, Morality and Law: The Philosophy of John Finnis* (above, n. 133), 460.

[138] Matthew 16:24–26.

[139] Nyanatiloka, *The Word of the Buddha*, 14th edn (Buddhist Publication Society, 1967), 15.

[140] Nietzsche, *Thus Spoke Zarathustra* (1883–1885), Fourth Part, 'On the higher man', §3 (trans. Walter Kaufmann) (emphasis in original).

While these recommendations are hard to accept, we should consider seriously the possibility that we *are* persistently deluded about what is good for us. After all, as Finnis himself admits,

> 'isn't it clear that one's thoughts about the values of one's objectives ... could be mistaken? That they can be mistaken is something we have all learned, or at least come to presume, from experience, by the very dawn of the age of reason – by six or seven or whenever it was.'[141]

If children can be persistently mistaken about what is good for them, why not adults? That even reasonable adults can be mistaken is something Finnis also admits in an essay on whether a couple having sex that cannot result in the procreation of a child (and not because one or both of them are sterile) can ever be said to be participating in a basic good while having sex:

> '*in reality*, whatever the generous hopes and dreams and thoughts of giving with which some ... partners may surround their sexual acts, those acts cannot express or do more than is expressed or done if two strangers engage in such activity to give each other pleasure, or a prostitute pleasures a client to give him pleasure in return for money.'[142]

The difficulty is – if we *are* persistently deluded about what is good for us, how could we ever tell? Perhaps the only test is provided by death: If someone had lived a life that was flourishing in Finnis's terms, might they still think, as their life came to an end, that they had wasted their life?[143] Might they think: 'I failed to get closer to God' (a Christian regret), or 'I was too attached to worldly things' (a Buddhist regret) or 'I lived too conventionally, too narrowly' (a Nietzschean regret)? We will let the reader decide.

To sum up, then, Finnis's account of human flourishing is not as uncontroversial or as self-evident as Finnis might have hoped or expected.[144] This has an important implication for whether we accept his legal theory. If it is a controversial issue what human flourishing consists in, it might be *dangerous* for the law, or the state, to seek to bring into existence the ensemble of material and other

---

[141] Finnis, 'Foundations of practical reason revisited' (above, n. 77), 117–18.

[142] Finnis, 'Law, morality, and "sexual orientation"' (above, n. 122), 29 (emphasis in original). This statement was rebuked by Michael Perry in 'The morality of homosexual conduct: a response to John Finnis' (1995) 9 *Notre Dame Journal of Law, Ethics and Public Policy* 41, at 60: 'The reader can decide for himself whose "reality" is an illusion:' that of heterosexual couples who practise 'mutually affirming and nurturing' non-vaginal or contracepted sex and homosexual couples '– or instead that postulated by John Finnis, for whom [such sex] ... is *equal in moral worthlessness* to the commercial sex of a prostitute.' Either way, someone is under an illusion. (In a footnote, Perry concedes that 'large numbers of people in our society ... *are* in the grip of one or another "sexually liberal" illusion' (ibid, fn. 46) (emphasis in original) – he just can't see how lifelong, monogamous, faithful, loving couples having non-procreative sex can be said to be deluded about the worth of what they are doing.)

[143] Cf. the poem written by Michelangelo – who, by Finnis's standards, definitely lived a flourishing life – just before he died, where he despairs: 'Making all those big dolls [that is, his sculptures], I wonder what the point was ...': Mortimer (ed.), *Michelangelo: Poems and Letters* (Penguin Books, 2007), 57 (poem 267).

[144] NLNR, 81–86.

conditions required for people to flourish as human beings. Because if those responsible for the law or the state turn out to be *wrong* about what human flourishing consists in, then they could do more harm than good.

FINNIS'S ILLIBERALISM

Of course, the fact that a particular theory is illiberal is neither here nor there in determining whether it is sound. The heading is merely meant to capture a common theme in three sets of criticisms that can be, and have been, made of Finnis's legal theory. However, for those for whom labels are important, it might be worth noting – before we discuss the respects in which Finnis's legal theory is illiberal – the respects in which Finnis's legal theory can be described as 'liberal' in nature.

(1) The incommensurability of the basic goods means that there are a vast number of different kinds of lives that are reasonably open to us.
(2) The incommensurability of basic goods across persons, and the injunction that we should never intentionally damage a basic good, means that sacrificing individuals in the name of the 'greater good' is both senseless and wrong.
(3) Finnis does not believe that the role of the state is to compel people to live virtuous lives, but rather to provide the conditions (which he calls 'the common good') that will allow people to live virtuous lives. So the state should not coerce someone into acting reasonably unless the public and interpersonal nature of their unreasonable action threatens the common good.

Finnis's theory of law therefore makes a place for the values of *diversity*, *dignity*, and *privacy* that tend to be cherished by liberals. However, there are two ways in which Finnis's theory of law can be accused of being illiberal in nature.

(1) *The central case of law.* As we have seen,[145] Finnis thinks we can best understand law through looking at the central cases of law – ones which best exemplify why we might 'choose to have [law], create it, maintain it, and comply with it'.[146] So, Finnis argues, the central case of law is law that, through promoting the common good, favours, facilitates and fosters our flourishing as human beings. But this implies that the central case of law is *perfectionist* in nature – that is, it seeks to help us to lead worthwhile lives. Many liberals do not believe that the state should help us to lead worthwhile lives.[147] They would object to the idea – implicit in Finnis's view of what the central case of law is – that a legal system that is neutral on issues of what counts a good life is a degraded, or watered down, form of legal system. Indeed, Finnis nowhere explains why we might not 'choose to have [law], create it, maintain it, and comply with it' for *more limited* reasons than that law can favour, facilitate and foster our flourishing as human beings. Why could someone

---

[145] See above, pp. 16–18.
[146] Finnis, 'Law and what I truly should decide' (above, n. 25), 129.
[147] For further discussion, see below, ch. 10.

not argue, on this basis, that the central case of law is law that simply allows each of us to pursue our own conceptions of what a good life is and that a legal system that pursues more ambitious, perfectionist, aims is a watered-down, or degraded, version of the simpler type of law that forms its central case? So the first 'liberal' criticism of Finnis's theory of law is that it illegitimately associates perfectionism with the central case of law, with the result that we are encouraged to think that there is something wrong or inadequate with legal systems that disdain perfectionist goals.

(2) *Finnis's certainty*. While Finnis embraces the idea that there is an almost infinite variety of forms that the common good could take, and therefore 'no right answer' as to how that common good is to be secured,[148] Finnis does not seem to accept that there can be any room for *reasonable* differences of opinion over what human flourishing involves, and what practical reasonableness demands of us (except in the case where practical reasonableness demands that we contribute to the common good), and therefore has no room in his legal theory for questions about how we accommodate those reasonable differences of opinion within a society where we share a common life under one set of rules that governs all of us.[149]

Take, for example, the issue – much discussed by Finnis – as to the value, or otherwise, of non-procreative sex. For our purposes, sex will count as non-procreative if: (a) it is between a homosexual couple, or (b) it is between a heterosexual couple but the *form* of sex that they are engaging in means that it *cannot* result in the conception of a child. There are three positions one could adopt on the value of any given act of non-procreative sex. (1) You could say that it is valuable. (2) You could say that it is neither valuable nor harmful. (3) You could say that it is harmful. Finnis argues in favour of position (3) and therefore opposes the state doing anything to encourage people to think that non-procreative sex is normal or acceptable.[150]

In order to see whether there can be reasonable differences of opinion on this issue, let's consider the situation where the case for saying that non-procreative sex is valuable seems to be strongest: where the sex is engaged in between a couple who are in a committed, loving, monogamous relationship and they each intend, by having sex with each other, to express their love for the other. Let's call this kind of sex: *committed*, non-procreative sex. Why does Finnis not say that committed, non-procreative sex is valuable? He seems to take the view that we cannot say that this form of sex is valuable because a couple engaging in it cannot say (whatever their intentions might be) that they are participating in a basic human good by having such sex. Critics of Finnis wonder why they cannot say that they are

---

[148] Finnis, 'On the Critical Legal Studies Movement' (1985) 30 *American Journal of Jurisprudence* 21.

[149] Jeremy Waldron has very much made these questions his own: see Waldron, *Law and Disagreement* (above, n. 50).

[150] Finnis, 'Natural law: the classical tradition' (above, n. 3), 44.

participating in the basic human good of friendship.[151] Finnis's response seems to be that the couple cannot say that they are participating in that good by having committed, non-procreative sex with each other because the only intelligible reason they can be having sex with each other is for mutual pleasure, with the result that they are using each other's bodies – and allowing their bodies to be used – for pleasure. Friends don't use each other, or allow their friends to use them – or at least when they do, they aren't at that moment participating in the good of friendship, but are rather engaging in a kind of business or relationship of utility.[152]

Why, then, does Finnis not say that committed, non-procreative sex is neither valuable nor harmful? Why does he take the further step of saying that it is positively harmful? Finnis identifies two principal reasons why a choice to engage in committed, non-procreative sex might be said to be practically unreasonable:

(A) 'it harms the personalities of its participants by its dis-integrative manipulation of different parts of their one personal reality.'[153]

(B) 'it treats human sexual capacities in a way which is deeply hostile to the self-understanding of those members of the community who are willing to commit themselves to real marriage in the understanding that its sexual joys are not mere instruments or accompaniments to, or mere compensations for, the accomplishment of marriage's responsibilities, but rather enable the spouses to *actualize and experience* their intelligent commitment to share in those responsibilities, in that genuine self-giving.'[154]

(A) seems implausible. If kissing or tickling someone to make them feel better does not have a 'dis-integrative' effect on the kisser or tickler, it is hard to see how it is necessarily true that performing a sex act on someone else, or allowing them to perform a sex act on you, will have such an effect.

(B) is a much more interesting claim. Without wishing to put words in his mouth, what Finnis seems to be getting at here is that people's willingness to act on the idea that sex can be engaged in *just* for pleasure threatens married couple's abilities to engage in procreative sex with the kind of attitude that would allow them, through that sex, to participate in the basic good of marriage. Instead of seeing procreative sex as a peculiarly apt way of celebrating the fact of their being engaged in a productive union of their identities – because it involves a (potentially) productive union of their bodies – they too might end up simply regarding sex as a matter of mutually pleasuring each other. So, on this view, the problem with non-procreative sex is its effect on what Robert George calls a community's

---

[151] Perry, 'The morality of homosexual conduct: a response to John Finnis' (above, n. 142), 55–56; Macedo, 'Against the old sexual morality of the new natural law' in George (ed.), *Natural Law, Liberalism and Morality* (Oxford University Press, 1996), 39.

[152] For discussion of the difference between 'business' communities and friendship, see NLNR, 139–44.

[153] Finnis, 'Law, morality, and "sexual orientation"' (above, n. 122), 32.

[154] Ibid.

'moral ecology'.[155] It becomes much harder for married couples to invest procreative sex with the kind of meaning that would allow them to participate in the basic good of marriage through such sex when they live in a society where it is widely accepted that there is no distinction between sex before marriage and after marriage, that abstaining from sex before marriage is deeply abnormal and a legitimate ground for resentment on the part of one's dating partners, and the chief point of sex is the pleasure one gets from it.

It seems to us that this is the strongest case that can be made for Finnis's position on non-procreative sex. But there is plenty – to say the least – that can be said on the other side. First, if we adopted a *Mixed Theory* of human flourishing, where the amount of pleasure and pain in someone's life is to be taken into account in determining how well they are doing as a person, then sex that is engaged in purely for pleasure might start to count as being valuable. And even if we stick to Finnis's *Objective List Theory* of human flourishing, it is not at all clear whether or not it is true that a general toleration – or even endorsement – by society of couples' engaging in non-procreative sex would impair a married couple's abilities to invest their procreative sex with the kind of meaning that would allow them to participate in the basic good of marriage when having such sex. It is perfectly possible that a general social toleration – or even endorsement – of non-procreative sex could end up investing procreative sex with huge significance for couples engaging in it. For example, in a society where contraception was widely available, a choice to engage in procreative sex may become hugely significant – a major step forward for the couple that indicates a heightened level of commitment to, and identification with, each other.

So it seems to us that it is possible for people reasonably to differ on the rights and wrongs of non-procreative sex, and other issues (such as abortion or euthanasia) where it is not clear what practical reasonableness requires of us. Finnis's failure to attend to this point – because of his confidence in the correctness of his own opinions[156] – means that he does not explain how we should deal with these reasonable differences of opinion. This seems to us to be a major weakness in his theory of law.[157]

CONCLUSION

Finnis's theory of natural law suffers from significant weaknesses. The weaknesses arise where Finnis has chosen to treat as clear what is controversial: what human flourishing involves, what the central case of law is (and that there is such a thing as the central case of law), and what practical reasonableness requires of us (outside cases where practical reasonableness requires us to contribute to the fostering of

---

[155] See below, pp. 209–10.

[156] See, for example, Finnis, 'Public reason, abortion, and cloning' (1997–98) 32 *Valparaiso University Law Review* 361.

[157] See Waldron, '*Lex satis iusta*' (1999–2000) 75 *Notre Dame Law Review* 1829, 1851–56.

the common good). However, that conclusion does *not* justify jettisoning Finnis's entire theory as a failure and not worth attending to. There are three major respects in which Finnis's theory of law is indispensable: (1) his account of human flourishing provides us with a vital starting point for thinking intelligently about what it means for a human being's life to go well; (2) his account of why we might need authority figures to solve co-ordination problems seems to us faultless; as does (3) his account of the features of law which mean that law is the most suitable vehicle for the exercise of authority to solve co-ordination problems. Any theory of law that does not build on points (1), (2) and (3) will suffer from far more significant weaknesses than Finnis's theory does.

Further Reading

Finnis, *Natural Law and Natural Rights* (Oxford University Press: 1st edn, 1980; 2nd edn, 1991), chs III–VI, IX–X, XII, Postscript (2nd edn only): 415–25, 446–59, 467–72.

Finnis, 'Law as coordination' (1989) 2 *Ratio Juris* 97.

Finnis, 'Law, morality and "sexual orientation"' (1995) 9 *Notre Dame Journal of Law, Ethics and Public Policy* 11.

Finnis, 'Is natural law theory compatible with limited government?' in George (ed.), *Natural Law, Liberalism and Morality* (Oxford University Press, 1996).

Finnis, 'Law and what I truly should decide' (2003) 48 *American Journal of Jurisprudence* 107.

6

ADJUDICATION AND INTERPRETATION

In this chapter, we move away from debates surrounding the nature of law to debates about what courts do and should do within a legal system. For some, debates about what courts do and should do *are* debates about the nature of law, as they identify law with what the courts do and should do. On one view (which is associated with Ronald Dworkin), the courts always apply the law to resolve the cases that are brought before them, and they should apply the law to resolve those cases. On another view (associated with Oliver Wendell Holmes[1] and the 'legal realist' school of legal theory), law is to be identified with whatever the courts do in resolving cases that come before them. As we will see, H.L.A. Hart was sceptical of both of these views, dubbing the first view 'the noble dream' of cases always being decided impersonally by application of the law, and the second view 'the nightmare' of cases being decided according to the personal predilections of the judge without any kind of legal regulation of how the judge decides the case.[2] For Hart, deciding cases sometimes involves applying the law to resolve the case, but at other times it involves a judge deciding what the law will or should say in the case at hand. Each of the two debates discussed in this chapter offer us an opportunity to see which of these views of how judges operate is correct. The first debate is about how judges decide 'hard cases' – that is, cases where it is not clear what the law says in relation to that case. The second debate is about how judges should interpret statutory provisions.

Debate 1

How do the courts decide hard cases?

This question was popularised by Ronald Dworkin, in seeking to attack the model

---

[1] See Holmes, 'The path of the law' (1896–97) 10 *Harvard Law Review* 457, 461: 'The prophecies of what the courts will do in fact, and nothing more pretentious, are what I mean by the law.'
[2] Hart, 'American jurisprudence through English eyes: the nightmare and the noble dream' (1977) 11 *Georgia Law Review* 969.

of judicial decision-making set out by H.L.A. Hart in Chapter VII of *The Concept of Law*. So we will give Dworkin the honour of defining what a 'hard case' actually is. Dworkin actually offered two definitions; either one is fine for our purposes:

> A case 'is a hard case [where] no settled rule dictates a decision either way ...'.[3]

> A hard case is one 'in which reasonable lawyers will disagree about rights, and neither will have available any argument that must necessarily convince the other.'[4]

The available literature actually provides us with four models of how courts decide hard cases.

THE FOUR MODELS

The first model is *Hart's Model*. For Hart, a case would count as hard because the law had run out to determine the outcome of the case – either because there was literally no law governing that case (a 'gap' case) or because the language in which the legal rule applying to that case was expressed was such that it was uncertain how the rule applied in that case (an 'uncertainty' case). Whatever the reason, when the law ran out to determine the outcome of a case, a judge could only decide that case by determining what the law *should* say in that case. The judge, in deciding the case, would exercise a law-making power, whereby he not only got to determine what the law said in the case before him, but all like cases that would come up in future.

The second model is *Dworkin's Model*. As has already been noted, Dworkin's Model was developed in reaction to Hart's Model. For Dworkin, even in a hard case the law *never* runs out to determine the outcome of that case. While the existing precedents and statutes might not expressly say how the law applies in a hard case, the *principles* underlying those precedents and statutes have legal force and point to what the legally right answer will be in a hard case. We determine what principles are part of our law by seeing which principles provide the best explanation of the existing precedents and statutes, where what counts as the 'best' explanation is determined along two dimensions – does a given principle 'fit' the existing precedents and statutes, and does it provide an appealing explanation of why the precedents and statutes say what they say? Dworkin came to dub this theory of how one determines what the law says in a particular case – even a hard case – 'law as integrity':

> 'Judges who accept the interpretive ideal of integrity decide hard cases by trying to find, in some coherent set of principles about people's rights and duties, the best constructive interpretation of the political structure and legal doctrine of their community. They try to make that complex structure and record the best these can be. It is analytically useful to distinguish different dimensions or aspects of any

---

[3] Dworkin, 'Hard cases' in *Taking Rights Seriously* (Duckworth, 1977), 83
[4] Dworkin, 'Introduction' in *Taking Rights Seriously* (Duckworth, 1977), xiv.

working theory. It will include convictions about fit and justification. Convictions about fit will provide a rough threshold requirement that an interpretation of some part of the law must meet if it is to be eligible at all ... That threshold will eliminate interpretations that some judges would otherwise prefer, so the brute facts of legal history will in this way limit the role any judge's personal convictions of justice can play in this decisions. Different judges will set this threshold differently.'[5]

The third model is *Raz's Model*. As we will see, one of Dworkin's main criticisms of Hart's Model is that it seems to give judges too much discretion to decide for themselves what the law should say in a hard case. Moreover, that feature of Hart's Model runs counter to what judges say in deciding hard cases: that even if the case is not covered by the existing precedents and statutes, they are still constrained by the law in how they decide that case. Raz's Model was designed as an 'upgrade' on Hart's Model to overcome these criticisms. On Raz's Model, when the courts decide a hard case they are – contrary to what Dworkin argued – exercising a law-making power: they are determining what the law should say in that case and exercising a power to make the law say what they think it should say in the case they are deciding. However, that law-making power is what Raz calls a *directed power*: the law-making power is coupled with a duty to exercise it in a particular way, to achieve certain objectives.[6] What those objectives might be would depend on the legal system. The objective could be to develop the law in a way that is coherent with the present state of the law: in which case, judicial decision-making in a hard case under Raz's Model would not differ that greatly from decision-making under Dworkin's Model, in substance though not perhaps in form. However, the duty might be to develop the law in a way that will make things go best – in which case, judicial decision-making in a hard case under Raz's Model would strongly resemble judicial decision-making under Hart's Model. It would all depend on what had been adopted as the common practice by judges in exercising their law-making powers in deciding hard cases.

The fourth model is the *Realist Model*. In presenting the Realist Model, we have to acknowledge that it does not correspond precisely to the claims made by legal realists about how judges decide cases. For legal realists claim that judges decide *all* legal cases primarily in response to the facts of those cases.[7] So a legal realist would reject the distinction between an easy case and a hard case, because such a distinction presupposes that the law can have a role to play in determining the outcome of a case. For legal realists it never does: it is an illusion to think that the outcome of a particular case can ever be determined by the law. Ultimately, it is the facts of a case, rather than the law, that primarily determine who wins and who loses that case. It is this 'nightmarish' vision of judicial decision-making that H.L.A. Hart

---

[5] LE, 255 (see list of abbreviations, p. xiii).

[6] Raz, 'The inner logic of the law' in his *Ethics in the Public Domain* (Oxford University Press, 1994), 242.

[7] Brian Leiter calls this the 'Core Claim of Legal Realism': '*judges respond primarily to the stimulus of facts.*' (Leiter, 'Rethinking legal realism: toward a naturalized jurisprudence' in his *Naturalizing Jurisprudence* (Oxford University Press, 2007), 21 (emphasis in original).)

sought to rebut, first of all in Chapter VII of his *The Concept of Law* and then in his 'nightmare and the noble dream' piece.[8] Hart attacked the legal realist view of judicial decision-making as a distortion of what goes on in most cases where a judge decides a case:

> 'It is possible that, in a given society, judges might always first reach their decisions intuitively or "by hunches", and then merely choose from a catalogue of legal rules on which, they pretended, resembled the case in hand; they might then claim that this was the rule which they regarded as requiring their decision, although nothing else in their actions or words suggested that they regarded it as a rule binding on them. Some judicial decisions may be like this, but it is surely evident that for the most part decisions, like the chess-player's moves, are reached either by genuine effort to conform to rules consciously taken as guiding standards of decision or, if intuitively reached, are justified by rules which the judge was antecedently disposed to observe and whose relevance to the case in hand would generally be acknowledged.'[9]

However, even if Hart's criticism of the general claims of legal realists hit their mark, those claims can be recast as limited claims about how hard cases are decided, where Hart would concede that the law is of limited relevance to the outcome of the case. It is this version of legal realism that we refer to as the Realist Model. According to the Realist Model, judges decide a hard case primarily in response to the facts of that case. How is this view different from Hart's Model? Well, on Hart's Model judges decide a hard case by determining what the law should say in that kind of case and apply that understanding of the law to decide in favour of one of the parties to the case. On the Realist Model, judges don't decide hard cases in such a forward-thinking way. Instead, they focus on the past – what happened in the case – and their reactions to what happened in the case govern their decision as to which party will win.

THE DEBATE JOINED

Now that we have some familiarity with these four models for how judges decide hard cases, we can trace the main paths of the debates over which of these four models is correct. The debates in this area were primarily between Hart and Dworkin over which of *their* models was correct. As we have seen, Dworkin criticised Hart's Model on the basis that it does not correspond with the way judges actually decide hard cases.[10] But Dworkin made a further criticism of Hart's Model, which was that if Hart's Model were correct, then judges who decide hard cases always do an injustice to the party who loses the case. This is because on Hart's Model the judges decide who wins a hard case according to an understanding of the law that was not actually in force at the time the events that gave rise to that

---

[8] See above, n. 2.
[9] CL, 140–41.
[10] See Dworkin, 'The model of rules I' in his *Taking Rights Seriously* (Duckworth, 1977), and LE, 130–31.

case took place.[11] So, for example, in a hard case like *Riggs* v *Palmer*[12] – where the issue was whether a nephew should be allowed to inherit under the will of an uncle whom he murdered in order to stop the uncle making a new will and disinheriting him – if Hart's Model were correct, the judges who decided that case in favour of preventing the nephew inheriting under his uncle's will were doing so not on the basis of what the law *did* say at the time Elmer murdered his uncle but on the basis of what they thought the law *should have* said at that time.

Let's call the first objection to Hart's Model the *unreality objection*, and the second objection to Hart's Model the *retrospectivity objection*. In response to the unreality objection, Hart wondered how seriously we should take the idea that there are no legally unregulated cases and pointed to the many judges who have said extra-judicially that their function does involve a law-making function, contrary to the popular image of judges as always being concerned to apply the law.[13] Hart did admit in the Postscript to the second edition of *The Concept of Law* that:

> 'It is true that when particular statutes or precedents prove indeterminate, or when the explicit law is silent, judges do not just push away their law books and start to legislate without further guidance from the law. Very often, in deciding such cases, they cite some general principle or some general aim or purpose which some considerable relevant area of the existing law can be understood as exemplifying or advancing and which points towards a determinate answer for the instant hard case.'[14]

But this practice need not cause us to reject Hart's Model of how judges decide hard cases. Given the fact that hard cases only arise interstitially – in between areas where the law is clear and determinate – and that the responsibility of a judge in deciding a hard case (according to Hart's Model) is to decide that case in accordance with what he thinks the law *should* say in that case, it would be odd if a judge, in determining what the law should say in that case, did *not* have regard to the surrounding law within which his decision is going to have to fit in future.

In response to the retrospectivity objection, Hart argued that retrospectively applying a legal rule to a case is only objectionable where doing so would disappoint the legitimate expectations of the parties to that case that such a rule would not apply in that case. In a hard case, Hart pointed out, the parties could not have had any such legitimate expectations: the difficulty of knowing what the law said in that case meant that they could not have legitimately expected their case to be decided in a particular way.[15] Timothy Endicott has also addressed the issue of when it will be objectionable to change the law and apply the new law to an old

---

[11] See Dworkin, 'Hard cases' (above, n. 3), 84.
[12] See above, pp. 49–50.
[13] CL, Postscript, 274.
[14] Ibid.
[15] CL, Postscript, 276.

case. He has argued that doing so will not be objectionable so long as the change in the law does not make it impossible for people to be confident that acting on their current understanding of what the law says will not prove counter-productive or land them in trouble.[16] For example, consider the change in the law (if such it was) that was brought about in *Sorenson's Case*.[17] In that case – hypothetical, but based on a real case – 11 drug companies were all in the business of manufacturing and distributing a drug, inventum; the drug companies negligently failed to warn consumers of inventum of the possible and very serious side-effects from taking inventum; the claimant was injured as a result of taking inventum and suffering these side-effects; and it was impossible to determine which drug company produced the particular dose of inventum taken by the claimant. The courts found (in a novel ruling for which there was no precedent) that all the 11 drug companies were liable for the claimant's injuries in proportion to their share of the market for inventum. Endicott argues that it was not objectionable for the courts to change the law on when a claimant will be allowed to sue a defendant in negligence, and apply that new law to the old facts of *Sorenson's Case*, because holding the drugs companies liable for Mrs Sorenson's injuries *reinforces* rather than undermines the drugs companies' understandings of what they were required to do under the law, which was to take reasonable steps to ensure that people like Mrs Sorenson were not injured in taking inventum.[18]

With arguments such as these, Hart was able to fend off Dworkin's challenges to Hart's Model of how judges decide hard cases.[19] However, Hart's arguments indicate that Raz's Model of how hard cases are decided is clearly superior to Hart's. Raz's Model is able much more easily than Hart's Model to explain why judges might feel *legally* obliged (as opposed to morally obliged) not to 'push away their law books and start to legislate without further guidance from the law'[20] in deciding a hard case. Raz's Model is also able to *guarantee* that a judge will not exercise her law-making power in a hard case in a way that would give rise to objections of retrospectivity – because that law-making power could come with a legal duty not to exercise it in such an objectionable way – whereas all Hart could say of his model is that it wouldn't necessarily be the case that deciding a hard case according to his model would give rise to objections of retrospectivity.

So Dworkin's criticisms of Hart's Model may lead us to prefer Raz's Model to Hart's. But if the unreality objection and the retrospectivity objection lead us to prefer Raz's Model to Hart's, then we might prefer Dworkin's Model to either Raz's

---

[16] Endicott, 'The impossibility of the rule of law' (1999) 19 *Oxford Journal of Legal Studies* 1, 9.

[17] See above, pp. 19–20.

[18] See Endicott, 'Adjudication and the law' (2007) 27 *Oxford Journal of Legal Studies* 311, 317–18. Though could no objection from retrospectivity be made to a law that was passed in response to *Sorenson's Case*, requiring officers of the law to smash up the cars of the CEOs of the drugs companies that made the type of drug that injured Mrs Sorenson?

[19] Hart's response to a separate challenge, that giving judges law-making powers is undemocratic, can be found at CL, Postscript, 275 (that giving judges such powers might be an acceptable price to pay to deal with problems that cannot be easily dealt with at a legislative level).

[20] CL, Postscript, 274.

or Hart's, as Dworkin's Model makes perfect sense of the idea that the outcome of a hard case is legally regulated, and Dworkin's Model allows a judge to reassure an unsuccessful party in a hard case that his lack of success was due to the fact that the law *as it existed at the time of the facts that gave rise to the case* was not in his favour. However, before we leap to endorse Dworkin's Model, we should consider two objections to Dworkin's Model of how judges decide hard cases.

The first objection was made by Hart, as well as others; it goes as follows. If Dworkin's Model is correct, then the law determines the outcome of a hard case. But if that is right, then there must be one right answer to the question of what the law says in a hard case. Hart doubted whether one could say this.[21] For example, is it possible to say that the right answer in *Sorenson's Case* was that the negligent drug companies in that case should be held liable to Mrs Sorenson in proportion to their market share, and that any other answer in that case was wrong? (Other answers that could have been given in *Sorenson's Case* were: (1) don't allow Mrs Sorenson to sue anyone; (2) allow her only to sue the drug companies that did the research into inventum's side-effects and allow her to sue them jointly and severally for the full extent of her injuries; (3) allow her to sue all 11 drug companies for compensation for her injuries in proportion to their wealth on the basis that the wealthier companies were in a better position to detect the side effects of inventum than the less wealthy; (4) assess how much money each drug company should be made to pay to punish them for their negligence in manufacturing and distributing inventum, order the companies to pay their 'fines' into a common fund, and then divide the sum between Mrs Sorenson and anyone in the same boat first on the basis of need, and then, if anything is still left over, equally.)

Dworkin tried to argue, in response to this criticism, that there had to be one right answer to legal questions like 'Is there a valid contract here or not?' as lawyers are committed to the idea that contracts are either valid or invalid, and there is no space in between for someone to say either (1) that a contract might be neither valid nor invalid (but something else), or for someone to say (2) that the concept of a contract being valid or invalid is inherently vague so that there will sometimes be contracts where it is not possible to say with certainty whether the contract is valid or invalid.[22]

This is correct, but not all legal questions come as neatly packaged as the question 'Is there a valid contract here or not?' The question in *Sorenson's Case* 'Is anyone liable to Mrs Sorenson here, and if so for how much?' does not admit of only two opposed answers, one of which must be right and one of which must be wrong. Moreover, a lot of legal cases involve disputes about what question the case turns on, with one party arguing that the case turns on the question 'Is there a

---

[21] Hart, 'American jurisprudence through English eyes: the nightmare and the noble dream' (above, n. 2), 984–85; Hart 'Problems of the philosophy of law' in his *Essays in Jurisprudence and Philosophy* (Oxford University Press, 1983), 108.

[22] Dworkin, 'Is there really no right answer in hard cases?' in his *A Matter of Principle* (Oxford University Press, 1985).

valid contract here or not?' and the other party arguing that the case turns on the question 'Whether or not there was a valid contract here, was it reasonable for me to rely on the other party's promise?' It is unclear that there can only be one right answer to questions about what questions are relevant to the outcome of a case.

Questions about what questions are relevant to the outcome of a case are questions about what legal rules and principles apply to that case. John Finnis has argued that if we adopt Dworkin's theory of how we determine what legal rules and principles apply to a particular case then we *have* to reject the one right answer thesis:

> 'Hercules himself, no matter how superhuman, could not justifiably justify unique correctness for his answer to a hard case ... For in such a case, a claim to have found the right answer is senseless, in much the same way as it is senseless to claim to have identified the English novel which meets the two criteria "shortest and most romantic" (or "funniest and best", or "most English and most profound"). Two incommensurable criteria of judgment are proposed – in Dworkin's theory, "fit" (with past political decisions) and "justifiability" (inherent substantive moral soundness) ... [I]n the absence of any metric which could commensurate the different criteria (the dimensions of fit and inherent moral weight), the instruction to "balance" [these criteria] ... can legitimately mean no more than bear in mind, conscientiously, all the relevant factors, and *choose*.' [23]

The second objection made to Dworkin's Model is that in arguing that there is one right answer to hard cases, Dworkin is being disingenuous. The one right answer that Dworkin argues determines the outcome of any given case always magically happens to be the one that corresponds with Dworkin's own political views. So – the objection goes – Dworkin's Model is not intended to help us understand how judges decide hard cases, but to help Dworkin smuggle his political views into the law by persuading judges to adopt his model of how judges decide cases.[24]

Dworkin responded to this objection by arguing that: (1) applying his theory to determine what the law says on a particular issue did not always produce results that corresponded with his own views as to what the law should say on those issues;[25] (2) when Dworkin applied his model for deciding hard cases to determine what the law said on a particular issue, it was inevitable that the conclusions *he* reached would be influenced by *his* political views as Dworkin's Model requires people who want to determine what the law says in a hard case to take their own political views into account in deciding what interpretation of the law cast the community's past political decisions in its most appealing light.[26]

---

[23] Finnis, 'Reason and authority in *Law's Empire*' (1987) 6 *Law and Philosophy* 357, 372, 374.

[24] See Kennedy, *A Critique of Adjudication: Fin de Siècle* (Harvard University Press, 1997), 127–28 for an example of this criticism.

[25] Dworkin, 'Introduction' in his *Freedom's Law: The Moral Reading of the American Constitution* (Oxford University Press, 1996), 36.

[26] Ibid, 37.

Point (1) is not really relevant to this second objection to Dworkin's Model: the accusation is not that Dworkin's theory of law is designed to ensure liberal conclusions to all legal questions, but just to legal questions arising in hard cases, where legal argument might make a difference to the outcome of those cases. And point (2) hardly refutes the critics' case against Dworkin; if anything it simply restates it. Moreover, it would be easier to accept point (2) in the way Dworkin wants us to take it – as saying that Dworkin is inviting people of *all* political persuasions to interpret the law in light of *their* views of what justice, fairness and procedural due process require, in the same way that Dworkin interprets the law in light of *his* views of what these values require – if Dworkin had not been so savagely critical of conservative judges who took up his invitation and sought to interpret the American Constitution in light of a conservative view of what justice, fairness, and procedural due process require.[27]

Given these criticisms, there does not seem much of a case for preferring Dworkin's Model to Raz's Model. Under Raz's Model, we have no need to endorse the one right answer thesis as the law does not determine what the outcome of a hard case will be; the law merely prescribes various objectives and conditions that a judge has to take into account in deciding what the law will say in that case. And there is no possibility of anyone arguing that Raz's Model has been reverse engineered to encourage judges to decide hard cases in a particular way, as Raz's Model is perfectly neutral on *what* objectives and conditions judges will have to take into account in deciding a hard case – that will depend on the particular legal system within which a judge is operating, and what conventions have been adopted among the judges in that legal system as to how the job of deciding a hard case is to be approached.

So if we had to choose between Hart's, Dworkin's, and Raz's Models as to how hard cases are decided, we would favour Raz's Model. However, there is a fourth model available to us – the Realist Model. Should we prefer Raz's Model to the Realist Model? At this point, we need to remind ourselves of what this debate is about – it is a debate about what *does* happen when judges decide hard cases, not about what *should* happen. There is no doubt that we should normally prefer judges to decide hard cases in accordance with Raz's Model rather than the Realist Model – in a reasonably just legal system, fairness to the parties to a case demands that the law regulate (though it may not determine) the outcome of the case, rather than allowing the outcome of a case to be determined simply by the judges' reactions to the facts of the case. However, it must be admitted that *in practice* the Realist Model seems to give a more accurate account of how judges decide hard cases than Raz's Model does. For example, Robert Goff – one of the most distinguished and articulate judges of the past 40 years – remarks that:

[27] See, for example, Dworkin, 'The Court's embarrassingly bad decisions', May 26, 2011, *New York Review of Books*.

'If I were asked what is the most potent influence upon a court in formulating a statement of legal principle, I would answer that in the generality of instances it is the desired result in the particular case before the court.'[28]

And Brian Leiter observes that:

'Recently I had occasion to ask a litigation partner at a local firm – a very capable attorney – with no jurisprudential instincts or training whatsoever – whether he thought appellate courts decided cases on the law or based on what they thought were the right results given the underlying facts of the case. He thought it was obviously the latter, not the former. A systematic empirical study on this point would be interesting, but all my anecdotal evidence to date – combined with my own litigation experience – makes me confident that the Realists had it right.'[29]

Leiter's experience corresponds with our own: all practising judges and barristers that we have met seem to endorse the Realist Model. If this is right, then the conventions that Raz sees as regulating the outcome of a decision in a hard case may really just be conventions as to how the decision in a hard case – which has actually been arrived at in response to the facts of that case – should be explained and presented to the outside world.

CONCLUSION

Our conclusion will be an unpopular one. The Realist Model seems to provide a more faithful account of how judges actually decide hard cases than any other model on offer. However, if we are unhappy with this conclusion, the solution is not to deny the truth of the Realist Model but to encourage judges to approach hard cases in a different way. Recruiting fewer judges from the ranks of barristers – who are past masters at framing legal arguments to fit the results that they want to achieve – may be a good start in this direction.

Debate 2

How should the courts interpret a statute?

Before launching into this second debate, we should note a difference in the way this debate is framed as compared with the previous one. As we have just noted, the previous debate was a debate about what *does* happen, rather what *should* happen. This debate is about what *should* happen. So why the difference? The difference arises out of the significance of these two debates for American legal theorists.

---

[28] Goff, 'The search for principle' (1984) 69 *Proceedings of the British Academy* 169, 183.
[29] Leiter, 'Legal realism and legal positivism reconsidered' in his *Naturalizing Jurisprudence* (Oxford University Press, 2007), 77, fn. 70. Though it cannot be ruled out that the judges are unconsciously guided by the values immanent in the law in responding to the facts of a particular case.

For such theorists, the first – descriptive – debate about how judges actually decide hard cases promises to shed some light on the nature of law. (It should be noted that most non-American legal theorists would deny that inquiries into how judges decide hard cases will tell us anything about the nature of law.) For American legal theorists, the second – normative – debate is of vital importance because of the way the United States Constitution controls the exercise of governmental power in the United States, to the extent that legislation passed by both Houses of Congress and signed by the President may be declared invalid by the US Supreme Court if it violates some provision of the Constitution – in particular, the Bill of Rights (which is made up of the first 10 amendments to the Constitution) and the Fourteenth Amendment to the Constitution, which was passed in the aftermath of the American Civil War and provides that no 'State [shall] deprive any person of life, liberty, or property, without due process of law; nor deny to any person within its jurisdiction the equal protection of the laws.' The question of how provisions like these should be interpreted is therefore a highly political issue in the United States, as the answer to that question has major implications for what the American government is, and is not, allowed to do.

Let's now turn to the major schools of thought in this debate. Just as with the previous debate, we can identify four different models of statutory interpretation that different theorists think should be adopted when we interpret a statute.

FOUR MODELS OF STATUTORY INTERPRETATION

We can call the first model the *Plain Meaning Model*. According to this model of statutory interpretation, we should simply give effect to the statute's plain meaning; in a situation where it is not clear what the statute says, it does not apply. This model of statutory interpretation[30] is most closely associated with Justice Antonin Scalia, who was appointed to the US Supreme Court in 1986. Scalia's preferred model of statutory interpretation is, however, a variation on the Plain Meaning Model – he seeks to interpret provisions of the US Constitution in a way that gives effect to the *original* meaning of those provisions at the time they were incorporated into the Constitution.[31] So, for example, Scalia would never interpret the Eighth Amendment to the US Constitution (which, among other things, forbids the government from inflicting 'cruel and unusual punishments') as forbidding

---

[30] Though it is questionable whether simply giving effect to a statute's plain meaning involves any interpretation at all. For the view that the need to interpret only arises when there is room for argument as to what a legal rule says, see Endicott, 'Legal interpretation' in Marmor (ed.), *The Routledge Companion to Philosophy of Law* (Routledge, 2012), 112, 121; also Dummett, 'A nice derangement of epitaphs' in LePore (ed.), *Truth and Interpretation* (Oxford University Press, 1986), 464: 'when the hearer does not have to search for the speaker's meaning, but takes for granted that he is using words in just the way with which he is familiar, there is ... no process of interpretation going on' (quoted with approval in Marmor, *Interpretation and Legal Theory*, 2nd edn (Oxford University Press, 2005), 16).

[31] Scalia, *A Matter of Interpretation: Federal Courts and the Law* (ed. Gutmann) (Princeton University Press, 1997).

the use of capital punishment, as at the time the Eighth Amendment was incorporated into the US Constitution (1791), the death penalty was in common use. So in 1791 whatever 'cruel and unusual punishments' meant, that phrase did not cover capital punishment.

The second model is *Hart's Model*. Hart's Model tells judges that they should give effect to a statute's plain meaning where its meaning is clear, but if it isn't clear how the statute applies in a given situation, the judge should determine what the statute *should* say in the case at hand and give effect to the statute on the basis that it *does* say what it should say. So Hart's Model distinguishes between 'core cases' where it is clear how a given statutory provision applies, and 'penumbral cases' where it is not so clear.[32] To illustrate this point, Hart often referred to a rule forbidding vehicles from entering a park: 'No vehicles in the park'. A core case where it is plain that the rule will be violated is where someone drives a car into the park. Penumbral cases would occur where an ambulance is driven into the park to pick up someone who is having a heart attack, or where someone rides into the park on roller skates, or where a child brings a toy car into the park. In these cases, it is not certain whether the rule 'No vehicles in the park' applies or not. The Plain Meaning Model would say that the rule does not apply to these penumbral cases, as it is not clear that it does apply. However, Hart thought that it was open to a judge to *determine* whether or not the rule applied in these cases, by asking himself 'what the law ought to be'[33] or whether the penumbral case sufficiently resembles the core cases where the rule does apply, where the judgment of whether the resemblance is sufficiently close 'depend[s] on many complex factors running through the legal system and on the aims or purpose which may be attributed to the rule'.[34]

The third model is the *Intentionalist Model*. Under the Intentionalist Model, a judge will seek, in interpreting a statute, to give effect to the intentions of the law-makers who created that statute unless it would be unfair in some way to do so. On the Intentionalist Model, judges should normally give effect to the plain meaning of a statute as that is normally how the law-makers who created that statute intended it to be read. But if, in a particular case, it is not clear what the statute says or there is evidence that giving effect to the plain meaning of the statute would be inconsistent with the intentions of the law-makers who created that statute, then the judge should interpret the statute in a way that gives effect to those intentions unless doing so would be unfair because, for example, people reasonably believed that the statute would be read in some other way and they relied on that belief.[35]

---

[32] Hart, 'Positivism and the separation of law and morals' (1958) 71 *Harvard Law Review* 593, 607–608; CL, 126.

[33] Hart, 'Positivism and the separation of law and morals' (above, n. 32), 608.

[34] CL, 127.

[35] See Duxbury, *Elements of Legislation* (Cambridge University Press, 2013), 125–26.

The fourth model is *Dworkin's Model*. According to Dworkin's Model for interpreting statutes – as set out in his book *Law's Empire*[36] – his ideal judge, *Hercules*, must seek, in interpreting a statute, not only to come up with an interpretation that will 'fit and explain the text of the statute itself'[37] but also one that will cast the process of enacting that statute in its best light. In other words, the judge's interpretation will assume that that statute was enacted in accordance with 'his convictions about the ideals of political integrity and fairness and procedural due process as these apply specifically to legislation in a democracy'[38] and his interpretation of the statute will seek to live up to that assumption. This means that not only will the words of the statute be relevant to its interpretation, but also the legislative history of the statute and statements made about the statute in the course of its passage through the legislature:

> '[Hercules] acknowledges that legislation is seen in a better light, all else being equal, when the state has not misled the public; for that reason he will prefer an interpretation that matches the formal statements of legislative purpose, particularly when citizens might well have made crucial decisions relying on these statements.'[39]

THE DEBATE JOINED

Which of these four models of statutory interpretation should we prefer? Debates over this issue have tended to involve an advocate for one model criticising another model. So, as we will see, Hart attacked the Plain Meaning Model as inferior to his model. Lon Fuller attacked Hart's Model as inferior to the Intentionalist Model. And Dworkin sought to show that anyone who signed up to the Intentionalist Model would have to end up giving effect to his model of statutory interpretation. If Hart, Fuller and Dworkin were all correct in their arguments, then that would indicate that we should prefer Dworkin's Model, on the basis that:

Plain Meaning Model < Hart's Model < Intentionalist Model < Dworkin's Model

However, as we will also see, while Hart scored a convincing victory over the Plain Meaning Model, it is not clear whether Fuller was successful in undermining Hart's Model. Given this, even if Dworkin was successful in showing that his model of statutory interpretation is superior to the Intentionalist Model, all that we can say is that:

---

[36] It is necessary to make it clear that when we are talking about Dworkin's Model, we are talking about the model for statutory interpretation set out in *Law's Empire*, as in Dworkin's later writings on statutory interpretation (most notably, his 'Comment' in Scalia, *A Matter of Interpretation* (above, n. 31), at 115–27, and 'Originalism and fidelity' in Dworkin, *Justice in Robes* (Harvard University Press, 2006)) he seemed to switch to an Intentionalist Model of statutory interpretation. For further discussion of this point, see Goldsworthy, 'Dworkin as an originalist' (2000) 17 *Constitutional Commentary* 49.

[37] LE, 314.

[38] LE, 338.

[39] LE, 346.

Plain Meaning Model < Hart's Model
Intentionalist Model < Dworkin's Model

We cannot infer from this that Dworkin's Model is superior to Hart's Model. The question of which model of statutory interpretation is correct has to be determined some other way.

Hart's criticisms of the Plain Meaning Model

Scalia's principal argument in favour of the Plain Meaning Model is a democratic one: under the Plain Meaning Model, the legislature gets to determine through its choice of language how its statutes will be read and an unelected judiciary is not allowed to add to or subtract from the enacted statute by determining what that statute *should* be read as saying in cases where it is unclear how the statute applies.[40] Hart argued against the Plain Meaning Model on the basis that:

> 'we should not cherish, even as an ideal, the conception of a rule so detailed that the question whether it applied or not to a particular case was always settled in advance, and never involved, at the point of actual application, a fresh choice between open alternatives.'[41]

The reason[42] why Hart thought that we should positively avoid thinking of rules as providing no opportunity for choosing how the rule should apply in penumbral cases was that legislators *always* labour under two handicaps in seeking to subject human conduct to rules.

The first is that they cannot anticipate every conceivable situation in which a given rule might apply and specify how the rule should apply in every conceivable situation.[43] The second is that a legislator who lays down a rule (say, against vehicles in the park) will do so because various considerations will indicate a need for the rule in the central cases where that rule will apply, but as we move to more peripheral cases, that balance of considerations may shift in favour of no rule applying – but the legislator will be unable, in framing the rule, to consider at what point that balance shifts. So legislators *need* the help of the judiciary to overcome these handicaps and ensure that a rule created by legislators is applied in a way that will take into account the facts that there will be (1) situations where the rule might seem to apply which were not anticipated by the legislators, and (2) situations where it will be difficult to tell whether the balance of considerations that was responsible for the rule being created in the first place counts in favour of the rule applying in those situations.

---

[40] Scalia, *A Matter of Interpretation* (above, n. 31), 13.

[41] CL, 128.

[42] See CL, 128–29.

[43] And ss. 44–50 of the Serious Crime Act 2007 show that if they try to do so, they may well end up producing something incomprehensibly complicated.

Hart went on to point out[44] that there will be occasions where wise legislators will recognise that these twin handicaps – of being unable to anticipate every situation where a rule might apply and of being unable to identify at what point the balance of considerations in favour of the rule start tipping in the opposite direction – are particularly severe, and on those occasions the legislators might lay down a general rule (such as that an employer should take reasonable care to ensure her employee's safety) and expressly invite the judiciary to determine how that rule will apply in concrete situations.

So the Plain Meaning Model of statutory interpretation is positively undesirable: it prevents judges providing legislators with the help they need to subject human conduct to rules in an intelligent way.

Fuller's criticisms of Hart's Model

While Hart rejected the Plain Meaning Model, his own model of statutory interpretation did not reject the idea that a statutory provision could have a plain meaning. His model was primarily concerned with how judges should handle penumbral cases where it was not clear how the statute applied. Fuller's criticisms of Hart's Model focused on the distinction Hart drew between cases where it was plain that the statutory provision applied and penumbral cases. Fuller argued that it was simply not possible *ever* to determine how a statutory provision applied without first asking what the purpose of that provision was. Cases where it seems obvious that a statutory provision applies are cases where our knowledge of what the purpose of that provision is *makes* it obvious that the provision applies.[45] So, Fuller argued, the Intentionalist Model of statutory interpretation is superior to Hart's Model as we cannot understand how a statutory provision applies without first inquiring into the intentions of the legislator in creating that provision.

Fuller gave two hypothetical examples where, he argued, applying Hart's Model would produce a counter-intuitive result. Only applying the Intentionalist Model will allow us to achieve the 'right' result in these examples. The first example took as its starting point Hart's imaginary ban on 'vehicles' in the park. Fuller asked whether the rule against vehicles in the park would apply to bar some war veterans from creating a war memorial in the park by mounting a fully working World War II truck on a pedestal.[46] A fully working motor vehicle would seem clearly to fall within a rule against vehicles in the park, but it seems counter-intuitive that the rule against vehicles in the park would apply in this kind of case. The Intentionalist Model tells us why: the purpose behind banning vehicles in the park is not engaged by the war veterans' plans. Under the Intentionalist Model, it seems obvious that the truck will *not* count as a 'vehicle'.

Fuller's second example was a rule against sleeping in a railway station. He contrasted two cases: (1) a passenger who was forced at 3 am to wait for a delayed

---

[44] See CL, 131–32.
[45] Fuller, 'Positivism and fidelity to law – a reply to Professor Hart' (1957) 71 *Harvard Law Review* 630, 663.
[46] Ibid.

train and who was found by a policeman sitting upright on a bench, snoozing gently; and (2) a man who had settled himself down in a railway station with a pillow and blankets, but had yet to fall asleep when he was found by a policeman.[47] On Hart's Model, a breach of the rule against sleeping in a railway station would plainly seem to have occurred in (1), but not in (2). Again, this seems counter-intuitive, and the Intentionalist Model tells us why: the purpose behind banning sleeping in railway stations would seem to indicate that the only person who should be held to have committed an offence in these situations is the man in (2), not the passenger in (1).

While Hart was initially resistant to the idea that interpreting a statute always involved (even subconsciously) considering what the purpose of that statute was,[48] in his later writings Hart seemed to concede Fuller's point.[49] However, other legal theorists – writing after Hart's debate with Fuller – have sought to defend the idea that words and sentences used in a rule can have a 'core' or 'settled' meaning that we can understand without inquiring into the purpose of the rule.[50] As Frederick Schauer points out, Fuller's example of the veterans seeking to create a war memorial actually helps to make this point. We know without thinking that the veterans' fully working truck counts as a 'vehicle' – and thus poses a problem for a rule banning vehicles from the park – because the conventions of our language establish that a fully working truck *is* a vehicle.[51] If this is right, then the superiority of the Intentionalist Model over Hart's Model cannot be established by arguing that we have no choice but to be intentionalists if we are to understand the words and sentences used in a rule. It must be established some other way.

Dworkin's modifications of the Intentionalist Model

In *Law's Empire*, Dworkin is not so much concerned to attack the Intentionalist Model[52] as to show that a judge – Dworkin calls him *Hermes*, after the Greek god of language – who is committed to the Intentionalist Model will eventually end up adopting something like Dworkin's Model of statutory interpretation. Dworkin's argument goes as follows.[53]

In order to give effect to the Intentionalist Model, Hermes will need to resolve a number of issues: (1) Whose intentions does he look at? (2) How does he determine

---

[47] Ibid, 664.

[48] See Hart, 'Positivism and the separation of law and morals' (above, n. 32), 614–15.

[49] See Hart, 'Introduction' to his *Essays in Jurisprudence and Philosophy* (Oxford University Press, 1983), at 7–8, conceding that the question of whether a rule applies to a particular situation does not depend on settled linguistic conventions, that 'the obvious or agreed purpose of a rule may be used to render determinate a rule whose application may be left open by the conventions of language', and that his 'failure to make this clear amounts, as Fuller argued ... to a defective theory of statutory interpretation ...'.

[50] Waldron, *Law and Disagreement* (Oxford University Press, 1999), 129; Schauer, 'A critical guide to vehicles in the park' (2008) 83 *New York University Law Review* 1109; Raz, *Between Authority and Interpretation* (Oxford University Press, 2009), chs 10–11.

[51] Schauer, 'A critical guide to vehicles in the park' (above, n. 50), 1122.

[52] This may be why Dworkin was so relaxed (in the writings adverted to at n. 36, above) about presenting himself as an intentionalist.

[53] LE, 315–37.

what their intentions were? (3) How does he decide whose intentions to give effect to when those intentions differ? Hermes' answers to questions (1) and (3) will be affected by his political convictions. On (1), he will look at the intentions of those he thinks should have a say in the political process, and will disregard the intentions of those who he does not think should have a say. On (3), where the intentions of the relevant law-makers and officials differed in relation to a particular piece of legislation, his views as to whose intentions with regard to that legislation should be allowed to prevail will depend on when he thinks it will be legitimate for the legislature to change the law – the intentions that make it legitimate to change the law will be the ones that count for Hermes.

On (2), Hermes will conclude that one can only determine what a law-maker's intentions were in passing some legislation by looking at that law-maker's general convictions, as revealed by the law-maker's record: 'He will ask what system of convictions provides overall the best justification for what she has done in office.'[54] And in summing the intentions of the law-makers and officials whose intentions count for Hermes in applying the Intentionalist Model, Hermes will need to find a way of determining what their collective convictions are. He finds this way when he realises that looking at 'the record of the legislature itself' will reveal the collective convictions of the law-makers and officials he is interested in. All he has to do is to ask 'what coherent system of political convictions would best justify what [the legislature] has done' to arrive at a fair view of what those law-makers and officials' convictions are.[55]

By this time, Dworkin claims, Hermes 'has become Hercules' twin'.[56] Hermes will, in interpreting a statute, seek to do so in a way that sees the statute as the product of a set of political convictions that both justify the process by which the legislature changes the law, and which present the legislative record of the legislature that passed that statute in its best light.

Dworkin's argument that Hermes must end up employing Dworkin's Method to interpret a statutory provision has recently been challenged by Richard Ekins in his book *The Nature of Legislative Intent*.[57] Ekins argues that a bill that is presented to a legislature for approval represents a coherent and reasoned plan for the community that is governed by that legislature.[58] If a majority in the legislature vote in favour of the bill, turning it into law, then they intend to adopt the plan that the bill sets out. So in interpreting a statutory provision, Hermes simply has to give effect to the plan that the statute containing that provision represents. One difficulty with this suggestion is – How is Hermes supposed to find out what the plan represented by the statute was?[59] Ekins denies that finding out what this plan was

---

[54] LE, 335.

[55] Ibid.

[56] LE, 337.

[57] Ekins, *The Nature of Legislative Intent* (Oxford University Press, 2012).

[58] Ibid, 230.

[59] See Goldsworthy, 'Legislative intention vindicated?' (2013) 33 *Oxford Journal of Legal Studies* 821, 828–29.

requires us to determine what anyone's intentions were in putting the plan together,[60] but this seems to suggest that the only thing that can tell us what the plan is, is the text of the statute that represents the plan. But then we are back where we started, with a problem about how the text of the statute is to be interpreted. And if finding out what the plan represented by the statute was *does* require us to inquire into the intentions of the plan-makers, then we are back with Dworkin's three questions that are designed to lead us ineluctably towards his model of statutory interpretation. So Ekins' arguments ultimately fail to show that Dworkin was necessarily wrong to claim that Hermes will become Hercules.

CONCLUSION

If Dworkin is right, and Hermes is destined to become Hercules, then we have at least winnowed down our four models of statutory interpretation to two contenders for the title of *the* method that we should adopt in interpreting a statute: Hart's Model and Dworkin's Model. Which of these we should choose probably comes down to what we value most. If we value integrity in our political institutions, then Dworkin's Model will come closer to achieving the integrity we prize than Hart's Model will. However, if we acknowledge – as Hart did – the importance of meeting

> 'the need for certain rules which can, over great areas of conduct, safely be applied by private individuals to themselves without fresh official guidance or weighing up of social issues, and the need to leave open, for later settlement by an informed, official choice, issues which can only be properly appreciated and settled when they arise in a concrete case.'[61]

then we will prefer Hart's Model.

Further Reading

Hart, CL, ch. VII.

Hart, 'American jurisprudence through English eyes: the nightmare and the noble dream' (1977) 11 *Georgia Law Review* 969.

Dworkin, *Taking Rights Seriously* (Duckworth, 1977), chs 2, 4 and 13.

Dworkin, LE, chs 7–10.

Fuller, 'Positivism and fidelity to law – a reply to Professor Hart' (1957) 71 *Harvard Law Review* 630.

Schauer, 'A critical guide to vehicles in the park' (2008) 83 *New York University Law Review* 1109.

---

[60] Ekins, *The Nature of Legislative Intent* (above, n. 57), 13.
[61] CL, 130.

7

THE OBLIGATION TO OBEY THE LAW

No work of Plato's better exemplifies Alfred North Whitehead's *dictum* that 'the European philosophical tradition ... consists of a series of footnotes to Plato'[1] than the *Crito*. The dialogue described in the *Crito* takes place in jail, in 399 BC. Socrates has been sentenced to death by an Athenian jury for corrupting the youth of Athens and for impiety. Crito, an elderly friend of Socrates', visits Socrates in jail two days before he is due to be executed, and urges Socrates to escape the death penalty by fleeing into exile. Crito will bribe Socrates' guards to induce them to let Socrates go, and will arrange for Socrates to live with friends of Crito in Thessaly, a region of Greece that resembled the American Wild West (without the guns or the hats). Socrates refuses to escape. He imagines what the Laws of Athens would say to him were he to do as Crito suggests, and concludes that it would be morally wrong not to submit to the death penalty imposed on him under those laws. In other words, Socrates concludes that he is morally obliged to abide by the laws of Athens.

The *Crito* is one of the first[2] discussions in Western literature of whether there is a moral obligation to obey the law that is in force in your country. One of the most remarkable features of that discussion is that virtually every single argument that has been made over the past 2,400 years in support of the idea that there is a moral obligation to obey the law can be found in the *Crito*. In this chapter, we will examine how strong those arguments are. The first debate we will look at is about whether there is a moral obligation to obey the just laws of a reasonably just state. If the answer is 'no' then there can be no such thing as a moral obligation to obey the law, because the case for saying there is such an obligation would be strongest in relation to the just laws of a reasonably just state. The subsequent debates that we will consider in this chapter focus on variations of the situation considered in the first debate. In the second debate, we look at whether there is a moral obligation to obey an unjust law of a reasonably just state. The third debate

---

[1] *Process and Reality* (Macmillan, 1929), 63.

[2] Not quite *the* first: Sophocles' play *Antigone*, written about 40 years before Socrates' execution, also deals with the same issue.

is about whether there is a moral obligation to obey the just laws of a wicked state. (We take it for granted that there can be no moral obligation to obey the unjust laws of a wicked state.)

Before we get into these debates, we need to make three points about the nature of the obligation we are looking at in this chapter. First of all, when we ask whether there is a moral obligation to obey the law, we are simply asking whether there is a *prima facie* obligation to obey the law, so that breaking the law would be morally wrong so long as everything else was equal.[3] We are not trying to establish – and no one has ever tried to establish – that there is an *absolute* obligation to obey the law, so that breaking the law would be morally wrong *in all circumstances*.

Secondly, when we ask whether there is a moral obligation to obey the law, we are asking whether – in a case where the law requires A to do *x* – it would be (prima facie) morally wrong for A not to do *x because* he is required under the law to do *x*. So establishing that it would be morally wrong for A not to do *x* because *x* is a good thing to do does not go anywhere near establishing that A has a moral obligation to obey the law that requires him to do *x*. That A has a moral obligation to do *x* is neither here nor there: we need to establish whether A has a moral obligation to do *x* simply because A happens to be required under the law to do *x*.

Thirdly, John Rawls followed H.L.A. Hart in making a peculiar[4] distinction between *duties* and *obligations*. *Obligations*, they both argued, arise because of the voluntary act of the person subject to the obligation.[5] *Duties* (or *natural duties*) are something that someone is subject to irrespective of what that person did. When *we* consider whether someone has an *obligation* to obey the law, we are *not* following the way Rawls and Hart used that term. We are *not* asking whether some voluntary act performed by A can result in A being morally required to obey the law. We are using the word obligation as a *synonym* for duty and could easily have entitled this chapter 'The duty to obey the law'. The reason we didn't is that most discussions of this topic use the word 'obligation' rather than 'duty'.

[3] In Smith, 'Is there a prima facie obligation to obey the law?' (1973) 82 *Yale Law Journal* 950, Smith says (at 951) that 'a person S has a prima facie obligation to do an act X if, and only if, there is a moral reason for S to do X which is such that, unless he has a moral reason not to do X at least as strong as his reason to do X, S's failure to do X is wrong.'

[4] See Green, 'Associative obligations and the state' in Burley (ed.), *Dworkin and His Critics* (Wiley-Blackwell, 2004), at 268–69, observing that the problem with Hart's and Rawls' distinction between obligations and duties 'is not that the distinction ... is incoherent but that it is unimportant ... [and] substantively idle ...'.

[5] Rawls, *A Theory of Justice* (Harvard University Press: 1st edn, 1971; rev'd edn, 1999), 113 (1971 edn), 97 (1999 rev'd edn): 'obligations ... arise as a result of our voluntary acts ...'; Hart, 'Legal and moral obligation' in Melden (ed.), *Essays in Moral Philosophy* (University of Washington Press, 1958).

Debate 1

Is there an obligation to obey the just laws of a reasonably just state?

In addressing this question, we have to be very careful to observe the second point made above about the obligation to obey the law. When we are asking whether there is an obligation to obey the just laws of a reasonably just state, we are asking whether there is an obligation to obey them not because they are just (and it would therefore be a good thing if those laws were complied with), but because they are laws. The literature on this question reveals seven basic arguments that have been made in favour of the proposition that there is a moral obligation to obey the just laws of a reasonably just state. We will consider in relation to each argument: (1) whether the argument is valid or not; and (2) if the argument is valid, how far does it go – does it indicate that *all* the just laws of a reasonably just state should be obeyed, or just *some* of them?

CONSENT

The first argument is that people living in a country have a moral obligation to obey the laws of that country because, by staying in that country, they have consented to obey the country's laws. This is a point repeatedly made by the Laws to Socrates, when he imagines in the *Crito* what they would say to him if he were to try to escape the punishment imposed on him by the Laws:

> 'any Athenian who wishes, once he has been admitted to adult status, and has observed the conduct of city business and ourselves, the Laws, may – if he is dissatisfied with us – go wherever he pleases and take his property. Not one of us Laws hinders or forbids that ... We do say, however, that if any of you remains here after he has observed the system by which we dispense justice and otherwise manage our city, then he has agreed with us by his conduct to obey whatever orders we give him.'[6]

The same argument was made by John Locke in §119 of his *Second Treatise of Government* (1689):

> 'every Man, that hath any Possession, or Enjoyment of any part of the Dominions of any Government, doth thereby give his tacit Consent, and is as far obliged to Obedience to the Laws of that Government, during such Enjoyment, as any one under it ...'

However, there are two problems with this argument. The first is that it is questionable how far someone can be said to have consented to obey a country's laws merely because he or she is living in that country. As David Hume observed in his 1748 essay 'Of the original contract': 'Can we seriously say, that a poor peasant or

---

[6] *Crito*, 51d-e; see also 52c: 'you emphatically opted for us, and agreed to be a citizen on our terms.'

artisan has a free choice to leave his country, when he knows no foreign language or manners, and lives, from day to day, by the small wages which he acquires?'[7] The second is that it is not clear how the mere fact of consent creates an obligation: if I consent to allow you to cut my hair, that does not mean that I am *obliged* to allow you to cut my hair. It is only if my consent is relied upon in some way that we could say that I have an obligation to do what I agreed to do. So we could say that a judge who agrees, through his judicial oath of office, to give effect to the laws of his country is then obliged to give effect to those laws because we, by allowing him to become a judge, are relying on him to give effect to those laws.[8] But there is no equivalent process of agreement plus reliance that could account for why an ordinary person has an obligation to obey the laws of the country in which he or she lives.

• GRATITUDE

The second argument is that someone living in a reasonably just country should be grateful for the benefits that he has received from living in that country, and as a result he should feel himself obliged to obey that country's laws which are, in part, responsible for his receiving those benefits. This argument can also be found in the *Crito*, where the Laws point out that 'We gave you birth, upbringing, and education, and a share in all the benefits we could provide for you along with all your fellow citizens.'[9] However, the problem with this argument was pointed out by Robert Nozick, who imagines that the people in your neighbourhood decide to set up a public entertainment system, with the entertainment being run each day by someone in the neighbourhood; a rota (which includes your name) determines who that is.[10] After 138 days of your enjoying the entertainment provided by your neighbours, your turn to run the entertainment system comes. Do you have an obligation to do your part? On these facts, Nozick does not think so and he seems to be right: when benefits are foisted on you without your asking for them, the mere fact that you have received those benefits cannot oblige you, even if you welcome those benefits being foisted on you when they come.

• HARM TO SOCIETY

The third argument is that someone living in a reasonably just country has an obligation to obey its reasonably just laws because disobeying those laws will encourage other people to disobey the law, with the result that the ability of the government to use law to provide us with various goods will be substantially

---

[7] The same argument is made in LE, 192–93 (see list of abbreviations, p. xiii).

[8] The judicial oath of office in the UK runs: 'I, ___, do swear by Almighty God that I will well and truly serve our Sovereign Lady Queen Elizabeth the Second in the office of ___, and I will do right to all manner of people after the laws and usages of this realm, without fear or favour, affection or ill will.'

[9] *Crito*, 51d.

[10] Nozick, *Anarchy, State and Utopia* (Basic Books, 1974), 93–94.

impaired. So the Laws in the *Crito* argue that if Socrates attempts to disobey the law, Athens will be 'overturned' and will as a result no longer 'exist'.[11] This seems very exaggerated. As Joseph Raz has pointed out:

> 'Law breaking is liable to undermine the effectiveness of the government in many cases. In others, violations of law have no such effect. Offenses never known to anyone or violating the interests of one private individual only, as with many torts and breaches of contract, generally do not diminish the government's effectiveness. There may be other reasons for conforming with the law in some of these cases, but the threat to the effectiveness of government and the law is not among them.'[12]

Critics of Raz's position have pointed to the undesirable effects that would result if everyone thought that they were free to disobey the law so long as doing so did not impair the effectiveness of government.[13] For example, Noam Gur has argued that when their own interests are at stake, people are unlikely to judge accurately what the effects of their law-breaking will be: their bias towards doing what is in their interests means that they may end up concluding, inaccurately, that their breaking the law will be harmless.[14] Given this, things would go best if people operated on the basis that they *always* have an obligation to obey the law. However, there is a difference between *thinking* that you have an obligation to obey the law and *having* an obligation to obey the law, and it does seem that arguments that purport to establish an obligation to obey the law based on the harm that law breaking does to law's ability to govern us do not go far enough to establish that someone *always* has an obligation to obey the reasonably just laws of a reasonably just state.

FAIR PLAY

There are actually three different versions of the 'fair play' argument for thinking that there is an obligation to obey the reasonably just laws of a reasonably just state.

The first version argues that someone who has initially agreed to let the law determine the outcome of a case in which he is involved has an obligation to abide by the law's verdict in that case. After all, if the verdict had been in his favour, he would have insisted on the law's verdict being respected; so fair play dictates that he respect the law's verdict if it is against him. This point applied particularly strongly in Socrates' case as he could have avoided the death penalty in his case, either by going into exile before his trial, or – after he had been found guilty – by

---

[11] *Crito*, 50b.

[12] Raz, 'The obligation to obey: revision and tradition' (1984–1985) 1 *Notre Dame Journal of Law, Ethics and Public Policy* 139, 149.

[13] See Boardman, 'Coordination and the moral obligation to obey the law' (1987) 97 *Ethics* 546; Finnis, 'Law as coordination' (1989) 2 *Ratio Juris* 97.

[14] Gur, 'Actions, attitudes, and the obligation to obey the law' (2013) 21 *Journal of Political Philosophy* 326, 337–43.

proposing that he be punished by being sent into exile. Instead, Socrates chose to stake his future on the Athenian legal process by first submitting to trial, and then proposing (after his initial proposal that he be punished by being given free meals by the city of Athens was rejected out of hand) that as his punishment he should be fined thirty minae of silver.[15] Given this, the Laws argued, Socrates had an obligation not to invalidate the verdict that was delivered in his case.[16] There does seem some merit to this argument, but it has very limited effect. It only establishes an obligation to abide by the verdict of a court where you in some way agreed to your case being taken to court.[17]

The second version of the fair play argument argues that you shouldn't be allowed to pick and choose which laws you will obey: it's unfair to take the benefits of the law when it is in your favour and refuse to assume the law's burdens when it is against you. If this argument is correct then we can recast Locke's argument in §119 of his *Second Treatise of Government* (1689) for there being an obligation to obey the law as being an argument from fair play rather than consent:[18] if you enjoy the benefits of living under a particular government by having 'Possession, or Enjoyment of any part of the Dominions of [that] Government' then fair play dictates that you should assume without complaint any burdens that that same government places on you. The difficulty with this argument is that it is not clear how much 'picking and choosing' is going on when someone benefits from the operations of the law. If *Driver* goes out for a drive in her car, she is benefiting from other people's observing the traffic laws, but *Driver* is not 'taking' those benefits: they are simply being thrust upon her as she goes out onto the road.

The third version of the fair play argument comes from H.L.A. Hart and John Rawls. This third version argues that you shouldn't refuse to shoulder certain legal burdens if you have in the past benefited from other people shouldering *those same* burdens themselves.[19] If this argument were correct, then that would establish that *Driver* has an obligation to obey the traffic laws when she goes out for a drive: having benefited from other people's restraint in obeying the traffic laws, she is now obliged to show the same restraint herself. However, there are two difficulties with this argument. The first is that Nozick's example of the neighbourhood public entertainment system[20] seems to show that the mere fact that you have benefited from other people taking on certain burdens does *not* mean that you have an obligation to shoulder those burdens yourself. The second is that this argument does

---

[15] This was equivalent to eight years' worth of the wages of an average Athenian at the time – so the equivalent of about £200,000 in today's money, given the average wage of someone working in the UK today.

[16] *Crito*, 50c.

[17] Given, as we will see later, that Socrates regarded exile from Athens as akin to death, there is room for questioning how voluntarily he was acting in both submitting to trial and in submitting to the possibility of being sentenced to death by failing to propose exile as his punishment.

[18] See Simmons, 'Tacit consent and political obligation' (1976) 5 *Philosophy and Public Affairs* 274, 291.

[19] Hart, 'Are there any natural rights?' (1955) 64 *Philosophical Review* 175, 185; Rawls, *A Theory of Justice* (above, n. 5), 96 (1971 edn), 111–12 (1999 rev'd edn).

[20] See above, p. 135.

not work to establish an obligation to obey a particular law where you have not benefited from other people obeying that law; nor does it seem to work where breaking a particular law will not actually harm the interests of people who have obeyed that law in the past.[21]

A DUTY TO AID JUST INSTITUTIONS

In *A Theory of Justice*, John Rawls thought that 'There is quite clearly no difficulty in explaining why we are to comply with just laws enacted under a just constitution.'[22] His main argument in favour of that view was not the argument from fair play that we have just considered, but his argument that we all have 'a fundamental natural duty ... to support and to comply with just institutions that exist and apply to us'.[23] One immediate problem with this view is the *locality* of this 'fundamental natural duty' – under it, we only have a duty to support the just institutions of the society in which we live. But why is this? – Why don't we have a duty to support just institutions wherever they exist?

Rawls thought that this fundamental natural duty arose out of the fact that if the members of a basically just society did not mutually acknowledge that they had a duty to do what they were required to do by that society's institutions, then the 'public conviction that all are tied to just arrangements would be less firm, and a greater reliance on the coercive powers of the sovereign might be necessary to achieve stability.'[24] In other words, if we could all trust each other to do our part under the rules of our society, then there would be less need for the government to intervene to make sure everyone does their part. So we have a special duty to support the just institutions of the society we live in because if we didn't acknowledge that we had such a duty then our society would become less stable and harder to maintain. No such harmful consequences would attend a failure to acknowledge that we have a duty to support the just institutions of some other society, such as France. However, Rawls' argument only seems to show that it would be desirable if we all *thought* we had a duty to support the just institutions of our society, not that we actually *do* have a duty to support those institutions.

Other theorists – notably Jeremy Waldron[25] and Christopher Wellman[26] – have sought to argue that we have a fundamental natural duty to support the just institutions of the society we live in because of the harms that would occur if such institutions did not exist. So Waldron argues that just institutions exist to prevent the conflicts that would otherwise occur between people, and that as those conflicts are likely to arise most often and are likely to pose most problems when

---

[21] See Smith, 'Is there a prima facie obligation to obey the law?' (above, n. 3), 956.

[22] Rawls, *A Theory of Justice* (above, n. 5), 350 (1971 edn), 308 (1999 rev'd edn).

[23] Ibid, 115 (1971 edn), 99 (1999 rev'd edn).

[24] Ibid, 334 (1971 edn), 294 (1999 rev'd edn).

[25] Waldron, 'Special ties and natural duties' (1993) 22 *Philosophy and Public Affairs* 3.

[26] Wellman, 'Samaritanism and the duty to obey the law' in Wellman and Simmons, *Is There a Duty to Obey the Law?* (Cambridge University Press, 2005).

the conflicts are between people who live near each other, it is especially urgent –
as a matter of justice – that people who live near each other create just institutions
to deal with the conflicts that will arise between them. This accounts for why
people who live in the same society have a special duty to support the just institutions of their society, as it is particularly important – again, as a matter of justice –
that people who live near each other are governed by just institutions. Wellman
argues that we would all be in peril if we lived in a state of nature, and if we are to
avoid that danger we need there to be 'general compliance with a single authoritative set of rules to secure peace and protect basic moral rights'.[27] The natural duty
that we all have to come to the aid of others in peril requires that we play our part
in ensuring that general compliance, and that means we have a moral obligation
to obey the just laws of the just institutions in our society.

Waldron's and Wellman's positions have been attacked by A. John Simmons.[28]
Simmons argues that Waldron's view that we pose a special threat to our neighbours, which accounts for why we have a special duty to support the just institutions that remove that particular threat, is 'inherently implausible and a bit
dated'.[29] It is people who are strangers to us who we are most likely to treat
unjustly. As for Wellman, Simmons asks why we cannot comply with our moral
duty to aid those who would be put in danger if we existed in a state of nature by
simply refraining from engaging in the violence, deception and other kinds of
harm-causing activities that would endanger people in a statute of nature.[30]
Wellman's arguments simply cannot support a general obligation to obey the just
laws of a just society, when such laws may do a lot more than just forbid us from
engaging in the sort of behaviour that would endanger other people in a state of
nature.

ASSOCIATIVE OBLIGATIONS

We have already seen that, for Ronald Dworkin, law – of its very nature – has *force*:
'law provides a justification *in principle* for official coercion.'[31] But it would seem
that for this to be true, there would have to be a moral obligation to obey the law.
If there were not, then law would provide a moral justification for coercing people
into doing what they have no moral obligation to do; which seems like a contradiction in terms. So the question of how there could be a moral obligation to obey
the law was of pressing concern for Dworkin's legal theory.

Dworkin sought to argue that legal duties were morally binding because legal
duties were forms of associative obligation – obligations that you have by virtue of
your membership of some group or community. The classic example of associative

---

[27] Ibid, 45.
[28] Simmons, 'The duty to obey and our natural moral duties' in Wellman and Simmons, *Is There a Duty to Obey the Law?* (above, n. 26).
[29] Ibid, 174.
[30] Ibid, 188.
[31] LE, 110.

obligations are the obligations that family members owe each other. So people have an obligation to look after their parents if the parents are now too old to look after themselves. A son or daughter whose parents cannot look after themselves never agreed to be subject to such an obligation, and never asked to be born to parents who now cannot look after themselves – but they are still obliged to look after their parents.

There is some support in the *Crito* for the idea that an obligation to obey the law can be spun out of the idea that legal duties are akin to other forms of associative obligation. So at one point in their imaginary dialogue with Socrates, the Laws of Athens compare themselves with Socrates' parents, saying that that they are 'more precious and venerable' than 'your mother and father and all your other forebears',[32] and that if Socrates disobeyed the law he would be 'disobeying us as his parents'.[33] However, Dworkin never actually establishes that legal duties are forms of associative obligation. All he does is set out[34] four properties legal duties would have to have *if* they were to count as forms of associative obligation: (1) they must be special to a particular group; (2) they must apply to individuals within the group; (3) they must reflect some kind of concern for the well-being of other people in the group; (4) they must reflect an equal concern for the other people in the group. But even if legal duties have all these properties – which is something that virtually no one other than Dworkin would accept – that does not necessarily mean they amount to associative obligations. It may be that having properties (1)–(4) is a necessary *but not sufficient* condition for something to amount to an associative obligation. It is likely that this is the case: that there are other properties that a given set of duties have to have to count as associative in nature. After all, we do not think that the duties we owe members of our families are morally binding on us just because they possess properties (1)–(4). If this is right, familial duties must have some other property that makes them associative in nature.

One possibility is that familial duties express and bring order to the emotional feelings that family members possess for one another. They help us express those feelings in a proper way by telling us what someone with those feelings for another is required to do for that other. They also tell us what we are not required to do, thereby safeguarding us from the kind of emotional blackmail that people with an emotional hold on us might otherwise be tempted to engage in. If this is right, then even on Dworkin's theory of law, legal duties cannot count as associative obligations as the members of the political communities that are governed by law rarely feel any kind of emotional bond towards each other.[35]

---

[32] *Crito*, 51b.

[33] *Crito*, 51e.

[34] At LE, 199–201.

[35] As Dworkin admits in LE, 201; see further, Simmons, 'Associative political obligations' (1996) 106 *Ethics* 247.

Another possibility is that familial duties owe their force to the fact that it is good for us to be subject to them: that being subject to these duties and trying to live up to them stretches our personalities in desirable ways by forcing us to try to develop certain desirable virtues (generosity, thoughtfulness, courage, objectivity) that will make it easy for us to live up to these duties.[36] Does living under the rule of law stretch our personalities in a similar way, so that we could say that legal duties share this property with familial duties, and can therefore count as associative obligations? If legal duties conform to Dworkin's account of them – as expressing a coherent conception of what it means to treat other people with equal concern and respect – then we might be able to say that they do. Living under the rule of law (as conceived by Dworkin) forces us to learn to live with other people on the basis that they are our equals, and it may be an intrinsically desirable thing for us to learn to live with other people on that basis, in the kind of society where, as Aristotle says, 'the honourable and just thing is to rule and to be ruled in turn.'[37] However, this assumes that legal duties *do* conform to Dworkin's account of them – and most legal theorists would argue that there is nothing in the nature of legal duties that *requires* that they give effect to a coherent conception of what it means to treat people with equal concern and respect.

IDENTITY

The seventh, and final, argument in favour of there being a general obligation to obey the just laws of a just society locates the root of that obligation in a duty to ourselves. The idea is that if you break the laws of the society you live in, you betray yourself by destroying your understanding of who you are. As a law breaker, you can no longer identify yourself as being an upstanding citizen of the society in which you live – you are forced, whether you like it or not, to abandon that understanding of who you are, and will find it very difficult to arrive at an alternative understanding of who you are. If you cannot, then you will be bereft of an identity, and will have destroyed the person you once were without being able to console yourself that, by doing so, you put a new and better version of yourself in its place.

There are strong echoes of this argument throughout the *Crito*. When Crito is urging Socrates to flee to Thessaly, he tells Socrates: 'don't let it trouble you ... that you wouldn't know what to do with yourself if you went into exile'[38] – thereby acknowledging the kind of rootlessness that Socrates would plant inside himself were he to disobey the law. The Laws of Athens later on make the same point in their imaginary dialogue with Socrates, arguing that 'Thessaly ... is a region of the utmost disorder and licence'[39] and asking Socrates what he would do there. Earlier

---

[36] For this suggestion, see Perry, 'Associative obligations and the obligation to obey the law' in Hershovitz (ed.), *Exploring Law's Empire: The Jurisprudence of Ronald Dworkin* (Oxford University Press, 2009).

[37] Aristotle, *Politics*, 1325^{b}7–8. Cf. LE, 189.

[38] *Crito*, 45c.

[39] *Crito*, 53d.

on in the dialogue, the Laws make an interesting comparison between the obligation to obey the Laws and the obligation of a soldier not to desert his position. The comparison is interesting because in Socrates' last dialogue before being executed (by drinking hemlock) – the *Phaedo* – Socrates makes a comparison between suicide and a soldier running away from his position.[40] So if these comparisons hold good, then for Socrates failing to obey the laws of his home country was a form of suicide.

Joseph Raz admits that someone can come to acquire an obligation to obey the laws of one's community by 'identifying with or belonging to the community'.[41] Someone who identifies with their community can acquire an 'attitude toward the community's organization and laws' that Raz calls 'respect for law'. This attitude involves 'a belief that one is under an obligation to obey because the law is one's law, and the law of one's country.' This attitude of 'respect for law'

> 'grounds a quasi-voluntary obligation. An obligation to obey the law is in such cases part and parcel of one's attitude toward the community. One feels that one betrays the community if one breaks the law to gain advantage, or out of convenience, or thoughtlessness, and this regardless of whether the violation actually harms anyone ...'[42]

This obligation, for Raz, is 'quasi-voluntary' because there is no 'moral duty to feel a sense of belonging in a community; certainly there is no obligation to feel that one belongs to a country ...'[43] So it is an entirely contingent matter whether one acquires the attitude of 'respect for law', just like it is an entirely contingent matter whether one becomes friends with a particular individual or not. Alasdair MacIntyre would question whether this is true. In his 1984 Lindley Lecture on the virtue of patriotism,[44] MacIntyre argued that you can only act as a moral agent – someone who is capable of reasoning about what you ought to do – within a moral community that gives you a life-long education in the moral rules that underpin life in that community, and allows you to experience various goods that result from observance of those moral rules. If this is right, then it follows that being loyal to one's community *is* a moral necessity: 'Detached from my community, I will be apt to lose my hold upon all genuine standards of judgment. Loyalty to that community ... is on this view a prerequisite for morality.'[45]

If MacIntyre's arguments are right, then breaking the law of the community we live in may trigger a sense of moral disorientation that should at least give one pause for thought before deciding to break the law. However, someone may be exposed to a variety of different moral communities in his life (at home, at school,

---

[40] *Phaedo*, 62b.

[41] All quotes in this paragraph are from Raz, 'The obligation to obey: revision and tradition' (above, n. 12), 154.

[42] Ibid.

[43] Ibid.

[44] MacIntyre, 'Is patriotism a virtue?' in Primoratz (ed.), *Patriotism* (Humanity Books, 2002). (The lecture is also available on the Internet.)

[45] Ibid.

at work, at church) and may end up identifying with one particular community and its traditions. As a result of identifying with that particular community, he may both be led to break the law of the country in which he lives, and be able to break the law without in any way endangering his identity as a moral agent. So as moral agents we would only *need* to identify with the country in which we grew up if that country was fairly homogenous in terms of the moral traditions and understandings maintained in that country. Needless to say, this tends not be the case in modern Western liberal societies.

CONCLUSION

None of the above seven arguments convincingly establish on their own that there is a general obligation to obey the just laws of a reasonably just state. However, it may be the case that these arguments, taken together, have enough going for them that in almost all situations we will have an obligation – for one reason or another – to obey the just laws of a reasonable just state, and not because of what those laws say, but because they are the law. It might, in fact, be morally taxing to work out, in any given situation when we are tempted to break the law, whether any of the above seven arguments apply to our situation to indicate that we have an obligation to obey the law we are tempted to break. Given this, we might do better – both in terms of doing the right thing and in terms of using our mental energies in the most productive way – if we simply *assumed* that we always had a moral obligation to obey the just laws of a reasonably just state. Certainly, it is difficult to think of situations where it is *obvious* that *none* of the above seven arguments apply to establish that one has an obligation to obey a reasonably just law of a reasonable just state. Consider the following example presented by M.B.E. Smith:

> 'let us assume that while driving home at two o'clock in the morning I run a stop sign. There is no danger, for I can see clearly that there was no one approaching the intersection, nor is there any impressionable youth nearby to be inspired to a life of crime by my flouting of the traffic code.'[46]

Smith thinks that, at worst, his running the stop sign amounts to a 'mere peccadillo'. However, it is arguable that various of the arguments canvassed above might generate a fairly strong obligation here to stop at the sign: while you 'can see clearly' that no harm will be done by running the stop sign, you might still be wrong and so stopping would be the morally wise thing to do; moreover, it might be desirable for you to subject yourself to the discipline of stopping even when – maybe especially when – there is no one else around to see what you are doing.

Timothy Endicott gives us an example of a 'wise electrician' who knows that the government has passed regulations requiring all home wiring to have Grade 5 insulation, but who uses the slightly cheaper Grade 4 insulation in connecting the ceiling light fixtures in his own home because when it comes to ceiling light

---

[46] Smith 'Is there a prima facie obligation to obey the law?' (above, n. 3), 971.

143

fixtures, Grade 4 is just as safe as Grade 5.[47] While Endicott thinks that the electrician does nothing wrong in disobeying the law when it comes to wiring his own home, it is possible to argue that doing so might result in people's disobeying the law on domestic wiring in future and make it harder for law-makers to achieve the goods that that law was directed at achieving. For this to happen, all it would take is for one of the wise electrician's customers to ask him 'So what wiring do you use for the ceiling light fixtures in your own home?' and the genie would be out of the bottle. The wise electrician would find it difficult to explain why he needs to use Grade 5 insulation in the customer's home while using Grade 4 insulation in his own home ('It's the law!' won't cut it, as the electrician has already shown that he is willing to break the law to save money when it comes to his own home) and would consequently find it difficult to resist the customer's demand that he use the cheaper Grade 4 insulation on the customer's ceiling light fixtures. And word might then spread from that customer to other customers that Grade 4 is all you need for your ceiling light fixtures, and the advantages of specifying a uniform standard for domestic wiring will be lost. Given this, the wise electrician might have quite a strong reason for using Grade 5 insulation on the ceiling fixtures in his own home.

Debate 2

Is there an obligation to obey an unjust law of a reasonably just state?

It might be thought that if the answer to the first debate was 'For all intents and purposes, we might as well assume that there is an obligation to obey the just laws of a reasonably just state', then the answer to this second debate must be the same. After all, we did say that when we are inquiring into whether there is an obligation to obey the just laws of a reasonably just state, we are trying to find out whether there is an obligation to obey them not because they are just, but because they are laws. So it would seem that the arguments that were made in favour of the view that there is an obligation to obey the just laws of a reasonably just state must apply with equal force to the unjust laws of a reasonably just state.

This is not true. Many of the arguments made above in favour of the view that there is an obligation to obey the just laws of a reasonably just state do not apply – or do not apply to the same extent – to the case where someone is tempted to break an unjust law of a reasonably just state. Let's go through these arguments again, more briefly this time as the basic ideas have already been explained.

---

[47] Endicott, 'The subsidiarity of law and the obligation to obey' (2005) 50 *American Journal of Jurisprudence* 233, 244–45.

CONSENT

Where someone has agreed to abide by the laws of a particular country, and their agreement has been relied upon, that agreement plus reliance may generate an obligation to obey a particular law, even when it is unjust. However, there are limits. If the law is particularly unjust, then even someone who has agreed to obey the law may be able to argue that their agreement did not cover this kind of law.

GRATITUDE

Even if we should feel grateful for the benefits we have received from living under the laws of a particular country, with the result that we have an obligation to obey those same laws, it is doubtful whether that obligation of gratitude extends to benefits that we have received from unjust laws. It might depend on the nature of the law. For example, someone might have an obligation to pay an unfair tax,[48] knowing that they have benefited from other people paying the tax in the past. But it would be hard to argue that a manager has an obligation to apply legislation that unfairly discriminates in favour of a particular section of the population just because he benefited from that legislation in the past.

HARM TO SOCIETY

It seems widely accepted that this argument – that there is an obligation to obey the law when a public act of disobeying the law might encourage people to disobey the law generally and thereby impair its efficacy as an instrument for governing people – applies just as much to unjust laws as it does to just laws.[49] An objection might be made that if people see someone disobeying an unjust law, they will not be encouraged to disobey the law generally, but only to disobey unjust laws – and that this would not be a bad thing. However, if everyone adopted the maxim 'I will only obey just laws', that could be as bad for a legal system's ability to govern people as people's adopting the maxim 'I will only obey the law if it is in my interests to do so'. The reason is that different people will have different ideas of what is just and unjust: so if everyone acted on the maxim 'I will only obey just laws', general compliance with the law would be impossible to achieve.[50] Given this, it would be harmful to society to act in a way that might encourage other people to adopt the maxim 'I will only obey just laws'.

---

[48] Ibid, 242–43.

[49] NLNR, 361; Raz, *The Morality of Freedom* (Oxford University Press, 1986), 102; Endicott, 'The subsidiarity of law and the obligation to obey' (above, n. 47), 242.

[50] See, further, Rawls, *A Theory of Justice* (above, n. 5), 350 (1971 edn), 308 (1999 rev'd edn); Boardman, 'Coordination and the moral obligation to obey the law' (above, n. 13), 555 ('a colorable claim of injustice cannot cancel the prima facie moral obligation to obey legal rules'); Waldron, *'Lex satis iusta'* (1999–2000) 75 *Notre Dame Law Review* 1829.

FAIR PLAY

The first argument from fair play – where you have agreed to have your case decided by a court of law, and the decision in the case has gone against you – would apply strongly to generate an obligation to abide by the decision of the court even if the decision was unjust. However, the second argument from fair play – which forbids picking and choosing which laws you will abide by and which laws you will take advantage of, depending on what is in your interests – will probably not generate an obligation to obey unjust laws, as someone who refuses to obey an unjust law because it is unjust is not picking and choosing what laws to abide by and take advantage of according to what is in her interests. The third argument from fair play – which requires you to assume the same burdens that other people have shouldered in the past if you have benefited from their shouldering those burdens – will (assuming it has any validity in the first place) only apply to justify someone having an obligation to obey an unjust law in the same kind of situations that the argument from gratitude would justify such an obligation existing.

A DUTY TO AID JUST INSTITUTIONS

If there is such a duty, it is not clear that it applies to impose a distinctive obligation on people to obey the unjust laws of a reasonably just state. The reason is that if there is no danger that my act of disobeying an unjust law will encourage others to disobey the law generally (or, what is almost as bad, act on the maxim 'I will only obey just laws'), it is hard to see how disobeying an unjust law of a reasonably just state could violate one's duty (if it exists) to aid just institutions.

ASSOCIATIVE OBLIGATIONS

The issue of whether an unjust law can have 'force' given Dworkin's theory that legal duties are a form of associative obligation has already been discussed.[51] We concluded there that it was hard to see how an unjust legal duty could be said to have the properties that Dworkin himself insists that a duty has to have if it is to count as an associative obligation. If this is right, then the idea that legal duties are a form of associative obligation cannot justify someone's having an obligation to obey an unjust law.

IDENTITY

Will someone who identifies with their country with the result that they have the attitude that Joseph Raz calls 'respect for law' feel that they have an obligation to obey the laws of their country even when those laws are unjust? In principle, it seems that they would: after all, the sentiment 'My country, right or wrong' is quite familiar to us, and we have already seen that Socrates was impelled by

---

[51] See above, pp. 139–41.

identity-related considerations to accept a punishment that he acknowledged was unjust.[52] However, some remarks of Raz's on the nature of the attitude of 'respect for law' might make us doubt whether such an attitude can create an obligation to obey an unjust law:

> 'It is not difficult to see why practical respect [for law] might be thought of as a proper expression of loyalty to [one's] society. It is a manifestation of trust. A man who is confident that the law is just and good believes that he has reason to do as the law requires ... If a person places absolute trust in the law then he will acknowledge the authority of law. It is natural therefore that loyalty to one's society can be expressed by behaving as one would if one trusted the law implicitly.'[53]

If these remarks are correct, then it would seem that someone who has the attitude of 'respect for law' will not feel that they have an obligation to obey an unjust law. This is because, on Raz's account, someone who has the attitude of 'respect for law' is expressing their loyalty to their country by acting *as though* the law of their country is 'just and good'. But it would be impossible to maintain this attitude if they *knew* that the law they were obeying was *not* 'just and good'. In such a case, they would have to find some other way of expressing their loyalty to their country; they might even think – as officers in the German Army who conspired to assassinate Adolf Hitler did – that disobeying the unjust law would be the best way of expressing their loyalty. However, Raz's account of the foundations of the attitude of 'respect for law' is too restrictive. In the same way that someone's loyalty to a friend can lead them to help the friend to do something which they know to be wrong but which the friend is insistent on doing – for example, stealing money to fund an operation that the friend needs – there seems no reason why someone's loyalty to their country could not lead them to obey a law which they know to be unjust. However, there are limits. Should the injustice be sufficiently serious, it may be that someone who formerly identified with their country would no longer do so and would no longer feel any identity-based pull to obey his country's laws: they would feel that their country had committed suicide, and so could no longer command their loyalty.[54]

CONCLUSION

It is not incoherent to think that we have a much stronger obligation to obey the just laws of a reasonably just state *qua* laws than we do the unjust laws of a reasonably just state. The main argument for finding an obligation to obey such unjust laws is the 'harm to society' argument, which indicates that we should avoid acting in ways that will encourage people to disobey the law generally. And where you have benefited in the past from compliance with an unjust law, then you *may* have

---

[52] *Crito*, 44d, 49c, 54c.

[53] Raz, 'Respect for law' in his *The Authority of Law*, 2nd edn (Oxford University Press, 2009), 261.

[54] It may be that Socrates' execution had this effect on Plato's attitude towards Athens: he left Athens soon after Socrates' death and did not return for 12 years (in 387 BC).

an obligation to do your part when your turn comes – though it is hard to think of examples where this applies other than the unfair tax example. Arguments from consent or identity may also, on occasion, generate obligations to obey even an unjust law. However, this still leaves plenty of room to think of examples where it is unlikely any case can be made for saying that someone has a moral obligation to obey an unjust law even where the country they live in is reasonably just. For example, there is no basis for arguing that there is an obligation to obey a law forbidding couples from engaging in certain sex acts in the privacy of their own bedroom.[55]

Debate 3

Is there an obligation to obey the just laws of a wicked state?

There is not much of a debate on this issue: we only raise it for the sake of completeness. The question arises because even the most wicked state will have some laws that are relatively just. During the whole period of Nazi rule in Germany, contracts were entered into under the provisions of the *Bürgerliches Gesetzbuch* (or 'BGB' for short) – the civil code that has been law in Germany since 1900, and the provisions of which are relatively just. Timothy Endicott[56] points out that regimes that are 'as murderous and vile as you wish' are very likely to have relatively just traffic laws. And while, he observes, 'Life would be simpler if we could say that unjust legal systems impose no moral obligations, because abusive regimes deserve no obedience ...', the truth is that it is hard to see why people have *less* of a moral obligation to obey the just laws of a wicked state than they have to obey the just laws of a reasonably just state (assuming, of course, that they do have such an obligation), at least where those just laws regulate the relationships of people who occupy relatively equal positions, such as contracting parties, or car drivers.

Greater difficulties arise in a wicked state where members of a particular minority are subjected to systematic disadvantages, and those disadvantages are reinforced by relatively just laws, such as laws against theft and fraud. The question would then arise whether members of the disadvantaged minority have an obligation to obey the relatively just laws that happen to have the effect of preventing them helping themselves to get out of their plight. It is actually very difficult to find an argument in favour of the view that members of the disadvantaged minority have an obligation to obey the relatively just laws against theft and fraud in this kind of situation. Arguments from consent, gratitude, fair play, associative obligations and identity seem to have no application here – the systematic disadvantage under which the members of the minority labour prevent them applying. (For example, there is little chance of the members of the minority identifying with the

---

[55] Cf. *Griswold* v *Connecticut*, 381 US 479 (1965); *Lawrence* v *Texas*, 539 US 558 (2003).

[56] All quotes from Endicott, 'The subsidiarity of law and the obligation to obey' (above, n. 47), 243.

country they live in, given the way it treats them.) The only arguments that might apply are the arguments from 'harm to society' and the duty (if there is one) to aid just institutions. Both arguments gain some traction from the thought that if the members of the minority break the laws against theft and fraud then that might encourage other people to think (incorrectly) that they too are allowed to break the law when it is in their interests to do so, and whatever good the members of the minority might be able to do for themselves by engaging in theft and fraud will be outweighed by the evils unleashed by the rise in lawlessness that their decision to break the law might trigger. If this line of reasoning is correct, then that would establish that even in this very difficult case there is an obligation to obey the just laws of a wicked state. However, the obligation is much harder to make out than would be the case if we were considering the just laws of a relatively just state.

Further Reading

Plato, *Crito*.

Smith, 'Is there a prima facie obligation to obey the law' (1973) 82 *Yale Law Journal* 950.

Raz, *The Authority of Law*, 2nd edn (Oxford University Press, 2009), chs 12–13.

Finnis, 'Law as coordination' (1989) 2 *Ratio Juris* 97.

Endicott, 'The subsidiarity of law and the obligation to obey' (2005) 50 *American Journal of Jurisprudence* 233.

Wellman and Simmons, *Is There a Duty to Obey the Law?* (Cambridge University Press, 2005).

Gur, 'Actions, attitudes, and the obligation to obey the law' (2013) 21 *Journal of Political Philosophy* 326.

8

MORALITY AND RIGHTS

Debate 1

Is morality 'subjective'?

When one makes a moral claim – for example, that a possible act is morally wrong – it is often said in response that such claims are merely 'subjective' opinion. This debate is about whether that response is true.

Precisely what it means to say that a moral claim is subjective is itself disputed.[1] A useful working definition is:

(1) Moral claims are 'subjective' if they are not capable of being true or false in a significant sense of 'truth' and 'falsity'.[2] We can call people who make this claim *subjectivists*.

Conversely:

(2) Moral claims are 'objective' if they are capable of being true or false in a significant sense of 'truth' and 'falsity'. We can call people who make this claim *objectivists*.

We will have occasion later to consider in what ways a claim might succeed or fail to be true or false *in a significant sense*.

SUBJECTIVIST ARGUMENTS AND THEORIES

We can first consider three main arguments that have been offered for subjectivist views,[3] before examining different subjectivist theories.

---

[1] See, e.g., Lillehammer, *Companions in Guilt: Arguments for Ethical Objectivity* (Palgrave Macmillan, 2007), 5–7.

[2] See, similarly, Parfit, *On What Matters: Volume Two* (Oxford University Press, 2011), 413: 'That is what it [objectivity] means. Like answers to mathematical problems, moral judgments can be objective in the sense that they can be right or wrong, by being true or false.'

[3] The first two arguments are those identified by Parfit in ibid, chs 28–29.

(A) *The naturalistic argument.* The naturalistic argument claims that we cannot make sense of the idea that there are moral truths from a natural-scientific world-view. If all that exists, fundamentally, are the kinds of facts described by the natural sciences like physics and chemistry, this makes it puzzling how there could be moral truths.

The puzzle arises because of the *normative* nature of moral claims. Moral claims tell us what we *ought* to do. Consider the moral claim that one ought not to torture people for amusement. If this claim stated a truth, it should state a *fact*: the fact that it is wrong to torture for fun. But if all facts are natural, what kind of fact could this claim state? Scientists have not yet discovered and are unlikely to discover any normative particles or *ought*-matter floating around in the ether. As Dworkin remarks, it would be rather odd to believe in moral particles (which he jokingly dubs 'morons').[4] So it seems that the existence of moral facts – like the fact that I ought not to torture for fun – would have to be inconsistent with a scientific picture of the world.

Now, if one accepts this argument so far – if one accepts that the only facts in the world are natural facts and that moral claims do not state such facts (they proclaim the existence of some queer non-natural, normative fact) – there are two options.

One option is to say that moral claims are all *false*. On this option, when we make a moral claim we are *intending* to state something which could be true, but because there are no real facts in the world which will back up our claim – there are no normative particles – our claim is *false*. On this view, when we make a moral claim, we are like people who make claims like 'Mermaids live on the Isle of Man'. These claims *can* be true or false, but they are false (because there are no mermaids, just as there are no moral particles). This view would then be a form of *moral nihilism*: nihilists believe that all moral claims are false. This would not be *subjectivism*.

The other option leads to *subjectivism*. This other option is to reject the claim that moral claims state the existence of strange, non-natural, normative entities. On this option, moral claims do not state the existence of facts at all. Rather, moral claims *express attitudes like disapproval or certain kinds of desire*. On this view, when I say that torture is *wrong*, I am expressing my *desire* that torture not be done. I am *not* reporting the existence of a fact. If moral claims are simply expressions of these kinds of attitudes, there's no problem about reconciling morality with a scientific worldview. Things like desires are just psychological facts about people.

So the naturalistic argument points towards subjectivism insofar as it allows us to understand morality from within a modern scientific worldview, which does not postulate weird non-natural, normative, entities, and it does not commit us to saying that all moral claims are *false*. Or so this argument claims.

---

[4] Dworkin, *Justice for Hedgehogs* (Harvard University Press, 2011), 42–43.

(B) *The motivation argument.* The motivation argument, as we can call it, runs as follows:[5]

(a) It is inconceivable that we could be genuinely convinced that some act was our moral duty and not be motivated at all to do that act.
(b) According to *objectivists*, when we make a moral claim that some act is our duty, we are stating our *belief* about a fact (namely, that the act is our duty).
(c) But we can have a belief about a fact and yet be entirely unmotivated to act on that belief. I might be entirely unmoved by my belief that the cat is on the mat.
(d) Therefore, if moral claims state our beliefs about facts, *it is conceivable* that we could be convinced that some act was our duty and yet not be motivated to do that act at all.
(e) Therefore, given (a), it cannot be the case that moral claims state our beliefs about the facts; they must rather express some kind of motivating attitude, like a desire to act in a certain way.

The basic point of this argument is that since moral claims are intimately connected with *motivation* to act in certain ways, when we make a moral claim, we can't simply be stating our *belief* about some facts, as *objectivists* would have it, because that allows the possibility that we could have some moral view and yet be entirely unmotivated by it. But given the intimate connection between moral claims and motivation, that must be inconceivable.

(C) *The argument from disagreement.* It is often argued that given the fact of widespread moral disagreement, we cannot rationally believe that there are moral truths. Such an argument attempts to show that the best explanation of the existence of widespread moral disagreement is either that (1) all moral claims are false because there are no moral facts *or* (2) that moral claims are really disguised expressions of *attitudes* like desires or preferences which can be neither true nor false. (2) is a subjectivist thesis.

We can now consider some subjectivist theories, which rely upon one or more of these (or closely related) arguments:

Emotivism

According to A.J. Ayer, an Oxford philosopher writing in the 1930s, when we use moral language, we do not use it to say something that can be true or false. Rather, we are just venting or evincing our emotions. An emotion can be sincere or strongly felt, but it cannot be true or false.

As Ayer writes:

'[I]f I say to someone "You acted wrongly in stealing that money", I am not stating anything more than if I had simply said, "You stole that money." In adding that this

---

[5] Hume seems to have relied upon a similar argument: see Hume, *Treatise of Human Nature*, Book III, Part I, Section I. The argument is discussed by Dworkin, *Justice for Hedgehogs* (above, n. 4), 56–58.

action is wrong, I am not making any further statement about it, I am simply evincing my moral disapproval about it. It is as if I had said, "You stole that money," in a peculiar tone of horror, or written with the addition of some special exclamation marks. The tone, or the exclamation marks, adds nothing to the literal meaning of the sentence. It merely serves to show that the expression of it is attended by certain feelings in the speaker.'[6]

Few philosophers today are *emotivists*. There are a number of reasons for this.[7] First, *emotivism* is focused upon the use of moral language in *speech*. It is not clear how the emotivist can give an account of moral *thought*. When a person thinks to herself, 'Murder is wrong', this cannot be accounted for straightforwardly in terms of *venting* or *evincing* emotions. Secondly, *emotivism* seems to be unable to account for many of the ways in which moral language is used. Consider the sentence: 'if murder is wrong, then stealing is also wrong': this sentence makes sense but what emotion it evinces is unclear. Thirdly, we appear to disagree about moral questions, but emotivism struggles to explain this appearance. According to *emotivism*, when we disagree about a moral claim, we are like people at a football match who cheer for different teams, one group shouting 'Hooray: Reds' and one group shouting 'Hooray: Blues'. We wouldn't normally say that these people, in cheering for different sides, are *disagreeing* about anything, however.

Expressivism

Expressivist theories are the modern successors to *emotivism*. The basic idea behind expressivism is that the meaning of a sentence, S, is given by explaining what it is to *think* that S.[8] Unlike *emotivism*, expressivism is not therefore a theory necessarily concerned with moral *speech*. It is primarily concerned with what it is to *think* about some moral sentence.

In the case of *moral* sentences, expressivists argue that the meaning of such sentences is given not by the *belief* that sentence expresses, but fundamentally by other mental attitudes like *desires* or *desire-like attitudes*. Unlike beliefs, desires and similar attitudes cannot be true or false.

Expressivists have developed theories to explain how sentences like 'If murder is wrong, then stealing is also wrong' could express a desire-like attitude, rather than a belief. So Simon Blackburn, a leading expressivist, claimed that the sentence 'If murder is wrong, then stealing is also wrong' expresses a higher-order attitude which expresses disapproval of the lower-order attitude of 'disapproving of murder and not also disapproving of stealing'.[9]

Blackburn also purports to be able to explain the existence of *disagreement* about moral claims. On Blackburn's theory, our desires *conflict* when one person is in

---

[6] Ayer, *Language, Truth and Logic* (Penguin, 2001), 67.
[7] See Schroeder, *Being For: Evaluating the Program of Semantic Expressivism* (Oxford University Press, 2008), 3–6.
[8] See Schroeder, 'What is the Frege-Geach problem?' (2008) *Philosophy Compass* 703, 704.
[9] See Blackburn, *Spreading the Word* (Oxford University Press, 1984).

favour of some act and someone else is against this act. These people disagree, Blackburn claims, in that their desires cannot both be fulfilled; they cannot both get what they want.

Prominent expressivists make an interesting further claim about expressivism. Blackburn claims that, even though our moral views are fundamentally expressions of certain kinds of desire, expressivists can '... earn our right to talk of moral truth, while recognizing fully the subjective sources of our judgments'.[10] On this view, even if expressivism is true, and so, fundamentally, moral claims are just expressions of desire-like states, in themselves incapable of being true or false, we can *nonetheless* justifiably go on saying things like 'It is true that murder is wrong' and we could also justifiably say things like 'Even if I didn't desire it to be the case that murder is wrong, murder would still be wrong'.

Blackburn's account of such statements is that they also express desire-like attitudes. To say that *it is true* that murder is wrong is just to reiterate one's disapproval that murder is wrong. It is like the situation where you say that 'Mushy peas are disgusting' and I say 'that is true' as a way of expressing the same dislike. To say that murder is wrong even if one didn't have such an attitude is also just to express another higher-order attitude towards murder.

Blackburn's theory is an example of an account which, though it claims that we can continue to say that moral claims are true and false, arguably does not allow that moral claims can be true or false *in a significant sense*. According to Blackburn, for a moral claim to be true is just for certain people to adopt a certain kind of attitude towards it. But that is quite different from the sense in which it is true that 2+2=4 or that water boils at 100°C. These claims are true independently of anyone's adopting any kind of attitude.

OBJECTIVIST ARGUMENTS AND THEORIES

We can first consider some objectivist arguments, and objectivist responses to the arguments for subjectivism, before considering some objectivist theories.

(A) *Objectivism as the 'ordinary' view.* Objectivists typically claim that objectivism is the view assumed by most participants in moral discourse. It is said that we regularly assume that moral claims can be true or false.[11] Not many people think that it is neither true nor false that 'The Holocaust was wrong' or that 'Torturing children for amusement is wrong' is neither true nor false. As Dworkin writes:

> 'Someone who sticks pins into babies for the fun of hearing them scream is morally depraved. Don't you agree? You probably hold other, more controversial opinions about right and wrong as well ... You think that your opinions on these matters report the truth and that those who disagree with you are making a mistake ... You

---

[10] Ibid, 197.

[11] See, for example, Dworkin, *Justice for Hedgehogs* (above, n. 4), 27. See, similarly, Enoch, *Taking Morality Seriously: A Defence of Robust Realism* (Oxford University Press, 2011), 8.

also think, I imagine, that sticking pins into babies ... would be wrong even if no one actually objected to it or was repulsed by the idea. Even you. You probably think, that is, that the truth of your moral convictions does not depend upon what anyone thinks or feels ... This attitude toward moral truth – that at least some moral opinions are objectively true in this way – is very common. I shall call it the "ordinary" view.'[12]

(B) *Objectivism as the best explanation of the possibility of disagreement.* Subjectivist theories have a hard time explaining how it can be that when one person says 'Murder is wrong' and another says 'Murder is not wrong' they are really disagreeing. It can be hard to see how emotions 'disagree', just as it is hard to see how, say, my having a headache and your not having a headache means that we disagree. But if 'murder is wrong' can be true or false then it is easy to explain this. One person believes it is a fact that murder is wrong; the other denies the existence of this fact.

(C) *Responses to the naturalistic argument.* Various responses to the naturalistic argument have been made.

One strategy is to deny that moral claims refer to strange, non-natural, facts after all. According to *moral naturalists*, when we say that an act is wrong, we are in fact referring to a *natural property of the world*. According to such views, much as 'water' is identical with 'H_2O', so it is true that moral properties like 'wrongness' are identical to some natural property. For example, say one accepts the view that an act is wrong if it does not maximise happiness. On this view, what it is for an act to be wrong is for it to have some natural property – namely, its not maximising happiness.

One difficulty with this suggestion is pointed out by Nagel:

'If values are objective, they must be so in their own right, and not through reducibility to some other kind of objective fact. They have to be objective values, not objective anything else.'[13]

Nagel's objection to reducing moral claims to claims about matters of natural fact is that we lose the sense in which moral claims are *normative*. If we say that an act's being wrong is reducible to some natural fact – like causing pain – we lose the sense in which moral claims give us *reason* to act in certain ways.

Another strategy is to argue that there are indeed *non-natural facts*. Such arguments typically proceed by drawing analogies to non-moral domains of reasoning. The aim of these arguments is to try to show that it would not be so 'queer' after all if there were non-natural, moral, facts.

Parfit argues that moral truths are like mathematical truths. He writes that:

---

[12] See also Parfit, *On What Matters: Volume Two* (above n. 2), 380: 'Moral beliefs, most of us assume, are *beliefs*, which might be true or false.'

[13] Nagel, *The View from Nowhere* (Oxford University Press, 1986), 138.

'Nothing could be truer than the truths that 2 is greater than 1, that 2+2=4, and that there are prime numbers greater than 100. Not even God could make these claims false. For such claims to be true, there must be a sense in which there are numbers, or in which numbers exist.'[14]

Even although mathematical truths do not exist in space and time, even although no amount of empirical evidence will establish a mathematical truth (think especially of the truth that 2+2 *must* equal 4), we can still sensibly speak of the existence of mathematical truths and mathematical facts. Parfit's claim is that the sense in which moral facts exist is the same sense in which these mathematical facts exist.

Another argument for the existence of moral facts draws a different comparison. Cuneo argues that if one rejects the existence of (non-natural) *moral facts* (on the ground that these are strange creatures), one must also reject the existence of *epistemic normative facts*.[15] An epistemic normative fact is a reason for believing something to be true. For instance, if the cat is on the mat, I have an epistemic, normative, reason to believe the cat is on the mat. If we reject the existence of these epistemic normative reasons, then we are committed to being *skeptics*. That is: we will have to say that there are *no reasons to believe that anything is true*. That is implausible.

(D) *Responses to the motivation argument.* In response to the motivation argument, many have pointed to the existence of *amoralists*. Dworkin quotes from *Richard III*, where Richard declares that 'I am determined to prove a villain' and judged his own plans 'subtle, false, and treacherous'.[16] The point of such examples is to show that it is conceivable that a person can judge some action to be morally wrong and yet be entirely unmotivated to abstain from doing it. This amounts to a denial of the first premise of the argument.

One counter-response to *amoralist* examples is to deny that *amoralists* like Richard *sincerely* endorse their moral convictions. If Richard was entirely unmotivated not to murder his relatives to become king, he could not have *sincerely* believed that murdering them was wrong. This counter-response is irrelevant, however. The issue is simply whether someone can have a moral belief without being motivated by it. The issue is not whether someone can be *sincerely* convinced of some moral proposition and not be motivated by it. As Parfit points out, people who are depressed may take themselves to have decisive reasons to do something – for example, something which would protect their future well-being – even though, due to their depression, they are unmotivated to do so.[17]

(E) *Responses to the argument from disagreement.* A number of responses have been made to the argument from disagreement.[18]

[14] Parfit, *On What Matters: Volume Two* (above, n. 2), 479.
[15] Cuneo, *The Normative Web* (Oxford University Press, 2007).
[16] Dworkin, *Justice for Hedgehogs* (above, n. 4), 57.
[17] Parfit, *On What Matters: Volume Two* (above, n. 2), 382–83.
[18] Almost all of these responses are made by Parfit, *On What Matters: Volume Two* (above, n. 2), 552–63.

First, it can be pointed out that widespread disagreement in other domains does not lead to subjectivism. For example, physicists disagree about whether string theory is correct. This is not usually taken to suggest that there can be no fact of the matter about whether string theory is true.

Secondly, it is often the case that when people make conflicting moral claims, this is because they disagree *not about morality*, but about *non-moral* facts. Imagine the following conversation:

A: It is morally wrong to allow same-sex couples to adopt children.
B: That's nonsense!

A and B need not be disagreeing about what morality requires. A and B might both agree that it is morally wrong to allow same-sex couples to adopt children *if that caused harm* to the child's upbringing. A might believe that this would cause harm, whilst B believes that it does not. This is a disagreement over the relevant *empirical*, non-moral facts. An important instance of this is arguably disagreement which arises due to differing religious beliefs. If it is an empirical question whether God exists, then when people are disagreeing about morality based upon their differing religious beliefs, they may not really be disagreeing about morality. They are disagreeing over the empirical question of whether God exists.

Thirdly, it is often the case that conflicting moral beliefs arise due to distorting influences upon the way those beliefs are formed. If we ask people who stand to profit from some claim's being true whether it is true, these people are likely to give self-serving answers.

Fourthly, many moral disagreements are about borderline cases. We might agree that it is morally wrong to kill innocent persons, but disagree about what constitutes a 'person'. That is so in debates about abortion. This disagreement need not cast doubt upon the basic principle that it is wrong to kill innocent persons, however.

Fifthly, it may be that moral truths are sometimes by their nature imprecise. For example, there might only be very imprecise truths about whether one person's life is going better than another's.

We can now consider some objectivist theories, which give accounts of how it can be that moral claims can be true or false.

Response-dependence theories
On these views, a moral claim about whether an action is right or wrong can be true or false depending upon how a human agent would respond to the action under certain conditions.

Response-dependence theorists, such as David Wiggins, claim that what determines the truth of whether an action is right is whether it would cause a particular sort of response – a desire, emotion, or some other feeling – in some human observer.[19] For example, one view might hold that an action is wrong if it produces

---

[19] See Wiggins, *Needs, Values, Truth* (Blackwell Publishing, 1987).

a sensation of *disgust* in a person where they are fully aware of the action's properties.

There are two main problems with response-dependence theories. First, such theories seem to imply that if people had different psychological make-ups, the truth of our moral claims would be different. Lewis explains this objection:

> 'Psychology is contingent. Our dispositions to value things might have been otherwise than they actually are. We might have been disposed, under ideal conditions, to value seasickness and petty sleaze above all else. Does the [response-dependence] theory imply that, had we been thus disposed, those things would have been values? That seems wrong.'[20]

Secondly, it can be objected that we think actions are wrong not because people actually do respond to certain acts with disgust or certain emotions but because such responses would be *warranted* or *justified*. If that is right, response-dependence theories are *vacuous*. In virtue of what would disgust be *warranted*? Presumably, *if the action is wrong*. But the theory tells us nothing about what makes this true.

Constructivism

The core idea of constructivism is that the truth of moral claims depends upon what follows from or is entailed by an agent's perspective, where an agent's perspective is constituted by the agent's values. What a person ought morally to do depends entirely, according to constructivism, on what the values they accept entail. Suppose, for example, that you deeply value counting the blades of grass in your garden. From that perspective, you might have a reason to buy a calculator – to make the task easier.

Constructivism might be thought to lead to a pervasive relativism about what morality requires. On the one hand, if agents differ relevantly in their perspectives, then it seems morality could require different things of them. On the other hand, there seem to be no rational limits on what a person can value – mightn't they only value caring about the number of blades of grass on their lawns?

Not so, according to *Kantian constructivists*.[21] Korsgaard argues that every human agent is committed, as a matter of *consistency*, to accepting certain substantive moral claims. Her argument 'is intended to show that if we take anything to have value, then we must acknowledge that we have moral obligations'.[22] The argument, in outline, runs as follows.[23] If a person acts on the basis of what she considers herself to have *reason* to do, rather than acting simply instinctually on brute impulses, she necessarily places value upon her capacity to choose on the basis of reasons. Korsgaard calls this the value of 'humanity'. If you accept the importance of living according to reasons given by your values and commitments,

---

[20] Lewis, 'Dispositional theories of value' (1987) *Proceedings of the Aristotelian Society* 132.
[21] This terminology is borrowed from Street, 'What is constructivism in ethics and metaethics?' (2010) *Philosophy Compass* 363, 369.
[22] Korsgaard, *The Sources of Normativity* (Cambridge University Press, 1996), 92.
[23] See ibid, ch. 3.

you accept the value of humanity. If you accept the importance of your own humanity, she argues, there would be a kind of inconsistency in not accepting the importance of *other people's humanity*. This leads to moral obligations to respect other people's humanity.

Street identifies another kind of *constructivist* position, which she calls *Humean constructivism*. This kind of constructivism *does* countenance the possibility that people's moral obligations could diverge considerably depending upon their differing values. On this view, I only have reason to do some action if that action is suitably connected in some way to my values or desires. The extent to which morality requires the same of all of us depends, then, on the extent to which we have similar values and desires. It is open to doubt whether *Humean constructivism* is really a theory of what makes *moral* propositions true or false. Morality's claims upon us are not *conditional* in nature: morality demands that we not torture children for fun even if we have no desire not to do so. So it may be that this form of constructivism fails to provide an account of how moral claims could be true or false in a significant sense.

Realism

Realism comes in many forms.[24] The essence of most varieties of realism, however, is that there are moral facts whose existence is in no way dependent upon the attitudes, emotions, feelings, or perspectives of any agent.[25] Just as the truth of 2+2=4 in no way depends upon on any perspective being taken up, realists claim that the truth of moral claims does not depend upon anyone's perspective.

Realist theories are typically met with two main objections. First, there is the naturalistic objection: the idea of moral facts, directing what we must do, which exist independently of anyone attitudes, desires etc. is inconsistent with a naturalistic picture of the world. We have already seen above that it may be possible to meet this objection either by claiming that moral facts reduce to natural facts (*naturalistic realism*) or by drawing analogies to mathematical truths or epistemic reasons.

Another objection to realist theories is epistemological – that is, it's concerned with how we come to have *knowledge* of the moral facts which realists claim to exist. The objection is that it's entirely unclear how we *could* come to have knowledge of moral facts. One response, made by *naturalistic realists*, is that the natural properties which are identical with moral properties like rightness and wrongness *cause* us to have certain moral beliefs. So it might be that our experience of pain or seeing others in pain causes us to come to the belief that causing pain in certain ways is wrong. Another response is that coming to know moral truths is like coming to solve a mathematical problem. Even if numbers and mathematical operations do

---

[24] For an overview of different realisms, see FitzPatrick, 'Recent work on ethical realism' (2009) 69 *Analysis* 746.

[25] See, for this characterisation of realism, Street, 'Objectivity and truth: you'd better rethink it' (unpublished, available on her website), 3.

not *cause* us to reach answers to mathematical problems (since these are non-empirical properties, they don't *cause* anything), we can nonetheless still come to reasoned answers to such problems and learn mathematical truths.

CONCLUSION

In our view, some version of objectivism is likely to be true. This is because we accept the *ordinary view argument* and *best explanation of the possibility of disagreement argument* for objectivism, and the objectivist responses to the *naturalistic argument, motivation argument,* and *moral disagreement argument* seem more than adequate.

Debate 2

Is morality consequentialist or non-consequentialist?

General theories have been offered as answers to the question: 'What ought I, morally, to do?' These general theories are usually divided into two families: consequentialist theories and non-consequentialist theories. Consequentialism may be characterised as follows:

> *Consequentialism.* Whether an action is morally right or wrong depends only upon facts about what would produce the most value.[26]

Non-consequentialist theories deny this. In this debate, we describe and assess different kinds of consequentialist and non-consequentialist theories, in order to determine which kind of theory is true.

CONSEQUENTIALIST THEORIES

Recall our general characterisation of consequentialism:

> *Consequentialism.* Whether an action is morally right or wrong depends only upon facts about what would produce the most value.

Consequentialist theories differ depending upon (1) what they count as value; (2) how they claim that moral rightness or wrongness depends upon what would produce the most value.

Consequentialist theories differentiated by their theory of value

Consequentialist theories can therefore be differentiated by reference to what they count as 'value'. According to *utilitarianism*, for the most value to be realised, is for people (and in some cases, other animals) to have the greatest amount of overall

---

[26] See, similarly, McNaughton and Rawling, 'Deontology', in Copp (ed.), *Oxford Handbook of Ethical Theory* (Oxford University Press, 2006), 424. A similar definition is also used by Parfit, *On What Matters: Volume One* (Oxford University Press, 2011), 373.

happiness. Happiness can be understood in different ways, giving rise to different kinds of utilitarianism. The great utilitarian, Henry Sidgwick, understood happiness in *hedonistic* terms.[27] *Hedonism* is the view that the only thing which is intrinsically good is *pleasure* and the only intrinsically bad thing is *pain*.[28] Thus *hedonistic utilitarians* believe that for the most value to be realised is for people (and in some cases, other animals) to have the greatest amount of pleasure minus pain.

Consequentialists need not, however, be *hedonistically utilitarian*. Thus even if one rejects the view that pleasure (alone) is intrinsically valuable, it is still possible to be a consequentialist. This is important as there are well-known objections to the view that pleasure is intrinsically valuable. First, it might be questioned whether the pleasure that a slave owner obtains from owning slaves or the pleasure that a rapist takes in rape should be counted as valuable. Secondly, hedonist theories are subject to an objection made by Nozick – the experience machine objection.[29] The objection invites you to imagine that you could plug into a machine which allows you to experience many pleasures – for example, the joys of friendship, love, winning competitions – without realising that these pleasures are only provided by the machine and not *truly* experienced. If pleasure were all that mattered, the objection goes, it would be rational to plug into the machine. Yet people typically have an intuitive revulsion to plugging in; it seems that having real friendships matters in a way not entirely captured by pleasure experienced.

Other utilitarian consequentialisms include: *preference consequentialism*, according to which happiness or well-being consists in the satisfaction of people's preferences.[30] This view is distinct from *hedonism*, since the satisfaction of a preference need not involve a sensation of pleasure. One might prefer simply that one have a true friend, even if this brings no conscious pleasure. This view is also subject to significant objections. First, it cannot be said that the satisfaction of every preference constitutes an increase in well-being. Even if I prefer to eat this bar of chocolate which, unbeknownst to me, is laced with deathly poison, it would not benefit me to do so. This leads to a revision of this account, whereby only satisfaction of *well-informed* preferences counts as contributing to well-being. However, this reformed account is faced with a second objection. This objection has it that we prefer to have certain things only because they are good for us – i.e. they improve our well-being. If so, then we can't hope to explain well-being in terms of *preferences*.[31]

If one rejected both hedonist utilitarian and preference utilitarian consequentialism, one might endorse some form of objective list consequentialism.[32] Such a view holds that there are certain things which are objectively valuable in the sense

---

[27] See Sidgwick, *The Methods of Ethics*, 7th edn (Hackett Publishing, 1981), ch. 14, especially 398–407.

[28] See Sinnott-Armstrong, 'Consequentialism', in E Zalta (ed.), *Stanford Encyclopedia of Philosophy*, section 1.

[29] Nozick, *Anarchy, State and Utopia* (Basic Books, 1974), 42–45. See above, p. 104.

[30] Sinnott-Armstrong, 'Consequentialism' (above, n. 28), section 3.

[31] See, for this objection, Scanlon, *What We Owe to Each Other* (Harvard University Press, 1998), ch. 3.

[32] See, for example, Ewing, 'Utilitarianism' (1948) *Ethics* 100.

that their value does not consist either (wholly) in the sensation of pleasure or in the satisfaction of an individual's well-informed preferences. Such an account might list things like life, health, friendship, enjoyment, and achievement. To the extent that such lists include things whose value does not contribute to an individual's well-being or happiness, they are examples of non-utilitarian consequentialism.

Although different theories of value lead to different forms of consequentialism, it should be noted that consequentialist theories usually accept that, whatever theory of value one adopts, the value of an outcome is determined impartially. Imagine that you can either save your own child or five strangers' children, where all children have as much to lose in dying as each other. In determining whether it would produce most value to save your own child or the lives of the five other children, most consequentialist theories do not allow greater value to be placed upon the life of your own child simply because the child is your own. The value of saving your child's life cannot be enhanced, above the value of the life of each other child, simply because it is your child. This is often put by saying that consequentialism involves agent-neutral judgments about value.[33] An outcome's value, for consequentialist theories, is the value that the outcome has for any agent – it is neutral amongst agents.

Consequentialist theories differentiated by how they relate the right action with facts about what produces the most value

Consequentialist theories differ according to *how* they claim the right action is determined by facts about what produces the most value. Thus there is a difference between:

> *Act consequentialism*: an action is wrong if and only if it does not produce the most value.

and, in one formulation of it,

> *Rule consequentialism*: an action is wrong if and only if it is prohibited by the set of rules whose acceptance by everyone would produce the most value.

Act consequentialism focuses directly upon *acts* and assesses these in terms of whether they produce the most value, whilst *rule consequentialism* focuses only indirectly upon acts, and directly upon *rules* and assesses these in terms of whether they produce the most value. We will later explore the motivations for these different forms of consequentialism.

Arguments for consequentialism

A number of different arguments for consequentialism have been made. First,

---

[33] McNaughton and Rawling, 'Value and agent-relative reasons' (1995) *Utilitas* 31, 31: 'It is central to all ... consequentialist theories that value is determined impersonally; the real value of any state of affairs does not depend upon the point of view of the agent ... Consequentialism thus provides an agent-neutral account of both the right and the good.'

consequentialism seems to capture and develop the common thought that moral-ity requires us to 'make the world a better place'.

Secondly, the idea that everyone's good is judged and weighted from an impar-tial perspective is intuitively appealing. The idea that everyone 'counts for the same' seems to express a powerful idea of equality. Most consequentialisms endorse this idea insofar as they endorse agent-neutral theories of value.

Thirdly, to the extent that non-consequentialist theories may permit or require an agent to act in a way which is less than or significantly less than best, it may seem that these theories permit or require *irrational* actions. Conversely, as Mulgan puts it:

> 'the most rational way to respond to any value is to promote it. For instance, if we believe that happiness is valuable, then it is rational to seek to maximise the amount of happiness in the world. Consequentialism is thus the most rational moral theory, as it always tells us to promote value.'[34]

More generally, much of the appeal of consequentialist positions has been said to lie in 'alleged difficulties about the foundations of alternative views'.[35]

Fourthly, many people seem to have a strong intuition that all that fundamen-tally matters is how individuals' lives go – all that matters is individual well-being. Consequently, the only moral facts, on this view, are fundamentally ones about how some act or rule affects well-being.[36] What else could matter, in moral terms, other than how something affects the life of some human being (or other crea-ture)? This argument directly supports *utilitarianism* and, indirectly, therefore, *consequentialism*.

Fifthly, consequentialist theories seem to capture our moral intuitions in impor-tant kinds of case. Suppose that you can either save the life of one stranger or the lives of 10 strangers, in either case at no cost to yourself. It would seem to be wrong to save the life of the one. This can be explained on the basis that saving the one would not produce the most value.

Sixthly, *contractualist* arguments have been offered for forms of consequential-ism. (A contractualist argument, as we'll see later, is an argument which purports to justify some moral principle or rule by reference to whether rational agents would *agree* to it or *choose* it under certain circumstances.) For example, Parfit has recently argued that some version of *contractualism* supports rule consequential-ism.[37]

Objections to act consequentialism

We'll now consider some objections to *act consequentialism* (AC). To focus our thoughts, it will be helpful to focus upon

---

[34] Mulgan, *The Demands of Consequentialism* (Oxford University Press, 2001), 14.
[35] Scanlon, 'Contractualism and utilitarianism', in Sen and Williams (eds), *Utilitarianism and Beyond*, (Cambridge University Press, 1982), 103.
[36] See ibid, 108.
[37] Parfit, *On What Matters: Volume One* (above, n. 26), 377–403.

Act utilitarianism (AU): An action is right if and only if it produces the most benefits to people (that is, if it leads to the greatest amount of overall well-being).

(1) *The existence of constraints.* The standard objection to AU is that it fails to account for the existence of *moral constraints*. Most people think that there are constraints in the sense that we are morally required in certain situations *not* to produce the greatest overall benefit. Here is a classic example of a case where most people would say that morality requires us *not to produce the most benefit.*

> *Transplant. Patient* is in hospital for a minor operation. *Patient's Doctor* knows that if she secretly killed *Patient*, *Patient's* transplanted organs would be used to save the lives of five other people.

The 'secrecy' built in to this example is intended to ensure that no other consequences would ensue other than the killing of one and the saving of five. Although it would benefit people most if *Doctor* killed *Patient*, few people think this is the right thing for *Doctor* to do.

Some constraints seem to arise between any individuals, regardless of whether they have any special relationship to each other. For example, many people think that it would be wrong for *Stranger* to push *Bystander* in the following case:

> *Bridge.* A runaway train is heading towards five people. The only way to stop the train is for *Stranger* to push *Bystander* off a bridge under which the train is passing, thereby triggering the train's automatic brakes.

Even though *Stranger* and *Bystander* are unknown to each other, most people still think it is wrong for *Stranger* to push *Bystander*, though this will produce the most overall benefits.

Other constraints seem to arise by virtue of special relationships that people bear to each other. This is illustrated by the following case:

> *Father and Son. Father* can either save *Son* or the lives of two strangers' children. All children have as much to lose by dying as each other.

Here most people would think not only that *Father* is permitted to save *Son* but also that *Father* is morally *required* to save *Son* rather than the other children. This duty would not be owed by a stranger, who, most people would say, would be required to save the greater number. Hence, this is a constraint which arises from a special relationship between *Father* and *Son*.

In summary, AU is faced with the problem that most people would think that we have moral obligations *not* to behave in the way that AU requires. These obligations exist as constraints upon producing the best outcomes, where the constraint may be relationship-dependent or relationship-independent.

(2) *The existence of options.* Another objection to AU is that there are situations where it seems that, though we do not have a moral duty *not* to act as AU requires, we are morally *permitted* to act in that way. In other words, we have moral *options* not to behave in accordance with AU. Consider this simple example given by Mulgan:

Affluent's Tale. Affluent is an affluent citizen of a developed country, who already makes significant donations to charity. She is sitting at her desk with her cheque book. In front of her are two pamphlets: one from a reputable international aid organization, the other from her local theatre company. Affluent has enough money either to buy theatre tickets or to make a donation to the charity, but not both. Because of her love of the theatre, she buys the tickets, even though she knows that the money would have done far more good if sent to the charity.[38]

The moral of *Affluent's Tale* is supposed to be that Affluent does *not* act wrongly in going to the theatre rather than giving more money to charity, yet AU implies the contrary. Mulgan calls this the *demandingness objection*. Indeed, it seems that AU requires us to make very large sacrifices. If you can give away all or most of your salary to effective third world charities, charities which save people from serious injuries and death, then AU seems to imply that you should, so long as giving away that amount will not reduce your ability to give more later overall.

(3) *The integrity objection(s)*. Williams objected to AU on the basis that AU undermines the *integrity* of an agent's life. As Crisp has observed, Williams seems to make a number of different arguments under the heading of 'integrity'.[39] Two arguments may be discerned. The first focuses upon the idea that each of us is particularly responsible for what *we do* and has special reason to be concerned with outcomes that occur through our agency. Consider this case, made famous by Williams:

> *Jim and the Indians*. Jim, a botanist travelling in South America, comes upon a public execution in a small town. A military captain has lined up twenty Indians to be shot. He explains to Jim that the Indians are to be shot because they have been protesting against the government. The captain offers Jim a visitor's privilege. He says that he will let nineteen of the Indians go free if Jim shoots one of them. Otherwise, the execution of all twenty by Pedro, the captain's henchman, will go ahead as planned.

Williams doesn't intend this case as a refutation of AU. In fact, he agrees with what he takes to be the AU conclusion here: that Jim ought to kill one of the Indians to save the nineteen. His point is that AU makes this conclusion seem *obvious*, when it is not. What AU seems to miss is the idea that we are *specially* responsible for what *we* do. Jim seems to have a special reason that *he* not be the one who kills one of the prisoners. Yet AU seems to be indifferent as to how the deaths of the Indians come about: it is just concerned with the end-states of either 20 deaths or one death.

The second, closely related, argument focuses more directly upon 'integrity'. The claim is that AU denies the value of a person's 'sticking by what that person regards as ethically necessary or worthwhile'.[40] Consider this other example from Williams.

---

[38] Mulgan, *The Demands of Consequentialism* (above, n. 34), 4.

[39] Crisp, *Mill on Utilitarianism* (Routledge Publishing, 2006), 136.

[40] Williams, 'Replies' in Altham and Harrison (eds), *World, Mind, and Ethics: Essays on the Ethical Philosophy of Bernard Williams* (Cambridge University Press, 1995), 213.

George. George, a qualified chemist with wife and young children to support, is finding it hard to get a job. An older colleague tells George that he can get George a reasonably well-paid job in a laboratory where research is done on chemical and biological warfare. George turns down the job because of his opposition to such warfare. His colleague points out that the work is going to be done anyway, and that, were George not to take the post, the person appointed would probably be more zealous in advancing research than George.

Williams claims that AU doesn't give adequate weight to people's commitments and as a result it requires people like George simply to renounce their commitments because that will produce the most value. Yet, Williams claims, having some commitments is central to having a meaningful life.

(4) *The separateness of persons.* AU, it is objected, only cares about the *aggregation* of benefits, but not about the *distribution* of benefits. Suppose that a burden which will reduce overall welfare by 100 must be suffered. AU is indifferent between whether that burden falls on *one* individual or whether five individuals each suffer burdens of 20. In both cases overall welfare is reduced by 100. Yet the second distribution seems fairer. By looking only at the overall sum of welfare *across* all persons, AU ignores the separateness of persons.

(5) *The self-defeating objection.* It can be objected that if each person took their decisions about how to act directly by reference to AU, then the world would be worse than if people took their decisions by reference to some other principle. In this way, AU would be self-defeating.

Imagine a world in which everyone thought to himself or herself: 'I must try to maximise welfare.' In such a world people would, for example, lie to each other where they thought it would produce greater benefits. This would lead to an absence of trust and co-operation, with significantly detrimental effects for all. In such a world, people would be likely to deceive themselves into thinking that some action would produce the greatest benefit, out of self-interest. And in such a world, people would be constantly anxious that they would be sacrificed to produce greater benefits.

According to the *self-defeating objection*, then, if everyone tried to apply AU in their decisions, this would be counterproductive, and produce fewer benefits than if people used some other decision procedure in deciding how to act.

Responses to the objections
Let us first consider an objection to AU to which AU-supporters have a reasonably good answer. In our view, this is objection (5): the *self-defeating objection*.

There are at least two responses to this objection. First, as a matter of fact, it is highly unlikely that everyone will ever adopt AU in their decision-making. Most people care too much about their loved ones, for example, to consider impartially trading off their loved ones' welfare for the greater welfare of others. Secondly, as a matter of principle, it is no objection to AU that if people adopted AU in their decision-making that this would make things go worse than otherwise. As Parfit has argued, AU does not itself imply that AU be used by everyone in making deci-sions.[41] AU says: you ought to do what will produce the most benefit. It may be that you are unlikely to produce the most benefit if you try to take your decisions consciously by reference to AU itself. The general lesson here is that, as Bales points out, it is crucially important to maintain 'a sharp distinction between (a) decision-making procedures, and (b) accounts of what makes right acts right'.[42] AU is an instance of (b), not (a).

Now let's consider some responses to other objections. Consider objection (1) – that there are plausibly moral constraints on acting to maximise benefit. Some AU supporters try to meet the objection by altering their theory of value. To illustrate this strategy, it'll be helpful to focus on the example of *Transplant*. In *Transplant*, *Doctor* can either kill *Patient* or save the lives of five. Some AU supporters claim that in determining which outcome is worse – the death of *Patient* or the five other deaths – we should take into account that one death is a *killing*. The claim is that the existence of a *killing* is significantly worse than the existence of a natural death.

This is implausible. Suppose you can choose whether to save someone from being murdered or save someone from being killed in an earthquake and that there is a very slightly greater chance of saving the person from the earthquake than saving the person from being murdered. It seems that if there were just the slight-est greater chance of saving the life of the potential earthquake victim, most people would say that you should try to save that person. If that is true, then the existence of a *killing* cannot be significantly worse than the existence of a *natural death*.

Even if one did not accept the last argument, the claim that *killings* are worse than *natural deaths* will not deal with a modified *Transplant* case.[43] Suppose that the five people whose lives could be saved in *Transplant* need the organs because they have been the victims of an attempted murder. Thus, if they die, there will be five *killings*. Here it still seems wrong for *Doctor* to kill *Patient* even though this will lead to a greater number of killings than otherwise.

This leads some AU supporters to say that a *killing by the agent* is worse, *from their perspective*, than a *killing by another person*. So in *Transplant*, it would be worse over-all *for the Doctor* to kill the patient than for the *Doctor* to bring into existence the killings of five other people. In this way, these people give up on the traditional insistence of consequentialist theories upon an *agent-neutral* theory of value. Sen tries to motivate this kind of idea with the question: '... why should the moral value of the state of affairs as seen from Othello's position – husband, lover and killer of Desdemona – have to be no different from its value as seen from the posi-tion of another who is not thus involved?'[44]

[41] Parfit, *Reasons and Persons* (Oxford University Press, 1984), 40–43.

[42] Bales, 'Act-utilitarianism: account of right-making characteristics or decision-making procedure?' (1971) 8 *American Philosophical Quarterly* 257, 257.

[43] See Sinnott-Armstrong, 'Consequentialism' (above n. 28), section 5, for this case.

[44] Sen, 'Evaluator relativity and consequential evaluation' (1983) 12 *Philosophy & Public Affairs* 113, 118.

But even if we were willing to grant that that there is some coherent sense in which an outcome's value can vary according to perspective in this way, this strategy will still not reach the intuitively right results in other cases. Consider another modification of *Transplant* where *Doctor* has herself tried to kill the five other people and could kill innocent *Patient* in order to save the other five. It still seems intolerable to think that *Doctor* should kill *Patient*, even though this would prevent the existence of five killings *by herself*.

We conclude that the prospects of dealing with the existence of constraints by modifying AU's theory of value are bleak.

What about objection (2) – which points to the existence of moral options not to behave in the very demanding ways that AU requires? Some AU supporters bite the bullet and accept that morality just is very demanding. Thus Kagan responds that we should *expect* morality to be very demanding in a world in which there is a huge amount of great and avoidable suffering. As he writes:

> 'Now the extremist[45] will certainly concede that luxuries might enrich an individual's life, so that the best sort of life of all would be one which included them. But this is only to consider what the good life would be in a utopian fantasy world with unlimited resources for all. It is quite another matter to ask whether this is the best sort of life to have in a world in which others are suffering and one can do something about it.'[46]

There is force in this reply. However, the *demandingness objection* can be posed in a stronger form, focused upon cases involving special relationships. It can be argued that to treat everyone's interests equally and not to favour those of one's loved ones or one's friends is inconsistent with being in love, or *mutatis mutandis*, with being someone's friend. If that were true, accepting AU would preclude one from enjoying the benefits of love and friendship. Kagan's reply to this type of *demandingness objection* is that it is not an essential aspect of love or friendship that one favours the interests of one's loved ones or one's friends above the interests of strangers.[47] That is implausible.

What about objection (3) – Williams' *integrity objection*? It seems to us that this objection is weak. Though there is some value in not allowing some evil to come about *through one's own agency*, this value can be accommodated within AU or some version of AC. In some cases, and perhaps *Jim and the Indians* is one, this value can be outweighed by the greater good.

Rule consequentialism
The objection from *constraints* and some version of the objection from *options* seem to be powerful. These objections lead some to develop a version of *rule consequen-*

---

[45] This is Kagan's non-pejoratively intended term for someone who accepts that morality is very demanding.

[46] Kagan, *The Limits of Morality* (Clarendon Press, 1991), 361.

[47] Ibid, 368.

tialism (RC). It'll be helpful to begin with a formulation of RC by a prominent rule consequentialist, Brad Hooker:

> *Rule Consequentialism*: 'An act is wrong if and only if it is forbidden by the code of rules whose internalization by the overwhelming majority of everyone everywhere ... has maximum expected value in terms of well-being.'[48]

Before considering some features of this formulation, it is worth noting that it has some intuitive appeal. The basic idea is familiar – when we are thinking about whether some act is wrong, we often appeal to the thought – 'What if everyone did that?' Picking pretty flowers in the public park? What if everyone did that! RC asks us to imagine what the consequences would be if everyone felt free to act in a certain way. Acts are wrong if they are forbidden by rules whose internalisation by everyone – or by the 'overwhelming majority' – would have the best consequences.

Consider now some features of Hooker's definition:

(1) *Forbidden by a code of rules.* As we noted earlier, RC is distinguished by its direct focus upon *rules* not *acts.* RC assesses whether the internalisation of certain *rules* would produce the best consequences. It is possible that the rules which would produce the best consequences overall would require individual *acts* which do not produce the best consequences.

(2) *Internalisation.* Versions of RC differ depending upon whether they assess whether an action is wrong by reference to the consequences of people's *compliance* with rules or by reference to the consequences of *acceptance* of the rules. Acceptance of a rule includes feeling disposed to comply with the rule, to encourage others to comply with it, and to feel regret or shame when one fails to comply with it.

(3) *Overwhelming majority of everyone.* Hooker's reason for focusing upon the 'overwhelming majority' rather than *everyone* is that

> 'if we assume absolutely universal internalization, we eliminate any room for rule-consequentialism to make prescriptions about how to deal with people who completely lack moral motivation.'[49]

If we are asking about which rules would be best if people felt morally motivated to abide by the rules, this doesn't allow us to ask, Hooker claims, what rules we should have to deal with people *who are not morally motivated to abide by the rules* – people like psychopaths and so on.

Now we can consider how RC deals with the *constraints objection* and the *options objection.* Consider, first, the *constraints* objection. Here the basic RC claim is simple: things would go worse if there weren't generally accepted rules prohibiting torture, slavery, physical attacks and so on:

---

[48] Hooker, *Ideal Code, Real World: A Rule-Consequentialist Theory of Morality* (Oxford University Press, 2002), 32.
[49] Ibid, 83.

'On the whole, the consequences will be far better if there are generally accepted rules forbidding physical attack, torture, theft, promise-breaking, lying, and the like. Indeed, at least minimum forms of these rules are indispensable to society.'[50]

This claim seems plausible generally. However, it will not justify *absolute* constraints – constraints against doing some action regardless of how good the consequences are. Suppose that the only way to save the entirety of the human race is to torture a child. On one view, this would be wrong – no matter the consequences. Here RC would have difficulty in claiming that general acceptance of a rule prohibiting torture in this case would produce the best consequences. RC would need to claim that the inculcation of such a rule would not produce the best consequences because people might mistakenly misapply the rule or be too willing to torture people for self-interested reasons. However, given that the cost of not torturing the child in the imagined situation is more or less *infinite* (even if the probability of the event's occurring is virtually nil), it is difficult to argue against the inclusion of such a rule in the code. Therefore, RC could not justify absolute constraints.

Most people, however, think that constraints, or many constraints, are *not* absolute. So this is not a grave objection to RC. Few people would agree with Kant that if a murderer comes to your door asking you the whereabouts of his future victim, you are not permitted to lie about his whereabouts in order to save the person. Hooker therefore allows that the rules can be overridden in 'disaster' situations, where the destruction of humanity is one such situation.[51] What else counts as a 'disaster'? Here only very general guidance can be given:

'It takes the threat of a small disaster to justify breaking a small promise, a larger disaster to justify stealing, and a much larger disaster to justify inflicting serious physical harm on innocent people.'[52]

RC's strategy for justifying special obligations to our loved ones and friends is similar.[53] Love and friendship are central to human well-being. But these relationships are inconsistent with treating the well-being of loved ones and friends as on a par with the well-being of strangers. Furthermore, people in these relationships need reassurance that each other will favour their interests. Therefore, it is likely that things will go better if we have rules which morally require us to give favour to the interests of our loved ones and friends. This is plausible since, if there are no such rules, there can be no love or friendship in the world.

Finally, RC's strategy for dealing with the *options* objection is along the following lines. Hooker claims that his version of RC supports the following rule:

---

[50] Ibid, 126.
[51] Ibid, 135.
[52] Ibid.
[53] See, again, ibid, 136–41.

Hooker's beneficence rule (HBR). 'Over time agents should help those in greater need, especially the worst off, even if the personal sacrifices involved in helping them add up to a significant cost to the agents. The cost to the agents is to be assessed aggregately, not iteratively.'[54]

In an ideal world, RC would not imply HBR – in an ideal world, where everyone *followed* the rules, RC would entail that people who are relatively well off by world standards all give something between 1% and 10% of their income to effective third world charities. However, in a non-ideal world where many people will fail to comply, HBR is likely to be the optimal rule. The point that 'cost' is to be assessed aggregately, not iteratively, is built in so that people are not required to make a small sacrifice in every situation where they could produce considerable good in doing so. There are so many lives one could save by giving to charity – in a world where there is much less than full compliance – that a rule that ignored one's previous contributions (i.e. was *not* aggregative) would require one to impoverish oneself. Such a rule, Hooker claims, would have immense psychological costs and so would not be optimal compared to HBR.

Objections to rule consequentialism

Three objections are commonly made to RC.

(1) *Collapse*. The standard objection to RC is that it ultimately collapses into AC and thereby faces all of AC's problems.[55]

Here is the objection. RC says that an act is wrong if it is prohibited by the rules whose general internalisation would produce the best consequences. But won't this ultimately require agents to act in ways that produce the best consequences? If so, RC requires the same as AC.

This objection is unsuccessful, at least against Hooker's RC.[56] Consider the case where one can either break a promise and gain a little in happiness (say, 10 units) but cause just a little less unhappiness (say, 5 units), or keep the promise and not gain any happiness and cause minor unhappiness (say, 2 units). AC says that you should break the promise, which is intuitively incorrect. You ought to keep your promises even if breaking them would lead to slightly greater happiness overall. But according to Hooker's RC, if everyone internalised a rule that promises should be kept (unless there is a disaster), this would lead to much better consequences than if *everyone* internalised a rule that 'promises should be kept unless better consequences can be achieved'. The latter rule would greatly undermine people's confidence that promises would be kept and thereby undermine trust and co-operation in societies. That rule would therefore not be included in the code. Therefore, AC and RC diverge, on some versions of RC.

---

[54] Ibid, 166.
[55] See Lyons, *The Forms and Limits of Utilitarianism* (Clarendon Press, 1965), 137–43.
[56] It is also convincingly shown to be unsuccessful against another version of RC by Gibbard, 'Rule-utilitarianism: merely an illusory alternative?' (1965) 43 *Australasian Journal of Philosophy* 211.

(2) *Incoherence.* The incoherence objection to RC says that, insofar as RC diverges from AC, it is internally incoherent.

The objection runs as follows. Ultimately, according to RC, all that matters is that things go as best as possible. If all that matters is that things go best, then how can RC coherently require agents to act in ways which *do not* produce the best outcome? As Kagan puts it:

> 'Rule consequentialism has seemed to many to be open to the charge of "rule worship". If the best act, as revealed via a direct appeal to the good, differs in some case from that prescribed the rules, isn't it irrational to continue to insist on compliance with the rules? ... If what is of ultimate importance is good consequences, shouldn't we evaluate acts directly in terms of their consequences?'[57]

This objection also probably fails. As Hooker explains, RC does *not* say that all that matters is that things go as best as possible.[58] RC claims that what matters is that the *rules* which are internalised by everyone (or the overwhelming majority) are the ones which produce the best outcomes.

The objection does have force if one tries to justify RC from the premise that 'all that matters is that things go as best as they can go'. If one accepted that premise, and some people find this premise very intuitively attractive, it would probably be incoherent then to require sub-optimal acts. However Hooker does not claim to be providing a justification of RC from this premise. He proceeds rather by trying to show that RC matches our considered moral convictions.

(3) *The wrong kind of reasons.* There is another objection to RC which is, we think, powerful. Even if someone could come up with an ingenious explanation of how *AU* would lead to the upholding of freedom of speech and prohibitions against slavery in all likely situations that human societies are likely to face, there would still be something deeply wrong with that explanation. What is wrong with it is that it *gives the right verdicts for the wrong reasons.* We know that slavery is wrong before we've worked out whether it is sub-optimal to bring about slavery. As Arneson points out, exactly the same can be said of *RC*.[59] RC cannot capture the idea that, fundamentally, the reason I should care about my friend is because he is *my friend*, and not because having rules requiring me to care about him will make everyone happier.

NON-CONSEQUENTIALIST THEORIES

Non-consequentialist theories deny that whether an action is right or wrong depends only upon facts about what would produce the most value – be it *acts* which produce the most value (AC) or *rules* which produce the most value (RC).

---

[57] Kagan, 'Evaluative focal points' in Mason, Hooker, Miller (eds) *Morality, Rules and Consequences: A Critical Reader* (Rowman and Littlefield, 2000), 135.

[58] See Hooker, 'Rule-consequentialism and internal inconsistency: a reply to Card' (2007) 19 *Utilitas* 514, 517.

[59] Arneson, 'Sophisticated rule consequentialism: some simple objections' (2005) *Philosophical Studies* 235. Though Arneson doesn't consider this objection to be decisive.

Whilst consequentialist theories define the right action *solely* in terms of the good, non-consequentialist theories place the right 'prior' to the good; rightness is not wholly exhausted by facts about the good. Non-consequentialist theories do not deny that consequences can be a factor in determining whether an act is right. They deny that consequences or the value of consequences are the *only* things that matter.

Non-consequentialist theories can be characterised as accepting: (1) the existence of moral constraints; and (2) the existence of moral options.[60] We'll now explore some different non-consequentialist accounts that accept (1) and (2).

Rossian non-consequentialism

According to Ross, we each have several, distinct, duties.[61] These include duties to keep promises, duties of gratitude, duties to repair wrongdoing, duties not to harm others, and a duty to promote the good. Each of these duties is what he terms *prima facie* – which means that one may not in fact be required to act in the way that the supposed duty requires because the duty may be outweighed in the circumstances by a more important consideration. For instance, the duty to keep a promise could be outweighed by the duty not to harm another. However, for Ross, there is no higher principle by which we can determine when one duty will be outweighed in the event of conflict. So it is not the case that these duties are outweighed simply in the event that this will produce the greatest good.

What distinguishes Rossian non-consequentialism is its denial that there is a master principle which explains why we have each of the duties we do. Rather, Ross claims that the *prima facie* duties are self-evident in the sense that we can come to realise their truth after reflection, but without reasoning from further premises.

Kantian non-consequentialism

Kant's moral theory is widely understood to be non-consequentialist. According to Kant, an action is wrong if it fails to satisfy the Categorical Imperative (CI). Kant gave a number of non-equivalent formulations of CI. Here are two versions of it (frustratingly, Kant gave many different versions even of these two formulas):

> *Formula of Humanity* (FH). We must treat all rational beings, or persons, never merely as a means, but always as ends.

> *Formula of Universal Law* (FUL). We must act only in accordance with maxims that we can will to be universal laws.

How do these formulas generate non-consequentialist conclusions? Here is an example of FH leading to a non-consequentialist conclusion. It is plausible to

---

[60] See Kamm, *Intricate Ethics: Rights, Responsibilities, and Permissible Harm* (Oxford University Press, 2007), 14: 'Nonconsequentialism is now typically thought to include prerogatives not to maximize the good and constraints on producing the good.'

[61] Ross, *The Right and the Good* (Clarendon Press, 1930).

claim that we would be treating *Bystander* in the *Bridge* case above[62] 'merely as a means' if we threw him off the bridge in order to stop the train to save the five others.

FH seems to lead to implausible results in other cases, however. For instance, if *Egoist* saves a child from drowning in a pond *solely* in order to gain some financial reward, *Egoist* treats the child *merely as a means*. FH wrongly condemns *Egoist*'s action here.[63] It might be that FH can be reformulated to avoid this objection by requiring that we not *harm* people merely as a means to achieve some end, unless that end could not be achieved in any other way, and given the goodness of this aim, imposing the harm would not be too disproportionate.

To understand FUL, we need to understand the concept of a 'maxim'. By this, Kant means, roughly, a policy of action. Examples would include: 'Avenge all insults', 'Strike children when they are disobedient', 'Never lie', 'Kill only in self-defence'. In what sense does Kant mean 'can' will in FUL? Can I will it to be the case that everyone acts on the maxim 'Do what's best for me'? In a trivial sense, of course, I *can*. Sometimes Kant speaks of whether one can *consistently* will that everyone act on a certain maxim. It's not clear in what sense it would be inconsistent for me to will that everyone tries to do what is best for them, though. At other times, Kant seems to mean that we should ask whether I could *rationally* will that everyone act on a certain maxim. A person who regularly acts on the maxim 'Do what's best for me' could not rationally will it to be the case that everyone acts on this maxim. As Parfit writes: 'Most Egoists could not rationally choose to live in a world of Egoists, since that would be much worse for them than a world in which everyone accepts various moral maxims.'[64]

How does FUL lead to non-consequentialist moral rules or principles? What Parfit says here is instructive and amusing:

> 'Many professional philosophers have told their students that Kant's Formula of Universal Law conflicts with Act Consequentialism. The Act Consequentialist maxim, these people assume, could not be rationally willed to be a universal law. Some students must have asked "Why not? Why can't we rationally will that everyone does what would make things go best?" We would expect that, by now, there would be some standard answer to this question, which would be repeated in many introductory texts on ethics. Surprisingly, that is not so.'[65]

Parfit's answer involves many steps. In brief, his argument is that, under a revised version of FUL, people could only rationally will principles whose universal acceptance would be *optimific*. That is: principles whose acceptance would make things go as best as possible (in the sense of produce the most value, from an impersonal

---

[62] See p. 164, above.

[63] See Parfit, *On What Matters: Volume One* (above, n. 26), 216.

[64] Ibid, 290. As Parfit also points out, however, FUL wrongly condemns the Egoist's action whenever he is acting on the maxim 'Do what's best for me' – so even if the Egoist is saving a child in order to gain a reward, his act is condemned by FUL.

[65] Ibid, 482, fn. 406.

point of view). But people could not rationally will that everyone accept AC because the universal acceptance of AC would not be optimific:

> 'if everyone always tried to do whatever would make things go best, these attempts would often fail. When predicting the effects of possible acts, people would often make mistakes, or deceive themselves in self-benefiting ways. It would be easy, for example, to believe that we were justified in stealing or lying, because we falsely believed that the benefits to us would outweigh the burdens that our acts would impose on others.'[66]

Scanlonian contractualism

Contractualist moral theories contend that what makes acts wrong depends upon facts about what principles people would or could rationally or reasonably *agree* upon.

In his book *What We Owe to Each Other*, Scanlon, a prominent contractualist, claims that:

> 'An act is wrong if its performance under the circumstances would be disallowed by any set of principles for the general regulation of behaviour that no one could reasonably reject as a basis for informed, unforced general agreement.'[67]

So the crucial question in determining whether an act is wrong, for Scanlon, is whether it is prohibited by a principle which no one could *reasonably reject*.

What constitutes reasonable grounds for the rejection of a principle? Scanlon is doubtful that we can be very precise about this. He writes that: 'moral principles that can be stated as definite rules and applied without significant appeals to judgment are rare at best'.[68] Nonetheless, Scanlon mentions some general considerations which go to determining whether a principle could be reasonably rejected.

(1) *Burdens and benefits.* One consideration is the extent to which a principle forbidding an action benefits and burdens people compared to the benefits and burdens of an alternative principle permitting the action. For example, on these grounds, the principle that you must take action when 'you are presented with a situation in which you can prevent something very bad from happening, or alleviate someone's dire plight, by making only a slight (or even moderate) sacrifice'[69] could not be reasonably rejected.

(2) *Fairness.* A principle which arbitrarily favours one person over others is reasonably rejectable.[70] For example, if a principle said that 'everyone earning over a certain amount except John is required to make a small contribution to pay for disability benefits', and no reason is offered to exclude John, this would be arbitrary and in that sense unfair.

---

[66] Ibid, 404.
[67] Scanlon, *What We Owe to Each Other* (above, n. 31), 153.
[68] Ibid, 246.
[69] Ibid, 224.
[70] Ibid, 206–13.

(3) *Individualist focus.* The consideration of the benefits and burdens imposed upon people by a principle compared to alternative principles might suggest that Scanlon's contractualism has a consequentialist flavour. Scanlon attempts to avoid some of the objections to consequentialism by requiring that when we ask whether a principle is reasonably rejectable, we consider only various *individuals'* reasons for rejecting the principle. This, he claims, 'is what enables it [contractualism] to provide a clear alternative to utilitarianism and other forms of consequentialism'.[71] For example, it is always in principle possible under utilitarianism for some individual to be made to bear some huge burden, in order that many people could obtain some small benefit, so long as those people are sufficiently numerous to produce an overall benefit. Contractualism blocks this because none of those *individuals*, taken on their own, could reasonably reject a principle which prohibited the imposition of a great burden on another individual in return for a tiny benefit. Scanlon provides the following example. Suppose that we can rescue an electrician in a television transmitter station from serious pain and injury, but only by switching off the transmitter for 15 minutes, with the result that millions of people are deprived of World Cup football for that time. No individual viewer could reasonably reject a principle that required us to 'save a person from serious pain and injury at the cost of inconveniencing others or interfering with their amusement ... no matter how numerous these others may be'.[72]

CONCLUSION

We suggested that the *constraints objection* and some forms of the *demandingness objection* provide strong arguments against act consequentialism. We then suggested that *rule consequentialism* is more defensible, but that it is subject to the *wrong kind of reasons objection*. This gives some support for the view that morality is likely to be non-consequentialist in character.

Debate 3

What are rights?

What is meant by saying that some entity has a *right*? There are different theories. According to Raz, such theories 'attempt to capture the way the term is used in legal, political and moral writing and discourse'.[73] In what follows, we explore different theories which can be construed in this way – as attempts to understand the nature of rights, both *legal* and *moral*.

As Leif Wenar has written, the analysis of the nature of rights can usefully be understood to involve two aspects: 'a description of the internal structure of rights

---

[71] Ibid, 229.
[72] Ibid, 235.
[73] Raz, *The Morality of Freedom* (Oxford University Press, 1986), 165.

(their form), and a description of what rights do for those who hold them (their function)'.[74]

THE FORM OF RIGHTS

There is considerable agreement about the best analysis of the *form* of rights – both legal and moral.[75] Most people agree that the form of rights is best represented by an analytical system developed by the American legal theorist, Wesley Newcomb Hohfeld.[76] Hohfeld argued that when we talk about legal rights, we could be referring to any one of a number of different things. In the Hohfeldian system, there are four basic forms of rights: (1) claim; (2) liberty; (3) power; and (4) immunity. Hohfeld defined each of these forms of right by reference to its relationship with other concepts, as follows:

Claim	Liberty	Power	Immunity
Duty	No-right	Liability	Disability

Each column contains 'jural correlatives': two legal positions which logically *entail* each other. The diagonal pairs in the first two columns (duty/liberty; claim/no-right) and the second two columns (power/disability; immunity/liability) represent 'jural contradictories' – legal positions which *negate* each other.

So, C has a *claim-right* against D that D do *x* if and only if D owes C a *duty* that D do *x*. So one form of right is a *claim-right*, a right which C has against D in relation to some action, if and only if D owes C a duty in relation to that action. For example, I have a (moral and legal) claim-right against you that you don't punch me in the face. My right and your duty are opposite sides of the same coin – *jural correlatives*. Claim-rights are usually understood to be the central or paradigm case of a right.

C has a *liberty* against D that C do *x* if and only if C is *not* under a duty to D *not* to do *x*. The existence of liberty rights is thus defined by reference to the absence of rights of others that one not do the action mentioned in the liberty. For example, I have a right, in this sense, to sit on an empty park bench – I am not under a duty not to do this action.

Powers and *immunities* are rights about claim-rights and liberty-rights. Powers and immunities are rights that allow people to introduce or modify their claim-

---

[74] Wenar, 'Rights', in E. Zalta (ed.), *Stanford Encyclopedia of Philosophy* (2011), section 2.

[75] See Kramer, 'Rights without trimmings' in Kramer, Simmonds, and Steiner, *A Debate over Rights* (Oxford University Press, 1998), 8: '... virtually every aspect of Hohfeld's analytical scheme applies as well ... to the structure of moral relationships.'

[76] We draw mainly upon Hohfeld, *Fundamental Legal Conceptions as Applied in Judicial Reasoning* (Yale University Press, 1923).

rights or liberty-rights. They are in this sense *second-order* rights. A *power* is the ability to alter someone's claim-rights or liberty-rights. If A has a power against B then B is *liable* to suffer some change in B's claim-rights or liberty-rights depending on what A does. An *immunity* is enjoyed insofar as another does *not* have the power to alter one's claim-rights or liberty-rights. So, for example, an employer may have a power to alter his employee's obligations under a contract.

Let's apply this analysis of the form of rights to Ronald Dworkin's famous characterisation of rights as 'trumps':

> 'Individual rights are political trumps held by individuals. Individuals have rights when, for some reason, a collective goal is not a sufficient justification for denying them what they wish, as individuals, to have or to do, or not a sufficient justification for imposing some loss or injury upon them.'[77]

We can use Hohfeld's analysis of the form of rights to flesh out this claim of Dworkin's. Dworkin seems to be claiming with his 'rights as trumps' idea that C will have a 'trumping' right when: (1) C has a claim-right against the government that it not harm C in some way in order to promote the public interest; or (2) C has an immunity from the government's depriving him of a particular claim-right or liberty-right in order to promote the public interest.[78] The right that UK citizens enjoy under the Human Rights Act 1998 that a public authority not subject them to 'torture or to inhuman or degrading treatment or punishment' contrary to Article 3 of the European Convention on Human Rights is an example of (1). The First Amendment to the US Constitution – which provides, among other things, that 'Congress shall make no law … abridging the freedom of speech, or of the press' – is an example of (2).

THE FUNCTION OF RIGHTS

The two main theories of the function of rights are the *will theory* and the *interest theory*. What these theories are trying to do is to isolate what, conceptually, rights do for right-holders.

According to the will theory, the function of a right is to give the right-holder control over another's duty. Hart distinguished three different levels of control a person may have over another's duty: (1) the power to waive the other's duty or not; (2) the power to enforce the other's duty or not; and (3) the power to waive the other's duty to compensate in the event that the duty is breached.[79] The will theory thus aims to capture the intuitively close connection between our having rights and our ability to determine what other people may and may not do to us.

---

[77] Dworkin, 'Introduction' in his *Taking Rights Seriously* (Duckworth, 1977), xi; see also Dworkin, 'Rights as trumps' in Waldron (ed.), *Theories of Rights* (Oxford University Press, 1984).

[78] See Waldron, 'Pildes on Dworkin's theory of rights' (2000) 29 *Journal of Legal Studies* 301 for a defence of the view that Dworkin's 'rights as trumps' idea reflects the idea that there are limits on the *reasons* on which the government may legitimately act. Our elaboration of Dworkin's claim gives effect to this view.

[79] See Hart, 'Legal rights' in Hart, *Essays on Bentham* (Clarendon Press, 1982), 183–84.

According to the interest theory, the function of a right is to further the *interests* of the right-holder. C's legal right that D not negligently run C over is not a right of C's (mainly) because C can *waive* the performance of D's duty, but rather (mainly) because that duty serves C's *interests* – for instance, C's interest in bodily integrity.

Problems with the will theory

The will theory seems to be unable to explain many of the rights that people tend to think exist.

First, the will theory seems unable to explain the rights of, for example, comatose adults, since these people cannot waive the performance of other people's duties to them. Yet, most would think that these people still have a right, say, not to be intentionally physically injured by others.

Secondly, the will theory cannot explain the possibility of *unwaivable* rights. A possible example is the right not to be enslaved.[80]

Thirdly, as Wenar has emphasised, the use of rights-talk within sports and games is difficult to account for under the will theory. According to Law 12 of the FIFA *Laws of the Game*, Fouls and Misconduct: 'All players have a right to their position on the field of play.'[81] Here players are ascribed rights and yet the players do not have a power under the rules of football to waive their right not to be fouled. However, it may be questioned whether a theory of rights needs to capture such non-legal, non-moral, uses of rights-language.

Problems with the interest theory

The interest theory also faces problems. Consider Raz's interest theory:

> *Definition of a right*: 'X has a right' if and only if X can have rights, and, other things being equal, an aspect of X's well-being (his interest) is a sufficient reason for holding some other person(s) to be under a duty.

> *Capacity for possessing rights*: An individual is capable of having rights if and only if either his well-being is of ultimate value[82] or he is an 'artificial person' (e.g. a corporation).[83]

Two sets of objections can be made to this view. First, it can be objected that we can imagine situations where X's interests would be sufficient to justify imposing a duty upon Y to take some action, yet X does not have a right that Y performs that action. For example, many of us plausibly owe some duties to aid people who are dying of easily avoidable diseases in third world countries. These duties are

---

[80] See MacCormick, 'Rights in legislation' in Hacker and Raz (eds), *Law, Morality, and Society: Essays in Honour of H.L.A. Hart* (Oxford University Press, 1977), 197.

[81] See Wenar, 'The nature of claim-rights' (2013) *Ethics* 202, 203.

[82] By 'ultimate value', Raz means, roughly, of 'intrinsic value' – so a human being is a core instance of an entity whose value is *intrinsic* – the value of a human being is not just a product of the instrumental uses to which he or she can be put. See ibid, 177.

[83] Raz, *The Morality of Freedom* (above, n. 73), 166.

justified by the great improvement in these people's welfare that some small sacrifice on our part would bring. However, as Kamm argues, though the interests of these people are sufficient to justify duties upon us, it need not follow that any such individual has a *right* against us.[84] By breaching one's duty to aid, one does not violate the right of any particular individual – one does not *wrong* an individual.

Secondly, it can be objected that it is conceptually possible to have a right that it is against one's interest to have or where one's interest plays no role in the reasons why one has the right. For example, a parent has a right to the obedience of her child, yet it is not clear that we need to say that it is the parent's interest which grounds this right. Similarly, a person might have a property right which is more trouble than it is worth. Or, to take another example, D might enter into a contract with C which, due to C's miscalculation, is not to C's advantage and whose fulfilment would make C's life go positively worse – yet nonetheless, C would have a right to performance under the contract.

Interest theorists have a response to this second objection. Raz claims that 'Though rights are based on the interests of the right-holders, an individual may have rights which it is against his interest to have.'[85] The justification of this within Raz's theory is that our rights always benefit us as persons who have certain characteristics as persons, even though they may be against our interests overall. So, even if C enters into a contract with D which is disadvantageous, and so C's obtaining a right under that contract is not to C's interest, C nonetheless has an interest, as a person, in being able to enter into special voluntary relationships with other people. As persons, we have an interest in entering into special bonds with other persons.[86] Similarly, Kramer's interest theory holds that rights need only be '*generally* advantageous for their holders'.[87]

Beyond the will and interest theories of rights
Alternative theories have been developed. Sreenivasan proposes that we should adopt a hybrid model of rights, which draws upon *both* the will theory and the interest theory:[88]

> *Hybrid model of rights.* Suppose X has a duty to do Z. Y has a claim-right against X if and only if: (1) Y has the power to waive X's duty; or (2) Y has no power to waive X's duty but (that is because) Y's disability advances Y's interests on balance.

This model avoids the *unwaivable rights* problem. It allows that Y has a right not to be enslaved by X, even if Y cannot waive this right – since not being able to waive the right would serve Y's interests overall. However, Sreenivasan's hybrid model struggles with the *comatose adult* problem. It is not obvious that a comatose adult's

[84] Kamm, *Intricate Ethics: Rights, Responsibilities, and Permissible Harm* (Oxford University Press, 2007), 244.
[85] Raz, *The Morality of Freedom* (above, n. 73), 181.
[86] Ibid, 175.
[87] Kramer, 'Rights without trimmings' (above, n. 75), 96 (emphasis added).
[88] Sreenivasan, 'A hybrid theory of claim-rights' (2005) 25 *Oxford Journal of Legal Studies* 257.

(CA's) inability to waive their right not to be intentionally injured advances CA's interests on balance. This seems to imply that it is better for CA to continue in a condition where they cannot consent to waive their rights – that is, for CA to continue to be comatose – than for CA not to be in that condition.

Another theory focuses upon the idea that rights are, or create, duties owed to persons *in virtue of their status as persons and the respect owed to them in recognition of that fact.* For example, consider the *liberty-right* to free speech. We might think that people have this right simply in virtue of their status as human beings. The idea that we need to suppose that this right exists because it is generally in the interest of the right-holder to have it, or because the right-holder has the ability to waive the right, might involve one thought too many. As Kamm writes:

> 'The right to speak freely may simply be the only appropriate way to treat people with minds of their own and the capacity to use means to express it. Even if their interests would be set back only slightly by interfering with their free speech, the permissibility of doing so (including their having no right that such interference not occur) would imply that they were beings of a quite different sort. Not recognizing a person's option of speaking is to fail to respect him.'[89]

This analysis of the *liberty-right to free speech* also gains force from the fact that the *stringency* of this right – the powerful pull it has upon our reasoning in deciding how to treat people – is outstripped by the interest that the right protects. Even if what someone says is valueless, many people think that there are nonetheless strong reasons, based upon their rights, to protect their saying it.

However, it is doubtful whether all rights need to be thought of as duties owed to us out of respect for our special status as human beings or because we are entities with non-instrumental value.[90] Surely the law can confer rights upon people without claiming that those rights are conferred out of respect for our status as human beings. Perhaps only (some) fundamental human rights need to be thought of in that way.

Wenar has recently developed a novel theory of *claim-rights.*[91] The basic idea behind his theory is not far from the idea that claim-rights are duties which are owed to us in virtue of our having a certain status. However, Wenar's theory is not restricted to the specific status of *being a human being.* It can usefully be explained by reference to the idea of a *role.* Different roles – teachers, parents, goalkeepers – imply different rights owed to the role-bearers. Wenar claims that something similar to the idea of a 'role' is built in to the idea of claim-rights. For example, a footballer has a right under the rules of football that other players not tackle him in certain ways. According to Wenar, the player enjoys this right in virtue of the fact

---

[89] Kamm, *Intricate Ethics* (above, n. 84), 247.
[90] Raz addresses the idea that rights may be justified simply as a recognition of our status as human beings as an objection to his interest theory. He responds that this is not really an objection since 'a person has an interest in being respected as a person. That shows that rights grounded in respect are based on interests': Raz, *Morality of Freedom* (above, n. 73), 188.
[91] Wenar, 'The nature of claim-rights' (above, n. 81).

that the other players have a duty not to tackle him in certain ways and that this is a duty which he, *in his role as a footballer*, has a reason to want to be enforced. In general terms, for Wenar, claim-rights correlate to the duties that relevant 'role-bearers' have reason to want to be enforced.

Wenar recognises that not all rights can sensibly be said to be enjoyed by virtue of our occupying some 'role'. As he observes:

> 'While it is tempting to construe all claim-rights as the rights of role-bearers, this can no longer be done. History has moved on. As Applebaum says, "There exists a whiff of the premodern in talk about role, making such talk suspect to liberals who have no nostalgia for societies divided into castes, estates, or classes, and who fear retreat from the idea of universal humanity".'[92]

Nonetheless, Wenar claims it is possible to extend the *role-based* theory so that it covers rights that are not plausibly based upon a role being occupied – like *human rights*. The more capacious theory he terms the *kind-desire theory* of rights. The basic idea is that rights are correlated with the duties which a certain *kind* of entity, or *class* of entity, has reason to want to be enforced. So the theory maintains the idea that we enjoy rights by virtue of our membership in some *class*, but the idea of a 'class' is not restricted to occupying a *role*.

Wenar's theory seems to deal elegantly with problems in the interest and will theories. Incompetent adults still have *reason* to want that the duty not to intentionally injure them is enforced (the incompetent adults problem). People still have *reason* to want the duty not to enslave others to be enforced against them, even if they consent to this (the unwaivable rights problem). Conversely, people have reason to want that a promise to them be fulfilled if they have not waived the performance of that promise (the right without an interest problem). Moreover, Wenar's theory can explain the use of rights-language in games and other normative systems.

CONCLUSION

The will theory is unsustainable in so far as it refuses to countenance that incompetent adults still have rights. The interest theory avoids this problem, but it seems unnecessary to explain the existence of some rights by the fact that people's interests provide sufficient reason to impose duties on others. Since Wenar's theory avoids these problems, it is a more promising theory of the nature of rights.

Further Reading

Ayer, *Language, Truth and Logic* (Penguin, 2001).
Blackburn, 'How to be an ethical anti-realist' (1988) 12 *Midwest Studies in Philosophy* 361.
Dworkin, *Justice for Hedgehogs* (Harvard University Press, 2011), Part One.

---

[92] Ibid, 218·

Hooker, *Ideal Code, Real World: A Rule-Consequentialist Theory of Morality* (Oxford University Press, 2002), chs 2, 4, 6–7.

Kamm, *Intricate Ethics: Rights, Responsibilities, and Permissible Harm* (Oxford University Press, 2007), chs 1, 8.

Mulgan, *The Demands of Consequentialism* (Oxford University Press, 2001).

Scanlon, *What We Owe to Each Other* (Harvard University Press, 1998), ch. 5.

Shafer-Landau and Cuneo, *Foundations of Ethics* (Blackwell, 2007).

Smart and Williams, *Utilitarianism: For and Against* (Cambridge University Press, 1973).

Sreenivasan, 'A hybrid theory of claim-rights' (2005) 25 *Oxford Journal of Legal Studies* 257.

Wenar, 'The nature of claim-rights' (2013) *Ethics* 202.

9

JUSTICE

Debate 1

What kind of thing is justice?

In his review of Amartya Sen's *The Idea of Justice*,[1] John Gardner notes that:

> 'one oddity of The Idea of Justice which is also an oddity of Rawls' A Theory of Justice [is that] [n]either book gives over many words to explaining the very idea of justice, i.e. what marks a question out as one of justice as opposed to diligence, decency, humanity, toleration, public-spiritedness, etc.'[2]

Let's not fall into the same trap. What exactly are we talking about, when we talk about justice? Justice seems to be a term that can be applied to a person, an act, and a community. The question is whether there is some underlying sense of what justice is that might account for these diverse ways in which the term justice is used. Three views on this issue can be identified.

JUSTICE IS ABOUT DISTRIBUTIONS

The first view is that justice is concerned with *distributions* of benefits and burdens among individuals. Three versions of this first view can be distinguished.

(1) *Gardner's view.* John Gardner argues that whenever we are concerned with the question of how a benefit or burden should be *allocated*, then that is a question of justice. However, he would insist that 'there is a question of justice ... only when something is up for allocation.'[3] If there is no need to *decide* who gets what, then justice has nothing to say about what we should or should not do. So, for example, it would be odd – on this view – to say that A is acting *unjustly*

---

[1] Sen, *The Idea of Justice* (Penguin, 2010).

[2] Gardner, 'Amartya Sen's *The Idea of Justice*' (2012) 6 *Journal of Law, Philosophy and Culture* 241.

[3] Gardner, 'Finnis on justice' in Keown and George (eds), *Reason, Morality and Law: The Philosophy of John Finnis* (Oxford University Press, 2013), 161.

when he tortures B.[4] Torture is not something that is up for distribution, and in relation to which someone can say '*he* should be tortured, but *she* should not be'.

(2) *Waldron's view*. Jeremy Waldron's view is wider than Gardner's. Waldron argues that:

> 'an interest in justice – defined generally – is an interest in distributive information across individuals. Justiciers [people who are interested in justice] look for information about distributions; these are the states of affairs they want to interrogate ... An interest in justice [is] an interest in distributive information: Who gets what.'[5]

Waldron's view seems to be wider than Gardner's because, for Waldron, *any* distribution of benefits or burdens among individuals may be tested for its justice. For Gardner, only those distributions of benefits and burdens that were *distributable* can be said to be just or unjust. Having said that, Gardner would agree with Waldron that a distribution of benefits or burdens does not have to have been deliberately brought about before we can say that it was just or unjust.[6] The distribution of those benefits or burdens may have been determined by impersonal rules; but so long as those benefits or burdens were 'up for allocation' then we can ask whether the distribution of those benefits or burdens was just or unjust.

(3) *An old-fashioned view*. An old-fashioned view, which is narrower than Gardner's, is that justice is concerned with how benefits and burdens should be distributed among individuals when those benefits and burdens are *initially* held *in common* among those individuals, or are *jointly owned* by those individuals.[7] On this old-fashioned view, an uncle's decision as to how much money to give each of his nephews and nieces for Christmas cannot be said to be just or unjust – even though it involves an allocation of a particular benefit among individuals – because the money he is distributing is not initially held in common among his nephews and nieces. The uncle's distribution of his Christmas largesse could be evaluated for its wisdom or considerateness, but not for its justice.

We will not seek to resolve these differences here. Instead, we will simply say that on this first view of what justice is about, a just person is someone who is concerned to distribute in the right way the things that it falls to him to

---

[4] Cf. CL, 157–58 (see list of abbreviations, p. xiii): 'A man guilty of gross cruelty to his child would often be adjudged to have done something morally *wrong*, *bad*, or even *wicked* or to have disregarded his moral *obligation* or duty to his child. But it would be strange to criticize his conduct as *unjust*' (emphasis in original).

[5] Waldron, 'The primacy of justice' (2003) 9 *Legal Theory* 269, 277, 278.

[6] *Contra* the position taken by F.A. Hayek in his *Law, Legislation and Liberty* (Routledge, 1976), ch. 9.

[7] See Aquinas, *Summa Theologica*, II-II, q.61, a.2: 'in distributive justice, something is given to a private individual, in so far as what belongs to the whole is due to the part, and in a quantity that is proportionate to the importance of the position of that part in respect of the whole.' See also NLNR, 166–67: 'A disposition is *distributively just*, then, if it is a reasonable resolution of a problem of allocating some subject-matter that is essentially common but that needs (for the sake of the common good) to be appropriated to individuals.'

distribute. A just act is one which distributes certain benefits or burdens in the right way. And a just community is, on one view, a community in which the benefits or burdens which it is within that community's power to distribute are distributed in the right way, and, on another view, a community in which the benefits and burdens that are distributed across that community are distributed in the right way.

JUSTICE IS ABOUT TREATING PEOPLE RIGHT

John Finnis disagrees with H.L.A. Hart's observation[8] that it would be 'strange' to criticise a man who is 'guilty of gross cruelty to his child' for having acted unjustly.[9] Finnis is of the same mind as the Roman jurist Ulpian who said that 'Justice is a constant and perpetual will to give every man his due.'[10] The father who abuses his child fails to act justly because he does something morally *wrong* to his child, and in that way fails to give his child what is *due* to him or her. So, in Finnis' view, 'justice concerns ... those relations and dealings which are necessary or appropriate for the avoiding of a *wrong*'.[11]

Some thinkers straightforwardly identify doing something wrong to someone with violating their *rights*. If this is correct, then we could re-characterise this view of justice as saying that justice is about respecting other people's rights.[12] It is this rights-based view of justice that Charles Taylor is referring to when he describes

> 'a mode of justice which holds between quite independent human beings, not bound together by any society or collaborative arrangement. If two nomadic tribes meet in the desert, very old and long-standing intuitions about justice tell us that it is wrong (unjust) for one to steal the flocks of the other. The principle here is very simple: we have a right to what we have.'[13]

However, as John Gardner observes, it may be an error to identify 'failing to give someone their due' with 'violating their rights': it may be that a particular benefit might be 'due' to someone because they deserve it, but that may not mean that they have a right to that benefit; and where someone deserves for a particular burden (such as a punishment) to be allocated to him, it is almost impossible to say that he has a right to that burden.[14] So it is probably safer to say that on this

---

[8] See above, n. 4.

[9] NLNR, 163; Finnis, 'Reflections and responses' in Keown and George (eds), *Reason, Morality and Law: The Philosophy of John Finnis* (above, n. 3), 503.

[10] Justinian, *Digest* I.1.10.

[11] NLNR, 162 (emphasis added).

[12] Cf. Finnis, *Aquinas* (Oxford University Press, 1998), 188, identifying 'the substantive issues of justice' with the question of 'When will everyone, some people, or someone be entitled to some action or forbearance of mine, or to some thing which I should provide, respect, or restore?'

[13] Taylor, 'The nature and scope of distributive justice' in his *Philosophical Papers 2: Philosophy and the Human Sciences* (Cambridge University Press, 1985), 289.

[14] Gardner, 'Finnis on justice' (above, n. 3), 156. Gardner's arguments led Finnis to concede in his 'Reflections and responses' (above, n. 9), at 505, that 'various of my writings [such as at n. 12, above] too quickly assimilate what is due to X with X's right'.

view of what justice is about, justice is concerned with what we should do for other people; a just person is someone who has a standing concern to live up to the moral obligations he is subject to that require him to treat other people a certain way; a just act is one that fulfils those moral obligations; and a just community is one that lives up to the moral obligations it is subject to in the way it treats its members, and those outside the community as well.

Definitional matters aside, it seems that it is this view of justice that people are referring to when they talk about *global justice*. The idea underlying the ideal of global justice is that we have moral obligations – individually and collectively – both to do things, and to forebear from doing things, for people who we otherwise have nothing to do with. So global justice might require us not to degrade the world's environment, or to open our borders to allow those in need access to our resources and amenities; and a failure to act in accordance with these requirements can be criticised as 'unjust'.

JUSTICE IS CONCERNED WITH THE PROPER FUNCTIONING OF POLITICAL COMMUNITIES

Each of the first two views of the nature of justice find an echo in Book I of Plato's *Republic*. In the conversation between Socrates and various interlocutors over the nature of justice that makes up the *Republic*, Cephalus says that justice involves performing one's legal obligations (such as returning property that you have borrowed)[15] and Polemarchus – Cephalus's son – is happy to take the position that justice involves doing good to your friends, and harm to your enemies.[16] Cephalus's position is akin to the second view of what justice is about; while Polemarchus's view is more consistent with the view that justice is about how things (harms and benefits) should be distributed.

In Book IV of the *Republic*, Socrates (or Plato, speaking through Socrates) advances his own view of what justice is about. His view is quite different from Cephalus's and Polemarchus's and provides the basis for a third view of what justice is about. Justice, Socrates argues, is what allows the 'best city' – a city that is marked by a combination of moderation, courage, and wisdom – to function in the way it has to function if it is going to be the 'best city'. Justice involves everyone in the city performing the roles that enable the city to be the 'best city', minding their own business, and not meddling with other people performing their roles.[17] In this way, justice provides

> 'the power by which [the city's riches in moderation, courage and wisdom] came into being; and once having come into being, it provides them with preservation as long as it's in the city.'[18]

---

[15] *Republic* I, 331b.
[16] *Republic* I, 332d.
[17] *Republic* IV, 432d-434d.
[18] *Republic* IV, 433c (trans. Allan Bloom).

Aristotle followed Plato in identifying justice as fundamental to the proper functioning of the *polis*, the city-state:

> 'justice is the bond of men in states; for the administration of justice, which is the determination of what is just, is the principle of order in political society.'[19]

> 'A constitution is a kind of justice. For a constitution is a partnership for sharing. And it is by its justice that every shared thing maintains itself.'[20]

So on this view, justice is peculiarly concerned with the question of what should be done to keep the political community in which we live functioning *properly*. Questions such as – How are our leaders to be selected? What powers are they to enjoy? What rules are to govern the way we treat each other? Can they be altered, and if so by whom? How are those rules to be enforced? – are all questions of justice.

Some of these questions are about *distributive justice*: how things should be distributed. But others are about what Aristotle called *corrective justice* and what Thomas Aquinas called *commutative justice*: how we should be required to treat each other. And other questions of justice (on this view of what justice is) may not have very much to do with either corrective justice or distributive justice; for example, a question about what procedures should be followed before the law can be changed. Whatever the nature of these questions, all of them can only be properly answered against a background understanding of what political communities are for, as we cannot know what is required to ensure the proper functioning of a political community unless we know what political communities are for. If one takes the view (as Aristotle did) that political communities exist in order to enable and help people achieve a kind of personal excellence that people cannot achieve on their own,[21] then one will take one view of how the above questions of justice should be answered. If one takes the view (as Hobbes did) that political communities exist in order to help people achieve a degree of physical security from the depredations of other people that they could not achieve on their own, then one will take another view.

On this view of justice, then, a just community is a political community that is functioning properly to achieve the distinctive goods that political communities exist in order to achieve. A just act is one that contributes to the proper functioning of a political community. And a just person is someone who is concerned that the political community in which he or she lives should function properly.

CONCLUSION

It is possible to argue that the third view of what justice is all about is *foundational*, and that the first and second views are derived from that third view. So the fact

---

[19] *Politics* I, 1253ª37.
[20] *Eudemian Ethics*, VII, 1241ᵇ13–15.
[21] *Nicomachean Ethics* X.9; *Politics* I, 1252ᵇ30; III, 1281ª3–5.

that justice is – on the third view – concerned *in part* with questions of how things like political offices and legal responsibilities should be distributed, accounts for the emphasis placed by the first view on justice as being concerned with distributions. And the fact that justice is – on the third view – concerned *in part* with questions of how we should be made to treat other people accounts for why the second view should see justice as being concerned with how we should treat other people. So one could argue that the third view of what justice is concerned with is *correct* and that the other views are misunderstandings, based on a failure to grasp fully what we are talking about when we talk about justice.

However, there is a problem with taking this stance. The third view of what justice is all about may not be one that we can adopt nowadays.[22] As we have seen, the third view of what justice is concerned with rests on the *teleological idea* that political communities exist for a particular purpose, and it is with that purpose in mind that we can determine what the proper functioning of a political community requires. However, what that purpose might be is controversial; and as a result any conception of what justice requires which is based on this third view of what justice is about must also be controversial.

Given this, it may not be helpful to adopt the third view of what we are talking about when we talk about justice – doing so would mire us in arguments about whether political communities exist for a particular purpose, and, if so, what that purpose is (survival? getting on as best we can? achievement of personal excellence?). The only way to avoid this fate would be to focus on what is required for a *particular type* of political community to function properly, and therefore what justice (in the third sense of that term) would require *within that particular type* of community. So justice (in the third sense) would require one thing in a country like the UK, something else in a country like China, and something completely different in a country like the Vatican City. However, this *relativising* of justice may not be something that we can accept, and we may prefer to reserve the term justice for something more invariable – such as (1) questions about how certain benefits and burdens should be distributed among a group of individuals, or (2) questions about how we should treat other people.

If we had to choose which of these sets of questions – (1) or (2) – should be classified as questions of *justice* – and it seems we do, as a failure to do so can only breed confusion – there is no doubt that we should reserve the term 'justice' for type (1) questions. This is for two reasons.

First, if we do not use the term 'justice' to describe what we are talking about when we are talking about questions of distribution, then we will have no good term to describe this kind of discussion. The same is not true of questions about how we should treat other people, which are commonly characterised as questions

---

[22] For a modern attempt to give an account of what justice requires that seem to be based on this third view of what justice is, see Wiggins, 'Neo-Aristotelian reflections on justice' in his *Ethics: Twelve Lectures on the Philosophy of Morality* (Penguin, 2006), discussing the views of Bertrand de Jouvenel as set out in *Sovereignty: An Inquiry Into the Political Good* (Liberty Fund, 1997).

about what 'moral obligations' we owe other people, or what 'moral rights' other people have against us. Re-characterising these questions as questions about 'justice' would do nothing to assist ongoing conversations about what we should do for (and forebear from doing to) other people, but would leave us grasping for words when we wanted to address the quite different issue of how certain benefits and burdens should be distributed among a group of individuals.

Secondly, reserving the term 'justice' for issues about how benefits and burdens should be distributed makes it clear why law and justice have for so long been thought to be related, and why people think that laws can be assessed as just or unjust. For if law is about anything, it is about distributions – and at two levels. At the doctrinal level, law determines what legal rights and duties people will have, what remedies will be made available when those rights are violated and duties breached, and when and how the violation of a right or breach of a duty will be punished. At the practical or administrative level, judges and other legal officials are charged with the task of ensuring that people get the legal benefits and burdens that are 'due' to them under the law. At both levels, the law is concerned with distributions, and so the language of justice can be used at both levels.[23] At the doctrinal level, we can ask whether the way the law distributes various legal benefits and burdens is just – in other words, whether the law is getting it right in distributing those benefits and burdens in the way that it does. And at the practical or administrative level, we might say that a judge or other legal official is acting 'unjustly' if he fails to give someone what they are entitled to under the law. While this latter use of the language of justice has been criticised,[24] the identification of justice with the proper distribution of benefits and burdens at least explains *why* we might say that a judge who fails to comply with the law acts unjustly.

Debate 2

Should we accept Rawls' theory of justice?

If we are going to evaluate the justice of law's distribution of legal benefits and burdens at a doctrinal level, we need to develop a theory of justice that would tell us what a proper distribution of legal benefits and burdens would look like. The most significant theory of justice that was developed in the 20th century was that advanced by the American political philosopher, John Rawls.

As the quote from John Gardner noted at the start of this chapter, Rawls' theory of justice straddles the various different views canvassed in the previous debate as to what justice is all about. Rawls' theory of justice is a theory of how certain benefits and burdens should be distributed and is in that sense consistent with the first

---

[23] See CL, 160, noting 'a certain complexity in the structure of the idea of justice', at least when it is applied to law.

[24] Lyons, 'On formal justice' (1973) 58 *Cornell Law Review* 833. For a defence of the idea of formal justice, see Kramer, 'Justice as constancy' (1997) 16 *Law and Philosophy* 561.

view of what questions of justice are about. However, Rawls' theory is relativised to a particular type of political community – a *democratic* society. Rawls' theory of justice is about how certain benefits and burdens should be distributed among the citizens of a democratic society, in a way that allows that society to function in a stable way and allows the citizens of a democratic society to maintain the view of themselves that their membership of a democratic society encourages them to adopt. So Rawls' theory of justice seems heavily influenced by the third view of what justice is about. And finally, the benefits and burdens that Rawls' theory of justice seeks to distribute include the rights and duties that citizens of a democratic society will have against each other. So Rawls' theory of justice is also consistent with the second view of what justice is all about, as it is – in part – a theory of how we should be required to treat each other, as fellow citizens of a democratic society.

No matter: Rawls' theory of justice is rich enough that it can serve whatever conception of what justice is about that we endorse. So let's now look at Rawls' theory of justice in more detail to see whether we should accept it as a basis for evaluating the justice of law in the way it distributes legal benefits and burdens among its subjects.

RAWLS' THEORY OF JUSTICE: AN OVERVIEW

Rawls' theory of justice ('TOJ') was first set out in his *A Theory of Justice* ('TJ').[25] It subsequently went through various refinements, as set out in his *Political Liberalism* ('PL').[26] Shortly before Rawls' death in 2002, a set of lectures on his theory of justice that he gave at Harvard in the 1980s was published as *Justice as Fairness: A Restatement* ('JF').[27] The following summary of Rawls' theory of justice is mainly based on JF, as that provides the most systematic and recent account of Rawls' TOJ.

(1) *The subject of Rawls' TOJ.* Rawls' TOJ deals with how (A) basic rights and duties, (B) the benefits arising from social co-operation, and (C) the burdens necessary to sustain social co-operation are to be distributed by the basic structure of a democratic society. Rawls aims to arrive at principles of justice ('PJ') that will specify how (A), (B) and (C) are to be distributed.

(2) *The basic structure.* The basic structure of a democratic society is provided by its main political and social institutions, working together to 'distribute fundamental rights and duties and determine the division of advantages from social cooperation over time'.[28]

---

[25] Rawls, *A Theory of Justice* (Harvard University Press, 1971), rev'd edn (Harvard University Press, 1999). The page numbering of the original 1971 edition of *A Theory of Justice* and the subsequent 1999 revised edition differ substantially. So in the footnotes that follow, the 1971 edition will be referred to as 'TJ (1971)', and the revised edition as 'TJ (1999)'.

[26] Rawls, *Political Liberalism* (Columbia University Press, 1993) (henceforth, 'PL').

[27] Rawls, *Justice as Fairness* (Harvard University Press, 2001) (henceforth, 'JF').

[28] TJ (1971), 7; TJ (1999), 6.

(3) *A democratic society.* Rawls' TOJ is worked up from certain key ideas that are characteristic of democratic societies: (i) a democratic society is viewed as being a fair system of social co-operation over time from one generation to the next; (ii) the citizens of a democratic society are viewed as being 'free and equal'; and (iii) a democratic society is a well-ordered society.

(4) *A fair system of social co-operation.* A fair system of co-operation is one under which people co-ordinate their activities by reference to publicly recognised rules and procedures which it would be reasonable for them to accept provided that everyone else did as well. Rules and procedures which satisfy this requirement (the requirement of 'reciprocity') are 'fair terms of cooperation'. Rawls' PJ are charged with the task of specifying what these 'fair terms of cooperation' are.

(5) *Free and equal.* The citizens of a democratic society are viewed as *free* because they are not dominated by whatever conception of what a good life entails that they currently endorse. So they are free to revise and change this conception should it seem reasonable for them to do so. The citizens of a democratic society are viewed as *equal* because they are regarded as all equally possessing two moral powers that enable them to engage in social co-operation over a complete life.[29] The first power (the power to be 'reasonable') is the capacity for a sense of justice – the ability to understand, apply and accept the PJ that determine the fair terms of social co-operation. The second power (the power to be 'rational') is the power to form and pursue a conception of what a good life entails. Rawls' PJ have to be consistent with the citizens of a democratic society's status as 'free and equal'. In other words, they have to be settled by an agreement between the citizens, made under conditions which ensure that they are unaffected by: (i) the vagaries of what conceptions of the good particular citizens happen currently to endorse; and (ii) any current differences in wealth or status between the citizens.

(6) *A well-ordered society.* A well-ordered society is one which is effectively regulated by a particular set of PJ. For that to happen, it will have to be true that: (i) all the society's citizens agree on what PJ will govern the operation of the basic structure of the society, and they know that they all agree; (ii) the basic structure of the society is publicly acknowledged to give effect to those PJ; and (iii) all the society's citizens act in accordance with those PJ.[30] Rawls' PJ have to satisfy these conditions. In other words, they have to be capable of being publicly recognised and mutually acknowledged by the citizens of a democratic society.

(7) *The argument.* We can summarise the above by saying that the PJ Rawls is trying to arrive at have to satisfy two key conditions:

(a) *The fairness condition:* the PJ must set out terms of social co-operation that are *fair* as between citizens who are conceived as being 'free and equal'.

---

[29] On the two moral powers, see PL, 18–20; JF, 18–20.
[30] PL, 35–40; JF, 8–9.

(b) *The stability condition*: the PJ must be *stable*, in the sense that when the basic structure of a democratic society gives effect to those PJ, the reasonable citizens of that society will support, give effect to, and affirm those PJ even in the face of temptations to violate those PJ.

Rawls argues that *his* PJ – *Rawls' principles of justice* – satisfy those two conditions. If this is right, then a democratic society should give effect to Rawls' PJ. It is only by giving effect to Rawls' PJ that a democratic society can simultaneously live up to: (i) its promise to amount to a fair system of social co-operation between citizens conceived as being free and equal; and (ii) its aspiration to be a well-ordered society.

(8) *The primary goods*. Before we set out Rawls' PJ, we should recall (see point (1), above) that the fundamental task of Rawls' PJ is to specify how (A), (B) and (C) are to be distributed by the basic structure of a democratic society. (A), (B) and (C) can be fleshed out and made more concrete through the following list of 'primary goods':[31]

(i)   The basic rights and liberties: freedom of thought and liberty of conscience, and freedom of association. 'These rights and liberties are essential conditions for the adequate development and full and informed exercise of the two moral powers.'
(ii)   'Freedom of movement and free choice of occupation against a background of diverse opportunities, which opportunities allow the pursuit of a variety of ends and give effect to decisions to revise and alter them.'
(iii)   'Powers and prerogatives of offices and positions of authority and responsibility.'
(iv)   'Income and wealth, understood as all-purpose means ... generally needed to achieve a wide range of ends whatever they may be.'
(v)   'The social bases of self-respect, understood as those aspects of basic institutions normally essential if citizens are to have a lively sense of their worth as persons and to be able to advance their ends with self-confidence.'

It is the distribution of these goods by the basic structure of a democratic society that Rawls' PJ seek to regulate.

(9) *Rawls' principles of justice*. Rawls' PJ are as follows:

(i)   *The first principle of justice*. The first PJ is that 'Each person has the same indefeasible claim to a fully adequate scheme of equal basic liberties, which scheme is compatible with the same scheme of basic liberties for all.'[32]
(ii)   *The second principle of justice*. The second PJ is that 'Social and economic inequalities are to satisfy two conditions: (a) they are to be attached to offices

---

[31] JF, 58–59. The primary goods are set out in much more sketchy form in TJ (1971), 92; TJ (1999), 79.
[32] JF, 42. Rawls' earlier formulation of the first principle can be found at TJ (1971), 60; TJ (1999), 53.

and positions open to all under conditions of fair equality of opportunity; and (b) they are to be to the greatest benefit of the least-advantaged members of society.'[33] (b) is known as the *difference principle*.

The first PJ is prior to the second PJ in that the second PJ is only given effect to against a set of background institutions that give effect to the first PJ.

(10) *Original position*. We can test for whether Rawls' PJ satisfy the *fairness condition* through the 'original position' (OP) device. This involves imagining that representatives of the citizens of a democratic society are determining the terms on which they will co-operate together under conditions where they do not know: (i) what comprehensive conceptions of the good the citizens they represent happen to endorse; and (ii) what positions in society are occupied by the citizens they represent.

These conditions (known as the '*veil of ignorance*') will help guarantee that the representatives' conclusions as to the terms on which the citizens will co-operate will reflect the citizens' status as 'free and equal'. First, they will not be affected by whatever conceptions of the good the citizens happen to have adopted today (when their 'free' status means they may adopt a different conception of the good tomorrow). Secondly, they will not be affected by variations in wealth and status among citizens of a democratic society (when their status as 'equals' means that such morally arbitrary factors should be irrelevant to the determination of the terms of co-operation between the citizens).

It follows from this that whatever terms of co-operation that are agreed upon in the OP are guaranteed to be fair terms of social co-operation as between citizens who are 'fair and equal'. So if the representatives in the OP would prefer the basic structure of the democratic society in which the citizens they represent live to be regulated by Rawls' PJ as opposed to any other competing PJ, then that shows that Rawls' PJ satisfy the fairness condition.

(11) *Maximin*. In deciding what PJ to adopt in the OP, it would be rational for the representatives in the OP to adopt a decision procedure known as 'maximin'. This decision procedure involves evaluating proposed PJ according to what their least worst outcome is.[34] (An example of making a decision under 'maximin': 'If I invest all my money in shares, I could make a lot of money, but I could also lose a lot of money. But if I put it in the bank, I won't make much money, but I won't lose it either. I'll put it in the bank.') It would be rational for the representatives in the OP to adopt this decision procedure because it is likely that not much might be gained – in the best case scenario – by opting for one PJ over another, but a lot could be lost – in the worst case scenario – by opting for one PJ over another.

---

[33] JF, 42–43. Compare TJ (1971), 60; TJ (1999), 53.
[34] For more on maximin, see TJ (1971), 152–54; TJ (1999), 132–33.

(12) *Rawls' PJ vs the principle of utility*. The representatives in the OP would prefer to adopt Rawls' PJ to a PJ – the 'principle of utility' – which says that the basic structure of society should be arranged in such a way as to maximise the average utility of the citizens of that society. It is reasonable to expect that in a society governed by the principle of utility that certain citizens' basic liberties will be curtailed in order to promote the average level of utility enjoyed by citizens generally. This is a much worse outcome than the worst outcome in a society governed by Rawls' PJ, where the average level of utility may be lower, but citizens' enjoyment of the basic liberties will always be protected. The representatives in the OP will always refuse to trade off the basic liberties against an increase in the average standard of living because they will recognise that those they represent may be deeply affected – in terms of not being able to free to practise their religion or pursue some other comprehensive conception of the good – by such a trade-off.

(13) *Rawls' PJ vs the principle of restricted utility*. The representatives in the OP would also prefer to adopt Rawls' PJ to a PJ – the 'principle of restricted utility' – under which the basic structure of a society is to be arranged in such a way as to maximise the average utility of the citizens of that society *so long as*: (a) every citizen's enjoyment of the basic liberties is guaranteed; and (b) every citizen enjoys a certain minimum, satisfactory, standard of living. To see why this is, consider the following scenarios:

(i) In the first scenario, we compare two societies. In the first (*Moderatia*), citizens are allowed to trade goods and services, and retain the benefits of their trades, subject to minimum wage laws and various controls on the prices that are charged for goods that are likely to be purchased in the main by the *less advantaged* in society and sold to them by the *more advantaged*. In the second society (*Libertaria*), citizens are allowed to trade goods and services free of any controls at all. The table below sets out the wealth each member of each section of the population will enjoy in either scenario.

	Moderatia	*Libertaria*
More advantaged (50% of population)	500	800
Less advantaged (50% of population)	150	120
Average wealth per head of population	325	460

Assuming that in both societies every person's basic liberties are respected, and that 100 represents a minimum, satisfactory, standard of living, then the principle of restricted utility indicates that we should prefer *Libertaria* to *Moderatia* as the average utility per citizen is higher in *Libertaria*. However, Rawls' PJ indicate that we should prefer *Moderatia* to *Libertaria* as the gain in wealth that the more advantaged experience as we move from *Moderatia* to *Libertaria* does not work to the benefit of the less advantaged in the population; indeed, it is – to some extent – obtained at the expense of the less advantaged. The representatives in the OP will also prefer *Moderatia* to *Libertaria* as allowing some citizens (the more advantaged) to enrich themselves at the expense of other citizens (the less advantaged) simply because they have been lucky enough to be endowed with the qualities that qualify them as more advantaged would be incompatible with the citizens' statuses as 'free and equal'.

(ii) In the second scenario, we compare two societies. The first (*Anomia*) is characterised by weak co-operation between all citizens of the society. Everyone tries to manage as best they can for themselves and their families, but occasionally have need to trade with other citizens. The second (*Privilegia*) is characterised by weak co-operation between the more advantaged and less advantaged citizens, but very strong co-operation between the more advantaged. So the more advantaged work together on developing new technologies and products that they then share between themselves, excluding the less advantaged from the benefits of those technologies and products.

	Anomia	*Privilegia*
More advantaged (50% of population)	350	2,900
Less advantaged (50% of population)	100	100
Average wealth per head of population	225	1,500

The principle of restricted utility would favour *Privilegia* over *Anomia* as the average utility of each citizen is higher in *Privilegia* and each citizen enjoys at least a minimum, satisfactory standard of living (100) in *Privilegia*. However, Rawls' PJ would not prefer *Privilegia* over *Anomia* as the increase in wealth enjoyed by the more advantaged as we move from *Anomia* to *Privilegia* does not work to the benefit of the less advantaged in society. Rawls claims that the representatives in the OP would also refuse to prefer *Privilegia* over *Anomia*, as the principle of restricted utility indicates that they should.

But note that here the more advantaged's increase in wealth is not obtained at the expense of the less advantaged: the less advantaged are simply left out in the cold as the more advantaged get wealthier and wealthier by co-operating together. However, the representatives in the OP would still refuse to prefer *Privilegia* over *Anomia* because it would be very difficult for the citizens they represent to think of the society they live in as amounting to a fair system of co-operation *between* citizens viewed as free and *equal* if the basic structure of their society allowed some citizens 'to take advantage of contingencies of native endowment, or of initial social position, or of good or bad luck over the course of life ... in ways that [did not] benefit everyone, including the least favored'.[35] The fact that the less advantaged are left behind by the more advantaged in the second scenario will make the less advantaged think that the idea that they live together with the more advantaged in a society where *everyone* co-operates together on the basis that *everyone* is 'free and *equal*' is a cheat and a lie. So as a PJ, the principle of restricted utility is unstable: in time, the less advantaged will 'feel left out; and, withdrawn and cynical' will be unable to affirm the principle of restricted utility as being a PJ.[36]

The only society that the representatives in the OP would prefer to *Anomia* is one (*Welfaria*) where strong co-operation between the more advantaged works to the benefit of the less advantaged through transfer payments being made to the less advantaged by the more advantaged out of the increase in wealth that increased co-operation between themselves brings them.

	Anomia	Welfaria
More advantaged (50% of population)	350	1,500
Less advantaged (50% of population)	100	1,000
Average wealth per head of population	225	1,250

The average wealth per head of population is less in *Welfaria* than it is in *Privilegia* because the fact that the more advantaged are no longer working exclusively for themselves in strongly co-operating together lessens their incentives to co-operate so much among themselves. So the principle of restricted utility would favour *Privilegia* over *Welfaria*. However, the representatives in the OP would favour *Welfaria* over *Privilegia* (as Rawls' PJ indicate they should) as in *Welfaria* the morally arbitrary distribution of talents and assets is not allowed to work exclusively for the benefit of those lucky enough to be blessed with those talents and assets, but instead works for the benefit of all.

So in scenarios (i) and (ii), the representatives in the OP will reject the idea of the basic structure of society being governed by the principle of restricted utility, and will instead prefer the basic structure to be governed by Rawls' PJ. (It should be noted that this preference for Rawls' PJ over the principle of restricted utility in scenarios (i) and (ii) does not rest on the adoption of a maximin decision procedure, but on considerations of what is entailed by the conception of citizens in a democratic society as being free and equal and engaged in a fair scheme of social co-operation.)

---

[35] JF, 124.
[36] JF, 128.

(14) *Rawls' PJ vs other principles of justice*. Rawls claims, but does not prove, that the representatives in the OP will prefer Rawls' PJ over any other competing principles of justice. Rawls' PJ will therefore be adopted by the representatives in the OP as determining the terms of social co-operation in a democratic society; and the conditions under which the agreement to adopt Rawls' PJ is reached will guarantee that those terms are 'fair'. This concludes the argument for thinking that Rawls' PJ satisfy the *fairness condition*; but it still has to be shown that Rawls' PJ satisfy the *stability condition* so that we can say that a society whose basic structure is governed by Rawls' PJ will be a well-ordered society.

(15) *The inevitability of reasonable pluralism in a democratic society.* It is inevitable that reasonable citizens of a democratic society will adopt fundamentally different conceptions of what a good life entails. This is because arriving at such a conception involves exercising one's judgment, and many factors ('the burdens of judgment') mean that people will exercise their judgment on this matter in different ways: (a) evidence relevant to the exercise of one's judgment may be hard to assess; (b) different people may put different weight on factors relevant to the exercise of their judgment; (c) any concepts that are relevant to the exercise of our judgment will be vague and be capable of being interpreted in different ways; (d) the life experiences that we bring to bear on the exercise of our judgment will inevitably be different; (e) where different, incommensurable, factors weigh on both sides of a issue, it is impossible to determine precisely how that issue should be resolved and different people will end up making different – and equally reasonable – decisions.[37]

(16) *The idea of an overlapping consensus.* This fact, and the fact that Rawls' PJ facilitate this pluralism by guaranteeing that each citizen will enjoy the basic liberties to an equal extent, may make it hard for Rawls' PJ to satisfy the *stability condition*. How can citizens who end up adopting radically different comprehensive conceptions of the good still all support, give effect to, and affirm Rawls' PJ? Despite this problem, it should still be *possible* for reasonable citizens of a democratic society, who all endorse different conceptions of what a good life looks like, to arrive at an 'overlapping consensus' under which they *all* acknowledge and give effect to Rawls' PJ. This is for two reasons.

(17) *The idea of public reason.* The first is that reasonable citizens will accept that when it comes to determining how coercive political power is to be used, the use of such power has to be justified in terms that other citizens could reasonably be expected to accept. So the use of coercive political power has to be justified in terms of *public reason*, and cannot be justified on grounds that would only be accepted by someone who adopts a particular comprehensive conception of the good which will, inevitably, not be shared by others.

---

[37] On the 'burdens of judgment', see further PL, 54–58; JF, 35–36.

As Rawls observes, 'if it is said that outside the church there is no salvation'[38] and therefore basic liberties such as freedom of speech must be abrogated where their exercise threatens the church's ability to save souls,

> 'the appropriate reply is that such a doctrine is unreasonable: it proposes to use the public's political power – a power in which all citizens have an equal share – forcibly to impose a view affecting constitutional essentials about which many citizens as reasonable persons, given what we have called the burdens of judgment, are bound to differ uncompromisingly.'[39]

Reasonable citizens will accept this, and seek to justify the use of coercive political power in terms that other citizens could reasonably accept. Rawls' PJ provide them with the ability to do this as Rawls' PJ do not rest on a particular comprehensive conception of the good, and instead rest on the idea – which reasonable citizens will accept – that the citizens of a democratic society co-operate together on the basis that they are free and equal. So reasonable citizens in a democratic society could be expected to support, give effect to, and affirm Rawls' PJ in determining how coercive political power is to be used, no matter what conceptions of the good they happen to adopt.

(18) *The virtues of a liberal society.* The second is that reasonable citizens of a democratic society, who all endorse different conceptions of what a good life looks like, may come to feel an allegiance to Rawls' PJ once they experience what life is like in a democratic society whose basic structure is governed by Rawls' PJ. They will see that such a society is free of on-going disputes and bargaining over the scope of people's basic liberties, that it operates in a stable and predictable way, and that by doing these things and by promoting the idea of citizens as being 'free and equal' it encourages 'the cooperative virtues of political life: the virtues of reasonableness and a sense of fairness, and of a spirit of compromise, and a willingness to meet others halfway'.[40] These are not mean achievements, and no reasonable person – no matter what concept of the good they happen to endorse – will lightly throw them away. Instead, it will be far more likely that where an individual's particular conception of the good runs up against adherence to Rawls' PJ, the individual in question will revise his or her conception of the good to accommodate the demands of Rawls' PJ.

(19) *Conclusion.* This concludes the argument for adopting Rawls' PJ in determining how the primary goods are to be distributed by the basic structure of a democratic society. Rawls' PJ, it is claimed, are both fair and stable, and should therefore be given effect to in a democratic society which – by definition – claims to be a fair system of co-operation between citizens conceived of as free and equal, and which aspires to be a well-ordered society.

---

[38] JF, 183, referring to Pope Boniface VIII's *Unam Sanctam* (1302).
[39] JF, 184.
[40] JF, 116.

Rawls' TOJ has been universally acclaimed. The libertarian philosopher Robert Nozick said – in his book *Anarchy, State and Utopia*[41] – that 'Political philosophers now must either work within Rawls' theory or explain why not.'[42] The socialist philosopher G.A. Cohen said that 'at most two books in the history of Western political philosophy have a claim to be regarded as greater than *A Theory of Justice*: Plato's *Republic* and Hobbes's *Leviathan*.'[43] However, Rawls' TOJ is not without its critics – Nozick and Cohen are two of the most prominent. Most criticisms of Rawls' TOJ are targeted at his 'difference principle'. We will discuss three criticisms that have been, or might be, made of that principle. (Criticisms of Rawls' first principle of justice – the equal distribution of basic liberties – will be dealt with in the following chapter.)

TITLE TO DISTRIBUTE

The first criticism was made most forcefully by Robert Nozick, three years after Rawls' *Theory of Justice* was published. It goes as follows: In distributing 'income and wealth' (the fourth primary good), Rawls' TOJ overreaches itself. It purports to distribute something that is not, in Gardner's phrase, 'up for allocation'. People are already entitled to the income and wealth that comes into their hands (so long as it was legitimately acquired), and not by virtue of any rules on the private ownership of property set up by the basic structure, but by virtue of natural rights that they have to property that they have legitimately acquired.

After all, we would not dream of adopting a 'difference principle' in relation to people's natural attributes, such as their looks or their physical skills. We would not say that inequalities in looks are only to be allowed if such inequalities work to make the least good looking in society better off than they would be if such inequalities did not exist. And that's because someone's physical appearance is not something that is 'up for allocation'. A person is entitled to their own appearance – and this not because the basic structure of our society says they are, but because they simply are.

Income and wealth are the same – so long as they were legitimately acquired in accordance with rules (laid down by Nozick in *Anarchy, State and Utopia*) for the just acquisition and transfer of property, then they are not 'up for allocation'. Accordingly, Nozick argues that Rawls' TOJ is fundamentally flawed: it wrongly treats income and wealth as 'manna from heaven'[44] – an unearned gift to the community that the members of the community are free to determine among themselves how it should be shared out.

How might Rawls' TOJ be defended against this attack? One way might be to say that virtually all the income and wealth produced in a democratic society is the

---

[41] Nozick, *Anarchy, State and Utopia* (Basic Books, 1974).
[42] Ibid, 185.
[43] Cohen, *Rescuing Justice and Equality* (Harvard University Press, 2008), 11.
[44] Nozick, *Anarchy, State and Utopia* (above, n. 41), 199.

fruit of social co-operation, and can therefore be legitimately distributed by rules that purport to govern the terms on which people will co-operate with each other. However, consider the situation[45] where a class of students take an exam. The teacher marks each student's paper and gives each paper a mark out of 100. Each student's mark will, in large part, reflect the social co-operation between the students and between the student and the teacher that has gone on within the class over the term, studying whatever is the subject of the exam. But no one would take that as suggesting that students who have done less well in the exam have a claim to any of the marks obtained by students who have done better in the exam. Each student is entitled to the mark that they have received, even though that mark could not have been obtained without a great degree of social co-operation.

The argument seems compelling, but can rebutted. The purpose of the exam is to determine how each student is doing in their studies; that purpose would be entirely frustrated if a student's mark did not reflect how well *they* performed in *their* exam. But if the teacher were handing out sweets to the students to reward them for their performance – with the number of sweets received by a student corresponding to how high a mark the student achieved in the exam – it might well be that the students who have done less well could legitimately make a claim to share in the extra sweets obtained by the high flyers on the ground that the high flyers could not have flown so high without their help. (And – if they were trying to be fair and objective – the students might unanimously decide that the high flyers should be allowed to retain *some* of their extra sweets on the basis that doing so will incentivise those who have done less well this time round to try harder next time, thus giving effect to a form of difference principle in their deliberations as to how the extra sweets should be distributed.)

In the absence of some further argument to the contrary, it seems then that the income and wealth produced by social co-operation can properly be regarded as a 'common asset' that can be legitimately distributed by the basic structure of a democratic society.

THE ROLE OF SELF-INTEREST IN RAWLS' TOJ

Some people read Rawls' TOJ as being based on the assumption that in the OP, each citizen's representative will seek to maximise the primary goods that would be enjoyed by that citizen, while being incredibly fearful that the citizen might end up being at the bottom of society.[46] Thus we get the difference principle: equal distribution of primary goods (other than the basic liberties) unless the worst off would be made better off under unequal distribution.

---

[45] Ibid.

[46] For such a reading, see Parfit, *On What Matters: Volume One* (Oxford University Press, 2011), 346–55; Simmonds, *Central Issues in Jurisprudence*, 4th edn (Sweet & Maxwell, 2008), 74–76.

If this reading is correct, Rawls' TOJ is open to the criticism that it is hard to see how agents acting in a purely self-interested fashion can tell us anything about what justice requires. We *can* use self-interest to try to get to an outcome which we *independently* know to be just (as we do when we attempt to divide a cake equally between A and B by inviting A to slice the cake in two, on the basis that B will get to decide first which slice he wants).[47] However, it seems implausible to think that we can use self-interest to determine what is just in the first place.

However, Rawls' later refinements of his TOJ seem to make it clear that this reading of his TOJ is incorrect. For example, the representatives in the OP do not – in the final version of Rawls' TOJ – prefer Rawls' PJ over the principle of restricted utility because they are fearful that the citizen they represent will end up materially worse off under the principle of restricted utility than he or she will under Rawls' PJ.[48] They do so because adopting the principle of restricted utility will be seriously damaging to a democratic society's conception of itself as being a fair scheme of co-operation between free and equal citizens.

G.A. Cohen made a quite different objection to the role that self-interest played in Rawls' TOJ.[49] Cohen's criticism was not so much a criticism of the difference principle, but the way Rawls justified inequalities by reference to the difference principle. Consider the following societies. We begin with an equal society, *Equalia*, where everyone has 100 units of wealth per head. Equality is maintained through a strict system of transfer payments which require those who are naturally blessed with greater talents to transfer some of their income to those less blessed. However, we start to think that we could actually increase the size of the pie that is available to be distributed by allowing the talented ones to retain a greater proportion of the fruits of their labours. So we transform *Equalia* into *Meritia* – a society where the rules on transfer payments are relaxed, so that the talented top 10% are incentivised to work harder and more productively, thus creating more wealth that they can keep for themselves, more wealth that 'trickles down' to the lower echelons of society, and more wealth that can be redistributed under the transfer payment rules that we have retained.

	Equalia	*Meritia*
Top 10%	100	500
Middle 80%	100	250
Bottom 10%	100	150

[47] An example used by Rawls in TJ (1971), 85; TJ (1999), 74.
[48] Rawls confessed in JF that the failure to make clear in TJ that the reasons for adopting the difference principle do *not* rely on maximin considerations was a 'serious fault': JF, 95, fn. 17. In Rawls' final version of his theory of justice, it seems that maximin considerations are much more relevant to adoption of the first PJ (which requires equal distribution of the basic liberties): PL, 310–15; JF, 104–105.
[49] See Cohen, 'Where the action is: on the site of distributive justice' (1997) 26 *Philosophy and Public Affairs* 3; and *Rescuing Justice and Equality* (above, n. 43).

The result is an unequal society, but one in which the bottom 10% do better than they would have done in an equal society. So Rawls' difference principle would see nothing unjust in moving from *Equalia* to *Meritia*; indeed, justice – as Rawls sees it – would demand that we make the shift.

Cohen did not think that *Meritia* is just. Why, he asked, can we not have a society where the wealth that is produced in the unequal society is equally distributed so that everyone gets 265 units of wealth each?[50] The answer is that such a society is not on offer to us because the talented top 10% will only be incentivised to produce the wealth that the unequal society enjoys if they are allowed to retain 500 units of wealth. But – Cohen argued – that answer shows that *Meritia* cannot be regarded as just. The only reason why we can't have a society where everyone has 265 units of wealth each is that the talented top 10% are not willing to work for others in society as well as themselves. The sort of society that *Meritia* is works with, and rewards, that attitude; and because its distribution of wealth is ultimately based on the self-interest of the talented top 10%, it cannot be said to be just.

Rawls might have sought to rebut Cohen's criticism by arguing that he is only concerned with the justice of the basic structure of a democratic society. The basic structure of *Meritia* can still be said to be just, even if individual actors in that society manifest greedy and grasping attitudes towards their fellow citizens. However, Cohen sought to counter this by arguing:

> 'why should we *care* so disproportionately about the coercive basic structure, when the major reason for caring about it, its impact on people's lives, is *also* a reason for caring about informal structure and patterns of personal choice? To the extent that we care about coercive structure because it is fateful with regard to benefits and burdens, we must care equally about the ethic that sustains gender inequality, and inegalitarian incentives. And the similarity of our reasons for caring about these matters will make it lame to say: ah, but only the caring about coercive structure is a caring about *justice*, in a certain distinguishable sense. That thought is, I submit, incapable of coherent elaboration.'[51]

So someone who cared about justice, Cohen thought, would care about taking steps to ensure that talented people in a society like *Meritia* were not so greedy and grasping that they would only be willing to produce more wealth on condition that they were allowed to retain more of that wealth than anyone else.

Two points can be made in response to Cohen's counter-argument. First, it is debatable whether it would be *legitimate* for the state to take an interest in reshaping people's basic attitudes about what they are prepared to do and for whom. This is a topic we will address in the next chapter. Secondly, it is not clear what is so wrong with the attitudes of the talented ones in the scenario we have been considering. Suppose that it were made clear to the talented ones in *Equalia* that 'If you

---

[50] We arrive at this figure by doing the sum (500 x 10) + (250 x 80) + (150 x 10) and then dividing by 100.
[51] Cohen, 'Where the action is: on the site of distributive justice' (above, n. 49), 23 (emphasis in original).

work harder and produce more wealth, the extra wealth you produce will be shared equally between everyone in society.' And suppose the talented ones respond in a self-interested fashion by saying, 'That's fine. In that case, we would prefer not to work harder. We know everyone would benefit if we did, but we prefer to enjoy the leisure time we would give up if we worked harder to the extra wealth we would make and be allowed to retain if we did work harder.' Is that so wrong? Are the talented ones *obliged* to give up the leisure time they enjoy in *Equalia* in order to move society to a state where everyone enjoys an equal share of a bigger pie? It is hard to see that they are.

THE SELF-CONCEPTION OF CITIZENS IN A DEMOCRATIC SOCIETY

As we have seen, the fact that citizens in a democratic society think of themselves, and are encouraged to think of themselves, as 'free and equal' does a lot of work in Rawls' TOJ. However, it is not – we think – a necessary truth that citizens in a democratic society *have* to think of themselves in this way. They could adopt a different conception of themselves. They could think of themselves as *unfree* in that they are always vulnerable, no matter what their position in society, to losing what they have as a result of accident or disaster (economic, man-made, or natural). And they could think of themselves as *unequal* in terms of their capabilities to satisfy their natural needs as human beings through their own efforts, or through co-operation with others. Just as some people are more talented than others, some people are more disabled than others.

A number of philosophers – notably Amartya Sen,[52] Eva Kittay,[53] Martha Nussbaum,[54] and Alasdair MacIntyre[55] – have started to explore what a just society would look like if we took seriously the idea of our being *equally vulnerable and unequally needy*. While this might not be an approach that any of the above mentioned philosophers would recommend, it might be worth asking what PJ would be adopted in the OP by the representatives of the citizens of a society were they to think of the society in which the citizens lived as being a fair scheme for co-operation between citizens who were equally vulnerable to losing everything through accident or disaster, and were unequally needy in terms of their abilities to fend for themselves.

The representatives would have to begin with a list of *capabilities*, the lack of which would severely hinder an individual in functioning properly as a human being. Equipped with such a list, the representatives would almost certainly decide that the basic structure of the society in which the citizens they represent live should seek to foster institutions concerned with: (1) the *acquisition* of those capa-

---

[52] Sen, 'Equality of what?' (Tanner Lecture on Human Values, 1979); *Inequality Re-Examined* (Oxford University Press, 1992); *The Idea of Justice* (above, n. 1).

[53] Kittay, *Love's Labor: Essays on Women, Equality and Dependency* (Routledge, 1999).

[54] Nussbaum, 'Beyond the social contract: toward global justice' (Tanner Lectures on Human Values 2002–3); *Frontiers of Justice* (Harvard University Press, 2006), chs 1–3.

[55] MacIntyre, *Dependent Rational Animals: Why Human Beings Need the Virtues* (Duckworth, 2009).

bilities (by someone who can acquire them but has yet to do so); (2) the *protection* of those capabilities (against being lost or damaged through accident, disaster, or other people's malevolence); and (3) the *replacement* of those capabilities (where lost by someone who once had them).

The first PJ the representatives in the OP would adopt, then, is that *the basic structure of society should care for those who cannot care for themselves.* But doing this could be expected to be very expensive. So the second PJ that the representatives in the OP could be expected to adopt is that *inequalities in wealth and income should be allowed insofar as they help the basic structure fulfil the first PJ.* So an economic system characterised by great inequalities of income and wealth would be tolerated under the second PJ only if that kind of system were capable in the long run of reliably producing the kinds of tax revenues needed to fund the institutions required for the first PJ to be fulfilled.

These speculations illustrate just how different the PJ arrived at by the representatives in the OP would be if we altered the way citizens in a democratic society think of themselves. However, it could be argued that by altering the self-conception of the citizens in a democratic society, we are no longer in the business of producing a theory of justice for a democratic society, but have started to try to produce a theory of justice for a quite different kind of society. That may be true. But the question then becomes – What sort of society do we want to live in? One which insists on regarding us as being free and equal and whose basic institutions seek to respect that view of who we are? Or one which recognises us as being equally vulnerable and unequally needy and whose basic institutions seek to help us in our vulnerability and need? If the latter, then Rawls' theory of justice may be a theory of justice fit for a society we would never want to live in.

Further Reading

Rawls, *A Theory of Justice*, Part One.
Kukathas and Pettit, Rawls: *A Theory Of Justice and Its Critics* (Polity Press, 1990).
Nozick, *Anarchy, State and Utopia*, chs 7 and 8.
Frankfurt, 'Equality as a moral ideal' (1987) 98 *Ethics* 21.
Cohen, 'Where the action is: on the site of distributive justice' (1997) 26 *Philosophy and Public Affairs* 3.
MacIntyre, *Dependent Rational Animals: Why Human Beings Need the Virtues* (Duckworth, 2009).
Gardner, 'Finnis on justice' in Keown and George (eds), *Reason, Morality and Law: The Philosophy of John Finnis* (Oxford University Press, 2013).

10

THE ENFORCEMENT OF MORALITY

The European Convention on Human Rights provides that a number of the rights set out in the Convention can be abridged, if it is necessary to do so, 'for the protection of health or morals'.[1] While no one disagrees with the state taking action to protect people's health, there is considerable debate over whether it is legitimate for the state to act with the object of (1) compelling people to comply with their moral duties; (2) encouraging or helping people to live worthwhile, meaningful lives; or (3) discouraging people acting in ways that will make it harder for other people either to comply with their moral duties, or to live worthwhile, meaningful lives. Let's say that a government that acts with the object of doing (1) or (2) or (3), or some combination of (1), (2) and (3), is in the business of 'enforcing morality'. The debates in this chapter are about whether it is legitimate for the state to be in the business of enforcing morality.

The first debate is about whether there is any reason for the state to be interested in enforcing morality. If there is not, then the case for the state getting involved in the business of enforcing morality doesn't even get to first base.

The second debate is about whether, even if there is a case for the state getting involved in the business of enforcing morality, it would simply be wrong for the state to do this. Most *liberals* argue that it would be. In their view, the state is morally required to confine itself to the more limited task of ensuring that people are in a position to decide for themselves what kind of lives they will lead. Others disagree, arguing that provided that the state can do more good than harm in doing so, there is no reason why the state should not get involved in the business of enforcing morality.

The third debate is about whether this proviso can ever be satisfied – Is it the case in practice that it is a bad idea for the state to get involved in the business of enforcing morality because by doing so it will do more harm than good?

If the right responses to the three debates considered in this chapter are, respectively, 'Yes – there are good reasons for the state to enforce morality', 'No – there

---

[1] This is true of the rights protected under Articles 8 (privacy), 10 (freedom of expression), 11 (freedom of assembly and association).

is no reason in principle why the state should not get involved with enforcing morality', and 'No – the state will not always do more harm than good by getting involved with enforcing morality', then we should support the idea of the state getting involved in the business of enforcing morality where it can do more good than harm. If any other set of responses (such as 'The state will always do more harm than good in enforcing morality') is correct, then we should reject the idea of the state getting involved in the business of enforcing morality.

Debate 1

Is there a reason for the state to enforce morality?

SOCIAL DISINTEGRATION

In his 1959 Maccabaean Lecture in jurisprudence, 'The enforcement of morals',[2] Lord Devlin argued that the state has a reason to enforce morality. The outline of his argument is as follows: (1) if a society's conventional morality is undermined, then the society will tend to disintegrate, (2) the disintegration of society would be undesirable, therefore (3) the state has reason to enforce that society's conventional morality in order to stop society disintegrating.

To understand Devlin's argument, it is crucial to understand the idea of a society's *conventional* morality. Following Hart, we can distinguish between the morality that a society *in fact* endorses and practises, which Hart calls its 'social' or 'positive' morality, and the morality which it *ought* to endorse – an ideal or 'critical' morality.[3] Devlin's argument is that the state has a reason to enforce a society's *positive* morality; thus the morality in question is that arrived at from

> 'the viewpoint of the man in the street – or to use an archaism familiar to all lawyers – the man in the Clapham omnibus ... It is what Pollock called "practical morality", which is based not on theological or philosophical foundations but "... the morality of common sense".'[4]

How, then, does Devlin support the first premise – that if a society's conventional morality is undermined, the society will tend to disintegrate? Devlin's main point is simply that it is part of the very essence of society that its members share a common morality, and so, if sanctions are not in place to incentivise against departures from that common morality, society, by definition, cannot exist:

> 'society *means* a community of ideas; without shared ideas on politics, morals, and ethics, no society can exist ... If men and women try to create a society in which there is no fundamental agreement about good and evil they will fail; if having

---

[2] Subsequently reprinted under the title 'Morals and the criminal law' in Devlin, *The Enforcement of Morals* (Oxford University Press, 1965), ch. 1.

[3] Hart, *Law, Liberty, and Morality* (Oxford University Press, 1968), 17–24.

[4] Devlin, *The Enforcement of Morals* (above, n. 2), 15. See also, ibid, 90: '... the fundament that is surely accepted ... what is acceptable to the ordinary man, the man in the jury box'.

based it on common agreement, the agreement goes, the society will disintegrate. For society is not something that is held together physically; it is held together by the invisible bonds of common thoughts. If the bonds were too far relaxed the members would drift apart. A common morality is part of the bondage. The bondage is part of the price of society; and mankind, which needs society, must pay its price.'[5]

As to premise (2) – that the disintegration of society would be undesirable – Devlin seems to have regarded this as more or less self-evident. He writes that 'it is generally accepted that some shared morality ... is an essential element in the constitution of any society'.[6] He does, however, make two specific points as to desirability of a society enforcing its shared morality and thereby, on his argument, preserving itself. First, there are situations where immorality can lead to harm: 'a nation of debauchees would not in 1940 have responded satisfactorily to Winston Churchill's call to blood and toil and sweat and tears'.[7] Secondly, without a shared morality there could be no 'cohesion'.[8]

H.L.A. Hart responded to Devlin's arguments in a series of essays,[9] and most fully in a set of lectures delivered at Stanford University in 1962, later published as the book, *Law, Liberty, and Morality*.[10] Hart points out that Devlin's first premise can be understood in two ways. At some points Devlin appears to be saying that, as a necessary truth, a society is identical with its common morality, so that, if that morality *changes* then that society necessarily no longer exists – it disintegrates.[11] In this sense of 'society', we might say that 'feudal society ceased to exist after 1500'. If this is what Devlin means, then there is no longer, according to Hart, any reason to believe (2) – that the disintegration of society is undesirable. After all, there is nothing objectionable about the *change* in a society's morality *per se*. If Devlin's argument required us to say that any and all changes in a society's common morality were undesirable, it would be absurd.

Premise (1) could alternatively be understood, Hart says, not as stating a necessary truth, but as making an *empirical* claim. It could be asserting that without shared agreement on morality, society, in the sense of any kind of arrangement whereby people live together, would disintegrate. To this, Hart objects that Devlin offers no empirical evidence to support his claims. In particular, Hart objects that Devlin's main example – deviation from society's conventional sexual morality – is particularly weak on empirical grounds: 'no evidence is adduced to show that deviation from accepted sexual morality, even by adults in private, is something which ... threatens the existence of society'.[12]

---

[5] Ibid, 10.
[6] Ibid, 114.
[7] Ibid, 111.
[8] Ibid, 114.
[9] Hart, 'Immorality and treason', July 30, 1959, *The Listener*, 162; Hart, 'The use and abuse of the criminal law' (1961) 4 *Oxford Lawyer* 7; Hart, 'Social solidarity and the enforcement of morality' (1967) 35 *University of Chicago Law Review* 1.
[10] Hart, *Law, Liberty, and Morality* (above, n. 3).
[11] Ibid, 51–52. See also Hart, 'Social solidarity and the enforcement of morality' (above, n. 9), 3.
[12] Hart, *Law, Liberty, and Morality* (above, n. 3), 50.

If we set aside all of the conventional moral norms in a society whose enforcement can be justified on the ground that they prevent serious setbacks to other individuals' well-being, it seems inherently unlikely that there needs to be enforcement of other conventional moral norms in order to prevent societal disintegration. That is: if we imagine a society which enforces laws against murder, serious physical injury, theft, promise-breaking, it seems unlikely that that society will disintegrate if it doesn't additionally agree upon moral matters such as prostitution, homosexuality, and adultery. Widespread disagreement on some of these matters in modern Western societies suggests that a prediction of disintegration is overly pessimistic.

MORAL ECOLOGY

Just as the environment around us can affect our health, so it might be argued that our environment can affect our ability to lead morally worthwhile lives. Specifically, our environment needs to allow us opportunities or options to pursue valuable activities. Consequently, it could be argued that the state has reason both to promote the existence of such valuable options and to discourage the immoral conduct of some people, which might be claimed to close off morally valuable options to other people, either by hindering those people from entering into valuable activities, or by undermining valuable institutions which make those options available. This is the idea of 'moral ecology', developed especially by Robert George:

> 'What is true of public health and safety is equally true of public morals. Take, as an example, the problem of pornography ... where it flourishes, [it] damages a community's moral ecology in ways analogous to those in which carcinogenic smoke spewing from a factory's stacks damages the community's physical ecology.'[13]

The idea, then, is that the state has reason to create and preserve a society's moral ecology by taking steps to provide people with a suitable *environment* in which they can pursue morally valuable activities and by taking steps to discourage immoral activities which might destroy that environment. This existence of this environment, George claims, is a kind of 'public good'.[14]

Here is a recent example that might illustrate George's point. Increasingly, it seems to be the case that, in the absence of much regulation of what can and can't be shown on screen, actresses need to be willing to be filmed engaging in (very) sexually explicit acts in order to be offered parts. A recent article in the *Guardian* refers to an advertisement for parts where the call was for actors who are 'the very definition of sluts'.[15] There is, then, a concern that actresses are increasingly being

---

[13] George, 'The concept of public morality' (2000) 45 *American Journal of Jurisprudence* 17, 17.

[14] George, *Making Men Moral* (Oxford University Press, 1993), 37.

[15] Saner, 'From *Nymphomaniac* to *Stranger By the Lake*: is sex in cinema getting too real?', February 21, 2014, *Guardian*.

asked to become 'sex objects' in order to pursue their conception of a good life. Here the state might have reason to intervene either by placing further limits on the kinds of sex which can be shown on screen, or by preferring, in the grant of public funds, film production companies which limit the kinds of sex shown in their films. Here, then, the state would be enforcing morality both in the sense that it would be discouraging the (arguably) immoral exploitation of actresses, and providing valuable – exploitation-free – options to the latter.

As an example of immoral activities that undermine valuable *institutions*, George cites pornography. His claim is that the dissemination of pornography is immoral in virtue of the harm it causes to the valuable institutions of *marriage* and of the *family*. The causal route by which it does this, he claims, is that it causes harm to people's character – their disposition to act in certain ways and to see others in a certain light – and it is these dispositions which maintain and protect the institution:

> 'The central harm of pornography is not ... that it shocks and offends people, any more than the central harm of carcinogenic smoke is that it smells bad. Rather the central harm of pornography is moral harm – harm to character, and thus to the human goods and institutions, such as the good and institution of marriage, which are preserved and advanced by the disposition to act uprightly.'[16]

It should be emphasised that the acceptance of this kind of argument does not entail that the state should, all things considered, enforce morality. The issue at stake is only whether the state has *a reason to enforce morality*.[17] It may still be that, as the next debate explores, it would be wrong in principle for the state to enforce morality, or that any good achieved would be outweighed by greater evils, as the third debate explores. Once qualified in this way, and on the supposition that we can say that some ways of life are more or less morally valuable than others, it is hard to deny that sustaining an environment in which morally valuable activities are promoted provides the state with a reason for action.

AUTONOMY

In his book *The Morality of Freedom*,[18] Joseph Raz develops an argument, centred upon the importance of autonomy to people's well-being, whose conclusion implies that the state has a reason to enforce morality. In the barest outline, the argument is that: (1) leading an *autonomous* life is central to people's well-being (in modern Western societies); (2) autonomy requires, amongst other things, the existence of a range of morally valuable options; (3) the state has a duty to ensure that

---

[16] George, 'The concept of public morality' (above, n. 13), 17–18.
[17] See also George, *Making Men Moral* (above, n. 14) 37: 'Of course, recognition of the public consequences of putatively private vice does not mean that liberalism is wrong to be critical of morals legislation ... It does mean, however, that a crucial premiss of the tradition's case against moral *laissez-faire* remains unshaken: societies have reason to care about what might be called their "moral ecology".'
[18] Raz, *The Morality of Freedom* (Oxford University Press, 1986).

we have the capacity to live an autonomous life and this means that the state has reason to be concerned that we live in a society where there is a range of morally attractive options open to us. Let's now consider the details of this argument.

(1) Autonomy as central to well-being in our society

According to Raz, the concept of well-being is concerned with evaluating how successful a person's life is going from his or her point of view.[19] Central to the success of a person's life, and so, central to their well-being, for Raz, is the fulfilment of various goals that the person has – where goals are understood broadly to include 'projects, plans, relationships, ambitions, commitments, and the like'.[20] Some of these goals are more important to well-being than others. What Raz calls comprehensive goals are particularly important: these are goals which permeate different important aspects of one's life:

> 'a comprehensive goal is not a long-term goal. I may desire to visit Venice on my sixtieth birthday, and I may have been working to save for it ever since I was twenty-five. It is still not a comprehensive goal. To be that it itself ... must have ramifications which pervade important dimensions of my life. This also entails that it does not consist merely of a repetition of one kind of activity. Going bell-ringing every Sunday is not a comprehensive goal in itself, but when it is conceived as a complex activity with social, sightseeing, architectural, and other interests, and when it assumes a significance which pervades other times than those when one is actually on a bell-ringing outing, then it is a comprehensive goal.'[21]

So, to take another example, a person's marriage may be one of their comprehensive goals – the success of that marriage will permeate many different important aspects of their life.

Raz claims that a person can have a comprehensive goal 'only if it is based on existing social forms, i.e. on forms of behaviour which are in fact widely practised in his society'.[22] Raz offers two kinds of reasons for believing that comprehensive goals are dependent upon the existence of social forms instantiating those goals.

First, some comprehensive goals require the existence of social institutions for these goals to exist as a possibility. Raz gives as examples the fact that one cannot pursue a career in the law unless one's society is governed by law; nor, until recently at least, could homosexual couples take advantage of the existing social forms of marriage relationship. There are more subtle examples: even an activity like bird-watching, Raz claims, acquires its character from social forms:

> 'Bird watching seems to be what any sighted person in the vicinity of birds can do. And so he can, except that would not make him into a bird watcher. He can be that only in a society where this, or at least some other animal tracking activities, are

[19] Ibid, 290.
[20] Ibid, 291.
[21] Ibid, 308–309.
[22] Ibid, 308.

recognized as leisure activities, and which furthermore share certain attitudes to natural life generally.'[23]

So some comprehensive goals depend for the very possibility of their existence upon there being social forms which instantiate them.

The second reason Raz offers for the claim that comprehensive goals are dependent upon social forms is that comprehensive goals cannot always be obtained by explicit deliberation, but only by social habituation. There are certain aspects of, for example, the relationship between spouses or friends that cannot be explicitly described, even by the people within these relationships. There are social conventions of appropriate behaviour which 'distinguish between business friends, personal friends, golfing friends, etc. They include clues by which one judges the intensity or intimacy the relationship has reached ... All these we describe inadequately.'[24] The point is that we cannot consciously pick up the nuances and richness of valuable goals without our being part of, being habituated within, the social forms which maintain them.

So the argument so far is: (a) well-being depends upon successful pursuit of goals; (b) comprehensive goals are particularly important to well-being; (c) comprehensive goals depend upon the existence of social forms. The next move in the argument is to assert that in our society, social forms are highly influenced by the ideal of *autonomy*:

> 'In western industrial societies a particular conception of individual well-being has acquired considerable popularity. It is the ideal of personal autonomy ... The ruling idea behind the ideal of personal autonomy is that people should make their own lives. The autonomous author is a (part) author of his own life. The ideal of personal autonomy is the vision of people controlling, to some degree, their own destiny, fashioning it through successive decisions throughout their lives.'[25]

How are social forms influenced by the ideal of autonomy? Raz claims that the ideal of the autonomous life is not simply one option amongst other options provided by the social forms in our society – the option of pursuing an autonomous life has 'special features ... which distinguish it from other ordinary valuable options, such as playing golf or becoming a nurse'.[26] Rather, our society's social forms are *generally* permeated by the notion of autonomy: it is part of the 'general character of one's environment and culture'. This means, Raz goes on to claim, that 'For those who live in an autonomy-supporting environment there is no choice but to be autonomous: there is no other way to prosper in such a society.'[27] This claim is already partly supported by Raz's argument that well-being depends upon social forms. If well-being depends upon social forms, and the social

---

[23] Ibid, 311.
[24] Ibid, 312.
[25] Ibid, 369.
[26] Ibid, 390.
[27] Ibid, 391.

forms in our society are permeated by the ideal of autonomy, then it will be hard to prosper in such a society without leading an autonomous life.

(2) Autonomy requires the existence of a range of morally valuable options

Raz claims that if we are to have the capacity to live an autonomous life – and thus (because of (1)) prosper in our society – a number of conditions need to be fulfilled.[28] First, we need to have the relevant mental capacities to live autonomously – for example, the ability to understand what options we have. Secondly, we need to have an adequate range of options available to us so that we have a meaningful choice as to what sort of life we will lead. Thirdly, we need independence from the coercive or manipulative conduct of others, conduct which subjects our will to theirs and thereby interferes with our autonomy.

For the purposes of the debate we are currently considering, the most important of these conditions is the second one – that we have an *adequate* range of options available to us – because this second condition requires, in Raz's view, that the options available to us are *morally valuable*.[29] Why is this so? Raz offers a somewhat artificial example to illustrate the point.[30] Suppose that you can pursue an occupation of your choice but only at the price of committing murder for any option that you reject. So you can decide whether or not to become an electrician – but if you reject that option, you must kill someone. If you choose to become an electrician, we would not say that your life path was chosen autonomously – because your alternative would have involved great evil. Hence, the existence of a choice between morally valuable options is necessary for autonomy.

(3) The role of the state in ensuring the autonomy of its citizens

Raz's argument is that if the state has a reason to promote autonomy, and if autonomy requires the existence of morally valuable options, then the state has a reason to help ensure that we have a range of morally valuable options available to us. But Raz goes further and argues that the state not only has a reason, but a *duty*, to help ensure that such morally valuable options are available to us: 'Autonomy-based duties ... require the use of public power to promote the conditions of autonomy.'[31]

Raz is not entirely clear on *why* the state has this duty. However, it is not too difficult to identify its sources within his arguments. First, as Jeremy Waldron explains, if the well-being of the citizens living in a particular country depends upon their leading autonomous lives, then a failure on the part of the government of that country to help those citizens to lead autonomous lives would 'make life unbearable for [those] citizens'.[32] Secondly, supporting the existence of valuable

---

[28] Ibid, 372.
[29] Ibid, 378.
[30] Ibid, 379.
[31] Ibid, 418.
[32] Waldron, 'Autonomy and perfectionism in Raz's *Morality of Freedom*' (1989) 62 *Southern California Law Review* 1097, 1129.

213

options is an inherently _social_ matter: it cannot be achieved by an individual acting alone. As Raz explains:

> 'Supporting valuable forms of life is a social rather than an individual matter. Monogamy, assuming that it is the only morally valuable form of marriage, cannot be practised by an individual. It requires a culture which recognizes it, and which supports it through the public's attitude and through its formal institutions.'[33]

The argument, then, is that the state has a reason, and a duty, to help people obtain what they, acting alone, could not achieve. If these two arguments work, then given (1) and (2), the conclusion follows that the state has reason to enforce morality, by dint of the contribution that the existence of a range of morally valuable lifestyles makes to people's being able to live autonomous lives.

CONCLUSIONS

Although Hart convincingly refuted Devlin's arguments for the enforcement of morality based upon social disintegration, the arguments from moral ecology and autonomy are far subtler.

The moral ecology argument rests upon an almost irresistible premise: that it is better that truly morally valuable activities are undertaken and prosper than that activities which have less or no moral value are undertaken and prosper. Yet to modern liberal ears this 'perfectionist' idea – the idea that the state has reason to promote morally worthwhile lives and to discourage engagement in morally worthless activities – sounds deeply suspect. As Raz writes, there is a 'threatening popular image of imprisoning people who follow their religion, express their views in public, grow long hair, or consume harmless drugs'.[34]

But this popular image, if it does exist, probably rests on at least three false misgivings. First, the creation of an environment favourable to certain valuable ways of life need not entail _coercion_. Secondly, it is consistent with _value pluralism_. Those who accept the moral ecology argument need not be committed to the idea that there is only _one_ worthwhile way of living. Most of us think that there are innumerable ways of pursuing a good life. Thirdly, the moral ecology argument is not committed to outlawing the ways of life which were targeted by Devlin's arguments – such as homosexual activities or partnerships. Once these misgivings are quelled, the fundamental premise of the moral ecology argument becomes very attractive.

Raz's autonomy-based argument can be construed as providing a deeper grounding for the moral ecology argument: the fundamental reason the state has to secure a morally advantageous environment is that the options provided by such an environment contribute to people's autonomy. Consequently, if one accepts the moral ecology argument, the issue is whether one ought to be an

---

[33] Raz, _The Morality of Freedom_ (above, n. 18), 162.
[34] Ibid, 161.

autonomy-based moral ecologist or not. It seems to us that there could be reasons to create a moral ecology even where the purpose in doing so was not to enhance *autonomy*. For example, the state could have a reason to fund artistic competitions, in order to enrich the lives of some of its citizens, even in situations in which the people who would enter these competitions, or who would benefit from the art produced through these competitions, already have an *adequate* range of valuable options at their disposal, such that their lives are already fully autonomous.

Debate 2

Is it wrong in principle for the state to enforce morality?

Even if the state has a reason to enforce morality, it may be that some moral principle or constraint[35] excludes the possibility of the state acting upon this reason. This debate explores various arguments that have been made for the existence of such principles or constraints.

INDEPENDENCE

H.L.A. Hart and Arthur Ripstein have both advanced versions of the claim that individuals have a right to be free from the coercion or restraint of others save only where coercing or restraining them is necessary to prevent or hinder them from coercing or restraining others. Following Ripstein, we can call this a *right to independence*. If each of us had such a right, then the only justifiable basis for restricting our freedom would be in order to prevent us coercing another person. Consequently, someone's freedom could not be restricted in order to encourage them to act morally or to help ensure that a range of morally valuable activities remain available to people who want to take advantage of them. Do we have such a right to independence? Hart and Ripstein both offer arguments that attempt to show that such a right is built into our ordinary beliefs and thought about rights.

(1) H.L.A. Hart

In his article, 'Are there any natural rights?', Hart defends the thesis that every adult human being capable of choice has a right to independence; that is, an equal moral right

> '(1) ... to forbearance on the part of all others from the use of coercion or restraint against him save to hinder coercion or restraint and (2) is at liberty to do (i.e. is under no obligation to abstain from) any action which is not one coercing or restraining or designed to injure other persons.'[36]

---

[35] On the idea of a moral 'constraint' against promoting the good, see above p. 164.
[36] Hart, 'Are there any natural rights?' (1955) 64 *Philosophical Review* 175, 175.

The basic structure of Hart's argument for this thesis is that *if* there are any moral rights, there must be a right to independence. This is because, he claims, the very idea of a moral right implies the idea that people have a right to independence:

> 'it is I think a very important feature of a moral right that the possessor of it is conceived as having a moral justification *for limiting the freedom of another* ...'[37]

Hart draws attention to questions such as 'What *right* do you have to do that?' in order to argue that the function of asserting a moral right is to assert that you have a justification for interfering with a person's freedom.[38] When someone asks 'What right do you have to do that?', they are asking for a justification for your interfering with their freedom. But such a justification would only be needed, Hart claims, if we had a right to be free from interference. So the special justification which rights provide would only make sense against the background that we have a right to be free.

Hart goes further than this. He also claims that:

> 'the moral justification for interference which is to constitute a *right* to interfere (as distinct from merely making it morally good or desirable to interfere) is restricted to certain special conditions and that is inherent in the meaning of "a right" ... Claims to interfere with another's freedom based on the general character of the activities interfered with (e.g. the folly or cruelty of "native" practices) or the general character of the parties ("We are Germans; they are Jews") even when well founded are not matters of moral right or obligation.'[39]

The claim here is that a *right* to interfere with a person's freedom can only be justified by special considerations that go beyond or are different in nature to the mere fact that the interference would be desirable or morally praiseworthy. It is this aspect of Hart's analysis which, if correct, may seem to make it impermissible for the state to restrict a person's freedom in order to encourage them to lead a morally better life, or to provide morally valuable opportunities for others.

There is reason to doubt whether Hart's argument establishes that we have the kind of right to independence that would make it wrong for the state to enforce morality. After all, in the above passage Hart admits that in 'certain special conditions' we are justified in limiting someone else's freedom. Hart asserts that these conditions only obtain when we are acting pursuant to some 'moral right or obligation'.[40] However, it is not clear why this is the only situation where limiting someone's freedom will be justified; and in any case theorists such as Joseph Raz would contend that the state, in preserving morally valuable forms of life, *is* acting pursuant to a 'moral right or obligation'.

---

[37] Ibid, 178 (emphasis added).
[38] Ibid, 189.
[39] Ibid, 190.
[40] Ibid.

(2) Arthur Ripstein

The right to independence for which Ripstein argues has a narrower content than Hart's.[41] For Ripstein, to interfere with a person's freedom is not merely to close off one or more of their options. The interferences prohibited by Ripstein's right to independence involve a kind of *domination,* whereby one person makes a decision which it was another's to make, either by *usurping* that person's powers (by *using* their body or property without their consent) or *destroying* their powers to pursue their own purposes (by *destroying or injuring* their body or property).

Ripstein seeks to prove the existence of the right to independence by providing examples of situations in which the intuitive wrongfulness of a person's conduct seems to be explicable only by reference to a right to independence. Consider the following example:

> 'Suppose that, as you are reading this in your office or in the library, I let myself into your home, using burglary tools that do no damage to your locks, and take a nap in your bed. I make sure everything is clean. I bring hypoallergenic and lint-free pajamas and a hairnet. I put my own sheets and pillowcase down over yours. I do not weigh very much, so the wear and tear on your mattress is non-existent. By any ordinary understanding of harm, I do you no harm. If I had the same effects on your home in some other way, no one would suppose you had a grievance against me ... Your objection is to my deed, my trespass against your home, not to its effects.'[42]

On the face of it, it is difficult to explain the fact that Ripstein wronged you in this case by reference to the fact that he *harmed* you. The deed caused you no harm. A plausible explanation of why you have been wronged by Ripstein's nap is that decisions about the use of your property are yours to make: 'The obvious explanation of what is wrong with my nap is [that] I wrong you by using your home for a purpose that you did not authorize.'[43] This violates your independence because: 'You are independent if you are the one who decides what ends you will use your powers to pursue, as opposed to having someone else decide for you.'[44]

Do examples such as the nap case prove the existence of a right to independence? Colin Bird disputes this.[45] Bird objects that prohibiting harmless trespasses like Ripstein's nap case can be justified by 'the overwhelmingly powerful interest each of has in personal security'.[46] This interest is so powerful because our ability to value other things would be radically diminished if we thought that our lives or property could be taken away from us at any moment by anyone stronger than us. If the state did not prohibit harmless trespasses, we would be anxious that our security would be invaded. Moreover, 'the fear that our persons and property are

---

[41] This section draws primarily upon Ripstein, 'Beyond the harm principle' (2006) 34 *Philosophy and Public Affairs* 215, but also Ripstein, *Force and Freedom* (Harvard University Press, 2009).

[42] Ripstein, 'Beyond the harm principle' (above n. 41), 218.

[43] Ibid, 227.

[44] Ibid, 231.

[45] Bird, 'Harm versus sovereignty: a reply to Ripstein' (2007) 35 *Philosophy and Public Affairs* 179.

[46] Ibid, 182–83.

insecure will seem particularly intense in the case of those holdings that provide us with safe shelter and personal space to which we may repair for the purposes of privacy and rest.'[47]

Bird's argument seems plausible in explaining why it would be permissible, and perhaps obligatory, for the state to prohibit harmless trespasses. However, it is questionable whether Bird's consequentialist concern that failure to prohibit such trespasses will lead to fear and anxiety is the best explanation of why Ripstein *wrongs* you in sleeping in your bed without your consent. It may be that the wrongfulness of his action can be more elegantly explained by the fact that Ripstein took a decision which was yours to make.[48]

If Ripstein's example succeeds in showing that there is a right to independence, what follows for the legitimacy of the enforcement of morality? This depends upon the circumstances in which interfering with someone's independence can be justified. Ripstein argues that the only circumstances in which such an interference is permissible is in order to protect the independence of others. The reason that interference can be justified in order to protect the independence of others is that, plausibly, each of us is entitled to *equal* independence. If I claimed to be free to walk on your land whilst insisting that you were unfree to walk on my land, then I would be claiming an *unequal* amount of freedom. So interfering with my freedom when I walk on your land without your consent in order to preserve your freedom can be justified as preserving a situation of *equal* freedom. However, if the interference with my freedom cannot be justified on the ground that it preserves equal freedom, then it amounts, on Ripstein's view, to deciding what purposes I shall pursue – it involves *dominating* me. This is the meaning of Ripstein's remark that 'Equal freedom and private wrongdoing form a closed set.'[49] Once we go beyond ensuring equal freedom, or in other words, prohibiting *wrongs* committed by one person against another, other limits to freedom amount to domination.

Yet it is questionable whether Ripstein's right to independence (if it exists) rules out all forms of enforcement of morality. It certainly seems to rule out *coercion* in the interest of improving the moral quality of people's lives, but it is far less clear that less invasive measures constitute 'domination' of the individual by the state. For example, if the state favoured certain valuable forms of life by subsidies or through advertising, it is not clear that it involves *domination* of any individual citizen. If the state nudges you towards one course of action rather than another, it need not act against the principle that: 'You are independent if

---

[47] Ibid, 183.
[48] This is a version of the 'right verdict for the wrong reasons' objection made to consequentialism, above, p. 172. However, Bird would counter that his anxiety-based explanation explains why we think there is a great deal wrong in Ripstein's napping in your bed, while we would not see very much wrong at all in Ripstein's taking a nap in a remote corner of a 60,000 acre 'uncultivated ... mountain wilderness' that you happen to own: ibid, 187.
[49] Ripstein, 'Beyond the harm principle' (above, n. 41), 238.

you are the one who decides what ends you will use your powers to pursue, as opposed to having someone else decide for you.'[50] You do decide.

RESPECT

In his 1981 essay 'Is there a right to pornography?', Ronald Dworkin claimed to have provided us with a basis for thinking that we have a 'right to moral independence'.[51] However, this 'right' has little to do with independence in the sense that term is used by Hart and Ripstein – as denoting someone's freedom to decide for themselves how they will deal with the things which they control. Dworkin describes the right to moral independence as the right:

'not to suffer disadvantage in the distribution of social goods and opportunities, including disadvantage in the liberties permitted to them by the criminal law just on the ground that their officials or fellow-citizens think that their opinions about the right way for them to lead their own lives are ignoble or wrong.'[52]

This right to moral independence would be violated, he explained, by a government that introduced a scheme for the regulation of pornography if:

'the only apparent or plausible justification for [that] scheme. ... includes the hypothesis that the attitudes about sex displayed or nurtured in pornography are demeaning or bestial or otherwise unsuitable to human beings of the best sort, even though this hypothesis may be true.'[53]

Dworkin's 'right to moral independence' is an outworking of his view that governments are required to treat their subjects with 'equal concern and respect'. To the extent that government favours one citizen's conception of a morally valuable life over another citizen's, for instance by restricting the latter's liberty in order to promote that conception, it treats citizens with *unequal* respect:

'Government must treat those whom it governs with concern, that is, as human beings who are capable of suffering and frustration, and with respect, that is, as human beings who are capable of forming and acting on intelligent conceptions of how their lives should be lived. Government must not only treat people with concern and respect, but with equal concern and respect. It must not distribute goods and opportunities unequally on the ground that some citizens are entitled to more because they are worthy of more concern. It must not constrain liberty on the ground that one citizen's conception of the good life is nobler or superior to another's. These postulates, taken together, state what might be called the liberal conception of equality ...'[54]

---

[50] Ibid, 231.
[51] Dworkin, 'Is there a right to pornography?' (1981) 1 *Oxford Journal of Legal Studies* 177. Reprinted in Dworkin, *A Matter of Principle* (Harvard University Press, 1985), ch. 17.
[52] Dworkin, 'Is there a right to pornography' (above, n. 51), 194.
[53] Ibid, 195.
[54] Dworkin, 'What rights do we have?' in Dworkin, *Taking Rights Seriously* (Duckworth, 1977), 272–73.

Most people would indeed accept Dworkin's postulates of political morality at an abstract level – that is, that governments should treat their subjects with 'equal concern and respect'. The crucial issue is whether showing equal concern and respect requires governments to refrain from enforcing morality.

It might be challenged both whether the enforcement of morality engages a principle of *respect* at all and, if it does, whether the enforcement of morality leads to *unequal* respect. The first type of challenge is made by Raz. Raz disputes that treating a person in accordance with sound moral principles involves a failure to respect the person:

> 'Is one treating another with respect if one treats him in accordance with sound moral principles, or does respect for persons require ignoring morality (or parts of it) in our relations with others? There can be little doubt that stated in this way the question admits of only one answer. One would be showing disrespect to another if one ignored moral considerations in treating him.'[55]

Finnis and George have offered different versions of the second kind of challenge – that the enforcement of morality need not treat persons with *unequal* respect. Finnis's point is that the *failure* to encourage or to assist people to lead morally valuable lives can itself be shown to involve an inequality of respect. Consequently, a principle of equal respect cannot be relied upon to exclude the enforcement of morality:

> 'there is no difficulty in supposing that a "paternalist" political programme may be based on a conception of what is required for equal concern and respect for all; for paternalists may well consider that, for example, to leave a person to succumb to drug addiction on the plea that it is 'his business' is to deny him the active concern one would show for one's friend in like situation; or that to fail to forbid teachers to form sexual attachments with their pupils is to deny the children of negligent or "wrong-headed" parents the protection that the paternalist legislator would wish for his own children, and is thus again a failure in "equal concern and respect".'[56]

George's point is slightly different. His objection is that in enforcing morality one is not treating some *people* more favourably than others. Rather, in enforcing morality, the state is acting on its own view as to what the correct moral *position* is. Judging that one moral *position* is sounder than another doesn't involve treating the individuals who hold those positions *unequally*.[57]

---

[55] Raz, *The Morality of Freedom* (above, n. 18), 157.

[56] NLNR, 222.

[57] George, 'The concept of public morality' (above, n. 13), 28: '... insofar as it is the *positions* as such being judged, they are in no way treating *people – including the people holding the positions* – unequally' (emphasis in original).

JUSTICE

It will be recalled from the previous chapter that John Rawls' *A Theory of Justice*[58] attempted to determine how (A) basic rights and duties, (B) the benefits arising from social co-operation, and (C) the burdens necessary to sustain social co-operation, are to be distributed among the members of a democratic society – which is conceived as being a fair system of social co-operation between people who are viewed as being 'free and equal'.[59] Rawls' first principle of justice (PJ) specified that 'Each person has the same indefeasible claim to a fully adequate scheme of equal basic liberties, which scheme is compatible with the same scheme of basic liberties for all.'[60] The basic liberties are:

> 'political liberty (the right to vote and to hold public office) and freedom of speech and assembly; liberty of conscience and freedom of thought; freedom of the person, which includes freedom from psychological oppression and physical assault and dismemberment (integrity of the person); the right to hold personal property; and freedom from arbitrary arrest and seizure as defined by the concept of the rule of law. These liberties are to be equal by the first principle.'[61]

In a society that adheres to Rawls' first PJ: (1) everyone will enjoy an equal measure of freedom to pursue their own conceptions of the good, and (2) the state is not allowed to take steps to make it easier for people to pursue certain lifestyles rather than others on the basis that those lifestyles are particularly worthwhile and fulfilling while the others are not. So the first PJ prevents people from 'using the coercive apparatus of the state to win for themselves a greater liberty or larger distributive shares on the grounds that their activities are of more intrinsic value'[62] and it prevents the state from 'subsidizing universities and institutes, or opera and the theatre, on the grounds that these institutions are intrinsically valuable, and that those who engage in them are to be supported even at some significant expense to others who do not receive compensating benefits.'[63]

So if Rawls' first PJ is valid, then it would be wrong for the state to get into the business of enforcing morality (at least in a democratic society). Rawls claims that his first PJ is valid because representatives of the members of a democratic society would agree to that first PJ in preference to any other PJ in the 'original position' ('OP'), where the representatives determine on what terms the members of a democratic society will co-operate with each other without knowing (i) what comprehensive conceptions of the good the members they represent happen to endorse; and (ii) what positions in society are occupied by the members they represent.

---

[58] Rawls, *A Theory of Justice* (Harvard University Press) (1st edn, 1971 (henceforth, 'TJ (1971)'; rev'd edn, 1999 (henceforth, 'TJ (1999)')).

[59] See above, pp. 191–92.

[60] Rawls, *Justice as Fairness* (Harvard University Press, 2001), 42.

[61] TJ (1999), 53. The equivalent list in TJ (1971) is at 61, but presented in a slightly different form.

[62] TJ (1971), 329; TJ (1999), 289.

[63] TJ (1971), 332; TJ (1999), 291–92.

Placing the representatives under this 'veil of ignorance' is supposed to ensure that whatever terms the representatives agree to will reflect the 'free and equal' status of the members of a democratic society.[64]

This raises two questions: (1) Would the representatives in the OP actually endorse Rawls' first PJ? (2) Even if they would, do the conditions under which the representatives in the OP operate mean that their endorsement of Rawls' first PJ does not actually tell us anything meaningful about how the state should operate in a democratic society?

On question (1), Rawls argues that the representatives in the OP would endorse Rawls' first PJ because not to do so would expose members of a democratic society to the risk that they would be prevented from pursuing their religious or moral convictions by a majority that thought differently from them. This would be too much of a gamble for the representatives to take: even to think about gambling 'in this way would show that one did not take one's religious or moral convictions seriously, or highly value the liberty to examine one's beliefs'.[65]

Against this, two points can be made. First, not all activities that a state might be interested in discouraging are undertaken as a matter of religious or moral conviction; for example, drug taking or watching pornographic movies. So it is not clear why the representatives in the OP would object to a PJ that permitted the state to place limits on people's abilities to engage in such activities, should it be determined that doing so would be desirable. Secondly, the representatives in the OP – if they were rational – would not object to a PJ that permitted the state to limit activities that are undertaken as a matter of religious or moral conviction if those convictions were demonstrably false. This is because people who hold certain religious or moral convictions do so because they believe them to be true: so they themselves would acknowledge that they have *no interest* in being permitted to act on religious or moral convictions that are untrue.[66] It follows that they would not object to their representatives agreeing to a PJ that did *not* guarantee that they would be allowed to give effect to religious or moral convictions that were demonstrably untrue.

On question (2), John Finnis has argued that:

'it simply does not follow, from the fact that a principle chosen in the Original Position would be unbiased and fair as between individuals, that a principle which would *not* be chosen in the Original Position must be unfair or not a proper principle of justice in the real world. For in the real world, as Rawls himself admits, intelligence can discern intrinsic basic values and their contraries.'[67]

Finnis is referring there to a passage in Rawls' *A Theory of Justice* where Rawls admits that:

[64] See above, p. 194.
[65] TJ (1971), 207; TJ (1999), 181.
[66] See George, *Making Men Moral* (above, n. 14), 134–35.
[67] NLNR, 109 (see list of abbreviations, p. xiii).

'Very often it is beyond question that the work of one person is superior to that of another. Indeed, the freedom and well-being of individuals, when measured by the excellence of their achievements and works, is vastly different in value. This is true not only of actual performance but of potential performance as well. Comparison of intrinsic value can obviously be made ...'[68]

The fact that the representatives in the OP – operating as they do behind a veil of ignorance – are deprived of all knowledge of these things brings into question the validity of their conclusions as to what PJs should govern a democratic society. If someone who was aware of the truths acknowledged by Rawls in the above passage would endorse a particular PJ, why should we reject that PJ just because it would not be endorsed by someone who was ignorant of those truths?

AUTONOMY

Unlike fellow liberal political theorists like Ronald Dworkin or John Rawls, Joseph Raz believes that it *is* legitimate for the state to seek to enforce morality generally, in the sense of helping to ensure that people enjoy a range of morally valuable options as to how they will live their lives, and encouraging people to pursue worthwhile comprehensive goals in deciding how to live their lives. However, at the end of *The Morality of Freedom*, Raz argued that it would be impermissible for the state to use *coercion* as a means of enforcing morality unless the state's object in doing so is to prevent someone harming someone's capacity to live their life autonomously.[69] So coercion can only be used to protect someone's capacity to live an autonomous life from being harmed.

Raz's main argument for this claim is that using coercion for any other purpose than protecting someone's autonomy from being harmed is self-defeating from the point of view of a political theory that places a high moral value on promoting individual autonomy: 'Using coercion invades autonomy and thus defeats the purpose of promoting it, unless it is done to promote autonomy by preventing harm.'[70] Raz identifies two ways in which coercion violates a person's autonomy (or, rather, a person's *capacity* to lead an autonomous life):

'First, it violates the condition of independence and expresses a relation of domination and an attitude of disrespect for the coerced individual. Second, coercion by criminal penalties is a global and indiscriminate invasion of autonomy. Imprisoning a person prevents him from almost all autonomous pursuits.'[71]

However, it is questionable whether either of these points *always* give us a good reason for objecting to coercion being used to enforce morality.

On the first point, Raz argues that:

---

[68] TJ (1971), 328; TJ (1999), 288.
[69] Raz, *The Morality of Freedom* (above, n. 18), 412–20.
[70] Ibid, 420.
[71] Ibid, 418.

'coercion invades autonomy not only in its consequences but also in its intention. As such it is normally an insult to the person's autonomy. He is being treated as a non-autonomous agent, an animal, a baby, or an imbecile. Often coercion is wrong primarily because it is an affront or an insult and not so much because of its more tangible consequences, which may not be very grave.'[72]

However, Raz immediately concedes that 'coercion by an ideal liberal state' is significantly different:

'its coercive measures do not express an insult to the autonomy of individuals. It is common knowledge that they are motivated not by a lack of respect for individual autonomy but by concern for it.'[73]

So a liberal state that uses coercion to enforce morality will not necessarily be guilty of insulting or disrespecting anyone in so doing. This point becomes even stronger if one accepts, as Raz does, that autonomously choosing bad options does not add anything of value to one's life.[74] But if this is so, Jonathan Quong wonders, 'why is it disrespectful or domineering to prevent people from making such choices?'[75]

Quong also questions whether the 'global and indiscriminate invasion of autonomy' that coercion involves identifies the *real* reason why using coercion to stop people making bad choices is objectionable. If coercion were objectionable because of its clumsy and blunt nature, then presumably it would be okay for the state to subject people to *Clockwork Orange*-style treatments that condition their brains to avoid making morally bad choices, or for a concerned *Neighbour* to lock *Lonely* up for a couple of hours to prevent *Lonely* getting back together with his 'mean and manipulative' ex-girlfriend.[76] If these carefully targeted interventions in people's lives to get them to avoid making bad choices are objectionable, it cannot be because they are 'global and indiscriminate' in their effects. They must be objectionable on grounds that have nothing to do with their effects on people's autonomy, but for some other reason – such as that they violate people's right to independence.

CONCLUSION

None of the theorists discussed in this section are able convincingly to argue that it is *always* wrong for the state to get involved in the business of enforcing morality. The most that can be said is that it *may* be wrong for the state to enforce morality *using coercion*. Raz unconvincingly attempts to argue that using coercion for any other purpose than to protect people's autonomy from being harmed will always be unacceptable to a liberal state that seeks to promote autonomy. The most prom-

---

[72] Ibid, 156.
[73] Ibid, 157.
[74] Ibid, 411.
[75] Quong, *Liberalism without Perfection* (Oxford University Press, 2010), 58.
[76] Ibid, 55.

ising explanation of why it might be wrong for the state to enforce morality using coercion lies in the idea that we all have a right to independence. However, whether there is any such thing remains controversial (even between the authors of this book).

Debate 3

Is it a bad idea for the state to enforce morality?

If you think that the state has a good reason for enforcing morality *and* that there is no principled reason why it would be wrong for the state to get into the business of enforcing morality, the debate as to whether the state should enforce morality becomes a pragmatic one and turns on the question of whether the state can ever do more good than harm by enforcing morality.

John Stuart Mill took the view that the state would do more harm than good by enforcing morality. In his 1859 book *On Liberty*, Mill argued in favour of what has come to be known as Mill's *Harm Principle* and which, in its original formulation, went as follows:

'the sole end for which mankind are warranted, individually or collectively, in interfering with the liberty of action of any of their number, is self-protection. That the only purpose for which power can be rightfully exercised over any member of a civilized community, against his will, is to prevent harm to others. His own good, either physical or moral, is not a sufficient warrant. He cannot rightfully be compelled to do or forebear because it will be better for him to do so, because it will make him happier, because, in the opinion of others, to do so would be wise, even right.'[77]

Because Mill was a utilitarian, he sought to defend this principle on the ground that departing from it would do more harm than good.[78] However, before we get into the pragmatic arguments that Mill made in favour of his Harm Principle – and other arguments that could be made for saying that enforcing morality will inevitably do more harm than good – we should immediately note one important feature of Mill's Harm Principle: it is a principle that seeks to limit when the state can use coercion to enforce morality. It does not purport to place any limits on the state's ability to use non-coercive means to encourage people to do the right thing or live worthwhile lives. This is not to say that Mill would have been in favour of the state's enforcing morality through non-coercive means. He simply did not consider the issue. We will discuss this issue in the second section of this debate, but in the first section we will consider – by drawing on arguments made by Mill and others – whether the state's enforcing morality through coercion will inevitably do more harm than good.

---

[77] Mill, *On Liberty* (1859), ch. 1, para. 11.
[78] Ibid, ch. 1, para. 13: 'I forego any advantage which could be derived to my argument from the idea of abstract right, as a thing independent of utility. I regard utility as the ultimate appeal on all ethical questions …'

IS IT A BAD IDEA FOR THE STATE TO USE COERCION TO ENFORCE MORALITY?

When we use the term 'coercion', we simply mean to refer to the state's using the criminal law to enforce morality. So the state uses coercive means to enforce morality when it criminally punishes people for doing such things as (1) watching, or making, pornographic videos; (2) taking, or supplying, hallucinogenic or highly addictive drugs; (3) engaging in underage but consensual sex, or sexual activities (such as necrophilia, or bestiality, or sado-masochism, or sex for money) that are regarded as degrading. The question is whether punishing people for engaging in these kinds of activities will inevitably do more harm than good.

Mill thought that it would. He made two basic arguments in favour of this view: the *experiment argument,* and the *character argument.* The experiment argument went as follows:

> 'As it is useful that while mankind are imperfect there should be different opinions, so is it that there should be different experiments of living; that free scope should be given to varieties of character, short of injury to others; and that the worth of different modes of living should be proved practically, when any one thinks fit to try them. It is desirable, in short, that in things which do not primarily concern others, individuality should assert itself.'[79]

Mill's fear was that if the state got into the business of enforcing morality, it would inevitably end up enforcing society's conventional morality – the moral standards widely accepted as such at any given time in a society's development – and in doing so, we would miss the opportunity of learning from people's engaging in 'experiments of living' that might be able to teach us something about how we should live. For example, we can only *know* that incestuous relationships, or polygamous marriages, are a bad idea if people are free to experiment with engaging in such relationships or marriages. And it may be that if people are freed to experiment in this way, we will learn that our negative views of such relationships or marriages are based on mere prejudice and that there is no reason to think that engaging in such relationships or marriages tends to be incompatible with living a fulfilling life.[80]

Mill's character argument was that if the state gets into the business of enforcing morality, then this will be bad for us. This is because if we are left to decide for ourselves how to live our lives, that will help us develop various desirable character traits such as courage, responsibility and initiative. In contrast, morals laws may well have the effect of encouraging us to develop 'the vices of moral infantilism, conformism, servility, mindless obedience to authority, and hypocrisy':[81]

---

[79] Ibid, ch. 3, para. 2.

[80] Cf. Mill's arguments for freedom of speech – that the expression of unconventional opinions should be allowed because the opinions, if wrong, will reconfirm us in our true beliefs and, if right, will help us see the truth – in ibid, ch. 2, paras 1 and 47.

[81] George, *Making Men Moral* (above, n. 14), 43.

'He who lets the world, or his own portion of it, choose his plan of life for him, has no need of any other faculty than the ape-like one of imitation. He who chooses his plan for himself, employs all his faculties ... It is possible that he might be guided in some good path, and kept out of harm's way, without any [of his faculties]. But what will be his comparative worth as a human being? It really is of importance, not only what men do, but also what manner of men they are that do it.'[82]

To Mill's experiment argument and character argument, we can add the *disrespect argument*, the *autonomy argument*, the *privacy argument*, and the *authenticity argument*. Each argument focuses on a distinct harm that might be done if the state gets into the business of enforcing morality through coercive means.

The disrespect argument focuses on the fact that the state's enforcing morality through coercive means may cause those whose life choices are sanctioned by the state to feel that the state is not treating them with respect. As Martha Nussbaum puts it:

'When the institutions that pervasively govern your life are built on a view that in all conscience you cannot endorse, that means that you are, in effect, in a position of second-class citizenship. Even if you are tolerated ... [the] government will state, every day, that a different view, incompatible with yours, is the correct view, and that yours is wrong.'[83]

It may be wrong for those at the sharp end of a state's morals laws to feel disrespected in this way,[84] but that does not change the fact that they will *feel* that they are not respected and this is a real harm that must be taken into account when considering whether enforcing morality through coercive means will do more harm than good.

The autonomy argument focuses on the fact that punishing people for breaching a morals law involves

'a global and indiscriminate invasion of autonomy. Imprisoning a person prevents him from almost all autonomous pursuits. Other forms of coercion may be less severe, but they all invade autonomy, and they all, at least in this world, do it in a fairly indiscriminate way. That is, there is no practical way of ensuring that the coercion will restrict the victims' choice of repugnant options but will not interfere with their other choices.'[85]

So punishing people in order to enforce morals laws will have the effect of hindering their pursuit of worthwhile options, as well as discouraging them and others from pursuing worthless or harmful (to them) options.

The privacy argument focuses on the fact that the enjoyment of certain human goods requires a degree of privacy that may be lost in a society that rigorously seeks

[82] Ibid, ch. 3, para. 5.
[83] Nussbaum, 'Perfectionist liberalism and political liberalism' (2011) 39 *Philosophy and Public Affairs* 3, 35.
[84] See the discussion of Dworkin's arguments against morals laws above, pp. 219–20.
[85] Raz, *The Morality of Freedom* (above, n. 18), 418–19.

to enforce certain morals laws that prescribe people from doing things in private (such as watching pornographic films or engaging in certain sexual practices in the privacy of one's own home).[86] So, for example, the lack of inhibition that is one of the valuable features of family life would be lost if people thought that their homes were under constant surveillance to check that they were not violating any morals laws directed at activities in the home.

Finally, the authenticity argument focuses on the problems that arise when someone (S) is forced to live a life (L) that she does not want to live. S will invariably be unhappy, and that unhappiness may trigger sudden outbursts of undesirable or positively harmful behaviour by S. Moreover, the goods that the state was trying to produce by pushing S into living life L will almost certainly not be present in life L if S does not identify with that life. So, for example, there is no doubt that the criminalisation of homosexual behaviour in the United Kingdom until 1967 was responsible for making a huge number of men and women unhappy by forcing them into living lives with which they could not identify.

If we take these six different arguments for not enforcing morality through coercive means together, they seem to indicate that enforcing morality through coercive means is *very likely* to do more harm than good where the state uses morals laws to target: (1) activities in the home; or (2) activities that are engaged in as a matter of deep personal conviction; or (3) activities that offend against conventional morality but where the costs and benefits of engaging in those activities are little understood. The state is also likely to do more harm than good where (4) it *severely* punishes those who breach its morals laws; or (5) its morals laws do not leave people with much room to judge for themselves how they will lead their lives. Conversely, enforcing morality through coercive means *may* do more good than harm where: (1) the state targets activities that are characteristically not engaged in at home, and (2) are characteristically engaged in for fun or money, rather than as a matter of deep personal conviction, and (3) long experience tells us that engaging in those activities is very likely to be associated with leading an unfulfilling and frustrating life rather than a fulfilling and worthwhile life, and (4) the punishments for engaging in those activities are not unduly onerous, and (5) preventing people from engaging in those activities leaves them lots of room to decide how they will lead their lives.

We leave it as an exercise for the reader to work out how these considerations apply to determine whether laws criminally punishing people for engaging in the kinds of activities listed at the start of this section are likely to do more harm than good or the opposite. But it seems unlikely that we will conclude that enforcing morality via the criminal law will *invariably* do more harm than good.

---

[86] See George, *Making Men Moral* (above, n 14), 212.

IS IT A BAD IDEA FOR THE STATE TO USE NON-COERCIVE MEANS TO ENFORCE MORALITY?

Mill never considered whether the state would do more harm than good by using non-coercive means to encourage people to do the right thing or lead worthwhile, fulfilling lives because it was only in the 20th century – with the growth in the powers of the state and changes in technology – that such non-coercive means of influencing people's behaviour became available. Whether or not such means should be used to change people's behaviour has become a hot topic nowadays thanks to Richard Thaler and Cass Sunstein's influential book *Nudge*.[87]

Nudge takes as its starting point the discovery by behavioural economists that human beings labour under certain *cognitive biases*[88] that consistently encourage them to make sub-optimal choices.[89] One such bias is *present-bias* which means that people tend to value things that can be enjoyed here and now over things that will only be enjoyed in future.[90] This means that people will tend to choose to eat fatty foods and sit around watching TV rather than diet and exercise – and this is so even if they acknowledge that dieting and exercising would be better for them than eating fatty foods and watching TV.

Thaler and Sunstein suggest that the state can capitalise on these cognitive biases to 'nudge' people into making good choices. For example, someone (S), who has resolved to give up smoking, will be tempted to give up on his resolution by his present-bias, which will make it seem that having a cigarette now will be so much more satisfying than not being addicted to cigarettes in the future. One way to help S to stick to his resolution is to set up a facility into which he can pay a certain amount of money: if he doesn't smoke for a certain period of time then he gets the money back; if he does, then it goes to charity.[91] This 'nudges' S into sticking with his resolution as it trades on another cognitive bias under which S will labour: the *loss aversion* bias, which makes us value avoiding a loss much more than making a gain. Similarly, we can trade on people's present-bias in order to encourage teenage mums not to get pregnant again by paying them a pound for every day they aren't pregnant: the immediate reward of getting a pound a day encourages them to take more precautions against getting pregnant than they might otherwise have taken.[92]

Nudges are not the only non-coercive means by which the state can encourage people to lead worthwhile, fulfilling lives. Public service announcements, advertising campaigns, tax incentives, subsidies, and even inserting storylines into dramas

---

[87] Thaler and Sunstein, *Nudge: Improving Decisions About Health, Wealth and Happiness* (Yale University Press, 2008).

[88] A comprehensive list of these biases can be found at <http://en.wikipedia.org/wiki/List_of_cognitive_biases>.

[89] Daniel Kahneman and Amos Tversky were pioneers in this field. For a popular summary of their work, see Kahneman, *Thinking, Fast and Slow* (Allen Lane, 2011).

[90] Thaler and Sunstein, *Nudge* (above, n. 87), 40–44.

[91] Ibid, 232.

[92] Ibid, 234.

on state-run TV stations, can all be ways by which the state non-coercively encourages people to make good choices. It seems unlikely that doing any of these things will inevitably do more harm than good. Many of the arguments canvassed above against coercively enforcing morality do not apply to enforcing morality through non-coercive means. The experiment argument and the character argument do not apply as the state is not – in using such non-coercive means – preventing people experimenting with alternative lifestyles or discouraging people from developing various desirable character traits by encouraging them to act in a servile or conformist way. Nor does the privacy argument or the authenticity argument apply here – non-coercively encouraging people into making good choices does not involve any intrusive surveillance or forcing people into leading lives that they cannot identify with. This leaves only the disrespect argument and the autonomy argument.

It has been argued that both of these arguments apply to the non-coercive enforcement of morality:

> 'Messing with the options that one faces, changing one's payoffs can be seen as manipulation ... If it is done intentionally, it also takes on the insulting aspect of manipulation, for it treats the agent as someone incapable of making independent moral decisions on the merits of the case.'[93]

However, a number of points can be made in response to this.

First, if it were true that giving some benefit to someone with the intention of getting them to make some choice were manipulative, this would lead to deeply counterintuitive conclusions. As Jonathan Quong notes, when Gideons International places free Bibles in hotel rooms to induce people who might not otherwise read the Bible to read it, they are not guilty of manipulation.[94] In fact, of the non-coercive means for encouraging people to make good choices considered in this section, only nudges are truly manipulative in the way they affect people's choices because only nudges try to influence people's choices through non-rational means.

Secondly, the interference with autonomy involved in nudging someone to make a good choice is not very serious because it only interferes with someone's ability to make a bad choice; contrast criminal punishment which – as we saw – limits people's ability to pursue worthwhile options. Moreover, Thaler and Sunstein are only in favour of nudging people to make choices that those people would want to make themselves were they free of the cognitive biases that lead them astray.[95] Provided this limit on nudging is respected, the interference with someone's autonomy in nudging someone to make a particular choice is pretty trivial.

---

[93] Waldron, 'Autonomy and perfectionism in Raz's *Morality of Freedom*' (above, n. 32), 1145–46.
[94] Quong, *Liberalism without Perfection* (above, n. 75), 63.
[95] Thaler and Sunstein, *Nudge* (above, n. 87), 4–5.

Thirdly, it is not clear whether there is any disrespect or insult involved in nudging someone to make a good choice. Nudging people to make good choices would not be necessary, or possible, if people did not suffer from cognitive biases, but recognising that *everyone* suffers from cognitive biases and trying to help them overcome those biases – as Thaler and Sunstein want the government to do – is no more insulting or disrespectful than pointing out that human beings are unable to fly unaided and making planes for them to get around in.

CONCLUSION

It is not likely that the state is doomed to do more harm than good if it attempts to enforce morality, either through coercive or non-coercive means. The dangers of doing more harm than good in enforcing morality are far greater when the state attempts to enforce morality using coercion, and in such a case there are only very limited circumstances where it can hope to do more good than harm by using coercion. In contrast, there seems little harm, and much potential good,[96] that could be done by using non-coercive means to enforce morality.

Further Reading

Mill, *On Liberty* (1859).

Dworkin, 'Is there a right to pornography?' (1981) 1 *Oxford Journal of Legal Studies* 177.

George, *Making Men Moral* (Oxford University Press, 1993), chs 1–2, 7.

Wall, 'Perfectionism in moral and political philosophy' in Zalta (ed.), *The Stanford Encyclopedia of Philosophy*.

Raz, *The Morality of Freedom* (Oxford University Press, 1986), chs 12, 14–15.

Conly, *Against Autonomy: Justifying Coercive Paternalism* (Cambridge University Press, 2013).

---

[96] However, see Rizzo and Whitman, 'The knowledge problem of new paternalism' [2009] *Brigham Young University Law Review* 905 for an argument that attempting to nudge people into making good choices will not in fact do any good because the state is not in a better position than anyone else to know what a 'good choice' for a particular individual will be.

11

THE VALUE OF STUDYING JURISPRUDENCE

It might seem strange to *conclude* an introductory book on jurisprudence with a chapter debating the value of studying jurisprudence. Surely this should have been the first question we debated, not the last?[1] However, the truth is that it is impossible to form a proper view as to the value of studying jurisprudence without some acquaintance with the sort of issues that mainstream writings on jurisprudence tend to focus on. Now that the reader has acquired some familiarity with those issues and writings, we can at last address the issue of whether all the intellectual effort that has been expended on the debates dealt with in the last 10 chapters – and all the intellectual effort that a student would have to expend to come fully to terms with those debates – is actually worth it. The first debate we will look at in this chapter is over whether there is any point in addressing the sort of questions that legal theorists – and in particular legal positivists – tend to focus on. The second debate is about the dark side of jurisprudence – whether studying jurisprudence actually has negative effects. The third debate is on whether we can hope to make any progress towards achieving a final answer on some of the issues debated in this book.

Debate 1

Do legal theorists ask the right questions?

Suppose that someone – *Anko* – became interested in defining what kind of fighting styles count as 'karate'. So *Anko* travels far and wide, looking at all sorts of different styles of fighting, and considers in each case 'Does this amount to karate?' He asks himself constantly, 'What would a fighting style necessarily have to

---

[1] Cf. CL, ch. 1 (see list of abbreviations, p. xiii), which begins by identifying 'persistent questions' that *The Concept of Law* is designed to answer; LE, the first sentence of which says 'It matters how judges decide cases' and follows that up on p. 3 with 'Since it matters ... how judges decide cases, it also matters what they think the law is, and when they disagree about this, it matters what kind of disagreement they are having'; and Shapiro, *Legality* (Harvard University Press, 2010), the first chapter of which is entitled 'What is law (and why should we care)?'.

include to count as karate? – If we subtracted this or that element from a fighting style, would it still count as karate?' He also asks himself, 'When would a fighting style that does count as karate stop being karate – If we added this or that element to a karate fighting style, would it still count as karate?' At some point, if we were kind, we surely would take *Anko* aside and say to him, 'What does it matter what counts as karate or not? Surely there are more productive questions for you to deal with, such as – Would a particular fighting style be improved in one or more dimensions if we added this element to it, or subtracted that element from it?'[2]

Can the same criticism be made of legal theorists – and, in particular, legal positivists – who obsess over what does and does not count as a legal system, or under what circumstances a rule will and will not count as a valid law? Are they wasting their time on irrelevancies in trying to answer such questions? For example, when a soft (or inclusive) legal positivist says:

> 'The separability thesis commits positivism to the proposition that there exists at least one conceivable legal system in which the rule of recognition does not specify being a principle of morality among the truth conditions for any proposition of law. Positivism is true, then, just in case[3] we can imagine a legal system in which being a principle of morality is not a condition of legality for any norm: that is, just as long as the idea of a legal system in which moral truth is not a necessary condition of legal validity is not self-contradictory.'[4]

we can legitimately ask, 'What is the point of knowing this? What is the point of knowing that there could exist a legal system on Mars where the validity of law does not depend on moral considerations where every legal system we have to deal with, and are ever likely to have to deal with, does make the validity of law dependent on moral considerations? More generally, what is the point of knowing that a certain set of institutional arrangements on Mars would count as a legal system, but a different set on Venus would not? Surely what matters is the *quality* of the legal system under which we live here, in this country – not the theoretical issue of whether we do or do not have a legal system (which is also a dead issue as we plainly do),[5] and not whether a quite different set of arrangements would or would not count as a legal system?'

A number of different responses might be made to this.

---

[2] Cf. MacIntyre, 'Is a science of comparative politics possible?' in his *Against the Self-Images of the Age* (University of Notre Dame Press, 1971), 260, comparing trying to come up with a theory of what politics is with trying to come up with a theory of holes.

[3] 'Just in case' is an incredibly irritating phrase used by philosophers when they really mean to say 'if and only if'. Of course, 'just in case' does not mean 'if and only if' but 'on the off-chance that'.

[4] Coleman, 'Negative and positive positivism' (1982) 11 *Journal of Legal Studies* 139, 143.

[5] Cf. Simpson, *Reflections on 'The Concept of Law'* (Oxford University Press, 2011), 80: 'In my own long experience as a teacher and to some modest extent a practitioner of law I have never once been asked the question "What is law?"'

(1) THE DEBUNKING RESPONSE

The first response – and one which may well have animated the writing of Hart's *The Concept of Law*[6] – might be that we need a general theory of what amounts to law and what amounts to a legal system in order to show that the ordinary person's perception that the law is something to be obeyed is incorrect. The fact that you can (in theory) have a legal system under which a grotesquely unjust rule still counts as valid law shows – it might be argued – that this ordinary perception is incorrect. As Jeremy Waldron observed, of Hart's statement that 'So long as human beings can gain sufficient cooperation from some to enable them to dominate others, they will use the forms of law as one of their instruments',[7]

> 'When the first year law student, hearing this, cries to his professor, 'Say it ain't so!' it is the professor's job to tell him that there is nothing in the concept of law that can provide the basis for any such assurance.'[8]

However, the problem with this debunking response is that you hardly need a general theory of law – particularly ones developed in as much detail as those which flow from the minds of modern legal positivists such as Joseph Raz – to debunk ordinary people's views about the nature of law. Simply pointing to some real life examples of unjust laws and asking people to reflect on how much influence they should have on people's decisions as to what they should do would suffice.

(2) THE NORMATIVE RESPONSE

The second possible response to someone who sceptical of the value of inquiries into the nature of law takes completely the opposite direction to the first, debunking, response. It asserts that law is an inherently normative concept, something which we are called upon to obey – or, in the language used by Lon Fuller, something that deserves our *fidelity*. The important job that legal theorists are called upon to do is to articulate a concept of law that can explain why this is – why law is something that deserves our loyalty:

> 'Law, as something deserving loyalty, must represent a human achievement; it cannot be a simple fiat of power or a repetitive pattern discernible in the behaviour of state officials. The respect we owe to human laws must surely be something different from the respect we accord to the law of gravitation. If laws, even bad laws, have a claim to our respect, then law must represent some general direction of human effort that we can understand and describe, and that we can approve in principle even at the moment when it seems to us to miss its mark.'[9]

---

[6] See Lacey, *A Life of HLA Hart: The Nightmare and the Noble Dream* (Oxford University Press, 2004), 225–27.
[7] CL, 210.
[8] Waldron, 'All we like sheep' (1999) 12 *Canadian Journal of Law and Jurisprudence* 169, 186.
[9] Fuller, 'Positivism and fidelity to law – a reply to Professor Hart' (1958) 71 *Harvard Law Review* 630.

The torch lit by Lon Fuller with these words was, of course, picked up by Ronald Dworkin, who argued that our concepts of law emerge out of debates over the nature of the value of legality, which 'insists that [the state's coercive power] be exercised only in accordance with standards established in the right way before that exercise'.[10]

> 'Conceptions of legality differ ... about what kinds of standards are sufficient to satisfy legality and in what way these standards must be established in advance; claims of law are claims about which standards of the right sort have in fact been established in the right way. A conception of legality is therefore a general account of how to decide which claims of law are true.'[11]

Of course, this kind of justification for doing legal theory is not open to legal positivists, for whom the concept of law is 'normatively inert'.[12] However, it should be noted that the more theories of law like Fuller's and Dworkin's gain traction, the more legal positivists will feel that it is important and valuable to come up with general theories of law that help to debunk the views of people like Fuller and Dworkin. So it may be that legal positivists are locked in a fatal embrace with their opponents – wanting to kill off their opponents' views, but also needing those views to survive and flourish in order to justify their own existence and work.

(3) THE 'WALK BEFORE YOU CAN RUN' RESPONSE

Perhaps legal positivists can escape this fatal embrace by taking advantage of a third response to those who worry that inquiring what does and does not amount to a legal system is a waste of time. This third response argues that you need to draw on a general theory of law in order properly to address important, normative, questions about what the law should say and what it should do. This response is made by Leslie Green,[13] who acknowledges that:

> 'If you come to law school with political curiosity but no prior training in the humanities or social sciences, and are then fed the typical first-year diet of doctrine, you are bound to arrive at your first legal theory course aching with hunger. To long for a first chance to debate liberty, justice or equality and then to be served up the practice theory of rules must be pretty frustrating. All the talk about general theory being the necessary preliminary to evaluation may just sound like more excuse for delay.'[14]

---

[10] Dworkin, 'Hart's Postscript and the character of political philosophy' (2004) 24 *Oxford Journal of Legal Studies* 1, 24.

[11] Ibid, 24–25.

[12] Gardner, 'Legal positivism: 5½ myths' (2001) 46 *American Journal of Jurisprudence* 199, 202. At the end of his Hart Lecture on Hart's Postscript (above, n. 10), Ronald Dworkin tells a funny story about a conversation with his successor as Professor of Jurisprudence at Oxford University, John Gardner: 'I said that I thought legal philosophy should be interesting. He jumped on me. "Don't you see?" he replied. "That's your trouble"' (36).

[13] See also Dickson, *Evaluation and Legal Theory* (Hart Publishing, 2001), 134–36.

[14] Green, 'The concept of law revisited' (1996) 94 *Michigan Law Review* 1687, 1716.

But, Green insists,

> 'The main interest in a general theory of law ... rests in the way that it helps us understand our institutions and, through them, our culture ... What is law that people take such pride in it? Is law a good idea? How and to whom do legal institutions distribute power? Is the rule of law always desirable? Can it help achieve justice? What might we gain, or lose, by limiting the reach of law? Those are deep and urgent questions for political theory, and also for political practice. Anyone who wants answers to them will need the help of a general theory of law.'[15]

However, there are two difficulties with this response. The first is that – with some creditable exceptions[16] – legal positivists seem unwilling to move on from their general theories of law to address these 'deep and urgent' normative questions.[17] They seem, for the most part, to be content playing games with words, and to make their students do the same.[18] The second is that we don't seem to need an incredibly complex theory of law in order to address adequately the 'deep and urgent' questions of political theory that Green identifies. For example, in order to start addressing these questions, we would not have to determine first who has the better view in the debate[19] between hard (or exclusive) legal positivists and soft (or inclusive) legal positivists over whether the rule of recognition of a legal system *can* include moral criteria for determining what does and does not count as a valid rule of law.[20]

(4) THE PHILOSOPHICAL RESPONSE

In a paper written for the Oxford Law Faculty's website on 'Why study jurisprudence?',[21] John Gardner offers us a more philosophical argument as to why 'investigating which propositions about law and legal life hold true universally, not just usually' is a worthwhile enterprise. Law students, he argues, (1) 'are at university and so should be studying at least some universals' and (2) 'should certainly study

---

[15] Ibid, 1717.

[16] Raz, *The Morality of Freedom* (Oxford University Press, 1986); Kramer, *The Ethics of Capital Punishment: A Philosophical Investigation of Evil and Its Consequences* (Oxford University Press, 2011); and NLNR, if one classifies Finnis as a legal positivist.

[17] See Dworkin's biting remarks about legal positivists in 'Thirty years on' (2002) 115 *Harvard Law Review* 1655, 1678: 'They make little attempt to connect their philosophy of law either to political philosophy generally or to substantive legal practice, scholarship, or theory. They teach courses limited to "legal philosophy" or analytic jurisprudence in which they distinguish and compare different contemporary versions of positivism, they attend conferences dedicated to those subjects, and they comment on each other's orthodoxies and heresies in the most minute detail in their own dedicated journals.'

[18] Even in Cambridge, which is hardly a hotbed of legal positivism, one of the few normative questions that was a focus of the jurisprudence course – whether the law should seek to encourage people to lead morally good lives – has now been dropped from the syllabus.

[19] See above, pp. 51–59.

[20] See Finnis, 'On the incoherence of legal positivism' (2000) 75 *Notre Dame Law Review* 1597, 1605: 'No truth about law is ... systematically at stake in contemporary disputes between exclusive and inclusive legal theorists. The central dispute is not worth pursuing.'

[21] <http://users.ox.ac.uk/~lawf0081/pdfs/whystudyjurisprudence.pdf> (accessed, December 1, 2013).

something other than parochial legal doctrine'. He elaborates on point (2) by saying that universities have a responsibility to their law students 'to remind [them] that there is more to life than legal practice. One way to do that is to study some philosophy.' And what better form of philosophy to make law students study than the philosophy of law?

There are a number of different problems with this position. Point (1) is undermined by the concession made by Gardner's mentor, Joseph Raz, that in determining what 'propositions about law and legal life hold true universally' we are always working with understandings of what law is that are inherited from our own culture, and are thus inescapably parochial in nature.[22] So an attempt to come up with a universal account of law that makes sense of *all* societies' understandings of the nature of law is doomed to failure. All we can do is make clear to ourselves what law is *to us*, and determine whether other societies do or do not have law according to our own understandings of what law is. So someone who studies the philosophy of law, as practised by masters such as Raz or Gardner, is not studying universals, but their own culture.

Point (2) is undermined by the fact that it is easy to think of other – and certainly more inherently interesting – forms of philosophy (and which *do* involve the study of true universals) that it would be natural for law students to study, if one wanted to make them study some form of philosophy. Moral philosophy, logic and epistemology (the study of how one can claim to know things) immediately spring to mind. Point (2) is also undermined by the fact that in a proper university, where law subjects are properly taught, law students are reminded that there is more to life than legal practice in every subject they study. For example, it is hard to see how one could properly study contract law or tort law at university without gaining some familiarity with basic economics. Or how one could study constitutional law without reference to political ideas about how society should be organised and power distributed within that society.

More generally, Gardner gives no reason why a *non-student* should be interested in studying the philosophy of law. There is no trace in his paper of an argument along the lines of 'This is why *I* have chosen to make the philosophy of law my life's work' with a view to then showing how the reasons he has for doing this might apply – albeit perhaps in an attenuated form – to students. Perhaps they don't and can't; but it would be surprising if this were the case – there is not such a huge distinction between a student of law and a teacher of law.

CONCLUSION

While not going so far as to endorse David Dyzenhaus' dismissal of legal positivism as a 'stagnant research programme',[23] there is clearly a problem in accounting for

---

[22] Raz, 'Can there be a theory of law?' in his *Between Authority and Interpretation* (Oxford University Press, 2009), especially 31–33.

[23] Dyzenhaus, 'Positivism's stagnant research programme' (2000) 20 *Oxford Journal of Legal Studies* 703.

why a legal positivist would want to delve as deeply into the nature of law as legal positivists tend to do. The truths pointed up by legal positivism – that there is, in the end, no way of guaranteeing that the laws of a particular state will be just – seem too obvious to need much argument to make them out. And the understanding of law promoted by legal positivists – determined by our own culture's understandings of what amounts to law, normatively inert, capable of saying almost anything (other than that it has no authority over its subjects) – makes the nature of law seem too abstract and uninteresting to be worth the effort of really coming to grips with its nature. It is only the more dashingly romantic visions of law propagated by theorists like Lon Fuller and Ronald Dworkin – of the law as in quest of itself,[24] or as working itself pure[25] – that make the enterprise of law seem something that is worth the intellectual effort of trying to understand what it is all about.

Debate 2

Does jurisprudence encourage us to adopt a false world view?

In 1991, Valerie Kerruish published *Jurisprudence as Ideology*,[26] in which she argued that the arguments of thinkers such as H.L.A. Hart, Ronald Dworkin and John Finnis legitimate law as an institution, and in so doing help to legitimate the social inequalities that law gives rise to. Mainstream writing on jurisprudence has this effect, she argued, because it portrays law as 'innocent'[27] of the evils that are done in its name, or because it portrays law as concerned to treat us all with 'equal concern and respect',[28] or because it endorses the law's self-presentation of its rules and doctrines as 'objectively' correct and justified.[29]

Jeffrey Goldsworthy rightly dismissed Kerruish's arguments as a 'travesty' and her book as a failure insofar as they and it applied to H.L.A. Hart.[30] This is because Hart emphasised over and over again in his writings the possibility that law might

---

[24] Fuller, *The Law in Quest of Itself* (Foundation Press, 1940).

[25] LE, 400ff. The concept of the law working itself pure comes from the case of *Omychund v Barker* (1744) 1 Atk 21, 26 ER 15. Before becoming Lord Mansfield, Sir William Murray was Solicitor-General and argued in *Omychund* that evidence given by Indian witnesses in an Indian court should be admissible even though the testimony was not preceded by the witnesses swearing an oath on the Bible. The relevant portion of his argument went as follows: 'Here is a ... court erected in *Calcutta*, by the authority of the crown of *England*, where *Indians* are sworn according to the most solemn part of their own religion. All occasions do not arise at once; now a particular species of *Indians* appears; hereafter another species of *Indians* may arise; a statute very seldom can take in all cases, therefore the common law, *that works itself pure* by rules drawn from the fountain of justice, is for this reason superior to an act of parliament.' (All emphases in the original.) 'Superior' here meant superior in the sense of being better able to adapt to changing circumstances.

[26] Kerruish, *Jurisprudence as Ideology* (Routledge, 1991).

[27] Ibid, 2.

[28] Ibid, 150–53.

[29] Ibid, 110–13.

[30] Goldsworthy, 'Is jurisprudence liberal ideology?' (1993) 13 *Oxford Journal of Legal Studies* 548, 560, 570.

be abused and used for illegitimate ends. For example,[31] he worried that in a modern society, the creation of a legal elite that determined what counted as a valid rule of a legal system might result in the population passively going along with whatever the law required them to do in a 'sheeplike' manner. In such a society, he warned, 'the sheep might end in the slaughter-house.'[32]

Kerruish never responded adequately to Goldsworthy's criticism,[33] and we are not concerned in this debate to see whether Kerruish's claims that mainstream jurisprudential writings have the effect of fooling us into thinking that law, and the inequalities that the law supposedly maintains, are legitimate. Instead, we want to address a more fundamental issue raised by Kerruish's book, which is whether by studying mainstream writings on jurisprudence we are inveigled into, and thereby encouraged to adopt, a way of thinking about the world that is straightforwardly false, or – at the very least – highly questionable. In order to explore this question, we will focus on the opening sentence of John Finnis's *Natural Law and Natural Rights*:

> 'There are human goods that can be secured only through the institutions of human law, and requirements of practical reasonableness that only those institutions can satisfy.'[34]

Let's call this sentence F for short (actually, for 'Finnis' or 'first' or 'false', according to preference). It is doubtful whether any mainstream theorist working in the field of jurisprudence would dissent from F. However, it seems to us that F encourages us to adopt a number of different assumptions about the world, all of which can be questioned.

LAW AND HUMAN NATURE

F first of all asserts that there is such a thing as 'human goods' – that is, a distinctive range of things, experiences and activities that can be counted as good for *all* human beings, wherever they exist. This, in turn, assumes that there is such a thing as *human nature*. If there were not, it would be hard to see how we could say that a particular thing, experience or activity is good for *all* human beings. And F assumes that law exists as an instrument to serve human nature – to help people enjoy the things, experiences and activities that count as good for human beings by virtue of human beings being the way they are and that could not be enjoyed in the absence of law.

---

[31] For further examples, see above, pp. 74, 85–86. See also Green, 'The concept of law revisited' (above, n. 14), 1699–1700; Waldron, 'All we like sheep' (above, n. 8).

[32] CL, 117.

[33] Kerruish's response to Goldsworthy is 'Worthy hearts of gold: ideology and intentions' (1995) 15 *Oxford Journal of Legal Studies* 141, but she evaded the challenge of dealing with Goldsworthy's points head-on on the basis that 'We work within different philosophical traditions, argue from different metaphysical and epistemological assumptions, and deploy different methodological techniques.' Debate and conversation becomes impossible with someone who adopts this kind of position. See, further, Nussbaum, 'Sophistry about conventions' (1985) 17 *New Literary History* 129.

[34] NLNR, 1; quoted in Kerruish, *Jurisprudence as Ideology* (above, n. 26), 56.

So, for example, H.L.A. Hart identifies five 'salient characteristics of human nature' which dictate that law must have a certain 'minimum content' if law is to help human beings survive while living together.[35] These are: (i) human vulnerability; (ii) approximate equality; (iii) limited altruism; (iv) limited resources; (v) limited understanding and strength of will.[36] These five features of human nature mean that if human beings are going to survive while living together, the legal system under which they live *has* to do such things as require people not to kill each other and to forebear from taking advantage of a temporary physical superiority over another, to recognise people as owning property and require other people to respect that fact, and to impose sanctions on those who fail to abide by the law's requirements.[37]

The relationship that *F* assumes exists between law and human nature – that there is such a thing as human nature, and law at its best exists to help us enjoy the things, experiences and activities that count as being good for us because of our nature that we could not enjoy in the absence of law – can be rendered problematic in two different ways.

First of all, it might be that there is no such thing as human nature. Someone who thinks this adopts an *anti-essentialist* position on human nature. On this view, just because we happen to share the same DNA as, say, the Ancient Greeks does not entitle us to think that we have anything else in common with them. They may have been, in every other respect other than DNA, radically different kinds of people from us, with the result that we cannot say that the sorts of things, experiences and activities that are good for us would also have been good for them. If anti-essentialism about human nature is correct, then what determines what kind of people we are and therefore what counts as being good for us? It would seem natural to assume that the kind of society we live in would play a large part in determining what kind of people we are, if anti-essentialism is correct. But if this is right, then a society's legal system will not – as *F* assumes it will, at its best – simply play an instrumental role in helping us get what is good for us; it may also play a big role in determining what is good for us in the first place by helping to shape what kind of people we are. And by depicting law, at its best, as simply servicing our needs as human beings, *F* makes it harder for us to see how law – in conjunction with other social institutions that shape what kind of people we are – helps to determine what those needs are in the first place.

Even if we reject (as we do) anti-essentialism,[38] there is a second way in which *F* might be accused of not giving us the full picture as to the relationship between law and human nature. If law, at its best, exists to help us enjoy the things, experiences and activities that we count as good for us by virtue of the kind of people

---

[35] CL, 193.

[36] CL, 194–98.

[37] Ibid.

[38] For a defence of essentialism about human nature, see Nussbaum, 'Human functioning and social justice: in defence of Aristotelian essentialism' (1992) 20 *Political Theory* 202.

we are, then law has to take a stand on what kind of people we are. In other words, it has to form a view about what human nature is. But once it has done this, there seems little doubt that the stance that the law takes on what kind of people we are will then play a major role in shaping our perceptions about what kind of people we are. But what if the law has got it wrong? – What if the law's view as to the nature of human nature is incorrect? In such a case, the law – in helping to shape our perceptions about what kind of people we are – would be complicit in deceiving us about what kind of people we really are, and the fear that first crops up in Western philosophy in Plato's allegory of the cave,[39] and which kick-started Descartes' philosophy[40] and which underlies films such as *The Matrix* and *Inception* – the fear that we might be trapped in an illusion about our condition – would be realised.

For example, Hart asserts of human beings that while they are 'not devils dominated by a wish to exterminate each other … neither are they angels, never tempted to harm each other … As things are, human altruism is limited in range and intermittent, and the tendencies to aggression are frequent enough to be fatal to social life if not controlled.'[41] But some[42] (though not us) would say that if people living in society are like that, it is because the social institutions under which they live – and in particular, their legal system – have made them that way by insisting on treating people *as though* they are only capable of limited altruism. For example, it could be argued that by giving us rights against other people that they not use violence against us, the law encourages us to distrust other people and think them capable of using violence against us. This negative perception of other people then becomes self-reinforcing: in a cycle that is familiar to students of international politics, our distrust of other people results in our seeking to make ourselves stronger to fend off any attacks on us, and this attempt to become stronger provokes fear and consequent pre-emptive attacks on us by other people who trust us as little as we trust them.

So even if we reject anti-essentialism about human nature, it is still possible to criticise *F* on the basis that by positing a simple relationship between law and human nature – that law (at its best) simply exists to serve human nature – *F* draws a veil over the ways in which law can work to shape our perceptions of what human beings are like, and potentially deceive us about our true nature.

LAW AS NECESSARY/NORMAL/NATURAL

But this is not the only basis on *F* can be criticised. *F* depicts law as necessary, or normal, or natural. We *need* law if we are going to enjoy certain goods that are

---

[39] See Plato, *Republic*, 514a-520a.
[40] See Descartes, 'First meditation: on what can be called into doubt' in his *Meditations on First Philosophy* (1641).
[41] CL, 196.
[42] See Rousseau, *Discourse on the Origins of Inequality Among Men* (1754) for the origin of all such views.

appropriate to our nature.[43] But we might question why this is so. If we recall, the pre-legal society that we have dubbed *Arcadia*[44] – a 'small community closely knit by ties of kinship, common sentiment, and belief, and placed in a stable environment'[45] – did not need law for its members to enjoy the human goods that *F* says *we* cannot enjoy except through law. And that is because we live in *Metropolis*, where unofficial and informally enforced rules of primary obligation would not work to enable us to enjoy the full range of human goods:

> 'problems arise when we try to apply ... informal solutions native to a world of transparent solidarity to *our world*, a world of few or repudiated kinship ties, in which sentiments are not shared, in which the environment is a maelstrom of change, where, as Marx says "all that is solid melts into air."'[46]

So law is not as necessary or normal or natural as *F* initially seems to suggest. *F* suppresses a conditional: that we only need law if we live in *Metropolis* and don't live in *Arcadia*. And in suppressing that conditional, *F* encourages us *either* (1) to think that living in *Arcadia* is simply not an option for us – that we have no choice but to live in *Metropolis*; *or* (2) to think that even if we did have a choice whether to live in *Arcadia* or *Metropolis*, the advantages of living in *Metropolis* so outweigh the benefits of living in *Arcadia* that no one could rationally want to live in *Arcadia* if they were given the choice.

(1) might be criticised for presenting us with what the legal and political philosopher Roberto Mangabeira Unger calls a 'false necessity' that limits our imagination as to how our society might be structured.[47] The examples of monasteries, the Amish in Pennsylvania, German Kommuja, and kibbutzim in Israel show that *Arcadia*-like societies can flourish even in modern times. However, whether they can do so as completely self-sufficient units, and not as communities that isolate themselves from the *Metropolis* within which they are located while simultaneously depending on the legal protections provided by that same *Metropolis* for their existence, is less clear. It might be that modern day *Arcadias* would require the support of legal systems outside their boundaries in order to protect and patrol those boundaries. If this is the case, then even someone living in a modern day *Arcadia* would have to agree with *F*. However, it is not completely obvious that this is the case, and an unthinking endorsement of *F* might blind one to the possibility that there may exist modes of social existence where we can enjoy a full range of human goods without the benefit of law.

Assuming that it might still be open to us to live in *Arcadia*, it might be – as (2) suggests – that no rational case could be made for choosing to live in *Arcadia*.

---

[43] See also CL, 42 depicting 'the step from the pre-legal into the legal world' as 'a step *forward* as important to society as the invention of the wheel' (emphasis added).

[44] See above, pp. 36–37.

[45] CL, 92.

[46] Green, 'The concept of law revisited' (above, n. 14), 1698.

[47] Unger, *False Necessity: Anti-Necessitarian Social Theory in the Service of Radical Democracy* (Cambridge University Press, 1987).

However, (2) is brought into question by the *communitarian* critique of modern societies, according to which while there may be disadvantages involved in living in *Arcadia*-like societies – chiefly, a suspicion of outsiders, and stifling pressures to conform on insiders – there are significant, and possibly graver, disadvantages involved in living in a society like *Metropolis*: chiefly loneliness,[48] aimlessness,[49] and selfishness.[50] So it is not at all clear that the only rational choice for a human being would be to live in *Metropolis* rather than *Arcadia*; and, indeed, many rational people choose to live in *Arcadia*-type societies.

In sum, we have no reason to think that (1) and (2) are necessarily true; but *F* discourages us from even considering that possibility, by making us think that law is necessary or normal or natural for the sort of people we are.

LAW AS POTENTIALLY BENEFICIAL

The final criticism that might be made of *F* is that it presents law as a potentially benign institution – one which *might* be used, and which (at its best) *is* used, to help us enjoy certain human goods that we could not enjoy in the absence of law. But suppose it were the case that law is almost always *ab*used, and its potential benefits are almost always never realised. If this were true, then *F* would present us with a very misleading picture of law: the equivalent of saying that strychnine helps to stimulate neural pathways in the brain without mentioning that it is almost always fatal to anyone who consumes it. So – it might be argued – by focusing exclusively on the potential benefits that can be obtained from law, *F* blinds us to the possibility that law is an inherently malign institution; something that is far more likely to be used to do harm than to do good wherever it exists.

Is this a possibility that is not worth considering? We know – as Hart repeatedly reminded us[51] – that there is a *chance* that law might be used for nefarious ends; but do we have reason to think that law will *almost always* be used for such ends? Jeremy Waldron observes that in a society with a developed legal system:

> 'primary rules come to have a presence in the lives of those subject to them that is quite different from their role in pre-legal society. On the one hand, ordinary people will not necessarily have the intimate familiarity with the rules that they used to have: they will be, in that sense, alienated from the rules. And the rules will begin to impact on their lives as much through the work of a dedicated apparatus of coercion as through the normative to-and-fro of a shared internal attitude, perhaps even more so.[52]
>
> Those who make and can recognize enacted law may use that capacity and that specialist knowledge for their own benefit, and to the detriment of the rest, who

---

[48] Putnam, *Bowling Alone: The Collapse and Revival of American Community* (Simon and Schuster, 2001).

[49] Himmelfarb, *The De-Moralization of Society: From Victorian Virtues to Modern Values* (Vintage Books, 1994).

[50] Bellah, *Habits of the Heart: Individualism and Commitment in American Life*, 3rd edn (University of California Press, 2007).

[51] See above, pp. 74, 85–86, 239.

[52] Waldron, 'All we like sheep' (above, n. 8), 179.

find they know less and less about the detailed basis on which their society is organized. The specialization of normative authority may thus exacerbate whatever exploitation and hierarchy exist in a given society apart from its legalization ... [So law's] existence in a society raises a real and serious prospect that it will be used to facilitate injustice and to confuse and mystify many of those who are subject to that injustice and who have no choice but to live their lives under its auspices.'[53]

A 'real and serious prospect', yes – but enough of a prospect for us to seriously consider the possibility that law is, at base, a malign institution?

The answer, we think, depends first of all on one's view of human nature – Are people who are given power over others in circumstances where they are unlikely to be held accountable for the way they exercise that power, because of the difficulties involved in understanding how they exercise that power, far more likely to use that power improperly than they are likely to use that power benevolently? It seems clear that the answer to this question is 'yes'.[54] However, the chances that the power that law gives legal elites over other people will be abused can be reduced by (1) adopting *procedures* for selecting who will and will not become a member of the legal elite so as to ensure that as few people as possible who are likely to abuse the power that being the member of an elite gives them become members of that elite; and (2) *diffusing* the powers enjoyed by members of the legal elite as widely as possible so as to minimise the amount of power vested in any one member of that elite.

So law is not an inherently malign institution – it is not far more likely to be used to do harm rather than do good *wherever* it exists. But law is very likely to *become* malign in a society where (1) and (2) are not true. Such a society will probably be better off without law. However, *F* encourages us not even to contemplate such a possibility: if we need law in order to enjoy certain human goods, how could any society possibly be better off without law?[55]

CONCLUSION

We hope we have said enough by now to show that there is a serious danger that current mainstream approaches to jurisprudence may well result in our adopting certain beliefs about the world – about who we are, about our need for law, and about the benefits of living under a legal system – that are, at the very least, highly questionable but which we never question because we are encouraged simply to assume that those beliefs are correct. So studying jurisprudence may well result in

---

[53] Ibid, 181.

[54] English law itself admits that the answer to this question is yes by subjecting people – *fiduciaries* – who possess power over other people and are unlikely to be held accountable for the way they exercise that power to special rules, disabling them from exercising those powers for their own benefit and from getting into situations where they are likely to exercise those powers unwisely.

[55] Cf. Endicott, 'The subsidiarity of law and the obligation to obey' (2005) 50 *American Journal of Jurisprudence* 233, 248: 'law in its historical manifestations through the ages, has always, or generally, been a morally valuable institution.'

our adopting a false world view, and we always have to be on our guard against that possibility.

Debate 3

Are debates in jurisprudence interminable?

The value of studying jurisprudence would be reduced, though not nullified,[56] if it were the case that there was no hope of achieving any progress in the debates on various issues relating to jurisprudence. So the value of studying jurisprudence might be put in question by the striking fact that in *none* of the debates discussed in this book has one side ever conceded defeat and accepted that the other side has the better view of the issue. (Of course, we have plenty of examples of one side claiming victory over the other side in a debate.)[57] We might put this down to professional pride – no one ever wants to admit that they were wrong – except for the fact that in *all* of these debates both sides plainly think that they are *not* wrong, and that they do have a better view of things than the other side.

So does this indicate that the *pessimistic conclusion* that debates in jurisprudence are doomed never to make any progress is justified? Our answer is 'Sometimes yes, sometimes no'. Sometimes the lack of progress in a debate is *justified*, and we cannot have much hope that the debate will ever reach a successful conclusion. In such cases, we have to wonder whether there is any point – other than for educative reasons – for bothering with the debate. But other times, the lack of progress is not justified, but can be *explained* by reference to factors that have nothing to do with the merits of either side's position in the debate. In such cases, we can have some hope that if the factor obstructing progress in the debate is removed (sadly, usually through the death of a participant in the debate who is affected by that factor),[58] then the debate can find its way to a successful conclusion.

So – when will a lack of progress in a debate be justified, and when will it merely be explicable?

---

[56] From the point of view of training one to think properly, there is some virtue in studying the progress of a debate over some issue in jurisprudence even if that debate does not end with a clear victory for either side, in the same way that there is some virtue in studying a chess match that culminates in a draw. Watching the moves that each side makes, and why, is an education in how to think for yourself in addressing an issue in jurisprudence.

[57] See, for example, Dworkin, 'Hart's Postscript and the character of political philosophy' (above, n. 10), claiming victory over Hart; and, claiming victory for Hart over Dworkin, Leiter, 'Beyond the Hart/Dworkin debate: the methodology problem in jurisprudence' (2003) 48 *American Journal of Jurisprudence* 17, 17–30, and Leiter, 'The end of empire: Dworkin and jurisprudence in the 21st century' (2004–05) 36 *Rutgers Law Journal* 165.

[58] Cf. Max Planck's remarks that 'A new scientific truth does not triumph by convincing its opponents and making them see the light, but rather because its opponents eventually die, and a new generation grows up that is familiar with it' and 'Science advances one funeral at a time'.

JUSTIFYING FACTORS

There are two factors that might justify the lack of progress in a debate in jurisprudence: (1) *indeterminacy*; and (2) *overdeterminacy*.

A debate is afflicted by indeterminacy if there are too few facts on the ground to allow us to say with any confidence which side in that debate is correct. It seems like the debate between hard (or exclusive) legal positivists and soft (or inclusive) legal positivists[59] may be afflicted by this kind of indeterminacy. What we know of how judges decide cases is not enough to enable us to say which side in this debate has the better view. When judges take into account moral considerations in deciding the outcome of a case, we do not know enough to be able to tell whether they are doing so because those moral considerations have been made part of the law by the rule of recognition of the legal system under which they operate or because there exists a secondary rule in that legal system directing them to take those moral considerations into account in deciding the case.[60] Given this, it is hard to see how either side can ever win this debate.

A debate is afflicted by overdeterminacy when there are enough facts on the ground to support both sides in that debate. This kind of overdeterminacy might account for why debates between those (such as Hart) who regard law as a *fact* and those (like Dworkin or Fuller) who regard law as a *reason* seem destined never to end. The examples of law that we work with in coming to terms with the nature of law contain enough features to support both analyses, and in-between analyses as well, such as those advanced by Raz (where law is a fact that purports to give us a reason) or Finnis (where the central case of law is a fact that, in conjunction with other premises, gives us a reason).

EXPLANATORY FACTORS

There are a number of factors that might explain, though not justify, the lack of progress in a particular debate. We will focus on three: (1) psychology; (2) biography; and (3) institutional pressures.

First, psychology. The literary theorist Harold Bloom coined the term 'the anxiety of influence' to describe the pressure that each generation of poets felt to distinguish themselves from the previous generation and demonstrate that they were their own men and not influenced by what had come before them.[61] Only by distinguishing themselves in this way could any generation have any hope that

---

[59] See above, pp. 51–59.

[60] In his *The Authority of Law*, 2nd edn (Oxford University Press, 2009), 47, fn. 8, Raz argues that positivists who believe that 'Sometimes the identification of some laws turns on moral arguments' have to provide 'an adequate criterion for separating legal references to morality, which makes its application a case of applying pre-existing rules, from cases of judicial discretion in which the judge, by resorting to moral considerations, is changing the law. I am not aware of any serious attempt to provide such a test.' But it is not clear why the burden is on Raz's opponents to supply such a criterion: for Raz to establish that *his* views are correct, he needs to supply such a criterion as well.

[61] Bloom, *The Anxiety of Influence: A Theory of Poetry*, 2nd edn (Oxford University Press, 1997).

their poetry would last, and would not be dismissed as a pale imitation of the previous generation's poetry. The same anxiety of influence might explain, though not justify, why one generation of legal theorists might pick a fight with the previous generation, repudiating the previous generation's teachings in favour of a radically different position. For example, it is not hard to imagine that Ronald Dworkin was afflicted by a serious case of anxiety of influence in relation to H.L.A. Hart. This would account for why Dworkin repeatedly kept shifting his line of attack on Hart's theory of law – first arguing that Hart's theory could not explain how principles figured in judge's decisions, then arguing that Hart's theory could not explain how judges decided hard cases, then arguing that Hart's theory could not explain theoretical disagreement in the law – in order to find some way of discrediting Hart's work. It would also account for why, in the words of Hart's biographer, Nicola Lacey, Hart had 'a sense that there was something wilful or even lacking in honesty about Dworkin's reading of his work'.[62]

The possibility that the different positions taken by legal theorists in a debate might be explained (though not justified) by reference to those theorists' life histories has received a considerable boost from the publication of Lacey's biography of Hart. For example, it does not seem so far-fetched to suggest that Hart's approach to analysing the nature of legal systems – always looking at them from the outside, while trying to understand the attitudes of the actors on the inside of the system – might reflect his feeling of being 'a perpetual outsider to the English establishment'[63] as shown by the following story about

> 'a striking comment which [Hart] made to Ronald Dworkin ... about the Oxford Chair of Jurisprudence. It was remarkable, [Hart] said, that no English person had held the chair in recent decades. Amazed, Dworkin replied, "But you are English." "No," [Hart] retorted, "I'm Jewish."'[64]

And Dworkin's insistence that a social practice can only be understood from the inside, through participants in the practice engaging in 'interpretive debates' about the nature of that practice[65] with the result 'that a social scientist must participate in a social practice if he hopes to understand it',[66] may reflect his status as the ultimate insider – Harvard graduate, Rhodes scholar in Oxford (with straight alphas in his Finals papers), clerk for Judge Learned Hand, Professor of Law at Yale Law School, Hart's successor as Professor of Jurisprudence at Oxford, while eventually and simultaneously maintaining various Professorships in New York.

Neither Hart nor Dworkin were subject to any institutional pressures in formulating their theories of law. The same is not true of modern legal academics, who – unless they occupy fairly senior, secure positions – have to show that they can

---

[62] Lacey, *A Life of HLA Hart: The Nightmare and the Noble Dream* (above, n. 6), 330.
[63] Ibid, 343.
[64] Ibid, 271.
[65] LE, ch. 2.
[66] LE, 55.

publish articles in distinguished law journals if they are going to be hired by a law faculty, and, once hired, come under pressure from their faculty to continue the process of churning out articles in order to boost the faculty's standing as a research institution. This institutional pressure to publish means that legal academics have an incentive both to pick fights with other academics operating in the same field of law, and to seek out new ways of analysing familiar legal issues by drawing on disciplines outside the law (such as epistemology, or the philosophy of action) that no one else has yet thought of applying to those issues. These institutional pressures can explain (though not justify) why a particular debate in jurisprudence might arise; and they also explain (though, again, they do not justify) why, having arisen, a jurisprudential debate may go on and on (because the participants in the debate are getting too many research credits to have any reason to bring it to an end).[67]

CONCLUSION

It would be presumptuous – and perhaps offensive – for us to pick through the debates set out in this book with a view to identifying which debates' interminability is justified (with the result that we cannot hope for much progress in those debates) and which debates' interminability is explicable, but not justified (with the result that we can hope one day that that debate will come to a successful conclusion). We leave that as an exercise for the reader. However, we are optimistic that progress is possible in a significant majority of the debates covered in this book, and hopeful that in some small way this book will have contributed to such progress being made.

Further Reading

CL, ch. 1.

Shapiro, *Legality* (Harvard University Press, 2010), ch. 1.

Dworkin, 'Hart's Postscript and the character of political philosophy' (2004) 24 *Oxford Journal of Legal Studies* 1.

Goldsworthy, 'Is jurisprudence liberal ideology?' (1993) 13 *Oxford Journal of Legal Studies* 548.

Green, 'The concept of law revisited' (1996) 94 *Michigan Law Review* 1687.

Green, 'General jurisprudence: a 25th anniversary essay' (2005) 25 *Oxford Journal of Legal Studies* 565.

Waldron, 'All we like sheep' (1999) 12 *Canadian Journal of Law and Jurisprudence* 169.

Perreau-Saussine, 'An outsider on the inside: Hart's limits of jurisprudence' (2006) 56 *University of Toronto Law Journal* 371.

Green, 'Jurisprudence for foxes' (2012) 3 *Transnational Legal Theory* 150.

---

[67] Though this is not, of course, true of all modern-day debates in jurisprudence that go on and on. Sometimes – as with the Kramer–Simmonds debate on the morality of legality (see above, pp. 66–81) – both sides will believe so fervently in the correctness of their position that they cannot allow the perceived errors of the other side to go unreproved.

INDEX